Caribbean Chemistry

A memoir from St. Kitts & Antigua 1942 to 1961

Christopher Vanier

Kingston University Press Ltd, Kingston University,
Penrhyn Road, Kingston upon Thames
Surrey KT1 2EE

Contents © Christopher Vanier 2009

The right of the above author to be identified as the author of
this work has been asserted in accordance with the
Copyright, Designs and Patent Act 1988.

British Library Cataloguing in Publication Data available.

ISBN 978-1-899999-45-3

Set in Palatino Linotype
Printed by Beamreach Printing (www.beamreachuk.co.uk)

Cover designed by Kerstin Arfwedson

Contents

Acknowledgements

A book is never entirely the work of its author, however much he has invested in it, and I am no different. I must first thank the many fellow writers who participated with me in various Paris workshops from 2002 to 2007 during the writing of this memoir. In particular, the poet Jennifer Dick was of great help when I was structuring my stories and my language; among my many readers, too numerous to remember over the years, I must cite my friends Chandrika Casali, Janet Skeslien Charles, Lizzie Harwood-Gohier, Arthur Greer, Marie Houzelle, Gwyneth Hughes, Dimitri Keramitas, Barry Kirwan, John Kohut, Kurt Lebakken, Ken Mackenzie, Alma Mecattaf, Laure Millet, Jane Verwijs, and Laurel Zuckerman, who all gave me vital feedback.

In a more formal context of work, I thank the creative non-fiction authors who looked at my writing during several July Paris Writers' Workshops: Laurie Stone, Mike Steinberg, Phillip Lopate, Floyd Skloot, and Vivian Gornick. These accomplished writers, and in addition Cara Black, gave valuable advice and encouragement. Thanks also to WICE, The British Institute of Paris, and the American Library of Paris for the numerous opportunities to present my work to the public.

My first draft was finished in 2006, but I could not have completed the task without the help of major readers who gave detailed comments on the entire manuscript: David Curzon, Felix Redmill, and Amir Taheri. Thanks friends, for all that fact checking and copyediting! This is not to escape my responsibilities – all errors or misjudgements remaining are mine alone.

It was my good fortune to be selected for a Life Writing prize by Kingston University Press, and I am extremely grateful for their help in publishing this book, in particular to Siobhan Campbell and her team.

Finally, thanks to my long-suffering family who have had to put up with my egotistical writer's preoccupations over the last seven years; to my siblings Hazel, Peter, and Noel, who gave me their affection and many suggestions; to my children Chloé and Cyril, who also commented wonderfully on difficult chapters; and above all to my wife Colette who passed away during the publication phase without ever being able to read my entire work.

Beyond thanks, my thoughts go out to the subjects of my memoir, my childhood friends of St. Kitts and Antigua, to whom I have endeavoured to be truthful and fair. And to my parents, engrained in these stories: I am happy that my mother at ninety was able to relive her early life by reading this memoir, and I regret forever that my father could not do so.

Preface

Vanier Family Tree

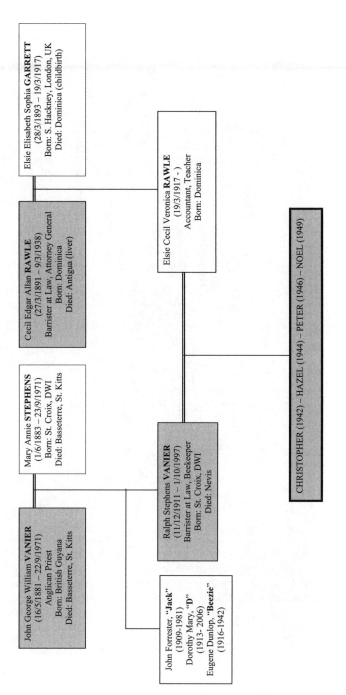

Elsie Elisabeth Sophia **GARRETT**
(28/3/1893 – 19/3/1917)
Born: S. Hackney, London, UK
Died: Dominica (childbirth)

Cecil Edgar Allan **RAWLE**
(27/3/1891 – 9/3/1938)
Barrister at Law, Attorney General
Born: Dominica
Died: Antigua (liver)

Mary Annie **STEPHENS**
(1/6/1883 – 23/9/1971)
Born: St. Croix, DWI
Died: Basseterre, St. Kitts

Elsie Cecil Veronica **RAWLE**
(19/3/1917 -)
Accountant, Teacher
Born: Dominica

John George William **VANIER**
(16/5/1881 – 22/9/1971)
Anglican Priest
Born: British Guyana
Died: Basseterre, St. Kitts

Ralph Stephens **VANIER**
(11/12/1911 – 1/10/1997)
Barrister at Law, Beekeeper
Born: St. Croix, DWI
Died: Nevis

John Forrester, "**Jack**"
(1909-1981)
Dorothy Mary, "**D**"
(1913- 2006)
Eugene Dunlop, "**Beezie**"
(1916-1942)

CHRISTOPHER (1942) – HAZEL (1944) – PETER (1946) – NOEL (1949)

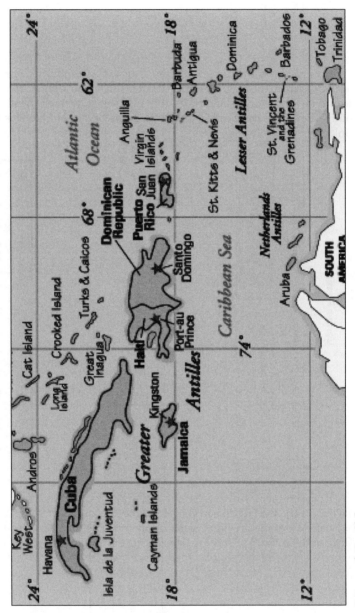

Map of Caribbean

A Caribbean Perspective

The sea boundary of an island simultaneously protects and imprisons its inhabitants. The Caribbean is a chain of such encircled territories, stretching from Trinidad in the south, only seven miles from the coasts of Venezuela and Guyana, through the Windward Islands, in a north-westwards arc to the bigger landmasses of Haiti, Jamaica, and Cuba. In the middle are the tiny island states of the Leewards, where I spent my youth. They have been called pinpricks in the ocean, but I prefer to think of them as mosquito bites.

Amerindians from the great South American continent migrated up this chain over two thousand years ago, caressing each island like a bright bead on a necklace. Successive waves populated the green-forested archipelago up to the 15th century, subject only to the gods of wind and fire. It is probable that the islands were periodically cleansed of bipedal life by hurricanes, prolonged droughts, or volcanic belches of destruction. The beauty and fertility of these clumps of earth nourished by a warm sea has always attracted strangers, but no tribe, ethnic group or occupying power has remained master of the fickle islands.

Until Columbus's fleet arrived from Spain in 1492, the sea had shielded the early islanders from the world. The Caribs, who called themselves Kalinagos, were busy absorbing another Amerindian people – the Tainos, or Arawaks. The Spanish claimed the region for their own and eliminated those who disagreed with them. The Tainos died out within 50 years, but Carib arrows kept some of the smaller islands free of the invaders for two centuries. However, from 1550 onwards, greed for the rich pickings of tobacco and sugar caused the arrival of other European predators – English, French, and Dutch – first as pirates and privateers, then as colonists. They brutally expropriated the small Carib strongholds. By 1700, the power of Spain in the region was definitively broken and the islands became a patchwork of European holdings, starting with my tiny island of Saint Christopher (St. Kitts) under Sir Thomas Warner, in 1623.

By the 18th century, the only Amerindians left were on the South American continent, with the exception of some stragglers in Dominica. The British and the French had completed the extermination – begun by the Spanish – of the previous island occupants. The sea had failed the Caribs and they had nowhere to flee. But the Europeans, being too lazy to tend their own crops under the hot sun, brought about their own long-term undoing by creating the slave trade and importing hundreds of thousands of blacks from Africa to reap the cane under appalling conditions. After many hard decades of plantation labour, when England abolished slavery in a fit of conscience in 1834, the blacks began to claim ownership of the islands in place of the white man.

During the 19th and 20th centuries, the European powers fought a rearguard action to keep political and economic control of their hard-won colonies. The islands became a new confinement for the ex-slaves, denied education, land, and emigration. Among the last colonial measures was the massive introduction of indentured labourers from India, who would later be as numerous as the blacks in Trinidad and Guyana, preparing yet another wandering people's claim to power. The 20th century brought times of great social strife (but no more than the bloodshed of the preceding centuries). Two world wars distracted attention from the islanders' goal of self-determination, but post-second-world-war Britain eventually accepted the decolonisation of the no-longer-rich islands and the birth of the present mini-states. They had become a burden to be relinquished, but could they be independent? The question was relevant both to communities and to individuals. I was born in the midst of this political upheaval, and like St. Kitts, I yearned for freedom while clinging to the protection of my known, small, sea-enclosed world and culture.

Part 1: Beginnings (St. Kitts, 1942-1951)

Flotsam and Jetsam

Ah, to be an embryo again, with the choice between turbulent existence and serene nothingness! What spaces we could glimpse from that forgotten frontier.

Let us then take a step back in time, and imagine the day a man and a woman were studying a ramshackle two-storey building in the capital of a small Caribbean island. The street was called Liverpool Row. The ground floor was occupied by a rum shop, from which came occasional loud voices and the heady smell of alcohol.

"This is the house," Ralph said to Elsie.

"I hope there aren't any rats," she said.

These were my parents: I was a red-skinned unborn baby, still nestling in my mother's womb.

"Could do with some work," Ralph said, as they climbed the wooden steps from the street to the upper level.

He fingered the brownish surface of the front door, and when he rapped his knuckles on the wood, a few flakes of paint came loose.

"Solid, though. A real wooden house – no corrugated iron – with a real roof over us. Won't blow down in the first hurricane."

They had been living in cramped quarters with a friend near the central town square until my father earned a little money and they found an affordable place for themselves. They went inside to shut out the odour of the rum shop and the town's open gutters. The main room was cooler than the baking streets outside, but dim.

"Ralph, where are the lights?"

He opened a few windows and let the sunshine in. "It has no electricity. We'll have to buy oil lamps."

Elsie turned on the tap in the small porcelain sink. "At least there's running water."

My father came over and held my mother around the waist.

I stirred in my intrauterine dreams, sensing the warm hand, and feeling the affection.

But who were they, these penniless parents, and my tiny precursor, soon to be promoted to fetus? They were not native to the island. The year was 1942, and they had just settled in Basseterre, St. Kitts. Here, sugar was king, rum was queen, and would be so for another two good decades of cane production.

A few weeks before my parents plunged into the unknown, my grandfather, John George, had warned my father, "You'll be like castaways! Why are you bobbing off to St. Kitts with your wife pregnant? You have no family there. And the sea trip may disturb your baby. Stay here with us in Antigua – in our rectory – until the child is born. Then you can decide what to do next."

"No, Daddy," Ralph said to him, "we won't stay. I can't find work. Just think, I passed my Bar exams in London, then risked my life zigzagging between German submarines, all for nothing! Much of my convoy was sunk before I got back home to the islands."

"But you have a job."

"No, that's nothing, it was all in vain: there's no opening for lawyers here. I have to leave. We're ready to take our chances; on St. Kitts, there are opportunities."

My father had a low-wage job in the Post and Telegraph Company of Antigua – that's how he would pay for the one-way tickets to St. Kitts. Doubtless, he didn't want to depend on his father's charity – an Anglican priest received little more than free lodging from his church.

"If you insist on leaving, may God protect you! All I can give you is fifty shillings and my love," my grandfather said. "It's a lot more than I got in similar circumstances."

Ralph's mother, Annie, called Mudsie by her offspring, put a hand on her son's shoulder. "I understand you, son. Go, if you must. You know, we were castaways too!

"It was 1907, when your father had just been ordained. He was posted to St. Croix and had nothing when we met, but we married anyway and started our family. And since then we've been wanderers, from island to island, as the Lord wills."

"And as the diocese pays," my grandfather said.

Perhaps I should have kicked my mother's stomach wall. I would have had a more secure start, born in Antigua where I had been conceived, in that rectory smelling of candles and preserved fruit. But my kicking muscles were not ready.

"I know where I'm going," Ralph said. "I'm neither a castaway nor a wanderer." I was sensitive to voices, floating in my liquid darkness, and my grandfather's reply was sharp enough to make me jump.

"We're all castaways," John George boomed, "thrown out from some other more favoured place – even my family in British Guyana, exiled French, never forget!"

The Vaniers had been intractable Huguenots, ejected from France after the revocation of the Edict of Nantes, and bounced from country to country until they landed in a place "no one" else wanted.

"Me too," said Annie. "If you live in the Caribbean, then you or your ancestors are by definition castaways or slaves, fleeing or forsaken. I'm Danish – my great-grandmother was exiled."

Annie had copper bowls decorated with the seal of the Danish royal family, which she would later give to me, inherited from this great-grandmother who was supposed to have lived in the Palace.

"Annie, don't fib! She was Irish, and worked in Copenhagen as a serving maid."

"It doesn't matter. The Prince took a fancy to her, and she was then paid a sizeable dowry to take the results of his fancy out to the faraway Dutch colonies."

"Results of his fancy, indeed!" John George said. "Why not call a bastard a bastard? I should know about that." Then he shut up.

"Well, we're going to start afresh and put down roots," my father insisted. "Apart from you, Daddy and Mudsie, you know whom I'll miss most in Antigua?"

"Your benefactress?"

This was someone I was not destined to meet, a philanthropist who had given my father money to study in England.

"No, my cat. I want you to take good care of him. He'll miss me, but there's an animal quarantine in St. Kitts, so we can't take him. If you see him moping, just ruffle his fur and call him Dickey Puss."

"He used to swim out to our raft at sea," Elsie said. "Most unusual for a cat to like water – a real will of his own."

I, too, could swim in my uterine space, learning to push against anything that restrained me.

A few days after moving in to that modest house in St. Kitts, Elsie was stirring vegetable soup on their kerosene cooker and saying, "Ralph, I wish *my* father were here to see our first home. I'm sure he'd be proud, whatever the conditions."

Ralph said, "Cecil would have been scornful of such a small beginning. He never approved of me."

"I'm sure Daddy secretly liked you."

"Hardly! Remember what he said when I told him Mrs Bell would pay for my legal studies, and I fancied marrying you on my return?"

Cecil Rawle's initial refusal to let Ralph marry Elsie had been the cause of my father's departure from Antigua to study in London. If Cecil had continued to say no, I would have remained for all eternity something less than a fancy, just a sweet whisper in the tropical night.

"He said you would never be a good lawyer, you were too honest."

"Said with a crooked smile."

"Anyway, he was wrong. Honesty is not fatal. But you know, when you were in England for so long, I began to lose trust and swore to become a nun."

This too would have annulled my story. There are far more ways *not* to be born than to be born.

"When Daddy died," she said, "I felt so guilty. He was ill and I betrayed him."

"By promising to marry me? No, his rum bottle killed him."

Alcoholism in my genes?

"Anyway," he said, "without your Mum, Cecil's passing was bound to be a blow."

My mother's mother, Sophia Garrett, a Hackney girl fresh out from England, had died at twenty-four in Dominica. She had married the mixed-race lawyer, Cecil Rawle, while he was studying in London. At Sophia's funeral, he dived into her grave in anguish, though this didn't stop him remarrying within the year. After an exceptional career as Attorney General and regional politician, he drank his liver to extinction twenty years later, leaving Elsie, like Cinderella, with an indifferent stepmother and six other half-siblings to fend for themselves.

The couple in Liverpool Row sat down, face to face, and tasted their soup.

A week later, having moved their few belongings into their new home, my father acquired a pet kitten. He admired the independence of cats, how they found their way to their owner's hearts by some magical process while never taking orders.

"I've decided to call our new cat 'Boley'," Elsie said. "Reminds me of Dickey Puss. He's adorable! Look how he sleeps on my tummy, right on top of baby, dreaming away. Maybe he swims, too."

This was not exactly news to me – I could hear the feline's deafening purr. Not quite Mozart, but erotic, nevertheless. And apart from curling up in bed with insolent freedom, Boley would be a great help in keeping down the population of St. Kitts rats.

"Elsie, we should find a doctor. The baby's due in four months."

"I've never felt better, but – if you want – a friend has recommended Doctor Strissiver. I'll make an appointment in a few days. My body is ticking just the way it should. Our baby will have no problems. I dream he will be as cuddly as our cat."

The doctor, when Ralph ushered him in, started by reassuring them. Home visits were the norm, so Elsie, now heavily pregnant, was reclining on a sagging spring mattress on their mahogany bed frame.

After the doctor had prodded and poked my mother's abdomen until I was quite jumpy, he inquired: "This is your first child, I take it?"

Elsie put her hand into Ralph's. "Yes, can't you tell?"

"Well, your weight gain is normal, and everything else looks all right, but I don't have any family antecedents for either of you. Are you eating well, taking lots of milk and fruit, and going for gentle walks?"

"Yes to all of that – except we can't get enough milk here in St. Kitts. And my baby is going to be beautiful!"

As the doctor was leaving, he asked, "How was it for your mother's first child?"

Elsie frowned. "That's me," she said, "and I'm the only one."

"Your mother stopped having children after just one? How odd. Did she have difficulties with you?"

"You could say so," interposed my father. "She died during a Caesarean childbirth."

"But that was twenty-five years ago in Dominica, my dear! Don't you worry! When the time comes, just send for me."

My mother should have been petrified by the thought of childbirth. Her life had been dominated by the loss of her mother on the day she was born. Little matter that she'd had an adoring father, while some children have neither parent; even less that she'd had a stepmother, a wet nurse, and a caring aunt, who had done all they could to fill the gap; and the steady stream of half-siblings only served to underline what a real mother meant. Nothing is as flagrantly absent as the one missing pearl in a well-formed necklace. Her only solution was to become what was missing – to be a mother herself – as quickly and categorically as possible. Though there was little to protect *her* against delivery complications, nature's forces combined so that she was superbly and irrationally confident.

"Fine, Doctor, but just remember, I don't fancy that Caesar thing!" she laughed.

The facilities were so scarce at the hospital in St. Kitts that most births took place elsewhere. Whether or not my mother would be better off at home, there was little choice. The infant mortality rate was three times as high as that in England.

On the other hand, whatever the state of the Caribbean hospitals in 1942, babies were born every day and most survived out there in the world of sun and music.

They still had to name me.

"I think it's a boy: let's call him 'Christopher'," my mother said.

"Just like the island?"

"No, before that, silly! There's a *Saint* in Saint Christopher. You know, the vision Columbus had when he first arrived."

"About the mountain range that looked like Christ being carried across a river?"

"Yes, Christopher meaning 'Christ Bearer', that's my son!"

"Quite a burden! But anyway, that story's all wrong," my father said. "I heard Columbus actually called the island 'San Jorge'."

"Well, who 'Christopherised' it then?"

"The British, much later. Look, let's compromise. Why don't we say our Christopher comes from Columbus himself? Better than 'Cristobal' in Spanish or 'Cristoforo' in Italian."

"If he can't be a saint, all right, I'll settle for him being an explorer."

"By the way, how do you know it will be a boy?"

"Well, I don't want a Christophene!"

Not a vegetable, then, but a choice between three Christophers: the island, the explorer, and the Saint. Thrice blessed – or thrice cursed?

It was a name to be wary of. The first of these three Christophers, the island of Saint Kitts, was a has-been place: once the jewel of Britain's Caribbean empire, then a forgotten little colony. The second, Columbus, was a thief, intrepid conquistador or not. He stole Arawak, Carib and later Aztec lands under the cover of Spanish Catholicism. As for the original Saint Christopher, the 3rd century patron of travellers, an eighteen-foot giant from Canaan, it seems he finished badly. To punish him for wild stories of carrying Christ across a raging river, he was tortured and beheaded by the nearest monarch.

I have made a balance sheet to work out how much I owe my parents for the whole project of being born. The moral mathematics is strange and I keep coming up with contradictions, as if I were dividing something by zero. Owe them everything? After all, they were the prime movers, whatever the results. Owe them nothing? I hadn't been consulted, and my prospects were uncertain out there in the Caribbean.

"Ralph, this is a sorry world, but we'll make it right for our child, won't we?"

Well, I'll work hard, so we won't be poor forever. Lawyers eventually make a decent living, even honest ones."

"But will he be happy?"

She was worrying about the icing before the cake had been baked.

"We'll do our best, love him, get him decent schooling, help him break out of the colonial system, encourage him to see the wide world like his namesake did." His hand stroked my mother's eight-and-a-half-month belly, giving me goose bumps inside.

She must have looked around the room, examining her world, creating little endorphin waves around me, taking in the plain wooden table and the books they had brought, attuning to the bright blue sky through the open window.

"You know, there are worse places. Maybe he'll like it here, after all. With a few changes, it could be paradise. I hope he succeeds in the islands, like my father."

"I hope he succeeds, full stop," my father said.

What counted was not the place but the determination of that couple, my parents. My mother was passionate not only about having children, but possessing them. Starting from zero, my father had had to struggle for an education like a barefoot boy squirming up a coconut tree. Both parents vowed to invest everything in their young ones, to provide them with the opportunities they hadn't had. Happiness would necessarily follow.

However, education can be a dangerous thing, possession can become jealous, and even the sunshine can be deceiving, so I suggest a last look around before we roll up the curtain on what happened. They were right to worry, surrounded by Caribbean torpor: people, projects, companies, crops, governments, and marriages – melting away in the tropical heat. In 1942, beggars flocked the streets of Basseterre, syphilis was widespread, and neglected racial inequalities were poisoning the society. Although still a profitable sugar producer, this island had become an imperial slum. The schooling at the centre of their hopes was non-existent for young children. And the Caribbean's British colonial legacy included whipping disobedient pupils, imprisoning homosexuals, and publicly hanging wrongdoers by the neck.

In addition, there was a ferocious world war going on in Europe, in which my father's brother Beezie would soon be killed, but not before sending my parents a crucial present: a little blue book on child rearing. Nearby in the Caribbean, in January of 1942, a German U-boat had sunk a Canadian passenger liner named *Lady Hawkins* with the loss of 350 lives. The day before my birth, St. Kitts had had a blackout because of submarine attacks on the not-so-distant island of St. Lucia. The heroes of the Normandy beaches had not yet landed, but my own private D-Day was upon me.

Lights, camera, action: I was ready for life, and I chose June 6th 1942 for my first appearance. There I was, a seven-pound, multiracial mixture from three continents, like a soup made of English and French greens, ground Arawak roots, and hot Angolan peppers. A descendant of the cast-offs from Europe, South America and Africa, thrown up on the shores of a fertile, bite-sized West Indian island – flotsam and jetsam.

The one unusual event, as the good doctor held me upside down and listened to my wails, was the appearance of a large birthmark, like a sprawling animal, running most of the length of my left leg. Superstitious Caribbean people say that whatever dreams inhabit a pregnant woman will be transmitted to the baby. That damned cat.

The Whistler

At three years of age, my world was kinetic and untrammelled. My mother whistled when she was happy, which was often. I couldn't whistle, so I kicked things, pulled the cat's tail, or shouted "Boo!" at all comers. My mother was proud of her first child; she would be tested by her second, resigned to her third, and surprised by her fourth.

In the late afternoon, when the sun was mild, she often took me to the park, a short walk from where we lived on Victoria Road. The sidewalks were cracked, the road was potholed, and much of the town's waste flowed by in open gutters. None of this mattered to me – not the heat, nor the sharp odours of cashew rinds, guinep skins, and mango seeds. The fruit I liked most was the tamarind: in my mouth the brown pulp was violent – acidic – stinging – faintly sweet – making me crave for more until my teeth were on edge. When I wasn't eating, my passion was for running: in circles, straight lines, or around corners. Movement entranced me. I couldn't have told you why I was running, but it felt good to leave one place and not to arrive anywhere else.

Despite the dry season, the park still offered patches of yellow-green grass for me to dive and roll on, but I wasn't allowed in the middle of it where it was greenest and cricket was played. Families with riotous young children stayed on the edge, under the red-flowered flamboyant trees. The mothers – white and black alike, but mostly the latter – sat on rough stone benches and looked occasionally at their little engines of destruction; some of them sweating in anticipation of the afternoon's mischief; others oblivious.

It was the year 1945, and the park was named after Sir Thomas Warner, the swashbuckling founder of this Mother Colony: St. Kitts, from which all the other British Caribbean islands were settled. I might bump into things, but the friendly sunshine discouraged thinking about past bloody collisions between English, Spanish, French, Dutch, Caribs, and Africans. The true history of my island surroundings was, as one English Captain put it, "a melancholy series of crimes and calamities." But the ghosts of the past had agreed to be silent during cricket matches, music festivals, and little boys' games in the park.

What to me was the challenge of speed and direction must have appeared haphazard to adults. A boy can run several miles like that without anyone noticing. In the oppressive world of childhood, craziness was one of the few means of power. I whirled my arms like an aeroplane hoping to take off into the blue beyond. When that didn't work, I ran and wobbled with my hands on my head to see of I would get dizzy and crash.

At length, my energy flagged, and I hoisted myself precariously upright onto an unoccupied stone bench. Rapidly, my mother zeroed in on me.

18

"Come down, Chris, don't climb the bench!"

A fuzzy-haired companion joined me and, disobedient together, we leaped up and down on our platform. Hop! I was a little nearer to the clouds. I ignored my mother. Hop! I could see men clad in white moving on the cricket pitch. My mother was coming closer. Hop! I wished I could climb those trees with the red flowers all the way up to the sky. My mother was walking fast. Hop!

Then the bench moved under me, or maybe the ground tilted, or maybe it was the whole world that wouldn't stay still. I was tumbling, then chop! My head slammed into the stone rail. The adults snared us, my mother's arms pulling me upright. My companion's mother, who had joined the little-boy chase, was all puffed up as she lunged for her son.

"Naughty! I said no! Now look at you!" My mother dabbed furiously at my face with a cotton handkerchief. Then she picked me up and hugged me while I cried my eyes out. My comrade – who had not fallen – was not so lucky.

"Bad bench!" my mother grimaced at the imperturbable stone.

"Leeroy, you going get it! Look what happen to you friend!" his mother grunted, and proceeded to smack Leeroy several times on the bottom. I wondered what Leeroy would do. He cried, even louder than I did.

It had been a short friendship of thirty minutes at most, and I hadn't even heard Leeroy's name until that moment, but, in a spirit of comradeship, I expected to be spanked next.

It didn't happen. Instead, my mother bundled me up and rushed me back home in her arms to wash and disinfect the cut. That was how the world worked, I thought. Leeroy got punished and I didn't, for being in the same place. Maybe because I was brown and Leeroy was black he was entitled to more spanks. Maybe my cut, which would later be a permanent scar on my left eyebrow, was enough of a punishment. Maybe my mother didn't know how to spank.

A giant-sized plaster, of which I was proud, covered my forehead for several days. From then on, it sank in that I wouldn't be spanked. Other boys could be punished, but not me. I was special. This came to seem entirely normal. Why should I doubt my special nature? I was special to myself, so why not to the others? And as a result, there was nothing wrong in climbing wherever I wanted.

I heard my mother explain it to the new nurse she had hired to take care of me, who by coincidence had the same name as the street we lived on.

"...and one more thing, Victoria."

We were in the kitchen of our home, and my mother had just shown her where the battered aluminium pots and pans were stored and how the kerosene cooker worked.

"Yes, Mistress?"

"The boy is not used to spanks. On no account must you hit him."

"But if he bad, Mistress? What I do to make him obey?"

"Talk to him, Victoria. He can understand. Explain what you want him to do, and he'll do it. Almost always."

"And if he don't?"

"Well, call me, then."

On other occasions, she would dress up these ideas for her friends. No one minded if I listened. She would take out a small, blue-covered book and read it to them:

"...physical correction – and in particular, spanking – inhibits the creativity of the developing child. He may come to fear that any experiment on his part will entail retribution and violence. He will thus be reluctant to try anything new. By eliminating vital learning situations, his intelligence will inevitably be handicapped. How much better for discipline to be accomplished by reasoned dialogue and tactful suggestion."

"What nonsense! How can you control a child of three if there is no threat?"

Were they talking about me? It sounded so complicated.

"I can tell you, it works on him. I never have a problem. He does what I say. Also, you must realise spanking may damage the parent-child relationship permanently."

"Parent-child what?"

And, more insidious, "But – don't you think – the lack of spanks will, well, not exactly *spoil* him, I suppose, but maybe *soften* him?"

"We all need *softening* – love is the only force that matters!"

My mother's friends never seemed to agree with her methods. I supposed this was because they didn't have her blue book.

In fact, my mother had come to regret her lack of higher education and the opportunities it brought. My father, as a lawyer, had considerable standing in our little island society, though not much money at first. Having been judged equally clever at school, my mother now found herself limited to running a home and raising children. A generation before it might have been sufficient, but, ever since the war, traditions had been breaking down, even in the colonies, and her role seemed insufficient. Her own origins had made her fervent about having children, so now she inflated her calling and made the job of bringing us up a revolutionary affair. The doctrine of the blue book suited her just fine.

In the meantime, we changed houses yet again, moving to the opposite side of the street, as my father's job got better. My mother said we were in our seventh home since arriving in St. Kitts. I was now four. Sometimes, briefly, I wondered where they had been, where I had been, before St. Kitts. Our newest house had an upstairs with a wide veranda. I could look down from it at the people in the bustling street.

One afternoon, my friend Rosemary came to visit. My mother went shopping for a while, and Victoria was left in charge. I climbed over the veranda railing to get nearer to the people below. I stood on a thin shelf of rain guttering, holding on with one hand behind my back. My! The people appeared curious and pointed at me. I smiled back.

"Mister Christopher, you come right back up here!"

That was Victoria on the veranda, petrified to see me suspended fifteen feet above the hard pavement of the street.

"No, no, I'm fine here. Let me play."

"He going jump," someone in the crowd said.

"No, I'm not."

"Come back, you hear, right now!"

"Rosemary, would you like to climb out here?"

"She ain't going nowhere!"

As I jigged on it, the guttering creaked enticingly. I did not intend to fall, but I loved the faces of the concerned people below. I was a king looking down on my subjects. It was so strange to be almost suspended in the air. Could I grow wings and fly? As for Victoria...

A delicious standoff ensued during the twenty minutes it took for my mother to return home. Victoria couldn't hit me or even threaten to hit me. So why should I give in to her requests?

Every time she came close to the hand I kept on the veranda railing, I removed it and changed my stance. The guttering creaked obligingly, and Victoria fluttered backward with a little cry. I looked at her eyes protruding like ripe hog plums, and I giggled.

"You mother going be vexed. You best come back now!"

We both knew it was an empty threat, so I giggled again.

Down below, several barefooted boys whom I knew – and avoided – were grinning up at me. A tall black woman selling peanuts, sugar cakes, and cigarettes from a tray kept repeating, "Lord a mercy, Lord a mercy." Several men stood arms akimbo, faces worried. More people arrived. Could I get a policeman to come?

But then another voice cried, "Chris! Stop! At once!"

I couldn't refuse *this* voice, not yet. My mother grabbed my arms and hauled me back to safety. The crowd cheered and dispersed.

That night, to my disappointment, my mother didn't read to me.

She or my father read to me every night, their stories more real than the humdrum world. I quivered to *Grimm's Fairy Tales*. I loved *Hansel and Gretel,* where the witch is roasted, and *The Fisherman and His Wife,* about why we should not get our wishes answered. There was also *My Book House* in twelve volumes. I felt for *Little Red Hen* who didn't want the sky to fall on her head and the native Indians who always lost out to the white settlers. It was not fair that only grown-ups could read books.

"Why can't I have a story tonight, Mummy?"

"Because you were naughty today and scared us all on the veranda. Suppose you had fallen?"

"But I couldn't fall. I held on tightly."

"That's not the point. You don't always know what's best. Why didn't you obey Victoria? Suppose the veranda had let go of you?"

My mother readily personified the everyday objects around her and I took happily to the game. On the positive side, it was exciting fantasy; but it could easily become a flight from responsibility.

"She annoyed me. And I'm stronger than the veranda." But now she had brought it up, I did feel a little worried the railing might come alive and betray me. Maybe next time I should use both hands.

"Well, what you did was not good. You must behave when I'm not there. Because you didn't, there'll be no story tonight. And Rosemary's parents were very upset that you asked her to crawl out on the railing. She won't be allowed to come back to play with you. Worst of all, Victoria has gone, and I have to find a new servant."

I didn't regret Victoria any more than I pitied the witch in the oven, but it was dastardly to deprive me of my story.

"Rosemary will invite me to her home."

"Only if you promise to obey her parents and servant."

I began speculating on new adventures using Rosemary's veranda, but my mother was relenting, so I pressed my advantage.

"And what about a little story, just a teeny-weeny story?"

My mother took a long look at me, and instead of picking up one of the usual books, she began:

"Once upon a time, there was a boy who wouldn't obey his parents. And his mother thought how good he had been when he was still in her tummy and wondered why he was so disobedient now. And how could he disobey her, when she loved him so much? So, she went to a powerful witch and asked how she could get her son to obey. 'Bind him with this magical rope, and tug on it every time he goes astray,' the witch advised. Think of my love as a rope, Chris." There was a lot more of this, but I stopped paying attention after a while and interrupted her.

"Is it true I was once in your tummy?"

"Yes, indeed. Snug as a bug in a rug."

"But how could I fit in? How did I get there?"

"You don't know how you got there?" My mother looked around speculatively, to see if there was anyone within earshot. Was four years old too young for an explanation?

"It all has to do with love, Chris.

"You see, Mummies and Daddies make babies together..."

My eyes widened. The next twenty minutes were much better than the usual story. There was no nudity ban in our home, so I was used to my parents' unclothed bodies, but I had never thought all the hanging appendages served any exotic purpose. Now I could imagine how grown-ups wriggled inside each other. I learned some new words.

The next morning, I looked with interest at my own appendage. So this was a penis – the thing I had previously called a diddy. I usually paid it little attention, hidden away in my trousers, except on Sundays at the beach, where I didn't have to wear clothes and sand got everywhere. Then I would jump into the sea to wash. My mother said everything came from the sea, so I put some back. I loved to pee in the sea.

My mother was daring in her Caribbean context, for sex education was taboo in polite middle-class circles. Only the cane cutters and the rum jumbies talked openly about such things. After "no spanking", her childcare book advised her not to hide important matters from children, and for the most part she followed this. I soon put this new knowledge to use.

We had a friend called Beryl. She was older than my parents, probably in her fifties. I remember her because she used to visit us quite often. She wore flowery tropical dresses and tied her greying hair in a tight bun behind her head. She smelled like the hibiscus flowers on her dresses with a whiff of perspiration added. I liked people who smiled as much as she did. Beryl lisped and called my mother "Elthie".

The next time Beryl came to tea with us, I walked to where she sat and noticed how fat she was. Her tummy made a large, comfortable mound when she sat down. I put my hand on it. She nodded at me, pleased at the attention.

"I know what this is," I said. "Shall I tell you?"

"Yeth, Chrithtopher, what do you want to thay?"

"I think you're pregnant. You've made love with someone!" I said, happy in my new knowledge. "His penis has wriggled in your vagina."

Grown-ups are funny. At first Beryl seemed pleased that I knew the way things worked, but then her quick smile crinkled and wore itself out until it became a sad look.

To my surprise, I was sent out of the room while the adults talked to each other. I walked around in circles in the garden and wondered when Beryl's baby would be born and if it would play with me. I was interested in wrestling. Things always seemed to take a long time to happen where adults were concerned. Anyway, with all the fat women around there would soon be a lot more babies. Or perhaps I had been rude, and now – at last – I would be spanked. Finally, my mother called me back in and everyone smiled.

Though my first diagnostic of childbirth was wrong, I did not have many weeks to wait for another occasion. My mother announced that she herself was pregnant, and I was going to have another baby brother or sister.

I already had one sister, Hazel, who spent most of her time in her playpen. I didn't remember when she arrived, since I was only two. I knew something had gone wrong, though: my mother said Hazel had survived by the grace of an angel. But this time I would see it all, I thought. It must have been hard work for my parents. They had been forced to wriggle together three times to have their three children.

Or maybe I was wrong about the hard work. As her tummy got fatter, I often caught my mother whistling, so it can't have been that bad.

To my great displeasure, I wasn't invited to the birth. As the day approached, my mother explained that neither Hazel nor I could be present. We would have to stay with our grandparents for a few days. They had come to live opposite us, across Victoria Road, in a place called Rest Harrow (now a bakery) with a tree-filled garden, where we had once lived ourselves. My mother told me these were my only grandparents left, like the last sweets in a bag. It seemed that God had taken the others. Grandpop was a busy priest who ministered in several parishes, while my Granny kept house with no second thoughts. One day in February of 1946 over lunch, she told us that we had a new addition to the family. At first, I was so upset to be left out of things that I wouldn't eat my chicken and rice. Then I became excited. My new sibling was a brother, Peter. I would have someone to wrestle with. It would be nice to imagine I loved my new brother from the start, but I simply liked the novelty. You don't get a new brother or a new cat every day. It didn't occur to me that if you could add people to our family circle, you could also subtract them.

My mother now had three children to look after, and her no-spanking regime began to show signs of strain. She whistled a lot less. She herself could command obedience (with growing effort) but the servants had no sympathy for her niceties. She became less and less satisfied with her role as the revolutionary-young-mother-who-doesn't-spank-her-children, and began to work part-time writing articles for newspapers. Thus, she was obliged to leave us increasingly in our servants' care. My sister and brother were too young to be conscious rebels, but at four I had learned I could do what I liked with no serious consequences – at worst a scowl and a story withheld by my mother, perhaps a serious look from my father. However, he was so busy establishing himself as a lawyer that he seldom intervened. Instead of discipline, I remember riding on his shoulders.

With so much that could go wrong, and three little pairs of hands to help it happen, our next incident was not long in coming. I was in the upstairs playroom admiring Baby Peter's determined crawl along the scrubbed wooden floor. How could he move so quickly? Elbow, knee, elbow, knee; like a naked, flexible rubber toy, he scuttled forward and I ran alongside. He seemed to know it was time for his bath and sped towards the little basin his nurse used to wash him in. She had left to fetch some cold water. The hot water was already there. Elbow, knee, elbow, knee; I paced beside him but – too late – I saw the crawler become a sitter and reach for the kettle. As he scalded much of the lower part of his body, I couldn't have said if his scream was louder than my shout.

The nurse flew back in a panic. She shouldn't have left the kettle within reach. Now, those servants we called nurses in St. Kitts at that time were not real nurses, which meant they knew little about medicine and nursing. They were nannies with a special responsibility for young children. This turned out to be lucky for Peter.

When my mother came home, she was horrified. "How could you take your eyes off him? And why didn't you use one of my creams to soothe the burn?"

This would have been a mistake, as the doctor told us later. Peter had first and second-degree scalds, and the nurse did the right thing by immersing him in cold water at once. Of course it didn't look pretty to see all his skin from the groin down turn ugly red and cover with blisters.

"My poor Peter, look at what the bad kettle did to you!"

But the cold-water treatment stopped even greater damage, we learned, and it all grew back nice and pink in a few weeks. None of his vital functions were affected. I thought it strange the kettle should be blamed, but that was my mother's way. From then on, however, my mother lost confidence in servants' ability to keep her "sweet" little barbarians in check.

"Ralph, what are we going to do? The children have gone wild, and I can't trust anyone to look after them. I'm especially concerned about Chris who seems to egg the others on and won't follow orders."

"Why don't we send him to school?"

"He's only four – there's nowhere for him to go until six."

"Maybe we could hire a teacher instead of a nurse."

"Do you want him to speak Kittitian patois or English? There's no one to teach him properly."

Children in the Caribbean grew up to speak a Creole variant of English (or French) – a dialect that used to be called, less politely, pidgin. Then they learned proper English at school, or not. But some families with pretensions, like ours, inverted the process and kept the Creole out until a later age. An older child, in any case, would master the whole spectrum, from pure patois to acceptable English, and would adjust his speaking according to the context and his family's mindset.

"Yes, there is."

"Who?"

"You. Remember what we always said about our children, that we would teach them ourselves if need be and give them every advantage. You used to teach in Antigua."

"But Ralph! I had teenagers, not infants. I know nothing about early education. I have no books for that. I'm no good for teaching a ruffian who can't read or write yet."

"We'll ask friends in England and find out how they do it. But it would be a shame to organise it just for one child."

"You mean, start a school?"

"Well, a pre-school."

So that was what my mother did, whistling again full throttle. She quit her outside work for two years and found other parents with four-year-olds who were also running out of control. The kindergarten project was surprisingly easy to sell in an island where education had always been regarded with suspicion – a luxury only rich planters indulged in. Times were changing.

Unlike my father, my mother could pass for white, which made people wonder who her parents had been. There was African blood in almost every family tree. With her soft brown hair and pale, heart-shaped face, she could either have been a vamp or a teacher, and the public rapidly accepted her in the second role.

She ordered children's books and equipment for drawing and painting from England, and my father built a climbing frame and a sandpit in the back garden of our eighth house in Basseterre. About a dozen other parents sent children to the school, and I mostly remember that having many friends during the day compensated for some boring exercises with crayons and paper.

But one day, a terrible injustice happened to me. My best friend was John. I was four and he was four, so we were equal. This was important to us because older children had more rights. Then John had a birthday. At school the next day, he announced he was five. We were no longer equal! Why couldn't I be five, too, I asked my mother? No one could explain this to my satisfaction. My father said I was four and three-quarters, but four was good enough, and John was three months older. I wasn't sure what that meant.

Next day, I yelled at John, "You're not five!"

We were inside the playschool but I couldn't see my mother nearby.

"Yes, I am!" he said. He tried – unsuccessfully – to tower over me.

"But yesterday you were four. I'm still four," I said.

"Well, I'm five and bigger than you now."

"No, you're not!" I shook my fist at him.

"I'm the boss."

"No, you're not!"

He pointed at my cat mark and said, "You have a boo-boo!"

Why did he have to elbow me when I grabbed him?

Thus began one of my first fights, to prove which one of us was bigger and more worthy, and, incidentally, to settle our mathematical problem of truncation.

John pushed me into a corner and we began struggling.

"Chris, stop at once!" my mother called.

But I was in no mood to listen; I preferred to sit on John's head for a while.

"Chris, you brute! Get off him!"

Then it was John's turn, as he flipped me over on the linoleum, and it became impossible to respond to my mother – had I even wanted to – with John planted on top of my back. It took several minutes to separate us, and my mother realised how limited her powers of persuasion had become.

"Go outside!" she said to me, while she looked after John.

I went into the far corner of the garden, taking care to not look over my shoulder, and lamented my fate. I thought I could hear my mother whispering to John and knew I wouldn't get any sympathy from that quarter. It would not be the first time she had sided against her own blood. Why did adults not understand? I had to fight John to make him admit he was lying. He couldn't be older than me today if we were the same age yesterday. We were both four, and that was that. And anyway, what was wrong with a little wrestling? How could I grow up strong if I didn't practice punches and arm-locks? I heard a sound from the house that might have been my name called, but I pretended I was deaf. I put my fingers in my ears and shut my eyes for a while. There was a place behind the bushes, near a small chicken pen, where I could not be seen. I stayed there, safe from intrusion, for a good while. When I thought school was over I sneaked back inside.

That evening at dinner, my mother said to me, "Why didn't you come when I called you? You should have apologised to John before he left."

"Didn't hear you."

"If you don't answer to your name, how can I get through to you?"

She turned to my father and continued, "Ralph, I'm going crazy. Nothing works with him. He won't stop fighting when I tell him, and he won't come when I call him."

I looked down at my dinner plate, suddenly fascinated by the chunks of yellow christophene that had been cut for me. How many could I spear at the same time with my fork?

Without looking up, I sensed my father studying me.

"Try an experiment. He needs focus. Train him to come when you whistle."

Maybe they looked at each other, maybe they didn't. At any rate, three chunks of christophene on my fork seemed to be the maximum. I tried to swallow the lot, but choked.

That evening, at the time when my mother used to call us for a bedtime fairy tale, she came to where I was playing, and said, "Listen, Chris."

Then she whistled, "Whee-whee-hoo." Like a train going through a tunnel: two sharp "whees" on intake, then a drawn-out "hoo".

"This is your sound," she said. "It's the same length as your name, see, 'Chris-to-pher' and 'Whee-whee-hoo'. Whenever I whistle like that, it's for you. It means, 'Chris, come at once.' It will be like an invisible cord between you and me. Remember the magical rope? Usually, I'll have something you like: sweets, a meal, or a story. But sometimes it might be because you are in danger: a car, a wolf, or a giant. Or maybe your Mummy might need help. Have you got the sound?"

"Yes," I said, "what sort of wolf?"

"Black, shaggy fur, and red eyes."

"And the giant?"

"Enormous, with just one eye, and a big club."

This looked like a good game despite the rope.

"When I'm ready for your bedtime story, I'll whistle."

She tiptoed out of the room for better effect, and I set myself to listen.

"Whee-whee-hoo."

I rushed to where she was waiting, and she read the promised story. Bluebeard certainly was a tricky husband. The next morning, I was called to breakfast by the same whistle. And after that, my whistle was for everything: meals, school, bath… My mother hardly used my name anymore. I was disappointed not to see any of the wolves or giants, but the call was irresistible.

"O, whistle and I'll come to you," said Robert Burns. Maybe if I had refused once, just once, the spell would have been broken. I didn't, and within a week I was conditioned (brainwashed, some might say), whatever the object of the call. Not only did the sound of my mother's whistle carry farther than her normal voice, but also it became imperative.

If I heard "Chris", it was like the beginning of a conversation; I could decide to respond or not. There were other Christophers out there in the world, after all. But the whistle was for me alone – it was an order with no possible response but movement to the centre of my universe. I had lost a part of my unruly freedom.

When playing with my friends in the garden, this whistle could yank me away from them, like a light being turned off. They were amazed. A magical rope has to be tied to something, so there was an invisible collar around my neck: impossible to escape. Once my friends could see how mindless my reflex was, they began to laugh at me. No one else I knew responded to a whistle. Unless, that is, you include dogs.

One day I realised that dog owners often called their pets in the same way my mother summoned me. I surprised myself on the street running towards a total stranger alongside his canine slave until I registered that he had whistled "Whee-whee" and not my full call "Whee-whee-hoo". That was the beginning of a certain shame and resentment, and perhaps explains why I have never liked dogs. But then again, could a boy with a link to cats ever be friends with the cat's enemies?

I didn't experience the bitter sweetness of the tamarind rod until boarding school, seven years later, when I questioned these chains and regained some of my stolen autonomy. I can't say that I missed being spanked, but during all that period, I was bound to my mother like an automaton. Her sense of fantasy inspired me but I think I never forgave her the humiliation of the whistle. It lodged around me, that magical rope, like a sleeping serpent, always waiting for its moment.

Buried Treasure

"What you got in that bag?" asked William.

"Nothing. Just a book." I swung it to my left hand.

"Where the book come from? Your parents give you?"

"No, I got it from the library."

"Library? They let you have a book? Small boy like you?"

"Yes, me!" I didn't tell him I had to give it back. I didn't want to show it to anyone. What it represented was mine alone, and a six-year-old is a proud animal.

"Let's see?"

"No, not now. It's just boring stuff, really hard to read."

"What's it about?"

"Oh, stupid animals – toads, moles and badgers."

"Badgers? What about mongoose, monkeys and goats?"

"No, just English-type animals."

"Must be boring then."

"Yes, hard to turn the pages." I shrugged my shoulders, turned my face to the sky, and feigned the most uninterested expression I could find. It wasn't easy.

"You know what I heard?"

"No," feeling I probably wouldn't like it.

"The more pages there are in a book, the better it is for toilet paper."

We both laughed, but then I felt annoyed. Why did he have to make fun of my secret project? No more questions from William. I touched my bag to make sure the book was still there. The most exciting day of my life had started badly.

William had been with me in my mother's kindergarten. He was black and younger than me, but just as determined to succeed. He seemed scornful of books that day, but appearances were deceiving. Reading would be vital to both of us. Although my friend would not benefit from an off-island boarding school, he would go all the way up the educational ladder, and on to a brilliant career.

My book out of the way, things got better. We trudged up Victoria Road under the oven-yellow morning sun, already damp from the heat in our short khaki trousers and blue shirts, kicking stones in the road. You had to kick straight to keep the pebble – or mango seed – on the paved surface and get a second crack at it. You couldn't retrieve a stone that went into a gutter. The overflow of household sewage went down those open gutters, and the sickly-sweet, green-and-brown algae growth was hard to clean off our shoes. On the other hand, the gutters were slippery and tempting. I often wondered how it would be to slide barefoot down a long stretch, skating on the slime.

I was one of the few boys in our group carrying a bag to school that day. We only had to bring writing material: exercise book, pen, pencil, eraser, and ruler. No homework. No books. Not yet. I was handicapped by my unaccustomed bag and missed several kicks.

We had nearly reached the gates. The school was at the top of Victoria Road, out of the heat and hubbub of central Basseterre. Time for a last game. Crowding to the right of the road, we ran as close as we could to the wire fence of the St. Kitts Lawn Tennis Club, not stopping, but looking. Yes, they had turned the sprinklers on. The parched grass drank its fill; the spray whirled round and round. The tennis courts would be moist, almost green, and ready for the portly businessmen and estate owners who played in the late afternoon. Swoosh, the spray rotated towards us. Rat-tat-tat, cascades of bright drops caught the fire of the sun, shot through the fence, and mowed down the rearguard of our little army, leaving our shirts speckled with delicious wetness. It would be dry before I sat down in class. Maybe William was right. This was more fun than books. It took a while to remember my secret project, but then I checked my bag had not been soaked.

I walked through the school gates and recalled that my *second* most exciting moment at the Basseterre Girls' High School had been cleaning out the drains. I mean, what's a small boy to do in a whole school filled with girls? Especially at an age when you are not at all interested in sexual differences. A girl was just a boy who couldn't run as fast and was more likely to cry if you hit her.

Curiously, I suppose the headmistress of the school, Miss Pickard, shared this point of view. Boys of five, six or seven were judged asexual. As a service to St. Kitts, the Girls' High School would take these boys in for a year or two and try to teach them to read. But not older than seven, please! The eight-year-olds would have to continue their schooling elsewhere. Thereafter it would be a pure girls' school. I attended for a year, from age six to seven. I didn't know whether the other children had all the bedtime stories I thrived on, but perversely I was determined that the school would *not* teach me to read. I didn't want to let them into my mind. I would learn on my own.

On the day of the drains, after a torrent of rain, I was puttering around with two friends not knowing what to do with my break period. I spied a metal grating overflowing with brackish water, water that hadn't been there the day before. The dirtier it looked the more it attracted us. We walked up to the pool and started kicking and splashing it.

"It must be blocked up," I said. "Let's dig it out!" It was something new. The pool was a sea, and there had to be a treasure to find at the bottom of it. An animal? Gold? Three dead men and a bottle of rum? Eagerly we strained to lift up the heavy iron grating.

It exposed a concrete-lined pit of unknown depth full of dirty water. We ran off and found sticks a few feet long. Anything that came to hand. It was fun to poke and probe with them. Soon we were all quite wet and almost as dirty as the water. None of us boys cared. Our digging dislodged some debris blocking the outlet channel, and the water in the pit started to subside. We cheered. More little boys and girls came to look. We didn't allow them to help. It was our game. Then the water went down far enough so that a small boy like me could climb right into the pit. I brought up handfuls of mud, stones and leaves. No gold, but it didn't matter. We took turns and piled the debris in a heap on the grass nearby. If we were wet and dirty before, now we were thoroughly mucky, absolutely filthy. I forgot the dull classroom, my next lesson due to start any minute, everything except the splendour of our earthworks. Rejoicing in the quantity of our excavation, we looked up to find the headmistress looming over us.

It could have gone badly. I imagine we might even have been expelled.

"What on earth are you doing there?" she asked, aghast. I explained we were only trying to help. We had seen the rain overflowing the drains and thought we could unblock them. No mention of the unfound gold. Nor how much fun it was to get so dirty.

Miss Pickard hesitated for what seemed a long while. Suddenly she beamed a smile at me. "Well done boys! You've saved us a lot of work. But never do things like this without permission. Now come along and get cleaned up for your next class."

Finally, we were heroes. I planned to tell the story in class. And find more adventures.

On the day of my first book, my first love, there was no rain, no playing in the school drains. Classes went by slowly, much too slowly – spelling, sums, pulling pigtails, standing in the corner, until it was time to go home. My bad moment came a little after lunch when the teacher, a jolly, round-faced, black lady, asked each of us to read aloud a page of a book. This was a painful exercise for many in the class, but I loved it. No wonder – pronouncing words correctly was what my father drummed into me every day at dinner. Of course, the teacher had meant it to be from the battered school textbook she had just handed out, "A Kindergarten Elementary Reader", with a brown paper cover and our school stamp on the front. There it was on my sloping desk. If I opened the reader, I would find the story about Jack's house and the malt and the rat. But since we could choose our page, my insidious thought was that I would secretly take my own book, the library book, and surprise the class with something different. My book began, "The Mole had been working very hard all the morning, spring-cleaning his little home..." This would surprise them – even William didn't know about moles.

"Your turn, Christopher," said the teacher.

I stood up and, instead of using the reader in front of me I opened the desk and fumbled inside. The reader slid backward on the wooden top.

As I got my hand on my library book, I realised the teacher would notice the different story. She would see straight off from the cover that it was not a schoolbook. The library book, though far from new, still had its illustrated jacket. Then I would have to explain. Confusion gripped me. It would be fun to show off, but I relished my secret too much. Did I really want to share my visit to the library with the class? Did I want the teacher to get credit for my hard work? I released my library book inside the desk and closed the top. My reader slid off and fell to the floor with a crash. The teacher looked at me in annoyance.

"Excuse me, Mistress," I said, picking the reader up. I banished the thought of my own book and read, "This is the house that Mole built…" No one noticed the mistake. My class would not finish this reader until the end of the school year.

At four o'clock, I waited until my classmates had left. The boys ran out, but to my annoyance, some of the girls dawdled. What did I care if they couldn't find their pencils? I had more important things to do. At last, I was able to open my desk in peace and take out my bag where my book had remained hidden. Thank goodness, I had avoided more questions about it, above all from the teacher. I wasn't sure why, because I was proud of the book. But the moment belonged to me, not to the school – a private thing that might be spoiled if someone else looked at it. Now I had to give the book back as promised.

So I packed my bag without anyone noticing and skipped out of the classroom, down the stone stairs, across the dry playground where little tufts of yellow grass were making a determined stand for survival against the impact of countless youthful feet – shod or not – and into Victoria Road.

"Hey, Chris, let's kick stones down College Ghaut."

William was waiting for me in the road. Nearby, College Ghaut was wider than Victoria Road so as to channel storm flows; it had a single large gutter in the middle. We could kick our mango seed from one side to the other of this centre line with abandon. It took a little longer to get home by that route and we ended up splashed with foul water, but it was well worth it. We didn't have to bother cleaning our shoes at this stage of the day – our mothers or their servants would (reluctantly) do it. I hesitated. I could go to the library another day. Surely, they wouldn't get cross if I didn't come on the day I was supposed to? Suppose I hadn't finished the book? Maybe it wasn't as important to return it as to get in a good game of kicking mango seeds. But I decided otherwise.

"Sorry, William, not today. Have to go somewhere else."

I ran down Victoria Road and Fort Street to the town centre. I consoled myself that kicking seeds with my friend had its limits. In the heat of the action, gutters were thrilling, but afterwards the smell *did* cling.

Meanwhile, my bag felt heavy, how could a book weigh that much? Then I headed along Central Street for the town library. It had taken me a fortnight – ages – to read the book. I thought I even understood most of the story. It wasn't the same, looking at the words, not as easy as listening to my mother or father's voice reading. I had been tempted to give up several times, but I had stuck with it. So many words I didn't know – despite all my parents' talk about dictionaries I couldn't stand interrupting the story to look something up, so I had to guess. My first book. Chosen and read by me, unaided. All of it. Not even my parents knew about it. Of course, there were other books in our house, but they had been read *to* me, so it wasn't the same. Two weeks before, the day I heard my parents talking about it, I had gone to the library all on my own, without telling anyone. The lady there had stamped this book, ticked my name, and smiled. Now she would replace it on the shelf, perhaps with another smile.

That library – today vanished in the flames of a never-to-be-elucidated criminal fire – now seemed so different. At the top of a worn wooden staircase, you could turn left and enter the book sections (starting with children's books), or you could turn right and walk around a small museum. Up to now, I had usually turned right, gazing at the Carib artefacts; the jars with preserved snakes, insects, and creatures I couldn't identify; rusting pistols and swords of forgotten British soldiers; and whitened skulls with their questioning eye-sockets. Now, I would turn left, to the books.

In my drawers at home, I had little treasures hidden – marbles, tops, sweets – and no one else knew about them. I felt this was another secret thing: the time I had spent reading the book, its story, were mine alone, not to be stolen by anyone. Soon I would show them all – brothers, parents, and grandparents – that I could read, but only when I was ready.

I couldn't anticipate that my choice that day – going to the library instead of playing a game – would render me hopeless at school sports, and have other disturbing consequences, but I did ask myself whether I would remember the wonder of the moment. I was breathing normally, yet I felt out of breath. Something internal was waiting for more words, more stories, before it would quiet down. That library was so big. How many stories were there to read? It might take me several visits to find all the interesting ones. What was the book's title anyway? I took it out and looked at the cover. *The Wind in the Willows*, it said, by someone called Kenneth Grahame. My hunger increased. Crossing the Pall Mall (today Independence) Square I looked at the tropical trees, the banyan, the palms, the mangoes, and the flamboyant, and I wondered what a "willow" was. And who would write a book like that, about talking animals? Who was this Kenneth person to tell such exciting tales? Books were like the school drains, full of buried treasures waiting to be discovered. And it thrilled me, vibrating to the core, to be carried far away, to new places and far horizons. This was what I was born for. I climbed the library stairs, looking for more.

Scars

I was a bit afraid of my grandfather, to tell the truth. They called him Father Vanier because he was an Anglican priest. Even off church duty, he wore a stiff, white collar that matched the close-cropped hair over his brown forehead. I couldn't imagine him without the white and black clothes of his office. Churchgoers in the small Caribbean islands must have been afraid, too. They never knew what he would denounce next: unbaptized babies, unneighbourly violence, or unbelieving attitudes; a strong voice striking out from his stone pulpit. His full name was John George William Vanier; my father called him Daddy and – later in life – The Old Man. I called him Grandpop, and even when his eyes were warm, his penetrating gaze made me wary. I suspected he did not agree with my mother's permissive upbringing of me. He was just itching for the opportunity to force some discipline into his eldest grandson.

Nevertheless, I couldn't avoid him. I was seven and he lived just opposite us with my grandmother, Annie. They often took care of my sister, my brothers, and me while my parents worked. We played in their back garden, under the mango trees and Granny's surveillance. No one had confidence in my ability to keep out of trouble.

Grandpop told stories, especially after lunch, or when he had lit up a cigar. He had a voice that carried me up and down each movement of his tale. And beyond his own voice – as I came to understand – was his divine Voice, which only he could hear. It was with great patience that he allowed me to question him in my own piping little voice – patience within limits. One day, to fix my erratic attention, he rolled up his left trouser leg and showed me his collection of scars. I was repelled, then fascinated. Grandpop was almost seventy years old, and from his thigh down, I witnessed a strange and terrible geography. My skin was light brown and smooth; his was darker and covered with gashes, cuts, white lines, pockmarks, discolorations, and more.

"You think it's ugly, don't you?" he asked.

When I nodded, he smiled. "These are not war zones, but holy shrines. God has put each scar there for a reason. Go on, feel them."

Not sure I wanted God to try his artistry on me, I fingered a long, thin gash near Grandpop's left shinbone.

"I did this one myself, Chris, with a machete, when I was hacking my way through a stretch of jungle. It's God's way of reminding me to pay attention."

His remark would come back to me many years later when I cut myself in the same spot, playing tennis with a sharp-edged metal racquet.

Then I tapped an elegant line of small black marks on his calf muscle, and his eyes lit up.

"That was the evil snake," he said.

"What snake?"

"It was brown and green, and a good ten feet long. We shouldn't call it a snake, really. It was a boa – a Red-tailed Boa Constrictor."

Now hooked, I asked why the boa had bitten him.

"Well, the Church had sent me on a mission to a remote Indian village. I went up the Demerara River into the jungle. I intended to visit the natives, and help them if I could. Bring the Word of the Lord, and perhaps medicines for the ailments their jungle potions couldn't cure. No one had been there for months. I took with me a bible, my pharmacy box, and a sharp hunting knife.

"When the river boat dropped me off at the village, I was greeted by shouts and confusion. The villagers were running into the jungle in a frenzy that had nothing to do with my arrival. Painted chests heaving, they shouted something about a boa. With difficulty, I found out the creature had stolen a small child from the village, and that the tribe was trying to get revenge. By the time I caught up with the main party, they had killed the monster by shooting arrows through its head."

"Didn't the boa fight back?"

"It should have, but just after eating the child, with its belly full, it was quite torpid and vulnerable. I saw it, agonising on the ground, with a huge, distended stomach. This wasn't my first encounter with a boa constrictor. I knew it first wrapped up its victim in its coils, breaking its bones, then swallowed it whole. It was fond of goats, pigs, and small mammals. It might take several weeks to digest its prey. Then I noticed how close the bulge was to the head of the boa – three feet of over-sated, slithery belly followed by seven feet of writhing, hungry tail. I realised the child had only just been swallowed – swallowed, not chewed – and I thought I could still do something useful. I brandished my hunting knife and asked the braves permission to dissect the snake. They must have thought I wanted the skin, and didn't stop me."

"You cut it open, Grandpop?"

"That's when I got this scar. I don't know whether I stumbled or the half-dead snake lunged at me, but its fangs whacked me painfully on the back of my leg. I was so concentrated on the possibility of extracting the child I didn't look at my own cuts until later. The boa wouldn't keep still, even with the arrows through its eyes and head, but my blade was quality Swiss steel, and at last, I made an incision in the tough skin. When the Indians saw the child's arm appear, many came and helped me to slit the rest of the beast down the middle like an unwholesome banana. Imagine our surprise to extract the entire body of the child – it was a boy of two or three – still in one piece. When we laid him on the ground and cleaned him up, he was obviously dead, eyes closed, ribs crushed in, but not dismembered or disfigured."

I pictured how I would have felt just out of the boa's belly, all gooey and slimy. Would the reptile's stomach acids be dissolving the soles of my feet?

"The parents of the child began wailing – indeed it seemed the whole village was wailing at the injustice of it – and I saw they were going to take him back for burial. Then a quiet Voice spoke to me, and said maybe there was still a chance for the boy. A young child's bones are more flexible than those of a goat, so why not try to wake him? I used every bit of the prestige I had gained when I had opened the boa, and insisted they let me treat the boy. I'll always remember the fear-struck faces around me as I administered first aid and breathed into the boy's lungs. I had saved people from drowning, lungs full of water, but never a boa victim, and I prayed to the Lord it would work."

Grandpop paused to look at me. I saw myself as that little boy, my breath sucked away by the vile snake, waiting in the darkness for my saviour.

"And?"

"God answered me, even though I wasn't a real priest. An electric shock ran down my back, and I knew the precise moment when the Indian boy started breathing on his own. He was in pain; he was injured; but he was alive. I put healing ointment on his bruises, and he began moving."

I felt the gratitude of the boy as he awoke.

"And what then? Did his eyes pop open?"

"I ignored the boy and I gave thanks to God, of course. I went down on my knees and prayed, surrounded by the Indians."

"Did they thank you?"

"More than that. They saw my God was great. With my bible and my cross, I converted the whole village to Christianity, that day. They were true believers, because they had seen. They, too, went down on their knees and prayed with me."

"How do you mean, you converted them? What did they believe before?"

"Some may already have heard of Christ from previous river evangelists, but most worshipped the jungle and its animal spirits, according to their ancestral rites. You can see how important this snakebite scar is to me. It shows faith can accomplish wonderful things. Do you understand faith, Chris?"

"Yes, Grandpop. Your faith in God caused a miracle and gave the boy new life."

I wanted the magic of Grandpop's faith. My sole reservation was a reluctance to go down on my knees like the credulous Indians; the church pews on Sunday had always seemed so hard.

Grandpop looked at me strangely. "I wouldn't put it like that. I prefer to say if I hadn't had faith, *and* hadn't known what to do, no one would have saved the boy."

I was puzzled that Grandpop seemed to be withholding and playing down his magic. It would be ten more years before I saw why he didn't like the word "miracle" when I read Oliver Cromwell's advice to his soldiers: "Put your trust in God, my boys, and keep your powder dry."

Some time later, when my grandfather was out of the island, I asked my mother about the snake story.

"You know, all of this took place in British Guyana when your Grandpop was quite young. Your father knows the story by heart."

Did he truly go into the jungle by himself? And what did he mean when he said he wasn't a "real" priest?

"Oh yes, the South American jungle exists, and he went there, and doubtless the boa constrictor existed. As for the Indian boy, we don't know if he lived very long; Grandpop never saw him again. Your grandfather had left school early to work in a pharmacy. That's how he knew so much about medicines. We still have the mortar and pestle he used for grinding powders. He hadn't had much school, but he could read, and the Church valued him for his enthusiasm. To their surprise, when they gave him a bible, he learned huge stretches by heart. He had a phenomenal memory, and so the Church recruited him to be a lay preacher. But, no, he wasn't a priest yet."

"How did he talk to the Indians?"

"Well, he was half-Indian himself, and got along well with the tribes, understanding their language even though he didn't speak it fluently, so the Church thought it wouldn't do any harm to send him out on missions."

"How old was he?"

"When he cut the boa open? About seventeen."

This didn't seem very old to me.

A few weeks after the boa constrictor tale, I asked my grandfather to show me his scarred leg again, hoping for a new story. He pulled up his right trouser leg and winked at me.

"What's happened Grandpop? Your scars are gone!"

Indeed, the skin on his leg was not as I remembered – it was almost without a blemish. What sort of prayer would a priest make to heal the scars of a lifetime? If he had this power, I wanted to know more.

He winked again, and pulled down the other trouser leg. Nothing had disappeared after all – I had been tricked – his left leg still showed these spectacular badges of honour. I wanted decorations like that for myself; adventures seemed indissociable from scars. I pursued my goal of a story, and grabbed his leg. I worked my fingers all around it. If size were anything to go by, the best story would be linked to the biggest scar. Triumphantly, I picked out a deep gouge under the knee, larger than the machete cut, and indicating a broken bone.

"How did this happen, Grandpop?"

"Ah, that's the fault of my horse."

This did not seem like a good beginning – horses were not my favourite animals.

"You remember my Church visits to the remote villages? Some of them were not accessible from the river, and I had to go on horseback. The Church gave me a sturdy brown colt, full of energy, which I came to love dearly. I followed paths, tracks, and trails. Some of the trails were broad enough to be considered roads where horse or oxen-drawn carts could pass. It was just after the turn of the century, about 1902."

I hoped he would meet some more exciting type of animal.

"On the day I got this wound, I never reached my destination. The trail was so good that a car overtook my horse. All this happened fifty years ago, and as I'm telling you this story, there must be several dozen cars all over Basseterre and St. Kitts. Why, even your father will have one soon. But cars had only just arrived in Guyana. And I hated cities like Georgetown, where the few vehicles had been imported. That day, I had the bad luck to be on the same road as a crazy new owner. The fool was showing off his new toy, driving as far as he could into the jungle."

I couldn't decide whether I'd prefer to be on the horse or in the car.

"You have to imagine how frightening it looked, this mechanical monster bearing down on me with its shattering roar, belching gasoline fumes and kicking up a dust cloud. It was worse than a herd of wild pigs, or a hungry boa. At least, my horse thought so. We were both scared out of our wits, but as my dear horse had less wit to lose, it went berserk. It bolted, and threw me out of the saddle. Unfortunately, one of my feet was caught in a stirrup and the horse dragged me for a mile before anyone could stop it.

"The man in the car had to shoot it, so I heard later, but I had blacked out by then. All I remember is falling, pain, and darkness. The car owner – curse him and bless him – picked up my battered body and transported me many miles back to the nearest hospital. I remained in a coma for days. Afterwards, I learned the doctors had diagnosed multiple fractures and serious internal injuries. When I woke up, they told me little, and especially not that my condition was incurable and I didn't have long to live."

I tried to put myself in my grandfather's body, waiting to die, but the idea was too fearful. Surely, I was not going to die, not any time soon?

"This is where the story really begins. Family and friends drifted by me saying goodbye. After days of floating in and out of consciousness, I realised I *was* dying. There was so much pain I didn't care at first. But then I wondered whether it was not too soon to leave. I felt guilty I had not done enough. I talked to my Voice, and I told God if He wanted me now, He could have me, but it was a pity because I wasn't even a real priest yet. If He wanted to keep me in the circuit, I would do all the studying necessary, whatever the sacrifice, to become a real priest. And then I would serve him for the rest of my life, as long as He needed me. I can't remember exactly what the Voice replied, but He must have said yes. I walked out of that hospital without crutches eight months later. Feel that broken bone again. Yes, the doctors gave me up for dead, and that was fifty years ago.

"Now you have had another whiff of faith, Chris. Faith can remake a life. Faith saved me. It gave me a future. Someday, this may happen to you. What do you want to do with your life?"

I no longer liked the way this story was heading. I didn't understand faith after all, and wanted to say no, I didn't want to wear starched white collars and go to church every Sunday. I would have preferred to be a swordfighter, or perhaps an assassin, and live forever. The incompatibility of these dreams did not give me pause. But I said, "I think, instead of a horse, I'll own a car when I grow up."

Of course, there were things missing from the horse tale that I didn't discover until much later. My grandfather would die at the age of ninety, more than seventy years after the horse had thrown him, and twenty years after he had told me the story of it.

I asked later, "How did Grandpop become a priest? Did his family help him?"

No, it was the Church," said my father, "always the Church. He had to leave Guyana to study. Less than two years after the horse incident, in 1903, the Church gave him a scholarship to Codrington College, a private Anglican seminary in Barbados. He must have worked incredibly hard to catch up on all his missed schooling. At Codrington he was an external student of Durham University in England, which awarded him a Bachelor's Degree in 1907. He dreamed of Northern England – far-off and cold – where his exams came from, he told me. He was ordained by the Bishop of Antigua in the same year as his B.A. and spent the rest of his life in the Church's service, preaching in the small Caribbean islands. One of his first postings was to St. Croix, which was Danish then but later American. There he met your grandmother Annie, and I was born."

"But what about Guyana and his people? Didn't he ever go back?"

"No," said my father, quickly. "Relations weren't good."

Not knowing how lucky I was to have my own secure home, I couldn't imagine anyone deserting his parents, and certainly not my wise grandfather.

"Why?"

"None of us are sure. You know he was half Amerindian? His mother was not part of the Vanier family in Georgetown – that made him a bastard. They brought him up, gave him board and lodging, but refused to acknowledge him as an heir. His siblings inherited the family estate – what there was – not him. When he understood this at age twenty, he slammed the door on his kin and left. Maybe the Holy Father became a substitute for his real father, John Henry."

"That was not the main reason for his anger," said my mother.

"Quarrels over money don't last. Years later, I talked to George Benson who knew the Vanier family in Guyana. The real problem was your Grandpop's girlfriend. He was in love with the daughter of the owner of the pharmacy where he worked, a rich girl from the Fonseca family. However, the Fonsecas were related to the Vaniers. When the girl's family found out her suitor was a half-Indian without money, and a cousin to boot, they refused to let her marry him, and it broke his heart. That's why he left home, and why he didn't return."

These internal scars were invisible when I was seven. But, later in life, I wondered how he could have failed to return home. I felt he must have yearned for reconciliation. I knew little about the fate of his Amerindian and French-named families, only that both parents were dead by the time he had finished his studies. And was he pained at the sorry state his country of Guyana fell into? On his sickbed in 1971, my father said Grandpop asked to go back, but his Voice was silent.

There were many more tales, about alligators with sharp teeth cutting through the green river waters, and animal traps that unwary travellers fell into, and Indians with blowguns who were not so friendly, but later in my seventh year, I became impatient with the way they all came back to God.

"Grandpop, tell me a different adventure story."

"About the jungle in British Guyana?"

I didn't want any miracles or faith games this time.

"No, something else. Were you ever a pirate? Did you ever rob or kill people?"

Grandpop paused at my impertinence, and his stern gaze lighted on a half-full cigar box. "Kill, no. Rob, not really. But do you believe in smugglers? Would smuggling be as good as piracy?"

That was tricky. Certainly, I believed in fairies, doctors, and lawyers. But smugglers? Did I see a gleam in Grandpop's eye?

"OK," I said, looking at his trouser leg.

"You don't mind if I have no scar to show you?"

"Not if I can have my own set of scars one day. I've only got the one on my eyebrow, where I fell down in the park."

"That's easier than you think. Well, this adventure happened between the two world wars, in the early 1920s. I was a real priest then, married to your Granny, with three children, including your father. Every few years the Anglican Church would change our ministry, and then we would have to travel by boat between the islands, with all our baggage, by whatever face the sea showed. When we arrived at port, the Customs men would search us."

"What were they looking for?"

"All sorts of things. We weren't free to bring in goods – and especially weapons – as we liked. You don't know about excise taxes, but let's say that if I had anything controversial, like liquor, the customs might confiscate it or fine me.

"There I was, at the port of St. Johns, Antigua, with Annie and the children, when a zealous brown-skinned customs officer cocked an eye at me. The native Antiguans were trying to be even tougher than their white, English Head of Customs.

"He asked, 'Well, Father, what you have to declare? Any gold or guns?'

"The mountain of our battered metal trunks, wooden crates, worn leather suitcases, and assorted objects must have looked impressive. You could have hidden anything under it. But the boat fare had taken all my savings, and I had no money in my pocket to pay any fines or duties. I decided to lie."

I thought I had misheard. Obviously, my grandfather, the priest, wouldn't tell a lie.

But he continued, "I adjusted my clerical collar and smiled slightly. 'Apart from our books, clothes, and some sacramental objects, I have 300 cigars, 60 bottles of wine, and a case of rum.'

"There was a moment of silence while I raised my eyes to the sky.

"The officer broke into huge guffaws. 'That's the best! And you be our next priest! I knows you don't drink or smoke. Can't fool me, Father, you all go on through.'

"He patted me respectfully on the back, expedited the family's belongings into the free zone, and vowed to tell all his friends what a tease I was.

"In fact, I had been over-truthful: I had tripled the real quantities of my contraband. May the Lord forgive me! I told you the story has no scar, but I do have this," and he showed me his tobacco-stained fingers.

I looked at Grandpop chuckling and felt much relieved. Scars without pain. I could go a little distance with this cheating God of his.

Boys Climb Trees

I was greatly attracted by trees as a way of escaping from the world. Adults don't climb trees. As a boy, even if I got a few scrapes, once perched high above the ground I saw things differently. I could spy the Indians creeping up on me from afar. The wolves could howl but I was safe from them in the high branches. Not that there were any wolves or Indians in St. Kitts; we could only boast of mongoose. But there were secondary advantages. Grown-ups couldn't find me, my small brother looked up in admiration, and there were fruit.

"Tree climbing" doesn't mean the same thing to a Caribbean boy as to a European or an American. For a start, it's a year-round activity, with no cold weather to distract us. Also, most trees of interest to small island children are fruit trees. We don't grow trees for wood – lumber is imported. Except for the grand old estate manor houses and public squares, we don't invest in decorative trees either. There are banyans, baobabs, mahogany, lignum vitae, royal palms, and sandbox trees in St. Kitts, but in the gardens of Basseterre, we plant trees for food. To a Caribbean, climbing trees really means "going for the fruit". I would only make an exception for the flamboyant, which bathes the island in such brilliant colours I confess to scaling them just to be in a sea of orange and red. To Kittitians, "flamboyant" is only secondarily an adjective; it is first and foremost the name of our national tree, *delonix regia*, also called *royal poinciana* after a charismatic French governor of the island, Philippe de Longvilliers de Poincy, from that long-vanished 17th century period when the French and the English shared things in an uneasy peace – but peace, nonetheless. Among the best fruit-bearers for climbing are plum, tamarind, guinep, almond, and fig. Breadfruit is too sticky; pawpaw can't hold your weight; guava and avocado grow too low to be daring; Caribbean cherry is too prickly; and mango doesn't need to be stolen – when the fruit is ripe, it falls off the tree by itself. Coconut and date palms are in a class of their own. Long ago, a teen-aged Madame de Maintenon, future wife of Louis XIV, lived in the Chateau de Poincy and adored the very same fruits that I did.

So, I climbed the easy trees around me and sometimes brought down fruit for the others. I kept these adventures secret. But things didn't always work out the way I wanted. Trees can be adversaries, and this is another reason to tackle them. While living in house number eight on Bay Road, I once climbed an enormous hog plum tree. The plums were small, yellow, and juicy. Some of them fell naturally to the ground but not nearly enough for my appetite.

The tree that bore them was thirty feet tall, with tiny green leaves and coarse grey bark. If I had lain down with my brother Peter and my sister Hazel and we had formed a circle, we could barely have touched fingers around the base. There were no low branches, but about eight feet from the ground, the huge trunk forked into two. In the middle, there was enough space for a small boy. Looking up, nothing seemed impossible. I had to get those plums, so I stood on a box and scrambled my way from side to side, using the rough bark for footholds. Right foot – push – left foot up – grab with hands – left foot – push – pull with fingertips – repeat. Only a modicum of skin was lost.

At last, I sat in the fork and was exceedingly proud for a while. Then I found I couldn't climb any higher, so I gave some thought to getting back down. Shame and panic! I couldn't descend. It is astonishing how forbidding an eight-foot drop can seem when you are only four feet tall yourself. It was unthinkable to go down forward, hands first, and backward I had nowhere safe to put my feet. I was afraid to jump.

Now climbing trees should be a reversible phenomenon. Go up and come down – at your own speed. At least, that's what I had always hoped. But reversibility is not guaranteed. Sometimes there's no going back – to your home, your lover, or your country – and here's where the inimical nature of the tree shows itself: it may impede your progress, make you lose control, gash you, or stop you entirely. The hog plum tree revealed a grim reality. I could be daring looking in one direction, but helpless in another. I hated moving backward into situations – I wanted to see where I was going before I started, and feel the result of my choice afterwards. Translated: for tree manoeuvres, I could never proceed butt-first. Going down a ladder was not a problem once I had placed my feet on the top two rungs, because I could see the next ones. But there was no ladder here. Backward descent would nevertheless have been my best plan for the plum tree. Had I simply lowered myself by my hands from the fork, it wouldn't have mattered if I couldn't find the old footholds in the bark. There would only remain a four-foot drop, and I was well padded. But I couldn't do it. I was always reluctant to trust what I couldn't see and hold. Yet, one day I would fall this distance in the black of night without caring.

I called to my little brother, who was following my exploits with curiosity, "Peter, can you find another box?" but this was beyond the resources of a three-year-old.

Negative. The more I thought of falling the more petrified I got. Should I stay there forever, perched like a sick monkey? Or should I risk punishment for going somewhere not allowed, and be dishonoured in the eyes of my brother?

"Peter, please call Grandpop and tell him I'm in trouble out here." Peter could do this with enthusiasm.

A few minutes later, my Grandpop shuffled slowly out of the house in pyjamas and slippers. He had been disturbed from his bed. An after-lunch nap is appreciated by all in the Caribbean, and sacred for the over-sixty.

"What is this nonsense? Why are you up there?"

"Looking for plums..."

"And why can't you climb down? Silly boy, here, get on my shoulders." And he helped me down.

I should have been relieved, happy to escape my imagined injuries, and glad to avoid a spanking from my grandfather. Instead, the knowledge of my frailty was too heavy and I burst into tears.

"Young man, let this be a lesson. Don't go back up this tree."

"Yes, Grandpop."

"Do you have any plums to show for it?"

"No, Grandpop."

"Don't ever go into places you can't get out of."

But there was no way I could obey his order as I grew up, and the hog plum tree problem was a small one compared with the volcano I would soon climb. I might have escaped falling, but that second scar was still in the making.

Brimstone

"A volcano can be a dangerous place, Chris," my father said to me. "You can come with us only if you promise not to stray."

It was 1949, and I didn't know much about volcanoes, but "dangerous" sounded good to me. The contrarian nature of little boys is always looking for ways to express itself. I didn't think the grown-ups really knew what was good for me. When they said, "Don't stray," I knew they were trying to keep me away from something interesting, and I resolved to find it. Perhaps there was more than my own nature involved. I was obedient about many things, but the volcano had a liberating and provocative influence on me from the start.

"I'm going to climb the volcano tomorrow," I said to my friends at school. "Bet you've never seen it!" No one in my class had climbed it, but they all seemed to know things about it.

"Jumbie going to get you," said one of them cheerfully. I gaped, because although my mother had told me all about the fairies, elves, and dragons I was quite likely to meet in life, we had never discussed the Caribbean jumbie. Surely, it didn't exist, I said to myself. I had read the legends of Perseus and the Gorgon, Hercules and the Cyclops, Theseus and the Minotaur – these were my preferred otherworldly companions. The jumbie was too local, too lower class. I knew nothing about the St. Kitts jumbie.

"What jumbie?"

"The jumbie on the mountain going to get you!" my friends repeated and ran away laughing.

"What's a jumbie?" I asked my mother that night.

She, too, was amused. Everyone seemed to think jumbies were funny. I was not so sure. "Who's been talking to you about jumbies, Chris? It's all nonsense! There aren't any jumbies."

"But what is a jumbie, anyway?" I persisted.

"Well, people believe a jumbie is the spirit of a dead person," she said. "It's supposed to be a troubled spirit, refused entry to an afterlife, which comes back to do mischief."

"In England, they would call it a ghost," my father added in the background. "But it's not so simple. Remember last Christmas at carnival we had Mocko Jumbies on stilts? The Mocko Jumbie tradition goes back to African religious beliefs, brought to the Caribbean by the slaves. You know how tall they are? That's for them to protect the village from evil spirits."

I was too young to understand that whereas well-filtered European folklore and fantasy were palatable in a religious Caribbean family, jumbies, Obeah and Voodoo had the disquieting smell of heresy, a competing system of beliefs.

"So it's real, then?"

My mother intervened. "It's time for bed, Chris, if you are going to come with us tomorrow. And there are no such things as jumbies. Think of fairies instead. Forget about jumbies. Who told you about them?"

But I held my counsel and didn't reveal what my friends had said, that there were jumbies on the mountain.

The collision of cultures was hidden from me. At that age, my mythologies were additive rather than substitutive. If jumbies met fairies, one wouldn't make the other vanish: they would simply cross swords or have tea together.

Subsequently I came to realise that the jumbie was associated with the ancient rites of passage from boy to man, but the night before the climb, I scared myself to sleep.

I dreamed of a full moon, and tombstones, which stood like white teeth in front of me. I advanced to touch. The stones cracked open, and grey-faced corpses clambered jerkily out. They tottered towards me, eyes blank, and I cried, "You're not alive. I don't believe in jumbies! Go back!" The ground opened in agreement and swallowed the dead bodies in slow motion, to a sucking noise, and then taut silence as their bent fingers disappeared into the earth. But then I smelled rotting matter, like the dead fish with flies crawling out of it that I had seen on the beach. Thin laughter came from behind me.

"Don't turn around. We aren't pretty, the real jumbies."

I ran and ran, but they kept on getting closer.

Once awake, however, I was ready for anything. I knew my father had done the volcano trek several times, with friends and with my mother. He had even climbed the peak itself (3792 feet), and said he knew the routes well. I had never been allowed on the climb, which he considered too difficult for a child of six or less. Most St. Kitts parents would have frowned on taking children a good deal older, but he was giving me my chance at seven; my brothers and sister had to stay behind.

My memories of this first climb are impressions of light and dark, of fatigue, of deliberately straying, and of perceived, delicious danger.

It began with an early morning bumpy ride in a truck through fields of cane. I couldn't see where we were going. Cane fields were the wallpaper of the St. Kitts countryside. Once you left Basseterre, green-and-yellow knotty cane stalks were everywhere, plastered over the roadsides, the skyline, and even underfoot; but the only way cane could interest me was if my parents would stop and cut some. Eating peeled cane joints is a serious pleasure for Caribbean youth. To my disappointment, this did not happen often, and not at all that morning on the way to the volcano. Later, I would remember my father saying it wasn't legal to cut cane from the roadside – it belonged to the estates and had to go to the factory to be crushed into sugar. I felt it was his mood; sometimes he would allow it and sometimes he wouldn't, but maybe it also mattered if we could be seen. He was, after all, Secretary of the Planters' Association.

I began to wake up when the estate truck dropped us off at the beginning of the rainforest. My parents had invited several friends who all hoisted packs of food and spare clothes on their backs. I carried only my weapons. I had a penknife and a slingshot, or "catapult" as we called it in the Caribbean. Of the forest on this first trip, I registered mostly the gloom. It seemed one minute a bright yellow morning sun was warming us up like toast, the next minute a mass of tangled trees and vines blotted out the light. The transition must have been more gradual, but I noticed nothing in-between. If I had known the expression "gothic atmosphere", I might have found it appropriate – a dark cathedral of giant trees with tiny rays of sunshine trickling through deep-green stained-glass windows to the sky. As I followed my parents up the winding path, the trees seemed to become bigger and bigger, their buttressed roots gnarled and encircling, and I was glad I had brought my catapult to protect us all from dangerous creatures. That there were no serious predators – snakes, tigers, or wolves – of any sort in St. Kitts didn't make me any less alert to the possibilities. And what about the jumbies?

The walk up must have taken three hours or more, rather than the two-and-a-half they advertise in the tourist brochures these days. But I didn't feel I was keeping them back. Most surely not my fault, I thought, but that of the adults, who would stop and talk too often. And if I went off the path from time to time, it was my right to explore. Why did they have to shout at me? I was not yet tired, I told myself, despite the annoying tendency of the rugged path to get steeper and steeper. Not tired, despite the ground that kept on slipping under my feet. It was normal to fall a few times. Not really fall, anyway – just skid a little and then stabilise on my knees. It was at this point, I think, that I started remembering the jumbies and wondered if they were tripping me up. What would they look like anyway? Would they be grey with sharp, black teeth, or black with red tongues and white incisors? I couldn't see far into the sombre undergrowth so I changed my tactics and decided to stick closer to the adults.

Neither myself at seven, nor my parents, were concerned with the real dangers of the volcano erupting. Our tropical world was full of these unnoticed risks – quiet volcanoes, buried earthquake fault-lines, and social dynamite inherited from the slave era, whose existence was suspected but which remained unfelt and unheard. I was perhaps the only one afraid of climbing the St. Kitts volcano, and this was because of the jumbies.

Then we halted, about halfway up to the crater, deep in the forest, where a wide section of the path overlooked a steep ravine. I could see down about thirty feet on my right, ferns and saplings covering a farther incline a lot deeper. I felt that if I fell there, I would roll forever. Overhead, giant tree trunks supported the heavy forest canopy. My father used his cutlass to chop the end of what looked to me like a thick, brownish-green rope entwined about one of those tall trees. I stopped thinking about jumbies.

"Watch this," he said, and took off his backpack.

He grabbed the rope with two hands and shook it free of the tree. Now I saw it went all the way up to the highest branches where it was attached in some intimate way.

"It's not a rope," said my father. "It's not even part of the tree. It's a liana, a plant of its own." He tugged on it hard and it didn't give any further.

With that, he kicked off the ground, adroitly swinging out over the void, ten, fifteen feet. My throat stopped up to see him in the air, hanging just by his hands, with an awful drop below. Then he was back, landing firmly on the path. All the grown-ups tried it, even my mother, each of them swinging more or less gracefully, out and back. I looked on with extreme fear and excitement. Would they let me do it? Could I hold on? Did I want to do it? At last, I was saved from my uncertainties.

"Let me try it," I said.

"You're too young to swing, Chris. Next time, I promise," my father said.

They all picked up their backpacks and continued. Outwardly, I was furious; they had not let me try. Inwardly, I was relieved; from now on, I would practice climbing ropes, I told myself. I wanted adventure, but it had to be in small doses. I hoped the volcano would give me other opportunities to exploit.

When we had walked up that slippery path a long, long way, it came to an abrupt end in a small open clearing on a ridge, and there we lunched. Not too soon for me. I gobbled my sandwich and wanted more, but they made me wait. It was deliciously cool, like putting my head in our kitchen refrigerator, but so moist that some adults changed shirts and my mother made me put on a sweater. I could see nothing because of all the mist around us.

"We're on the lip of the crater," said my father. "These are clouds, Chris. At three thousand feet, it's always cloudy and often raining up here."

I couldn't accept it. Surely, the clouds I looked up at every day in the sky were more solid than this? I punched the insubstantial white mist in frustration, but I got nowhere. My mother gave me another sandwich, perhaps to calm me down.

The clouds then cleared for a while, and looking past my sandwich, I saw the enormous hole in the ground the adults called the crater. Big, deep, scary, this was what we had come for. Was it the jumbies' home? I could see grass down there, something shiny like water, and brown unhealthy patches of ground. The bottom seemed impossibly far away. The crater walls were almost vertical – the green vegetation funnelling down more than six hundred feet to the heart of it.

Not just spectacular, our volcano is fearful, one of eighteen such volcanoes in the Caribbean. Some islands, like Nevis, where my father farmed, are nothing but volcano – nowhere to hide if it erupts. There are also submarine volcanoes in the region, new islands being born. "Kick'em Jenny" is a few miles north of Grenada, where an unpredictable stream of underwater eruptions shakes the sea surface from time to time like a giant electric mixer. Caribbean islanders get used to volcanoes early in their lives. We live on the backs of these monsters, oblivious, until something goes wrong.

In 1949, on my home island of St. Kitts, the central peak with its attendant volcano was called Mount Misery – the name given to it by Sir Thomas Warner, the first British colonist. Later in my life, it was gentrified into "Mount Liamuiga" – a Carib word meaning "fertile island". I approved the second version as a welcoming gesture to visitors and a belated recognition of the original inhabitants, but for me the volcano would remain Mount Misery; I couldn't change the name any more than I could erase a scar.

"Suppose the volcano blows up while we are here?" I asked.

"It can't do that," replied my father. "It's what we call a dormant volcano. Not yet quite extinct, but sleeping in a terminal coma."

"But it has blown up, hasn't it? With a big bang?"

"The last eruptions were in 1692 and 1843, a long time ago. It won't happen again."

My father was wrong, as I learned later. A volcanic island is a violent child, alive even when asleep. The deep Caribbean seabed was wounded long ago, and the crater is a scab on this wound. Every time the fiery child stirs in its tectonic dreams, the scab breaks, letting loose all manner of heat, sound, and violence. Mount Misery will erupt again. Worse, when their moment comes the Caribbean volcanoes of St. Kitts, Nevis, Dominica, St. Lucia, Guadeloupe and the rest will be "grey", like Montserrat. Unlike the "red" variety, which erupts with a spectacular but sedate lava flow (Mt Etna), the grey volcanoes explode violently, magmatic eruptions generating pyroclastic flows and surges, leaving sudden death in their wake (Mont Pelée). The eruptions my father had referred to were serious enough affairs, but he did not mention the catastrophic event of AD 400, which seems to have ended all life on St. Kitts at the time, covering even the current Basseterre site with a deadly stratum of volcanic ash. As for the eruptions that he had noted as being "a long time ago", the longer the period between these events the more violent is the later one.

I thought about the volcano not being dead, just sleeping. So, it didn't have a jumbie after all. My mother had said jumbies came from dead things. But still, something had been tripping me up and hiding in the bushes. Maybe the volcano had other tricks. I could find out if we went closer.

"Can we go down and see the lava?" I asked.

My father explained that the lava had solidified at the time of the last eruption and he showed me the shallow lake covering a part of the crater floor, the glistening area I had noticed.

"It's not hot down there," he said, "except for a few spots. You will find the lake quite cold."

Something tickled my nose, but I couldn't make out the smell. Vinegar? Surely not up here? Impatient, I begged him again to go down. He made me repeat my promise I would stay close to him and follow his instructions. With no more real footpath, we began slipping and sliding down the sixty-degree slope (I was wrong, it wasn't vertical) into the volcano's mouth. The other adults with their longer arms and surer footing went ahead. Every yard down was a triumph for me, gripping a large exposed root or a pliant branch and seeking desperately for my next toehold. Green from the torn leaves and brown from the mud stained my palms. My tree-climbing expertise was severely tested. Sometimes I got stuck, like in the plum tree – no way down or back – and had to be helped by my father, who may have regretted allowing a seven-year-old to attempt the descent. Near the bottom came the steepest stretch of all, and I had my first lesson on slipping down lianas while trying not to cut my hands.

Once down, things looked oppressive. We were surrounded on all sides by the volcano's green walls, isolated from the sea that islanders constantly use to position themselves. Later, I would come to recognise the crater form as a near perfect cone. What I had taken to be soft grass from above was green spiky reeds near the lake. Not a lake I could bathe in, they told me, because the water might be poisonous, and anyway it was barely a foot deep. Thinking of how difficult it was going to be to climb out of the crater, I wondered if we had been lured like flies into a trap.

"Come, let me show you what remains of the old volcano," said my father as he led us to a rocky, brownish area. The soil became prettily orange and yellow around me, the colours pulling me forward to see what was next.

A mass of white vapour flashed up in front of me, around me, in my face, much too warm. Never having seen a pressure cooker, much less having opened one prematurely, I didn't recognise it as escaping steam.

I wrinkled my nose: here was the vinegar thing again, an acrid, unpleasant odour.

"Smell that?" asked my father, smiling.

Had I known anything about rotten eggs, I would have had a basis of comparison. But I hadn't – eggs in my home in Basseterre were either fresh from our hens, or they didn't exist; you could hardly ever buy any in a shop.

So I said, "It smells like a rude noise."

"Ah," said my mother, "that's sulphur. It's just the volcano monster's bad breath. You can smell more of it near Brimstone Hill. They say that whole hill was spat out by the volcano, long ago. Take care now."

Thus, my mother was the first to refer to the volcano monster. She was mistaken about the origin of Brimstone Hill – it has a different geological history. But the cork-in-the-volcano-bottle theory was too cute for her to ignore. The jumbies retreated in my mind, replaced by this new mystery of a living mountain.

My father added, "Even a dormant volcano has some life left. Under a thick skin, there is still fire and brimstone. Watch your step and don't touch anything."

This last was one word too many, an opportunity I couldn't miss. I put my hands in my pockets and sidled away. I couldn't leave without a souvenir of the sulphur smell. As soon as I was sure no one was looking at me, I bent down and picked up a yellow stone.

"Put it back, Chris! It's brimstone, and dangerous." They were looking at me, after all.

I reluctantly put it down. How could a silly stone be dangerous? They wouldn't let me get any nearer to the steamy places, so I wandered huffily back to the lake. The adults were so absorbed that this time I really lost them. I took out my catapult to shoot something. Then I found an orange stone, almost as pretty as the yellow one, and then stones with stripes of several colours. By sniffing, I could tell they all came from the volcano monster and carried his body odour. Moving my weapons to the right pocket, I hid my treasure in my left pocket and walked back to the adults. They would never know.

Fatigue wiped most of the return trip from my memory. One hour and a half to climb back up to the lip of the crater, pushed and pulled by my father, then more than two hours to navigate back to the bottom of the volcano's slopes. As I trudged resolutely behind the adults, the stones in my pocket seemed to be dragging me down and heating up my leg. At the top of the cane fields, the truck was waiting. The same bumpy ride took us back to our car on the sugar estate grounds. They told me afterwards I slept most of the way home.

"Chris, get clean before going to bed," my mother said, later.

I felt pains all over, and my leg was sore. I didn't want to bathe, just to go to bed, but after dinner I obeyed and splashed water all over myself. It stung my left thigh like fury. When I looked at myself, it seemed like I had holes in me, showing the pink flesh underneath. My father had said the volcano had fire under its skin of earth. I didn't want to erupt and blow out noxious gases, so, reluctantly, I showed the injury to my mother.

"What have you done to yourself? Look at the patches of skin coming off! Did you fall?"

I told my mother I hadn't fallen.

She picked up my short trousers from where I had dropped them on the floor of the bathroom and found all my precious stones, still in my left pocket.

Sniffing the stones disgustedly, she said, "Oh no! Brimstone is sulphur, Chris. Sulphur! Didn't your father tell you it was caustic? You shouldn't have kept it in your pocket. It has worked its way through the cloth and attacked your skin. I'm afraid the volcano has marked you. What got into you, anyway? Your father told you not to touch anything."

A little bit of the volcano got into me, I thought, but I did not reply. I was far from possessing the chemical knowledge that brimstone – "burning stone" in old English – is more reactive with flesh than with cellulose. I just knew the volcano had a personal feud with me.

She threw the stones out of the window. "I'll patch the wound up with disinfectant and a dressing – it'll go away soon."

But it hurt for many days. I wasn't cross, not even sorry, but I was amazed the sleeping volcano could bite me like that, just because I had stolen its flesh. Maybe the grown-ups knew something after all. And now I had another scar, not in the same place as my grandfather, but one step nearer to his proud collection, nonetheless.

"What's that mark on your leg, Dad?" asked my son as I was dressing, one day some forty-odd years later.

He was pointing at my left thigh. I hardly recognised the marks at first. I hadn't examined them in years – the thirteen whitish half-inch circles on my brown skin, eight inches above the knee, just where the bottom of my pocket falls against the skin, and just where it fell with correspondingly smaller trousers and legs, years before. It was a legacy, a lifelong signature from the volcano monster, whether I liked it or not.

"It's all to do with St. Kitts, son. I'll show you where it happened one day." I pulled on my trousers rather more slowly than usual. I was remembering that guilt had been a foreign idea to me in those childhood years, perhaps because of my no-spanking regime, but that, on occasion, I had been forced to take responsibility for my escapades and misdemeanours.

Confessions

My first day at the St. Kitts Convent School in 1950, I wore a white shirt over my khaki shorts, a plain green tie, a button-down collar, and a buttoned-up lip. The school building was a two-storey wooden structure half-hidden by a wall of grey concrete, like the unwanted child of the sculpted Roman Catholic Cathedral of the Immaculate Conception next to it. I stared at the school and church from across the road, in Pall Mall (now Independence) Square – a run-down but still attractive reminder of the island's murky colonial past, with a chipped stone fountain in the middle, surrounded by palm, bamboo, and banyan trees, and a voluptuous red flamboyant right opposite the church.

My parents had insisted that it was quite all right to send me – an Anglican – to a Catholic school, just as it had been to send me – a boy – to an all-girls school. It was not that they sought out eccentric situations, or that they wanted to put me on the spot, but just that these incongruous schools were preferable to no school at all. St. Kitts in the 1940s was strong on sugar production, but weak on education.

"This arrangement is just temporary," my father told me, "until you're old enough for boarding school." I wasn't sure what he had in mind, but any school on the island seemed better to me than the prospect of leaving home.

"Watch out for the nuns – they're not ordinary teachers," he warned me on that first day. He told me that in a Convent School, daily religious instruction for Roman Catholics went hand-in-hand with reading, writing, and arithmetic. "But you're not one of them," he said, "so they've promised us you won't be included in their church indoctrination – your Grandpop would catch a fit if you were."

At the prospect of being shielded from a dangerous influence, I felt unease mixed with intrigue as to what the menace could be. I kept my mouth shut as I walked through the gates, content to scuff a little dirt with my shoes and wait to be noticed.

As it turned out, there were two of us non-Catholics in an entry-level class of twenty. Our names were called, and for a moment we felt like intruders, but soon we blended into the group. Then the Reverend Mother in charge of us appeared. She was clad in black, topped by a white hood, and wore a rosary with a crucifix on it. Over the next months, I never, ever, saw her hair. Her skin was pale, and I couldn't tell how old she was, but when she wasn't smiling, she had a severe case of wrinkles. She seemed to think I was scowling, and told me to cheer up. I wondered when the dangerous stuff would begin.

"Are you Father Vanier's grandson?" she asked.

Why had she mentioned my grandfather rather than my father?

"I'm just here for a year," I said, "then I'm going to another school."

"Let's find you a place then, while there's still time."

We all went into the classroom and I was given a desk at the back. Most of the other pupils seemed to know each other from Catholic elementary school and they prattled until the Reverend Mother took control.

"You're not just here to learn," she said, "you're here to obey."

No one crossed that firm voice. I was still in my low profile, not-talking mood, so I fitted right in, but the others shut up like clams. While the Reverend Mother explained about the school programme, and what behaviour was expected of us, I couldn't help asking myself how these Catholics were different from Anglicans. They looked the same as us, except for the Reverend Mother – black, brown, and occasional white skin. Both religions had "priests", though I got confused about the status of bishops, deacons, archdeacons, ministers, and cardinals. We worshipped the same God, I supposed. And went to church with the same reluctance most Sundays. But wasn't there a story about Catholics and chickens? That was it. My grandfather always said the sweetest part of a roast chicken, the part where the bird excreted, was called "The Pope's Nose". It was a joke, he said, about the Catholics who venerated the Pope almost as much as they worshipped God. Whenever my grandfather carved a chicken, he always served himself the Pope's Nose, and it made me quite jealous. I decided that when one day I had my own family and my own roast chickens, that I would take the prized morsel. Years later, I learned Catholics called this titbit "The Parson's Nose".

I was blissfully unaware of the awkward centuries during which these two religions had been at war. When the English drove the French out of the Leewards in the 18th century, they banned the Roman Catholic Church. Irish Catholics were not allowed to settle in those English islands for more than half a century for fear they would collude with the French or the Spanish in nearby territories. After the ban was lifted in 1753, the hostility and mistrust persisted. However, the Irish came back in sufficient numbers to have one section of Basseterre named "Irish Town". At one point, coloured people enjoyed civic rights the Catholics did not. Irish Town is now an all-black ramshackle zone, home to rum shops and crime where my parents forbade me to linger. These old conflicts had left something dark lingering in the Caribbean subconscious, a nasty carry-over of sectarian hatreds from Ireland itself. In 1938, when my mother changed her religion from Catholic to Anglican in order to marry my father, she outraged her family. One rare bond between Anglicans and Catholics in the 19th century was their mutual support for the maintenance of slavery in the islands. A slave should serve his master, the bible said; only Moravians and Methodists disagreed with this.

The next day, at the first lesson, the Reverend Mother said, "Time for our morning study of the Lord's scriptures. Open your bibles to the Old Testament…"

There was a rustling of pages, and I searched in vain for my bible. I hadn't been issued one. It must have been a mistake. I stuck up my hand and the Reverend Mother scowled at me. What had I done wrong?

"I don't have the book – "

"It's called the Holy Bible. Christopher, you and Francis come here," she said. "And bring your work books."

The Anglican brigade marched up to the front, and she spoke to us in a low voice.

"You two are excluded from this lesson at your parents' request. And since you can't benefit from the scriptures, you'll just have to make do with sums."

The way she said it, I felt intensely deprived of something.

"Now, go to the back of the room and try to complete these before the end of the class." She wrote out several arithmetic operations in neat columns in our books. "No noise from you – don't disturb what doesn't concern you." And she began reading stories from her bible to the other children.

I had thought – and perhaps my father had thought, too – that I would be allowed out of the room while the bible class was taking place. To play, for example. Instead, I had to do additions while the Reverend Mother was talking. This wasn't easy – I was sure I wouldn't finish. Arithmetic was boring enough as it was, and concentrating on it during story time was worse. However, the Reverend Mother must have been kind to us, and chosen simple exercises, because I finished in fifteen minutes. There was still half an hour of bible class to go, and I was forbidden to leave the room – so, I listened. I hoped my grandfather would never find out.

This was the pattern every day. The Mathematics exercises were always painless, and I had plenty of time to tune in to the Catholic stuff. Francis was my co-conspirator, although we never discussed it – why let the Reverend Mother know she wasn't giving us enough work to do? She told vivid stories, even thrilling ones. Many of these I had heard before from my grandfather, or in Sunday School, but Anglicans didn't believe in daily bible reading, even less in dramatising the texts, and I had found our Holy Book less interesting than Enid Blyton or G.A. Henty stories. The Reverend Mother had no scruples about embellishing her heroes and villains; it was much more personal. Her biblical characters were always fighting, killing, and being punished. There were famines, battles, mysterious voices in the desert, a sea that peeled back like a banana skin, and miracles. Warriors would wear their hair long to magically build up their strength, like the soon-to-be Rastas in our hills. Boys with slings could fight against giants. I began to equate "sling" with my catapult, which showed how poor a military observer I was. Behind it all was the same Jehovah my Grandpop often talked about. Sometimes I felt guilty, but it couldn't be wrong to listen a bit, surely? Just as long as I was not caught. I made sure to continue squiggling on my exercise page every few minutes, so it would look like work. It was enough to fool the Reverend Mother, I hoped.

But I was eventually betrayed by circumstances. The Reverend Mother had finished a quick tour of the Old Testament and had just started on the New Testament. I lapped it up every day. She got into the business of divine prophecy concerning the birth of Someone Important in ancient Palestine, and those who preached His coming. He could be seen as either a revolutionary or a King. Unfortunately, news of his arrival by the Three Wise Men led to Herod massacring all the two-year-old babies of Bethlehem on the Feast of the Innocents, just after Christmas day.

"But," said the Reverend Mother, "Jesus escaped to Egypt." Then she questioned the spellbound class, "Which prophet then announced the real coming of Jesus, the Lamb of God?" Having listened to the build-up, this seemed obvious to me, yet none of my classmates answered. I waited a bit, and the Reverend Mother repeated the question.

Wriggling in my chair, I shoved up my hand and said, "John the Baptist, Reverend Mother!"

It was curious the way she smiled at me. Maybe she hadn't been fooled by the pencil doodles after all. Suddenly, I was embarrassed. The whole class stared at me. I wasn't supposed to have been listening, so clearly I shouldn't have answered. Punishment would take the form of a ruler smacked over my open palm. But the Reverend Mother didn't punish me. She even smiled again and said it was "very good" I had been listening and would everyone please remember the answer. I saw by the look on Francis Gumbs' face he thought I had "got off lucky".

I never told my parents about the incident, yet it bothered me. Why had I been so foolish as to speak up? On the one hand, I felt I had been tricked; yet some part of me was proud to have answered a question the others couldn't – we weren't any dumber than the Catholics, after all. In class, I continued listening to the Reverend Mother. As time went by, she focused more on God and church matters, like communion, heaven and hell, and sin – especially sin. The flavour of things was different from my grandfather's religion, more dramatic.

"Confession," she said, "makes you truly Christian. Who has been to Confession?" I could tell the word had a capital "C" for the Reverend Mother.

One or two hands went up. She sighed, and the room was quiet.

"You must all go, but especially those who will take communion. It's so important – a matter of life and death. Here, if you don't think so, listen to what can happen."

I stopped my doodling so as not to miss a word.

"A group of children in a cold northern country used to play together and have great fun," she said. "One boy was very popular but he had an unfortunate habit of telling lies to his friends. He lied about his marks at school and he lied about his family's wealth. Everyone liked him, but he was a sinner because of his lies. He eventually became sorry for these lies and wanted to be forgiven. He knew it wouldn't do any good to be forgiven by the people he had lied to. Nor by Confessing to his parents. Lying is a "mortal sin" and he had to go to Confession and tell a priest about it. Then, maybe, the Holy Father, who alone can forgive a mortal sin, would absolve him. So, one day he resolved to Confess."

She paused to look hard at us. "But such a popular boy has many things to do," she continued, "so he put it off to the next day. That afternoon he went ice-skating with his friends. He was a good skater but there was an unexpected collision and he fell on his head on the ice. It was a terrible accident for one so young. He went into a coma for several days and then he died. Without ever having confessed his sins."

I felt the Reverend Mother's eyes boring into me, but doubtless all my classmates felt the same, so mesmerizing was her crowd control.

"The boy went straight to Hell," the Reverend Mother said, "where the Devil was delighted to torture him for all eternity with the fire of the damned. There is a lesson for you, children. Go to Confession as often as you can! Even heathens can confess. Death may come for you at any moment. Go today!"

A fever ran through the classroom infecting us all, Catholics and non-Catholics alike. When I thought of all the mischief I had done that might be counted as mortal sins, I shivered. Nobody in my Church had ever before insisted I go to Confession. Why had my Anglican family forgotten to warn me? According to the Reverend Mother, it wasn't enough to say daily prayers. Our Father who art in Heaven must be angry, I thought. I must, really must, go and see a priest to be forgiven. Of course, we didn't have any ice-skating rinks in the Caribbean, but what did it matter? At any minute, a bolt of lightning could strike me, or a runaway donkey could trample me, or a coconut could fall on my head, and that would be it. Straight to Hell.

I didn't know how to save myself, and I began to panic. I contemplated running to a Catholic priest that very day, where the others in my class would surely go. The Roman Catholic Church was next door. But it didn't seem fitting. I had already been caught out of place with John the Baptist – I squirmed at the memory. I began feeling I should go to my own Anglican Church. My grandfather was a priest, after all. Should I Confess to him? I rejected this instinctively, not wanting to open a war on two fronts, with both Grandpop and the Reverend Mother after me. Instead, leaving my classmates to their rendezvous with the Cathedral of Immaculate Conception, I trudged across the town after school and found a Minister I didn't know too well in St. George's 17th century Anglican Church, several times destroyed and rebuilt. He seemed surprised to see an eight-year-old boy enter his Church alone and ask to Confess.

"Confess? You want to confess?" From the start, his use of the word seemed different.

I could see him hesitating, so I repeated what the Reverend Mother had said in Convent School, and explained I didn't want to be struck dead before Confessing. He found a confession booth – that I later realised was little used – and put his robe on.

"What do you have to confess?" he asked. "It must be terrible – you seem upset."

My spirits plummeted, and I realised I didn't know how God was going to punish me, or even if he *would* forgive me. Just how hot was hellfire?

I told him about all the times I had punched my little brother and sister – not that I hadn't had provocation. And I told him about all the wrestling fights I had had with my friends; in my defence, sometimes I even let them win. And I told about all the times I had lied. This, according to the Reverend Mother, was the real clincher. But it had just been over-truths and under-truths, really.

Before I had finished reciting my list of what I thought were mortal sins, the Minister asked me, "Well, apart from this, have you done anything truly bad?" I was puzzled, thinking I had already confessed enough.

"Nothing more, Father."

It seemed unnecessary to tell him about the time I had burned some mice alive under our house – the smell was enough punishment. Neither did I tell him about the glass of urine I had once offered to a friend to drink – everyone thought it was funny except my mother.

He gave me his absolution, gently. He seemed almost disappointed. "A bit of advice, young man. Don't let that clever Reverend Mother know you're listening. Take out a book and read it."

No bolt struck me down; no fire scorched my feet. The man in front of me was all there was. And he said I shouldn't worry about the Reverend Mother's damnation story. The Minister's vision of God was kinder, a God who wouldn't send a boy to Hell just because he had missed a confession. My Anglican God didn't require this ordeal of confession – a sacrament, the Reverend Mother would have said. The Minister told me he was there to help, not as an intermediary between salvation and flames. A true confession – with a small "c" – was a personal affair, an examination of conscience. My feelings of guilt faded, replaced by a hearty respect for the Reverend Mother's tactics.

"We are all sinners," he said.

I wondered what a priest like him and the Reverend Mother had done to qualify as sinners.

"You can come back any time," he said, "but you don't need me – try mentioning these misdeeds when you pray. You do pray, don't you?"

I nodded, and smiled.

The Minister had just done himself out of a job

Kidnap

There was once a "Monkey House" on the Basseterre Bay Road, where people could feed the animals. It was built near the eastern end, across from the Pond's Pasture industrial site. This house was a wooden cage, a five-foot cube, and one could look at the monkeys through a wire front. The floor of the cage was a patchwork of slats to allow the discarded fruit skins to fall through. The sand below was covered with droppings. There was space enough to sweep under the cage if anyone had a mind to, but no one did. Three or four monkeys lived in the cage, sometimes more. Perhaps they were for sale, but I never saw the owner, nor noticed any price. At the approach of a sightseer, they would jump up and down and jabber wildly, hoping for food. The monkeys were a diversion for tourists, but children who got too close to them sometimes had their hair pulled. Mischievous, people thought. In later years, I felt it was wrong – even dangerous – to interpret the monkey's instinctive behaviour the way we did. They were wild animals. But as a boy, like many others around me, I was addicted to anthropomorphic ideas: the monkeys were human-like playmates.

That bay road in St. Kitts where the monkeys were caged is the emblem of Basseterre. It's one of the first things I would see of the island's capital when arriving by boat from the neighbouring island of Nevis, a two-kilometre-long curve of asphalt and concrete like the claws of a crab. The backdrop of mountains and cane fields masked the squalor. When I got closer to the pier, I could make out, next to gaily coloured homes, the alleys, the shacks, and the littered black-sand beach. Unclad urchins with navels popping out threw themselves laughing into the sea, and in the street markets, lined-faced peasant women sold overripe fruit to the latecomers. This sun-drenched poverty is the heart of exotic Basseterre, as much as the tourist shops touting off-island jewellery and the bustling grocery stores crammed with imported foods. At night, orange street lamps light up the bay road, hiding the untidiness from too close an inspection, dressing the town up. The effect is like the clothes the islanders wear to parties: gaudy. But gaudiness is not a crime in this part of the world – vivid colours are the lifeblood of the Caribbean, far from the subtle greys and pastels of Europe. As a teenager, I spent hours on our veranda at the Fortlands looking at the harbour and admiring the fascinating shoreline, trying to pick out the owners of the muffled voices pulsing across the water.

But Bay Road is also where the hurricanes strike. The most vulnerable sections are reinforced with a low concrete wall and piles of massive boulders. When I meandered past them as a child, I smelled the brown seaweed, I looked at the wavelets of the Caribbean Sea, and I used to think nothing could break through – nature was contained. But another type of tropical weather is waiting to assert itself. Every now and again, African storm winds whip up the waves, surprise us by their savagery, and destroy these defences, solid as they seem.

In 1950, when I was eight years old, I found it natural that St. Kitts was full of monkeys. My home was a tropical island, after all, and what could be more normal than to bump into an untethered goat, a contemplative mongoose, or a solemn-eyed monkey? I was drawn to these creatures and disappointed when I learned that, like the mongoose, the St. Kitts monkey is not original to the island but was introduced by French settlers several centuries ago. I felt they were *our* monkeys, and I had difficulty surrendering ownership to the African savannahs.

Today, what I find remarkable about the monkey population on the island is that, unlike the Caribbean humans, who form a mixed race, these animals have remained a pure species known as the Green Vervet Monkey, *Chlorocebus aethiops*, over 300 generations. And St. Kitts, together with Barbados, has a near Caribbean monopoly on them. What is more commonplace is that, as immigrants to the island, they have had to fight for a place under the sun just like the rest of us. But the monkeys reached the Caribbean before my family: the settlers who introduced them from West Africa did so somewhat before 1700, whereas our first genealogical traces date from 1729 in Paramaribo. There are resemblances: the Caribbean Green Vervet is healthy, having escaped the major pathogens that have infested contemporary African populations; my ancestors escaped with their lives from the debilitating religious quarrels of 18th century France.

Our Green Vervet Monkey has some near-human characteristics. It can even get blind drunk, something I learned first-hand.

When my parents drove us near the forest areas of St. Kitts, I would look up from my book and poke my head out of the car window to see whole tribes of Green Vervet Monkeys leaping and jumping on the roadside and in the trees, babies sometimes on a mother's back.

"What do they eat?" I asked, wondering how *I* would live if I had to scurry with the pack.

"Mangoes, bananas, and shoots," said my father. It didn't sound substantial. No ice cream and cake? No roast chicken?

Could they hang by their tails, I wanted to know? If I were a monkey, this at least would compensate for the monotonous diet. But my father was not sure they could use their tails in this way. My mother said "prehensile" three times, but they couldn't seem to agree on this, so I dropped the idea of becoming a monkey. My father always won his arguments with my mother, and I took my cue from this. His verdicts – when expressed – went unquestioned, whereas my mother's opinions could be contested.

As for the monkeys, what remained was an itch, a desire to get closer to these animals without frightening them. But all I could do was observe from afar. Areas like Brimstone Hill or the hills near Frigate Bay are favoured, even today, by monkeys. In the built-up parts of Basseterre, they sometimes hide in a leafy garden tree during the day and come out looking for food in the evening or in the early morning.

They were a lot bolder before most people, my family included, started keeping household dogs. Monkeys and dogs are natural enemies. At the time, the two species were also rivals for our family's affection. A good guard dog was expensive (people imported pedigree canines from England), and might attack friends, so we didn't have one, yet. Monkeys were cheap. I thought they were small and cuddly, even if some Kittitians said they could bite, and steal things. It seemed to me they deserved some special sympathy, because – unlike dogs – they are considered a delicacy. Kittitians eat monkey stew, although it is not served in restaurants for tourists. Throughout the Caribbean, and especially in Dominica, there are off-limits types of local game: iguana, agouti, manicou, crapaud (mountain chicken), and sea turtles. To forbid their hunting only makes them sweeter to the private Caribbean palate. Monkey hunting in St. Kitts was not forbidden, just frowned on, and that was sufficient for Kittitians to prize monkey meat, except those who considered them as pets.

In early 1950, we lived at the north-east corner of Church and Central Streets, now a grey office building. My father had recently given up his private law practice and taken a job as Secretary of the Sugar Association. He liked surprising us, and one afternoon he drove home from work at about five o'clock, while it was still light. "I've brought you a new playmate," he announced, carrying the creature in a wicker basket where it was shivering despite the tropical heat. "It's a monkey. It's called a Green Vervet."

I crowded round him excitedly with my brother and sister, and said, "He doesn't look green!" It was the first time I had come within touching distance of a monkey.

"Well, he's not *very* green, but if you look closely you'll see his brown fur is tinged with yellow, grey, and green."

Curiosity partially satisfied, I asked, "Why is he trembling like that? Is he ill?"

"No, he's just young and underfed. We'll get Virginia to give him some milk." Virginia was our black servant. She was a determined lady in her 30's, hair in a bun, eyes twinkling, used to getting her way with children and animals alike.

I made to poke the monkey with a finger, but he recoiled and tried to burrow through the bottom of the basket. "He's scared!" I said. I looked with sympathy at the small bundle of fur, tiny black face, delicate little fingers, and long tail. He needed taking care of. I sensed he had been snatched from his mother.

"He's yours to look after, Chris, and the rest of you can help, especially while he's weak. When he's bigger you can play with him in the garden."

My father handed me the basket. As I put my face close to the monkey, I smelled an acrid undercurrent.

"He needs a bath," I said.

My father promised that Virginia would hose him off to disinfect him.

Suddenly, I wasn't sure I wanted all that responsibility, although the monkey did sound like it might be fun later on. My father told me an estate manager had given it to him "for services rendered". He advised friends on legal matters on an informal basis.

"I can't very well give the monkey back," he said. I thought of the monkey returning to the hard place it had come from. Finally, I agreed to take care of it.

As for my mother, she was pleased with the monkey's arrival. She was working on articles for the Trinidad and Barbados newspapers at the time and anything that distracted her four children was good news. To her quick imagination, animals assumed human features, and I followed her inspiration.

We didn't put the monkey in a cage, so he was free to roam; our entire garden became a Monkey House. The property had high, stone walls and there were no adjoining gardens. It would have been difficult for the young animal to escape, even if it had wanted to. And later on, when it could climb anywhere, it didn't want to leave: it was too well fed.

The only person not happy with my new pet was Virginia, our maidservant. "Monkeys not pets," she said. Nevertheless, she put out its bowl of food every day on the kitchen steps.

Since I had no real chores concerning the monkey, my responsibility did not weigh heavily on me. It is not common to name a monkey in St. Kitts, as one would with a cat or a dog, and my mother simply called it "Monkey". We were all delighted with the new pet. I don't believe we knew monkeys live a lot longer than cats or dogs, up to twenty years. That's a long time for a family to honour a relationship.

My baby brother Noel, not yet two at the time, was bigger than the monkey and just as cuddly. But I soon discovered neither of them made good playmates for us older children. I couldn't make them understand my games. So maybe what happened was my fault. If I had taken more care of my brother, or the monkey, or both, they might not have become so attached to each other. On days when there was no school, my mother would put Baby Noel out into the garden after breakfast to play with us. He could crawl, even walk a little, but he often fell down. He was just beginning to talk.

One Saturday morning shortly after Monkey's arrival, I sat a pyjama-clad Baby Noel down at the bottom of the garden where I knew no one could see us. At this point, Monkey was about half Noel's size. Virginia had just bathed him. I picked him up and placed the squirming animal on Baby Noel's lap.

"Here's your new friend, Noel," I said, and stepped back to see what would happen.

A huge grin spread across Baby Noel's face, and he quickly clasped both hands around Monkey. At last – someone smaller than himself!

I expected Monkey to wriggle free but to my surprise, he didn't. I could have sworn the little animal was chuckling. I was wrong, of course, because monkeys don't look at the world as we do, and don't chuckle, but I hope there *is* a world somewhere in which they can laugh. I saw Baby Noel moving his fingers. He had found a patch of warm, blue skin on Monkey's tummy where there was no fuzz, and he was tickling his friend just the way his brothers would tickle him. After that, Baby Noel and Monkey got on so well that I left them alone together and went to play with the others.

My mother interrupted my game. "Where is Baby Noel?" she asked.

"Oh, he's playing with Monkey," I replied, pointing over my shoulder to the far end of the garden. In fact, I didn't know what they were up to. She didn't check.

Meanwhile, my brother and sister and I continued playing. That day it was pirates, with home-made wooden swords. I was trying to make my brother walk the plank. It didn't cross my mind the monkey would soon have similar game plans for Baby Noel. Virginia, at least, generally knew where the two babies were. At lunchtime, my mother would send her into the garden to bring Noel in for his meal and his nap.

This pattern continued for several months. What Noel and Monkey talked about and played at remained a secret, even to me. Baby Noel would often be naked in the garden – there were no Pampers in those days – and it was sometimes hard to tell which was the baby and which was the monkey. I would come home from school and find Monkey dancing around him, chattering gently, and Baby Noel clapping his hands. I told the others Monkey was teaching Baby Noel his language. Monkey would then take Baby Noel by the hand and walk with him, which charmed us all. I guess he looked on Baby Noel as a deficient fellow monkey who had to be taught his balance. Sometimes I would see the pair of them doing advanced exercises, walking along the little stone ledges and walls surrounding the flowerbeds. As time went by though, Monkey grew up faster than Noel. His baby fur, so downy to the touch, became thicker and rougher. He developed new traits.

"Look at how messy the garden is," said my mother one day.

"Virginia, the place needs sweeping. Why is there so much spoiled fruit on the ground?"

"It's Monkey, Mistress. He very wasteful. Eat half a mango and throw the rest. Peel a banana and let it rot."

"Well, don't give him so much to eat, then. I'm sure if you don't spoil him he can be neater."

"Better we should tie him up with rope, Mistress. Is no trouble that way."

But, of course, no one would agree to that.

I had sympathised with Monkey's behaviour up to this point. Since he was forced to eat fruit all the time, he might as well pick and choose. But there was worse. I examined the area where he slept, and I found strange little remains of insects. I suspected Monkey of eating cockroaches and spiders to liven up his fruit regime, or maybe just for fun. Monkey was not turning into the playmate I had hoped for. What did I have in common with an insectivore?

He began to show signs of aggressive behaviour towards the rest of us, but never towards Baby Noel. He would spit at us and run up trees instead of letting us pet him. We ignored this at first. Sometimes he would overturn his bowl of food, or climb the garden walls and throw stones at passers-by. Mischievous, I thought. Mind you, this had its good side: I could now throw things at people and blame Monkey.

One notable day when Virginia came for Baby Noel at lunchtime, Monkey made a fuss and spat at her. I didn't hear her report the incident. I laughed to myself – what prank would he pull next? The following day, Monkey wouldn't let Baby Noel go. He had assimilated my brother into his tribe and the new monkey was judged fit to spend time in the trees. When Virginia tried to pull Baby Noel away, Monkey decided to defend his territory. He bit her, hard, and monkeys have sharp teeth. She yelped. I came running to look on, maybe to help. But Virginia was bleeding and I cowered. Could this be my pet?

"I going kill it!" she screamed, and ran into the house to fetch my mother.

At this point, Monkey grabbed Baby Noel under his arms and started climbing the nearest tree with him – a large breadfruit tree. Despite being somewhat lighter than Baby Noel, Monkey was strong and looked at first as if he would succeed in kidnapping our brother. If Baby Noel had been an inert bunch of bananas, no doubt Monkey's strength and determination would have been enough to reach the higher branches. As it was, Baby Noel kicked and wriggled so much that the pair of them remained stuck at shoulder height. My mother had by now reached the scene.

"Ralph, Ralph, come quick! Monkey has gone crazy. He's got Noel!"

My father was the last to arrive. He took in the situation and looked for the nearest big stick. He grabbed a wooden broom.

Virginia repeated her war cry, "Hit monkey! Quick, kill the animal!" That was the moment when he lost his name, such as it was.

My father and Virginia approached the monkey, which was now gripping Baby Noel ever tighter and trying not to lose its hold on the tree. It spat, and Baby Noel looked seriously unhappy.

My mother began crying, "My baby! My baby!"

"You take it from the other side, Virginia," said my father, as he prodded the monkey's ribs with his stick. Virginia moved closer and got a hand on Baby Noel's foot. My father hit the monkey on the head and it fell in a heap with Baby Noel.

"Get the baby, Virginia, go!" yelled my father, holding the squirming monkey down with his stick. Virginia pulled Baby Noel by both feet and was rewarded by another bite.

"Aiee!" she cried, and shoved Baby Noel into my mother's outstretched arms.

The monkey – now unburdened – shot up the tree like lightning, hissing at us.

Baby Noel escaped with a few bruises and a bump on his head; my mother crushed him to her breast even harder than the monkey's grip. By now, I wanted vengeance against that crazy monkey. I began looking for rocks.

"Leave the monkey in the tree and go inside the house," my father ordered.

During lunchtime, the grown-ups discussed what to do about the monkey, and Virginia did not hesitate to join in. I had never seen a domestic taking charge, but this was different. She knew about monkeys. Meanwhile, we disinfected her bites.

"I'll have to get rid of it," said my father.

"Is simple, kill it," said Virginia, eyes gleaming, two bandages to her credit.

"We can't just kill our pet," said my soft-hearted mother, the fight already fading in her memory. I could see what she meant, although I still sided with Virginia. I wanted the monkey – no longer my pet – to be punished.

While I waited expectantly, Virginia said: "First, catch monkey. I make it special food, plenty strong. Can you give me some rum, Mister Vanier?" Rum was the cheapest alcohol available, but instead my father showed his sympathy by providing two bottles of his favourite beer while Virginia got the ingredients for a bowl of porridge. She mixed the beer with the oats, then added some sugar, and set the porridge in the monkey's usual bowl on the top of the kitchen steps. At mealtimes, the monkey would hop up the five stone steps from the garden and grab his food where Virginia had left it. I could see the monkey climbing down the tree now, hesitating, still angry.

"Baby Noel stay by bowl," Virginia said. It was true; lately the monkey had refused to eat unless Baby Noel sat next to it. A tribe eats together, even if Baby Noel wasn't allowed to take anything from the monkey's bowl until it had finished.

"Don't be frighten – no danger while monkey eating," Virginia insisted. "You others, keep back!"

So, Baby Noel was used as bait.

The monkey crossed the garden and climbed the stairs next to Baby Noel, who had recovered, was quite unfazed by the new events, and was still stark naked. The monkey stabbed a paw into the porridge and licked it. Baby Noel patted its back. The monkey gave in to hunger, and used its agile fingers to gobble down the porridge.

My father opened another beer for himself in the kitchen. "Chin-chin, monkey," he said quietly, raising his bottle.

After eating, the monkey just sat there, unmoving, on the top step. It looked at us ponderously. It seemed a long wait to me, but it was only a few minutes. Then it closed its eyes and fell over backward, down the stairs. Baby Noel trundled after it.

"Get me a crocus bag, Virginia," my father said.

Virginia produced a thick-woven brown burlap sack from a cupboard (Kittitians use crocus bags for bulk sugar and many other things). My father and Virginia shoved the drunken monkey into the bag and tied the top tightly with string.

"Say goodbye to the monkey," said my father. He walked to the garage with the bag, started his car, and drove off.

"How could we have known?" my mother asked.

"Monkey is as monkey does," Virginia said.

I felt no remorse for the monkey's exile despite my duty to take care of it, but then, Father Brown had not yet lectured me about responsibility. My parents replaced the monkey with cats and dogs. We realised that English-style pets – dogs in particular – were not only easier to keep, but a social gauge of rising family affluence. After a few weeks, we almost forgot about our simian friend. We still imagined human-like features in pets, but we no longer thought *all* animals could be domesticated. Some were part of the wild, and Monkey's fall from grace had been inevitable. But something remained unresolved. He had once seemed part of our loving family. What happens to the cast out? At dinner one day, I asked my father and mother about Monkey's fate.

"Well, your father drove all the way up into the hills above Basseterre where the tropical forest begins. He returned the monkey to the place where its real tribe lives," my mother said. "Like goes to like: I think it jumped up the nearest tree and swung away with its new friends. It's happy now."

Virginia disagreed, "That monkey never get away. No bush sense: drunk animal can't run far. I knows many farmers and others up there in the forest. Folks always hungry, and have cook pot just waiting. Skin it, and put onions, red peppers and tomato sauce. Feed eight people."

But, as I learned over two decades later, whatever the fate of our particular pet, some St. Kitts monkeys would have a more science-oriented destiny than playing in the trees or being hunted for dinner. In 1968, a new Monkey House came into being. A Canadian university research organisation – with the agreement of the St. Kitts Government, and complying with conservation policies – created the Behavioural Science Foundation for studying, breeding, and exporting our monkeys. Their farm, a mammoth wire shed open to visitors, manages 1000 Green Vervets at a time and culls several hundred more each year from the huge forest reservoir. There are more monkeys (50,000) than Kittitians on the island. Invaluable medical research is carried out on the exported monkeys to understand hypertension, Parkinson's disease, polycystic ovarian disease, dementia and anxiety disorders, alcohol abuse, and more; our monkey's relatives in Barbados are the leading source of the world's polio vaccine. Perhaps a team of Green Vervets are now chief tasters of Barbados Mount Gay rums.

My father, however, did not know all these things to come, and had yet another idea about our released monkey. "Actually, there was a problem," he said with a grin. "You remember we stuffed what we thought was the monkey into the crocus bag without really examining it? I drove as fast as I could up to the forest level, but when almost there I heard noises from the bag. I didn't want another fight. I stopped the car, cut the string, threw out the bag, and left in a hurry, without looking. So I'll never know who I set free, the monkey or Noel."

However, the monkey remained an animal for me, and not until too late, did I make any comparisons of its garden-confined state and my own island-confined one. I might have drawn conclusions about its growing-up conflicts with the world around it and my own. I might have concluded that its sad exile from home would one day be mine. I might have wondered if on leaving my home I would integrate with kindred spirits in the Caribbean, or be consumed by hungry political forces, or become useful as a sacrifice on the altar of science. I might have felt that Virginia's verdict on judging animals by their actions applied to all of us. But then, I didn't think of any of these things, and as my father joked about Noel, we should beware of cases of mistaken identity.

Mistaken identity: this was the playfulness we expected and loved in my father; it was always better to laugh our problems away. But how much did we know about *his* identity?

Hog Valley

My father, Ralph Vanier, needed all his patience. When he and my mother came to St. Kitts in 1942, he set up legal offices in Basseterre, near to Pall Mall Square. Fresh from the Inns of Court in London, he was articulate to a fault, wanting the right word for every occasion, and requiring its exact pronunciation. Few on the island spoke to his satisfaction. I recall his insistence that I say "Caribbean" the British way, with the accent on "*be*" and not the US version, with the accent on "*rib*". I was not allowed to use the Kittitian dialect – a sort of Creole English – that most of my friends spoke; it was the King's English or nothing.

He was as sincere in law as he was naïve in business. An industrious barrister, he won most of his cases. Standing five-foot-ten, with his broad forehead, neatly combed-back black hair, and relaxed smile, he radiated confidence in the courtroom. Whatever inner turmoil other people had, he always seemed calm, ready to quip his way through the storm. Elegant in his legal gown attire, the whiteness of the wig contrasted sharply with the nutmeg skin and broad nose inherited from his Guyanese father. Outdoors, his eyes were hooded in defence against the fierce sunlight, but indoors they opened with curiosity. He was excessively approachable by his clients; cases concerning the theft of a pig or a hen would be earnestly analysed to the last bristle or feather. It was not enough. The civil and criminal courts where he was allotted work didn't bring in much money. The outcome was usually a settlement between two poor people, and my father would sometimes not ask for any fee. Government prosecution cases weren't well paid either. Other lawyers compensated with more or less doubtful business deals – not him. By 1946, my father was having trouble supporting his wife and three – soon to be four – children. He searched for more stable employment and had two offers.

One of them was to provide legal services for the newly formed St. Kitts-Nevis Trades and Labour Union. The other was to become the Permanent Secretary of the St. Kitts Sugar Factory and Planters' Association. These were two organisations at opposite ends of the political spectrum. At age four, I was too young to be party to the family debate, of course, but it seems to have been a close decision. In the following years, I often questioned my mother about my father's motives, hoping to find my own keys to the universe. My mother would have preferred my father worked for the union; it seemed more "adventurous" and she was in tune with the pressure for radical social evolution in the colony. However, the factory option offered more money and security, so that's what my father finally chose. His legal expertise would be applied to industrial relations. In addition, the sugar factory job had aspects of technology that fascinated him. New machines were a luxury in the Caribbean, and since childhood, he had learned to repair almost anything in his workshop. The factory was one big machine he was fond of taking us to visit. He knew all the ins-and-outs of producing sugar, and sometimes wished he had studied engineering instead of law. The consequences of his choice of employer were far-reaching. When I think of it now, I try to imagine how the Labour movement might have been altered by his participation. He had the training and respectability; they had the drive and the sense of injustice. Perhaps he would have been too soft for the rough-and-tumble of politics, but more likely, he would have accelerated the movement to self-government.

It was a time when planters and cane cutters entered into deep conflict all over the Caribbean – a modern version of the emancipation from slavery a century before. St. Kitts had been named "The Mother Colony" because, in the 17th century, English settlers radiated out from this green haven to other islands. Despite its tiny size (68 square miles) St. Kitts has always been a source of change – a barometer of the region's social health. From being the richest of the sugar islands in the 18th century its fortunes followed the decline of world sugar prices and consequent neglect by its foreign rulers until it became one of the most miserable of the English-speaking Caribbean islands in the 1930s. In 1935, the island was at the origin of a titanic wave of labour and political unrest that swept the region (St. Vincent, St. Lucia, Barbados, Trinidad, Guyana, and Jamaica) with five years of strikes, riots, and several dozen deaths. The black masses were mired in poverty: poor pay, no land, no education, no political representation, no self respect, and no future; whereas the planters – though no longer as rich as before – enjoyed substantial privileges and fought to keep them.

The second world war brought a short-lived truce in this social upheaval (Britain paid more for wartime sugar), but not before a seven-week wage strike in St. Kitts in 1940 caused a firebrand young unionist, one Robert Llewellyn Bradshaw, then twenty-four years old, to be unfairly dismissed from his job at the factory. This formative strike should not be confused with the better-known strike of three months that Bradshaw would call in 1948 as union leader, bringing all cane processing to a halt. In 1940, I was not yet born and my father had not yet finished his law degree. The incident hardened the young Bradshaw's resolve and gave him indispensable credentials as the future political leader of St. Kitts during almost four decades. Bradshaw was charismatic and power-hungry, slated to become my father's adversary. The two men were vastly unalike. Bradshaw was a self confident and forceful speaker, although he had no more than a primary education: my father was a highly educated lawyer, always elegant in his speech, but averse to direct confrontation; outside of his structured

73

courtroom debates – I never heard him raise his voice in anger. Bradshaw had absorbed Marcus Garvey's influence and was inspired by anti-colonialist, back-to-Africa, semi-Marxist ideas: my father was a conservative, an admirer of Winston Churchill, hoping for gradual change, and wanting nothing from Africa – the yearly hurricanes the dark continent threw at us across the Atlantic were quite enough. But the two men were agreed on many basic things: a deep respect for English culture and law; belief in the Anglican Church; a horror of corruption; and a hope of progress for the people of St. Kitts. But what sort of progress?

Several years into his factory job, after tense salary negotiations concerning the cane cutters, the Labour Union press would trumpet headlines saying, "VANIER LIES AGAIN!" a title that has stuck forever in my memory. I am the son of a so-called liar. As British colonialism ran itself into the ground and Tate & Lyle (the UK owner of the sugar factory) slowly retired from the scene, the Labour Union would become the heart of political power in St. Kitts. The planters were mostly white and the trade unionists mostly black, with the allegiance of the coloureds like my father sprinkled evenly between the two camps. With the true masters of empire out of reach in Europe, there was no real adversary for Labour; the trade unionists could only take aim at the soon-to-be-expropriated planters, their friends, and the friends of their friends. My father became the planters' representative and a frequent Labour opponent. My family was thus placed squarely on the capitalist side of the political divide. Yet my father owned nothing at the time, not even his home, simply his legal skills.

When I was six, in 1948, my father's increased salary brought changes. The first I noticed was that we rented a bigger house and had more pets. Then, my father bought a car, because his office at the factory was outside of Basseterre. This was all positive, but one day my parents told me they had to leave us.

"Just for a short time, Chris. We're going to England for three months. It's part of your father's job," said my mother, as if it were an obligation.

In fact, it was what I would later call a "major employment benefit". The sugar factory and several large Kittitian trading firms gave their senior Caribbean employees "long leave" of several months every two years, with full pay. The tradition of these breaks came from a time when most managers had relatives in Europe and travel was by boat, too lengthy and costly for a short stay. This privilege (like most) was not abandoned when cheaper air travel became the norm and when few had any family left in Britain.

"But who will look after me?"

"Your grandparents, of course. You'll like that, won't you?"

I wasn't entirely sure. True, my grandmother was a good cook and spoiled us with her recipes from other islands, but there were times when I felt uncomfortable with my grandfather. I wasn't sure whether he would punish me, and how. And what sort of job was this where not only did the newspapers insult my father, but also his employers encouraged him to abandon his children for several months?

But it hadn't worked out too badly that first time; except for the Hog Plum tree incident, I was too young to concoct projects that would provoke Grandpop. On my parents' return we benefited from their tales of faraway places: pigeon droppings in Trafalgar Square, clothes dropping at the Moulin Rouge, and dropping water from the Mannequin Pis. St. Kitts was no longer my whole world. Tales from abroad were more concrete than books – one day, I, too, would visit these places.

Having more money had another effect that caused me to forgive my parents their long leaves. Two years later, in 1950, my father embarked on a farming project in the neighbouring island of Nevis, one of the two major agricultural ventures of his lifetime. Away from the abstractions of law, building and growing things were what he liked.

Nevis (pronounced "*Nee*-vis") is a smaller island than St. Kitts, round rather than club-shaped. It has fewer people but more fruit trees and beaches – a profitable exchange if you are searching for paradise. Like St. Kitts, Nevis is a dormant volcano, with hot water springs and a few sulphurous gas vents. The island's peak is perpetually covered with clouds, giving it a snowy look. There was no airport in those days, and the Nevis main roads were more potholes than paving. The volcano was not the only thing sleeping – the whole place was steeped with quiet, soporific memories of past glories. Alexander Hamilton was born there; Admiral Horatio Nelson was married at Fig Tree Church. But the sleeping kraken can awaken. Long before, in 1680, when the island had been fabulously rich with sugar, an ocean quake had quietly gobbled up the capital, Jamestown. Legend has it that on moonlit nights Nevisians can still hear its church bells tolling from the depths of the sea.

My father's farm project in Nevis began when I was eight. He felt sugar production was not the only way to use Caribbean land. He was able to buy some 400 acres in the Nevis mountains above Newcastle – an abandoned estate called Hog Valley. The very name tells you what he planned to do with it. The stony track leading up to it was so rough my father's car failed to climb it. A premonition of Hog Valley's intractability? He was obliged to acquire a four-wheel-drive vehicle. The terrain on the estate was too steep and uneven to grow sugar cane and, in any case, the island of Nevis had closed its sugar mills. But rainfall was plentiful, and the land lush and fertile, so Hog Valley could be used for farming – fruit, vegetables, poultry, and perhaps hogs. Included in the purchase was an independent lot of land known as Shaw's Estate – 100 acres of scrub and bush near the coast. This bit was flat and had potential for grazing cattle. Hog Valley Estate came with an old, six-room wooden house, badly in need of repairs, with no running water or electricity. There was, however, a large cistern nearby and a reed-filled, muddy pond about a half-mile away.

My father bought Hog Valley on a twenty-year mortgage, paying interest-only for the first years, with most of the capital to be reimbursed in a lump sum at the end of the period. He enrolled his elder brother Jack as a partner in the project. Jack had come to live in St. Kitts soon after Ralph arrived. He had married there, and he and his wife Iris had no children. The plan was that Ralph would continue his legal work at the factory in St. Kitts, visiting Nevis on weekends once or twice a month to help with the farm maintenance, whereas Jack would give up his job in Basseterre – an unappetising administrative function – and take up permanent residence at Hog Valley with his wife as soon as possible. He would run the farm on a daily basis while Ralph provided technical support, and marketed the farm produce in St. Kitts.

Jack's wife liked to say the bright idea of the Hog Valley farm really came from Jack. But he didn't have any money of his own to invest in the project, so Ralph was the legal purchaser. Jack considered himself an inventor, and was still talking about his bright ideas that would be appreciated some day when I last saw him in his seventies.

For both Jack and Ralph, it was not easy to stick to the plan for the farm.

The logistics took a long time to set up. The house needed *many* repairs. An extra room was added with bunk beds. A modern porcelain toilet was installed, complete with an outdoor cesspit in a nearby underground cave. A storage tank was built on the roof, to which water could be pumped. The window frames and shutters on the outside of the house were painted golden brown and white: Caribbean colours. Inside, the wooden walls and ceiling were left bare. On the farm, equipment had to be imported, livestock purchased, workers hired, and the land near the house cleared.

Jack lived there for a year but found it not to his liking. Hog Valley was isolated from other estates and residential housing. Having been abandoned for years, it was regularly trespassed by wandering woodsmen and vagrant villagers. Jack's wife, Iris, never joined him. She had her own job in Basseterre and their marriage was rocky. By all accounts, Jack was clever, but also lazy and totally undisciplined – in this last, just the opposite of a good farmer's profile. He was incapable of running any operation for more than a few days, the time it took him to get bored. No sooner had he and Ralph bought goats, rabbits, and poultry than they would be stolen from under his nose. Later on, they tried cattle – easier to keep track of. My father had to spend a lot more time in Nevis than originally planned.

When I thought about it as an adult, I asked my mother how she had felt about Jack during this troubled period. She often talked to Jack's wife.

"Iris, any news from Jack?"

"Not a thing, my dear. That man... But you and Ralph should know more."

"All we know is one of the cows died, and Jack wants more money."

"He going to pay for the cow's funeral?"

"No, no," Elsie said.

"Then watch out – he'll drink your money. Tell him to write me, anyway. He should be sending *me* money, not asking Ralph."

Her husband Jack was indeed fond of rum, including the illegal mountain stills, and not enough money was coming in to pay for his lifestyle. Ralph made up the difference for a while – but he couldn't support his lazy brother indefinitely.

Eventually Jack said, "I'm leaving this damned place and going back to St. Kitts where I can get more respect." He never returned to Hog Valley.

One person at least was glad to see him back in St. Kitts. Iris was fed up with Jack's absence on the farm, and hoped to moderate his drinking. But there was more, she confided to Elsie.

"I hear he's not living alone over there. If he's made any babies with those worthless Nevis girls, he'd better leave them behind. And get his arse over here where I can watch him."

Jack would always need a great deal of "watching" in this area – not that it would do much good. It would be decades before I discovered the existence of charming cousins whom Iris could never acknowledge.

Some considered Jack's desertion from the project a family betrayal; I was among them. How could he let his brother down like that? It was much simpler to find a scapegoat than to solve the farm's problems. I was sure my father could succeed alone. He tried. It put great stress on him to make it work by himself, but he hated failing at anything. His first step was to hire a foreman, Eddie James, of nearby Fountain Village, for the day-to-day running of the farm and the workers. This cost a lot less than paying for Jack's whims. He also decided, as he had to visit the farm more frequently, he would take his children along on a regular basis.

Until this happened, Nevis had been a distant place for me, a vague source of numerous heated discussions around the dinner table. From then on, the Hog Valley project became a glorious occasion to escape from St. Kitts and camp in the Nevis wilds. For almost ten years, it was my holiday and weekend home, and I remained blissfully ignorant of its profit-and-loss account. Our earliest crossings were in sailing sloops along with pigs, chickens, and farm equipment, but I remember little of that period. Later, my family would board a heavily packed, diesel-smelling launch run by Captain Anslyn from the Basseterre jetty and chug across the channel to the pier at Charlestown, the capital. I thought it took forever, but in fact, the trip was only two hours. Getting a good seat was important. Not waiting for my parents, I would scramble for a place on the open bow of the launch. Failure meant I would have to sit in the packed cabin where I would smell the engine fumes and be seasick. On deck, the air was tangy with salt and the worst that could happen to me was sunburn. Years later, in 1970, a similar launch, the *Christena*, would be so overcrowded it would capsize mid-channel, drowning over 240 passengers. Hardly anyone inside escaped.

But my crossings were pure magic. Basseterre retreated from us over the sparkling blue sea of the Eastern Caribbean. White foam frothed in our wake. The rocky brown St. Kitts peninsula rolled by, with a few white-sand beaches smiling here and there. Among the half-hidden coves, I noted one that the English cartographers had called "Shitten Bay", once prudishly removed from maps of St. Kitts, more recently resuscitated to titillate tourists. Bigger, rolling waves challenged us as we reached the open sea between St. Kitts and Nevis. Nevis with its head in the clouds, just like Columbus first saw it. A tiny hill called Booby Island, no more than 100 yards across, stuck up out of the channel between the two islands. The Brown Pelican is the Caribbean "Booby", and it mingles pell-mell on the island with Caribbean Coots and Black-headed Gulls. Birds and more birds. Then kilometres of the superior Nevis beaches appeared. Pinney's Beach was bare at the time; now it is dominated by the luxurious Four Seasons Resort. Charlestown – the capital – came into view with its quaint old wooden houses, a village compared with noisy, dusty Basseterre. Disembarked, we would unpack our cases and provisions, and stock up with fresh bread and tins of food. Finally, we'd find a jeep to make the rough ride up to Hog Valley. I'd count the ghauts (pronounced "gut") where the jeep would have to slow down to a crawl.

Even today, these ghauts are sometimes impassable after heavy rains. A quirk of colonial history has pasted this word (of Hindi origin, *ghât*) into the geography of many small Caribbean islands. Cat Ghaut, Cassava Ghaut, Soldier's Ghaut, Sulphur Ghaut, and Shallow Ghaut – they begin as watercourses down the sides of mountains and especially between hills and ranges in the tropical rain forest, turning into flatbed conduits lower down, not at all like the gentle English streams I used to read about. From February to August, most of the ghauts were dry-bottomed, filled with stones and debris. But when the rains came, they became quick-flowing torrents of water with no bridges. I didn't like our Caribbean rain. Not until later, when I would suffer the charming-but-insipid light rains of Europe that persist – grey and formless – for days, would I come to appreciate the savage tropical rainstorm. Action over hesitation. Nature unrestrained. We hardly ever used an umbrella in St. Kitts or Nevis: what good would it do to open such a fragile thing under a waterfall? Some of the ghauts converge from the mountains into inhabited areas. I was not the only one to dislike and fear the tropical rain. For the inhabitants of Basseterre or Charlestown, one single, violent downpour was enough to wash stray cars down the ghauts and right out to sea.

Between Camp Ghaut and Mount Lily Ghaut lies Fountain Village. We'd take a small, unmarked turning towards Nevis Peak and climb almost a mile of steep rocky road until the Hog Valley house came into view. Sleeping in its wood and concrete dreams, it came to life when we opened the doors and shouted from the windows.

No one lived within two miles of the Hog Valley house, and there were mysterious footpaths leading up into the mango forests or down into the guava fields and streams. In the absence of threats from predators, snakes, or poisonous things, our parents let us wander everywhere. While they strove to make the farm work, we were safe to entertain ourselves. Not that we couldn't invent our own dangers. My brother Peter stepped on burning ashes from a charcoal clay pot, and to this day hates pictures of Indian fakirs who walk on fire. Noel, aged three, climbed into the jeep – parked on a hill – and let the brake off. Only a determined sprint by my father saved Noel and my sister from disaster. Scolded one day, I ran off into the forest and got lost for many hours; a woodcutter found me and brought me home. More by luck than by design my brothers and I escaped injury during our Nevis adventures. I came to feel we were invulnerable, free to attempt whatever risky experiment we liked in the forest, without ever paying the consequences. It was this taste of freedom that made Hog Valley so attractive.

Water was essential in the running of the farm. My father dredged the nearby pond and laid pipes connecting it to the house for washing and bathing. He also pumped this water to livestock troughs, and used it for crops like corn, beans, carrots and tomatoes, which he hoped to cultivate even in the dry season. His vegetable produce was mostly sold in Charlestown, but some of it made its way back to St. Kitts.

For my brothers and me, the water was for drinking, not cultivation, and coming up the long hill to the house, I was always hot and thirsty. The rainwater from the cistern was judged clean and tasted sweet. There is an inland breeze on the small islands, bringing the freshness of the ocean. On the front veranda, which faced the wind, a large jug made of the red clay pottery of Nevis was always cooling. On arrival, my parents would pour us glasses of clear water from the jug. I would sit on that veranda, sipping, and look over the sea all the way back to St. Kitts, blue and green on the horizon.

I sometimes accompanied my father when he worked in the fields at Shaw's, tending the cattle. Once the herd was stabilised, my father began selling milk. But he needed to keep the whole area fenced in. It seemed strange the wire had to be repaired so often, and so many posts were knocked down between visits. Those silly cows didn't seem to want to stay on our land. Anyway, they didn't interest me nearly as much as the picnic lunch. My father and his team would cut up raw Nevis onions and spread them over slices of bread and butter. On top of the raw onions went little sardines, sliding out of their oily tin, and the grown-ups added hot red bird peppers. I had never thought a pungent vegetable like a raw onion could taste so good: it tickled the roof of my mouth and even my nose until the salty fish could slake the discomfort; the onion seemed to intensify the other flavours.

Willing to try any farming activity, my father stocked the pond with fish spawn and little crayfish. He added a small quay and the weeds and bushes around the perimeter were temporarily eliminated – but they would grow back every fortnight, a relentless invasion. We weren't allowed to disturb the young fish for the first six months.

"You have to wait for them to mature, son," my father said. "The first generation must become adult and give birth to a second generation."

At last the day came. All the stories of fishing I had read made it seem difficult, but I concluded that our lot of water-wigglers had been born stupid, because we could catch them – standing barefoot in the water – with just a bit of string, a bent wire, and a worm. So simple. Plop – nibble – jerk: from my trifling materials, I suddenly had a fish squirming in my hand. The catch of the day was grilled in the evening over a charcoal fire or small oil stove. Without electricity, after dusk we would ignite kerosene-based Tilley lamps that gave out an intense white light. Those Nevis days became steeped in memories of the food my father prepared. It was a male world, and my mother's cooking hardly entered into it. On some days, my father would stew the fish, filter out the bones, and make a soup, like a French *bouillabaisse.* Eating the crayfish with our fingers allowed me to discard eight or nine years of pretence at polite eating. My father constructed wooden cages in our pond to catch them, much like the sea-going lobster pots the local fishermen used, which we saw when we went to the beach to swim. This worked quite well, but one day we found strangers were helping themselves. The fish became scarcer, and little was ever sold, but my father didn't seem to care as long as there was some left for us.

Not all of my father's time in Nevis was spent working the farm. He became a keen hunter of game birds. He taught me early on a respect for guns, and told me what might happen if I wasn't careful. This was just as well, because my prior attitude to guns came from Lone Ranger comics and movies, and I was trigger-happy.

"You must never, never point your gun at a person," he said, "not even in fun. Accidents are so easy with firearms. And you, the gun owner, would be responsible. You can even have a single-person accident." This seemed impossible, but my father told us a story.

As a youth in Antigua, he used to go hunting with his brothers Jack and Beezie, armed with .22 rifles. Three brown-skinned young men at play, Jack being the tallest and fairest, almost white. They would compete for birds.

"First one to shoot that dove wins," challenged Jack one day.

The three aimed at a bird in a breadfruit tree. My father fired first. He missed, but scared the bird, which flew to a nearby branch. The other two fired and missed.

"Reload, it's still there," my father said.

All three reloaded, but before they could take aim and fire again, the dove flew off for good. My father lowered his loaded gun barrel and rested it on his shoe so that it wasn't pointing at anyone. His finger stayed on the trigger.

Jack was cross. "Why you scared the bird, Ralph? I had a perfect bead on it." And he punched Ralph playfully on the shoulder.

Caught by surprise and off balance, my father clenched his hand. The gun went off. He shot himself in the foot and blood oozed out of the hole in his shoe.

"Luckily," my father said to me, "my aim was perfect. I hit the gap between my two largest toes. I cleaned up the blood; Jack bought me a new pair of shoes; and all was forgiven, if not quite forgotten."

Of course, I blamed Jack for the accident to my father, but I might have had more sympathy if I'd only known how seriously *I* would one day put other people's lives at risk.

Thanks to my father's story, I did not shoot my brothers, though years later, on our front lawn, my youngest brother's friend, who hadn't heard the story, accidentally fired a pellet into another friend's throat, right alongside the windpipe. As soon as I was old enough, I was given a simple BB gun, and on my ninth birthday, I received a small compressed-air rifle that fired lead slugs. I jumped with joy. When my father went shooting mountain doves or pigeons, I was allowed to hunt ground doves – the smaller version. To my frustration, most of the time I returned empty-handed, my spent slugs embedded in trees or flattened on rocks. After a year of experience, I would be allowed to go out hunting on the Hog Valley lands on my own, and, if lucky, would bring home the two or three birds with poor reflexes that had not been able to avoid my slugs.

I yearned for the *real* hunting the adults did. "Why do you use a shotgun?" I asked my father, knowing he was an expert shooter in the St. Kitts rifle club.

"That's the fun of it," he said. "Doves often perch in groups of two or three on a coconut branch. The shotgun pellets spread out and – if you get the angle right – allow you to hit several birds at once."

I sensed the technique was as important to him as the result, and I dreamed of shooting *four* doves in one go, some day. It never happened. He had another reason for preferring a shotgun. I didn't realise it at the time, but a rifle is far more lethal than a shotgun; a spent bullet fired upwards can carry for over a mile. And rifles are dangerous weapons that can be used for other purposes than hunting.

The only way I could participate was as a camp follower, and I was grateful for that. My father would make up a party of three or four friends who would share the catch at the end of the day. I would follow one of them, preferably my father, and, after a shot, rush to collect the fallen birds. Often, a bird would still be alive, and I was taught how to dispatch it by wringing its neck. I didn't think I could manage this at first, and I dropped the bird, which fluttered into hiding.

"Don't let it suffer," said my father. "Grip the head firmly and swing the body in a circle. Remember – a wounded bird can't survive. If it gets away from you someone else will eat it."

With practice, killing them became easier. The knowledge that I was carrying out the role of a hunting dog in Europe would not have disturbed me in the least. At the end of the day, my father allowed me to help get the birds ready for cooking.

"Eat what you hunt. And prepare what you eat."

We plucked all the feathers, especially under the wings and on the neck, and chopped off the head and feet. I learned to cut open the stomach and the crop to remove the entrails, undigested seeds, and metal pellets. I would clean the heart and gizzard to be cooked separately. We seasoned the birds with thyme, pepper, salt and local herbs. Like the fish, we grilled the doves over a charcoal fire and ate them with our fingers like the original Carib Indians.

In those Hog Valley days of the early 1950s, no one bothered about who owned a gun, and you didn't have to register firearms with the police. There was less dove hunting in the following decade, but that's another story.

Time passed quickly, and Nevis remained a romantic dream.

I was shocked when my parents were forced to give the farm up or go broke. Afterwards, in the 1980s, I asked, "What went wrong with Hog Valley, Dad? Why did you have to sell it?" My father replied in a slow and deliberate way, with an easy smile. At the expense of spontaneity, he seemed to be thinking one sentence ahead. A lawyer's manner or introversion, it was hard to say.

He cleared his throat, "Well, I couldn't make money out of it, though it was worth the trouble, I think. Remember all those animals people stole from us? I couldn't protect them, so they ended up in the neighbour's cooking pot. And the fish. And the crops. That's why I became a beekeeper afterwards – the bees can protect their own hives."

My father explained that as the years went by his job at the sugar factory had become increasingly time-consuming, to the detriment of his other activities. He hadn't wanted to worry us with his troubles. What had been an uncomplicated role in the organisation of sugar production became a tense negotiation of labour problems. This in turn thrust him unwillingly into the political battlefield. The Labour movement's goal was to put an end to plantocracy in St. Kitts and nationalise the sugar industry. Naturally, the planters didn't agree to this. Prolonged conflict and strikes followed. Ralph, as the planters' representative, was needed.

"I could no longer afford to take off on weekends to piddle about on the farm in Nevis," he said. "But without constant supervision, things just disappeared.

"I had to admit even after ten years I was still not making any profits on Hog Valley. So, I stopped operating it. I hope you and the other children liked going there; I was sad to let it go."

I saw how hard it had been – even belatedly – to accept his lack of financial success. I also saw how blind I had been to my father's difficulties. He went on to say he had rented out some of the grazing ground, sold what he could of the equipment, and shut the house.

"But I couldn't leave it like that forever. When the lease on the land approached its end in 1970, my creditors requested repayment of the remaining debt. I had to sell. I dealt with a local lawyer who had off-island contacts. A group of Canadian investors bought Hog Valley from my lawyer friend, but not Shaw's. They did nothing at all with the land for years. I didn't get as much as I should for the estate because I didn't know what the land was worth. I never found out how much my lawyer friend made. Anyway, it paid off my debts and left some unexpected capital gains to distribute."

I don't think he realised that by selling the land he was severing some of the roots that attached us all to the islands; or maybe he did.

By "distribute" I guessed he meant to Jack. I knew they had maintained good relations through all those years, despite everything. It was just that my father spent less time with his brother, and refused to participate in any other projects with him.

I asked him why he had given half the profits to Uncle Jack. "I thought he quit the project," I said.

"He was my brother. You have to look after your brother," he replied. As for me, I could not regret a minute of the time I spent on my father's farm at Hog Valley. "Poor farmer, rich father," I said to myself.

Maybe my maternal grandfather Cecil Rawle was right; Ralph was too honest to make money in a normal "lawyerly" way. But then again… Time has strange ways of overturning hasty verdicts. The brilliant but not-so-honest lawyers of the Caribbean have a record of cheating on their associates, their health, and their wives. Cecil himself passed away at forty-seven, his liver overburdened with alcohol; three out of four of my own lawyer contemporaries have died prematurely. Ralph lived a long and satisfying life. In his late sixties, he needed money to repay another loan (his beekeeping business) and discovered that the plot of land he had kept at Shaw's Estate was now a coveted development site. Avoiding his former lawyer "friend", he sold it to an enterprising hotel builder for more than he had received for the whole of Hog Valley. At the last minute, he retained thirty acres out of the hundred, for future pocket money. This "pocket money" obligingly ballooned in value, and ten more years on, its sale provided for the late-life needs of my parents. Overall, Hog Valley made him a good deferred profit, quite by accident.

My father would think me a bit harsh concerning his fellow lawyers. I can hear him quipping, "Let's say the others were just too smart to grow old."

I remained curious about Hog Valley and visited it from time to time over the years. It was never fenced in. No hogs were ever seen there. The land just sat there in the sun and digested our human follies. Twenty years after my father had sold it, I went there for a last time with my children and had great difficulty finding any path up the hill from Fountain. No vehicle could penetrate – the way was overgrown with bushes and thorns. I had to leave the sturdy jeep and fight my way up by foot. At the top of a hill, I stumbled on a few concrete blocks, a bit of the old floor. It was all that was left of the house. No roof or walls standing. The piping, the steps, even the porcelain toilet: all gone. The cistern was abandoned and the pond seemed never to have existed.

In European cities, when the soul goes out of a building – from age, disease, or neglect – machines demolish and haul it away. In the Caribbean, green hands reach out of the dark, fertile soil and gently smother the ailing edifice, taking it apart stone by stone until, once again, the land is pure and savage, as if we had never been there.

Uneducable

Despite all my mother's efforts, I saw her hopes for my sister Hazel shatter in our veranda mirror.

"Hazel, look at your reflection! Keep your legs straight, and your arms on the rail! Hold the line – you can do it!"

I crept closer, wary of disturbing my mother's orchestrated exercises, but curiosity driving me to see Hazel's image. When I was almost directly behind her and my wobbling sister's reflection appeared on the far wall, I also saw myself in the glass, eyes scared.

Hazel walked towards the unattainable mirror, weaving from left to right, clutching at the bars of her walking frame, each bare foot stamping on the unyielding wooden floor, obliterating my mother's chalked foot marks, arms flexed in anger, hands clenched, neck jerking, face contorted, mouth popping half open. With just a few more steps to go, she came toppling down on her knees.

While I was wondering whether to laugh or cry, she shouted, "I can't do it, Mum! I won't poo any more of your ektherthith! Nod effer!" and she burst into tears.

My mother recoiled at these words before rushing to comfort my sister on the floor. She held her, and then, still bent over, froze as if remembering she should let her daughter pick herself up.

"Bon't help me – I bon't wand your help!"

We understood Hazel – my parents, my brothers, and me – but the rest of the universe was deaf. We were the rare initiates into Hazel's way of talking. I didn't know her garbled speech had a name: dysarthria. I had grown up with this secret tongue, so I was constantly surprised when strangers couldn't understand her. The consonants in her words were difficult to grasp; "but" might be heard as "put", "take" shifted to "bake", "Dad" to "bad", and "what" to "wad"; but also the "ch", "s", "r", and "v" sounds were distorted. And speech was only the beginning of her misunderstandings with the world.

"Ith too hart!"

My father was at work and would not learn of this drama until the evening. It was he who had built this walking frame for Hazel on our downstairs veranda, a physiotherapy contraption with two long, parallel, wooden rails leading to a large wall mirror, painted green to harmonise with our garden of mango and pawpaw trees. He would be disappointed.

I stared at my mother and Hazel, and thought how ungrateful my sister was. So much had been done for her, but here she was, ready to give up.

It was 1951; I was eight; she was six; it was a sultry tropical day in St. Kitts, just a few days since my mother and Hazel had returned from six months in America.

I remembered the day they had left. I had sulked, thinking it was surely not fair for my mother to go away, even temporarily. I was cross with my sister. Why couldn't she just be normal? Why did she walk and talk in such a funny way? And why couldn't we all have gone to America to see the cowboys and the skyscrapers? My father had said we didn't have enough money for that. But then, I thought, why had he sent my mother and Hazel over there in the first place?

When I searched for a culprit, I thought of Doctor Lake. Maybe it was his fault. He had visited us a lot at the time, and often talked about the clever surgeons in America, and their wonderful hospitals. They would cure her handicap, he said, and she would become like us. But I hadn't imagined it would take so long. My father had first said they'd only be gone for two or three months, just the time for the doctors to find the right treatment. I was having trouble with my new Convent School teachers, with their scary stories of damnation and hellfire. And, soon after my mother and Hazel left, my two brothers and I all caught whooping cough and were quarantined for several weeks. I missed my mother, who would have cared for us if she had not been away. While my father was at work during the day I had to make do with Granny and Grandpop, and all because of Hazel's problem.

I was stumbling, trying to find a meaning in my sister's "differences", sometimes brutally blind to the handicap, sometimes registering but not admitting the painful awkwardness, sometimes looking and pitying (the least acceptable to my sister), and then perhaps all of these at once.

After the whooping cough, my father told us my mother and sister couldn't come home yet, because Hazel's treatment wasn't finished. My mother was being trained to help her, but they had run out of money. She was working illegally in a supermarket in Kentucky, while we, back home in St. Kitts, unstuck postage stamps to help out. My father brought home huge boxes of envelopes – letters from his Basseterre law office. We would wet them, lift the precious stamps off, and dry them on blotting paper. Then my father would package these cancelled stamps off to my mother who sold them for food money. My mother and sister stayed with Aunt Dora, who wasn't really an Aunt but a Caribbean nursing friend. I remembered when she had lived in St. Kitts how she had helped my mother with Hazel. But then she had moved to America, so maybe she, too, was to blame for taking my mother away.

I had begun to doubt whether my mother and sister would ever come back to St. Kitts. They seemed pleased enough in America from the letters that my father read to us.

Finally, the money made them return – even the stamps weren't enough to shore up my father's modest revenues as a young lawyer with few clients. That return should have been a triumph.

We were all at the airport when the plane landed, except my baby brother Noel, and we were jumping with excitement. Of course, I shouldn't have expected Hazel to descend from the plane by herself, but I believed in fairy tales. When she was carried bodily down the stairs like a bundle of linen, I thought she was hurt. Then my mother set her on her feet and took her arm so she could stagger over to us. Hazel was overjoyed, but I had eyes only for the ragged gait and the wild head movements.

"Chrith! Beter!" she shrieked. "I'm pack!"

Now, my mother and Hazel had been back home for several days and my mother had begun their strange exercises with the rails and the mirror. I couldn't understand why, having been in America for a whole six months, Hazel wasn't already cured, as Dr Lake had promised.

At dinner that night, the day Hazel had fallen, I ate a few mouthfuls of stewed chicken and sweet potatoes, found the meal good, and turned to what was bothering me.

"When will Hazel be better?" I asked my parents.

We were seated around our large mahogany table and my mother was busy cutting Hazel's food into bite-sized portions. With a twitch of her head, my sister looked up from her plate and fixed me with a silent gaze.

I took after my father, being browner and more argumentative than my siblings. Hazel, on the contrary, had inherited my mother's light skin tone and oval face, and my father's dark hair. I noticed the painfully acquired scar on her forehead and imagined all the others. She, too, wanted an answer. My brothers, Peter and Noel, seated across the table from us, opened their eyes wide.

My father, the lawyer, spoke carefully into the silence: "We don't know, but we hope it will be soon." He was still wearing his white, short-sleeved shirt from work and he looked gravely at me. I would only know later how seriously he took his duty of analysis, trying to plan a future for his disabled Hazel.

"But Dr. Lake said… "

"I know, but it's more difficult than we thought – it will take months, maybe longer. Hazel suffers from cerebral palsy."

The name of this illness sat heavy on my tongue. "Can't she take a medicine?"

"What she needs is physiotherapy – that will correct her movements."

"You mean exercises like she tried today?"

Special exercises, like she had in America. Your mother has been trained by Aunt Dora and the American doctors to help Hazel."

"Well, she doesn't seem any better."

Hazel cast me a dirty look, if that was the right way to interpret her grimace.

"You're wrong, son. She's much better. You've forgotten how she was years ago."

I concentrated on eating a chicken wing with my fingers while puzzling more about my sister. Had she always been this awkward? Or even more so? Why hadn't I noticed?

"I cad *walk* now!" Hazel said.

"And that's not as simple as it was for you," my father said.

With the power of walking, however, comes the danger of falling, I thought. Hazel was inconspicuous when she could only crawl, but her handicap became much more evident on two feet because she could bump into things and crash onto the ground.

My mother stopped cutting up Hazel's food and raised her eyes to me.

"You don't remember her first trip to America, I suppose?"

"She hasn't been twice!"

"You were only four, sweetie, but you should remember. We took her when she was twenty-two months old, in 1946, just before my first playschool – the one I created for you two."

Vague memories of too much time spent with my grandparents and fighting with my friends in that playschool flitted through my mind.

My mother had always provided a volatile energy and enthusiasm in trying to come to grips with her daughter – sometimes it worked, but often it was misdirected, a sputter of flame quickly snuffed out. My father was the steady one. He folded his hands and looked at his four children from the end of the dinner table. He began to address his jury.

"Your mother and I were more worried when she was little. Hazel just lay there in her crib. She hardly moved, just wriggled, and couldn't sit up at a year and a half. Arthur Lake referred us to St. Luke's Hospital in New York. Do you know what they told us after weeks of testing?"

I shook my head.

"They said Hazel was brain damaged and uneducable. We couldn't accept that – we knew she was worth the effort of treatment. Your Grandpop would have sermonized them, 'O ye of little faith…' They called her ailment cerebral palsy – CP – but that's not polite. We prefer to say she's spastic. They even predicted she would never walk."

I preferred the more catchy word "spastic", like plastic, and I said, "But she *did* walk."

Hazel looked at me triumphantly this time, eyes wide, mouth tense, head cocked to one side. Now it was time for my father to establish the defendant's major success.

"So those doctors were wrong. That was tremendous progress, and it shows how important it is to believe in her and for her to keep on trying to develop. Hazel, do you remember that day, after the rough sea crossing to Nevis?"

"I boo!" she said. "I wath four, in Nevith, at the Arwood's houth. Mum held me, and Aunt Orwa wath on the far thide of the womb."

"You mean Aunt *Dora*," I said, "at the *Yearwood's* house."

"And the far side of the *room*," my father added, encouraging my sister.

Vewy far," Hazel said, "and Towa called, 'Come to me, Hathel,' and Mum gafe me a bush, so off I wend."

"A *push!*"

"Maybe it wath only a few thepth, mutt I bade them without a fall."

"*But* you *made* those important *steps* without a fall, indeed," my father said.

I remembered how fragile she had looked, like a newborn foal splaying its legs out for the first time. I hadn't thought she would complete the four steps on her own, but when she did, I was the first to clap. The gramophone was playing a song, *Alice Blue Gown*, just right for my sister.

"You see, children," my father said to us, "Hazel can do it. It doesn't matter if the rest of you walked three years younger – it's the end that counts."

We had by now almost finished eating. Only Hazel and Noel had food left on their plates.

"Like the tortoise and the hare!" I joked, and looked at my brothers for a response. Peter was four, light-skinned and dark-haired. Had I been as smart as I thought I was, I would have recognised a future scientist from the methodical way he went about eating his dinner. Noel was only two and quite the opposite: hard to control at the table, giggling as he played with his food.

"Don't laugh, this is serious. Your sister is just as clever as you are."

I must have frowned, for my father said, "She's lucky: some spastics *are* mentally deficient and others can't move their limbs at all. It's like a short-circuit in the brain."

My father loved electrical installations but these analogies made me uneasy.

Will it happen to the rest of us?"

"Not unless you hurt your head in an accident. Spastics are born that way, with their convulsions or paralysis, although we don't know why."

As if in response, Hazel stiffened in her chair and jerked her arms across the table. Her plate shattered on the floor, splattering chicken and sauce generously around.

Hazel made a distressed yelp. "Oh, dear!" my mother said, "Victoria!"

Before the servant Victoria could respond, something in Hazel's strangled cry made me explode in laughter. It rocketed through my mind that perhaps I could invent a game like that, where we all competed to give the best convulsion or jerk, and were allowed to throw plates and glasses around with abandon. There was no harm, after all, in having a good chuckle at my sister's expense.

But my father was less amused. "Stop right now, Chris! Never, NEVER, make fun of Hazel. You should know better! What if you were spastic too?"

I came back to earth as quickly as I had left it, hot and flustered. Angry, embarrassed, all I could think of was that this palsy thing was here to stay.

"Sorry, Hazel," I muttered.

My mother's eyes flashed at me as if I were responsible for the break-up of china and the downfall of grease. I could see she wanted me to pay.

"Help clean up the mess, Chris!" she ordered, but as I began to collect the pieces Virginia arrived with her mop, depriving me of my penance.

Then, fortunately, my father resolved things for us: "I want all you boys to promise me something – even Baby Noel. You have a mission: always believe in Hazel. She *will* drop and break things. Don't be scornful. Believe that she can achieve whatever she sets her mind to. Include her in all your games. Don't worry about her getting hurt – she'll learn how to fall. Have faith in your sister. Any time you doubt, just say 'she can do it', and we'll continue to make fools of those doctors in New York who said she was *uneducable*. Why, with the physiotherapy your mother will give Hazel, we can still hope for a cure. Some day."

I was an instant believer, not in the cure but in our duty. Until then, I had not realised how much my sister's handicap affected the whole family. It had been a pleasant feeling to be faster and surer in my movements than her, without asking why. Now, with my brothers, I had a mission. Our actions and support could do more for her future than all the crazy doctors in the world.

We were so excited by my father's brave words that we thought Hazel's moment of quiet meant acceptance. She was not happy with the exercises; perhaps she had less confidence in my mother's guidance than the Kentucky doctors'. I guessed later that the training did not seem useful to her. Her persistent rebellion soon destroyed my mother's plans. In that heady year of 1951, nothing could remove her jerks, facial tics, and awkward gait. But what did it matter within the magic circle of an activist family that had decided to reward effort over results? If only this cosy accommodation of her handicap could spill over into her school life, nothing could stop her.

I had faith but no perspective. Previous responsibilities for monkeys and assorted pets gave me no inkling of the future. I was as confident of my father's plans for my sister as a good foot soldier is of his general. But what of the enemy, the cold world so indifferent to its handicapped citizens, a world that would soon outlaw the word "spastic" in a frenzy of political correctness and yet ignore the affected? Could she take the hard knocks and could we make the sacrifices that might be needed for her survival? I would not learn the answers to these questions for years, because I was about to be removed from the family chessboard to play in an entirely new game, life at boarding school. From now on, I would see my sister only during the vacations.

The White Room

Usually, I felt I could trust my parents. They fed me and clothed me, sent me to school, and didn't get in my way much. But when I was nine they started making plans to improve me. It began with my snorts.

My throat itched. I didn't know why, and nor did anyone else, but one day I discovered a way to scratch it from the inside. I closed my mouth and moved my tongue and palate up and down so as to produce a sucking, grunting noise in my nasal passages. What mattered was the sharp pressure difference between the sticky surfaces near the back of my throat. I was able to rub the area around the larynx that was irritating me without actually touching it.

"Only pigs make that noise!" my brothers told me.

"And me!" I said. "Bet *you* can't do it."

We were playing in our garden, sitting on the grass, and Peter and Noel tried to copy me, without success.

"You're lucky," said Peter, "but I can move my ears," elevating his left lobe a good quarter-inch above the right. He knew this frustrated me – ear mobility was a family trait that my parents had not passed down to me.

"And I can move my nose as well," said Noel, dilating his nostrils. I laughed, because we could all do that.

During the day, my parents didn't care about the snorting. At night, however, when my grunting noises filled the house, they were bothered. I would continue grunting for hours and wake up with my throat sore.

"Stop it, Chris, and go to sleep!" they said. But I couldn't, even if I wanted to, because the grunting had become reflexive and my throat was irritated every night by the potent pollen from our garden. Some mornings, I rushed for a cooling drink of water as soon as I got up.

"He'll grow out of it," I heard my father say to my mother.

"But it will be a problem for his new school," she replied. "And later on, when he grows up, what girl is going to sleep in his bed if he makes such noises?"

I wondered what school they were talking about, surely not the insipid Convent School I was then attending. I wouldn't mind waking *them* up with a few snorts, but I wasn't sure how the Mother Superior would take it. I had had no confidence in her ever since she had scared me into going to confession. Maybe a new school was going to open in Basseterre, I speculated. And why should I allow a girl into my bed?

At lunchtime, I asked, "Where is the new school? Can I ride there on my bike?"

"Not unless your bike has wings," my father said.

I laughed. "Outside of town?"

"A bit farther: on another island. We want you to go to school in Antigua."

My father looked at me encouragingly, but I had misgivings.

"I don't want to go! Where'd I stay?" I said to my parents. We were eating mangoes Caribbean-style at the end of the meal, and I began licking my fingers noisily.

"It's a boarding school," said my father, "the best in the Leeward Islands. You're wasting your time in St. Kitts."

"I'm not! I get good marks!" It was not the first time I had heard talk of a boarding school for me, but now it seemed menacing.

My father and his father before him had pulled themselves up by their bootstraps thanks to their schooling in the Caribbean and further studies abroad; more than most, they understood the power of books. It would not be too strong to say that my father – the lawyer – was obsessed by learning.

A deep disquiet gripped me when I thought of leaving home. Life was plump and comfortable around me. I was never punished; I had lots of friends, and even a couple of expendable little brothers to wrestle with whenever I wanted. I read stories of buccaneers and privateers and daydreamed the time away.

"You've been to a Girls' High School and a Convent School – those are no places for a young Anglican boy."

This hadn't seemed a big problem to me until now.

"Why can't I keep on studying in St. Kitts? None of my friends is going away! I'd miss the weekends at Hog Valley!"

"You know, boarders come back home for vacations. We'll talk about all this later. Tomorrow we'll take you to see Doctor Lake for your throat. He'll get rid of that snorting before you go anywhere."

So, my parents passed me over to the doctors. The image of my first encounter with a hospital would stay with me for a long time. The only thing I knew about medicine was the avuncular face of our family doctor, Arthur Lake – a trusted family friend. He was tall and balding, with skin so light brown it was yellow, and when he smiled his whole face crinkled. My parents thought doctors were almost as holy as priests. Occasionally, a violation of my flesh with an injection needle would make me suspect that behind the pleasant smiles of doctors there might be something a little more sinister.

The truth, as I found out, is that doctors are just waiting for a provocation that will allow them not only to stick needles into you but also to slice and dice. Like a mechanic digging into the insides of a wheezing car, they justify surgery by removing some defective valve or sprocket and holding it up as a trophy in all its bleeding splendour. Unlike a garage technician, the doctor can't replace the parts he cuts out, not unless he finds a donor and cuts him up, too. So, he stitches your body together around the empty space and hopes it will get on with living.

Many things can be tolerated from a nine-year-old, but not loss of sleep. I'm sure everyone thought medical treatment was for my own good. Doctor Lake prodded and poked inside my mouth with a laryngoscope, and then returned his verdict, "Tonsils and adenoids – they must come out."

It seemed I might have tonsillitis and that my adenoids were enlarged and probably infected into the bargain. It was *the* thing for children's surgeons to do in the 1950s, never mind that the adenoids shrink on their own later on and have some value for disease protection. It was minor surgery and with luck not too difficult even for a place like St. Kitts.

"Trust me – it won't hurt, young man. We'll put you to sleep and when you wake up it will be all done."

"Will I have to go to school the next day?" I bargained.

"No, you can have two weeks of rest, just reading in bed."

"OK, then."

And so, a few days later, I was wheeled into the White Room. I called it the White Room, but those around me called it an operating theatre. It was in the depths of the grey Cunningham Road Hospital, since pulled down and rebuilt as offices. White walls, white ceiling, and bright white lights surrounded me. People in white gowns peered over me. A white cloth was clamped over my face and I was made to breathe in some nasty vapours. Then I had to count to a hundred, just like at school. Did they think they could trick me into mistakes? Then the white walls started expanding and compressing in waves of movement, like enormous hammers. Where there was quiet before, there was now a huge noise as my skull was caught and smashed between the hammers. It was a giant force, banging me into pulp every second. I was afraid. Where were my parents? Where was God? Where was I? And still the white walls of the White Room kept pounding at me. I forgot everything except my fear. My head wouldn't stay in one piece and my thoughts snapped apart. When I woke up my throat felt on fire.

I tried to say, "You didn't tell me I would have a bad dream, you told me to trust you," but it wouldn't come out. Nurses gave me lemonade to drink and my parents brought me books, but I didn't feel like reading for several days. I wondered whether I'd believe anyone, any more. I lay there, remembering the frightening whiteness, the giant hammers, the loss of identity, and the acid taste in my mouth.

After a week, I was sent home to convalesce, and things got better. I was just a little too old for the operation to be conveniently forgotten: for many years after, when I thought of how it would be to go crazy, I remembered being put to sleep in the White Room. At least it had served some useful purpose, I hoped. No more grunting like a pig and having sore throats because of infected adenoids. There was indeed a change. The air spaces around the back of my throat and nose – where the adenoids had been – had acquired a different geometry, and thus a different resonance. The pollen-rich air was as irritating as before. A few weeks after the surgery, my parents could tell the difference; I now sounded less like a pig and more like one of the mythical hogs on my father's Nevis farm.

"It hasn't worked," my mother said, looking at me reading a book and snuffling.

"Maybe he'll learn to control it."

"Do I still have to go to the new school in Antigua?" I asked.

"Try to understand – you've learned how to read and write and now it's time to go to a real school. You must discover languages, higher mathematics, poetry, and much more. And discipline, good discipline." My mother flinched at this.

"But I want to stay here in St. Kitts! My friends are here!"

My father clasped his hands together and said cheerily, "You're worth more than that. The secondary schools here have not yet found their feet. We want you to go to the same school I went to in Antigua. You'll make lots of new friends."

While I considered this, my father said, "But there's still the entrance exam."

"What exam?"

"Well, you're a year younger than the usual entry class and I suppose they don't have much confidence in St. Kitts schools, so they need to test you."

"I don't want to be tested for an Antiguan school!"

"Trust me – it's easy."

I glowered at him.

Years later, I heard you can only persuade someone who wants to believe. I had wanted my throat to stop itching, but I didn't want to leave home.

My family was not alone in the puzzle of finding adequate secondary school education for their children. Up to the end of the second world war, poor blacks and coloureds had been confined to primary education because the secondary schools were fee-paying; so it was mostly the planters' and merchants' children who could afford to continue their education and – perhaps – go on to university. But over the last ten years, all that had begun to change. Most of the Leeward Islands now had a public Grammar School that accepted brighter students of all colours at low cost, but resources were scarce, most of all qualified teachers.

It was difficult for parents. For the poor black families, where generations had been deprived of this opportunity, even a free Grammar School nevertheless meant feeding and clothing the child for up to seven more years instead of putting him to work. Was it worthwhile? The wealthier, mostly white families wondered how much quality would be lost in the expanded school system. Should they pay even more to send their offspring away to Barbados or even to Britain? Would the children ever come back? My middleclass but fortuneless family was caught in-between – preoccupied with good schooling but unable to pay for four children abroad. I was to be a test case.

My tonsillitis operation had been so traumatic it dwarfed smaller annoyances like an unwanted exam. It was my first real exam and I was not in the mood to take it since I was not happy at the idea of going to school on another island. This exam was just the first of a long series that would stretch my spirit almost to rupture and decide every future aspect of my life, even my country.

"At least I'll meet the other St. Kitts candidates," I thought. So, I was even less happy when I found myself alone in a sombre classroom on a Saturday morning, tapping my fountain pen on a battered desk. Also unhappy was the dark-skinned, hirsute examiner, come especially from Antigua. We took a mutual dislike to each other.

He frowned at me over his eyeglasses, "You look very young."

"I'm nine. Where are the other boys?"

"You seem to be the only one this year. Hardly worthwhile, is it?" he said, as he gave me the question sheet.

I agreed with him when I saw all the sums they expected me to do. "I'm going to fail," I thought, "but that's all right – I don't want go to boarding school anyway." To my disgust, the examiner took my answer sheet away before I had finished the long divisions. How could my father have said it was easy?

After the arithmetic, I realised there was a story to write, so I thought I'd tell them about the White Room and how difficult it was to hold my head together. Ether is full of evil spirits who will try to possess you, I decided. I got quite excited and even spelled "anasthetik" right, I hoped. I didn't know what the Antiguan school would think, but the essay felt good to me.

I looked up at the hairy-faced examiner with more enthusiasm than before. I gave him my paper. It flashed through my mind he looked like a black Blackbeard. I thought happily that I mightn't fail after all, and then I regretted it, because that would leave me with no excuse for refusing Antigua.

A few weeks after the exam, my father said to me, "You passed!"

"Don't want to go."

My father looked at me seriously for a long moment. Then, to my great surprise, he said, "OK."

"OK, I don't have to go to Antigua?"

"Yes, I guess we misjudged you."

"Huh?"

"It would be much too difficult for you."

"Hmm?"

"The classes are competitive, and boarding school is a tough life. Some children don't survive."

"How's that?"

"Well, they're not strong enough, not brave enough to live away from home. They have to be sent back after a few days."

"I wouldn't do that! I just don't want to go."

"Don't worry, we understand, you've had a soft life. Taking care of yourself and standing up for your rights requires courage."

"I could do it!"

"No, no, you don't have to."

"Yes, I want to! Let me show you. I can do everything for myself – be tough. I'm brave!"

"Well, if you really insist, maybe it's not too late…"

I thought so hard of all the possibilities for bravery that I hardly heard my father as he continued, "…and, by the way, you won a scholarship, all your fees will be paid by the government. That money will be useful."

From that word – scholarship – my father doubtless extracted "scholar", his hope for my future.

I only retained the word "ship", my ship of adventure. I would be a pirate.

"Trust me," my father said, "Antigua will be exciting."

I knew some promises led to unpleasant surprises, but suddenly I didn't care. I trusted my father, even after all that had happened; our real days of conflict would come much later. I stood up tall and breathed in a new freedom. "Francis Drake, Henry Morgan, William Kidd: all you has-beens, roll over!" I thought, "I'm off to sea to make my fortune."

I was too young to reflect that most pirates come to a bad end. The first of my heroes, Drake, a 16th-century Elizabethan privateer, the scourge of the Spanish Main, was also a thriving slave-trader, which I hadn't been told. He died of dysentery, off the coast of Mexico, his fleet defeated. The second, Morgan, a rascally Welsh 17th-century buccaneer, made his name by burning Spanish settlements from Santo Domingo to Panama, torturing and butchering the towns' inhabitants. The English gratefully knighted him in Jamaica, where he died of a mysterious yellow-skinned disease, and where the fierce earthquake at Port Royal four years later destroyed his tomb and all his works. The third, Kidd, a Scottish Presbyterian minister's son, interested me the most because he began his career brilliantly in St. Kitts by stealing a 20-gun French ship and donating his services to the English Governor of Nevis. Unfortunately for his later pirate's calling, he was not careful enough whom he robbed, and the same – ungrateful this time – English eventually hanged him in London, covering his body with tar and displaying it in an iron cage by a bend of the River Thames until it rotted. It was not a good foreboding.

Part 2: Boarding School (Antigua, 1952-1954)

The Pirate's Dreams

There was a first time for everything: my first flight in an aeroplane, a first moment when I breathed Antiguan air, my first sight of the school, and then my first night away from home. One moment I was in the family stronghold, cocooned with cats, dogs, rowdy siblings, and affectionate parents, all bearing gifts; the next I was on the rugged, open plains of boarding school life, alone in another country, with masters, bullies and other fierce spirits to be placated.

Almost ten years old, early in 1952, I stood at the Golden Rock Airport in St. Kitts (now R.L. Bradshaw Airport) and counted my clan: father, mother, sister, and two brothers. I knew they would all be there when I came back. I rolled my first nine years into a ball and put it in a trouser pocket, warm against my skin. Then I was led up the cramped metal boarding ladder of a twin-engine Dakota plane that would pitch itself into the air for a flight across the Caribbean Sea that seemed to me forever but was actually only a half-hour.

A few days before I went to Antigua that first time, I was subjected to an embarrassing homily from my mother. In my mind, this departure from St. Kitts was the start of a great adventure, a voyage during which I would distinguish myself. Not for nothing had I survived three elementary schools, learned to read, sat exams, wrestled with all comers, and generally shown the world what a tough guy I was. Perhaps not all my friends would agree with this. Perhaps had I bothered to check my face in a mirror – something I didn't do frequently for fear I would have to wash it – I might have noticed that, apart from an occasional tree-climbing scratch, my soft round features didn't exactly fit the pirate role. But now, proud of having been selected by examination for this new school on another island, I felt myself unleashed as a privateer of His Majesty, no longer restrained by petty parental recommendations. I would be master of my own ship. And a ship's captain doesn't take kindly to a woman's tears.

"Are you sad to go, Chris?" my mother asked, oblivious to my high ship's status. "Your Dad and I will miss you, you know."

I hated this idea of a parent "missing" me. Why could they not see I had my own life to live, my own dreams to find? If someone had tried to kill me with a musket or a sword and failed, then he would have "missed" me. I could accept that, and be appropriately afraid. But I couldn't stomach the mushy-mucky notion that I had no right to be out of sight and fighting my own battles for any length of time.

"Sad, me? Why should I be sad? I'm going to make lots of new friends at school."

"Yes, but you know you won't see *us* or your cat for three months."

Bringing up my cat was unfair; anyway, it didn't work. She might as well have said "three days" or "three years": three months didn't have any thickness for me.

"You can visit me in Antigua if you like."

"Yes, I'd like to, but I don't suppose your father and I can pay for a trip like that very often."

I owned a junior Post Office savings account in Basseterre but I had everything to learn about counting my pennies.

"Well, I'll be back." And then, with a nine-year-old's magnanimity, I added, "Don't worry."

"But you will write to me every week, won't you?"

Up to this point, the ship's captain had only been mildly irritated by the parental effusion.

"Write to you? Letters, you mean?" I had never written to my parents before, not even when they had gone to England on vacation a year previously, nor had I written to anyone else, not having any friends outside of my island. In fact, I didn't know how to write or to address a letter. The whole business of letter writing didn't seem to apply to me. I had never heard of an intrepid captain wasting his time to compose letters between attacks on enemy ships.

"Yes, letters. The Housemaster told us his boarders write home every Sunday morning after church."

I must have looked hostile at this. In addition, my hitherto neutral opinion of the Housemaster became tinged with suspicion.

"And you do write stories so beautifully. We'd love to hear from you each week. I'll keep all your letters. And we'll write back, of course, and tell you what's happening at home. Promise you'll write us."

Somewhat mollified, I promised. It was not so much the compliment, which I rightly took for bribery, but the strange idea that something might happen while I was not there. I had not thought the world I left behind could evolve in any way until I returned, but just in case…

"And if anything goes wrong, you know, if you have a problem with the boarding school, or your schoolmates, or the masters, just tell us. You've always confided in us while you were at home, so that's what we expect. We can help if you have any difficulties."

Was past practice any reason for me to bare my soul? I would have to think about that. The words "problem" and "difficulties" stuck in my throat. How could my mother imagine that a ship's captain like me, a buccaneer, could get into difficulty? I resolved never to use this resource, never to complain to her, and resigned myself with bad grace to write home now and again. Maybe I could tell jokes.

A stewardess mothered me to a window seat and strapped me in as the little plane took off. I looked down at the land and sea, eager for my adventures to begin.

I had lived until then with a small horizontal outlook of a few square miles. My framework was rows of old, colonial houses; shady trees; sunny gardens; dusty streets; and always a strip of blue sea on the horizon. And cane, of course. Where the houses stopped there were always green cane fields. That was my island world. Fifteen, maybe twenty thousand people lived in Basseterre, most of whom we knew, or knew someone who knew them. I had been into all of the stores in town (except the rum shops) and walked most of the streets. The smallness of my world didn't oppress me in any way, not at the time. Maybe it was little, but it was the same for everyone else on the island. It was only when I opened books and looked at maps that St. Kitts seemed little. Yet, the vastness suggested by the books and maps was somehow not real. What was real was my tangible neighbourhood of a few square miles.

Until, that is, I looked down on it from the plane. Then I could see so many more streets, and houses, and gardens, and trees, and people in the gardens, and goats in some streets, and small boats in the harbour, that my eyes filled up with the quantity of things under me, like a funnel pouring bright images into my brain. My small world exploded under me, and the higher we flew, the more I could see. But the more I could see, the fewer details I could discern, and soon I was given a picture I had never imagined before. It was the coastline of the island. My gaze was riveted on St. Kitts and its shores. It was the dry season. I could see the sandy beaches like icing around a fudge-topped cake, then the rocky bits like nuts and raisins as I glimpsed the Eastern peninsula. I could even make out the little waves ruffling the sand and the shifting greens on the offshore seabed. I shivered. Why had all this been hidden from me for so long?

The maps were right after all. My island world could be laid out on a sheet of paper and taken in with one blink. And since in this new reality my island world was so small, it was vulnerable, like an ant under my foot. I could stamp the whole island into the sea – squash the cake. It seemed to me suddenly that the greatest power in the world was to see things from above, to reduce all the dusty sprawling confusion of the horizontal to a new perspective, a few lines and colours far below me, not of any great importance.

"Maybe this is what God sees," I thought, promoting myself rapidly to omnipotence. But the Almighty became bored when we lost sight of land. The waters below turned a monotonous deep blue, and I could no longer make out individual waves. The sunlight glinted on formless, sliding things and, once or twice, I imagined there were ships there. But without a reference to fixed land, the plane didn't seem to be moving. I was stuck in the sky.

No longer captivated by the sight from the cabin window, I was tied down – bound – in a chair, suspended over dark waters, headed for an unknown destination. For a moment, this did not seem like a good thing to do. I knew the name of my destination: I was going to Antigua, to a boarding school. But what was Antigua, and how would this new school be? I didn't want to think right then about my family and friends left behind. That would keep for later. And my pirate vessel seemed to have sailed off into the fog, like the white clouds outside my cabin window, leaving me without support. I knew nobody in Antigua. My parents had friends who would "look after me" in case of need. But that, for me, was nobody. So, I took to imagining Antigua, which would, of course, be just like St. Kitts, with cane fields and streets and rows of old, colonial houses; shady trees; sunny gardens; and goats in the streets. And the sunny gardens would be full of fruit trees and my school would be so full of books I wouldn't even have to visit the town library. And certainly, the other boarders would make excellent schoolmates to replace those I had lost. I regained some confidence. I thought little about the Masters – surely that would take care of itself. More important, I counted on my fingers the new friends I would make on the first day, friends who would play my games. At least ten, I counted, before I ran out of fingers.

Then it became cool in the plane, and I fell asleep.

Someone checked my seatbelt and I woke up for landing in Antigua. I had the time to notice a long string of excellent sandy beaches. This new island seemed to have more of them than St. Kitts, I thought for a moment, but it couldn't be true, so I dismissed the idea. But where were the mountains, the peaks, and rainforests that remained green even when the drought painted the rest of the land in scorched brown and yellow? As we got in closer, I saw Antigua was a different place, flatter and drier, with hardly a cane field in sight.

Since I couldn't conceive of an island without abundant cane fields, the countryside took on an unreal aspect. I didn't know what was wrong, but every way I looked it seemed something was missing. What it was, I could not say. Perhaps this was not Antigua at all but some other place that the God who made aeroplanes had invented? This sense of displacement grew. A remembered story came to my rescue, and I did what I was supposed to do – pinched my arm. Nothing changed around me, but I verified I was still capable of feeling pain, even if the island didn't seem properly laid out.

Knowing everything around me in St. Kitts gave me confidence, even arrogance; taking the familiar sights away undermined these foundations. I peered uneasily at the stubbly fields a few hundred yards beneath the plane, the squiggly concrete and dirt roads, the lonely cows, and a few stray trucks. No cane. I imagined the cane fields were elsewhere, on another part of the island.

In this I was right: there *was* cane elsewhere. St. Kitts, only 68 square miles, was twice as densely planted as the larger Antigua. Sugar production in Antigua was declining in favour of tourism in the 1950s, and only amounted to about half that of the more fertile St. Kitts. On the other hand, Antigua did have more beaches.

My home had gone, and in its place was the Housemaster.

"You must be Christopher, the new boy from St. Kitts," he said, as he gathered up my small suitcase. "I'm Father Billington."

"Hello," I said. He was a large man in a white cassock. "You look like my grandfather."

"I doubt it," said Father Billington, with a small smile. "I'm English, you see, even if I'm dressed like him. How is old Father Vanier, by the way?" We took a taxi.

My grandfather hadn't said much about Father Billington, just that he was a decent chap, or something of that sort, and I was surprised this strange priest seemed to know him. But maybe all the Anglican priests on the islands knew each other. And why "old"? True, Grandpop had white hair, but I didn't think of him as old.

"Fine. Have the other boarders arrived yet?"

"You're the last. I gather this was your first flight in an aeroplane. Were you afraid?"

"Of course not!" I said. "Why should I be afraid?"

"Well, in my experience most small boys like you are afraid of leaving home. But it's worth it to come to a school like this, don't you agree? By the way, I'll excuse you because you are new, but you should address me as 'Sir'."

"Oh," I said. "Sir!"

There was a pause while I adjusted. I was confused. Had I been afraid in the plane? What a preposterous idea. Had my grandfather described Father Billington as decent, or peculiar? This man was weird, and I didn't know how to deal with him.

I got on well with the adults I knew in St. Kitts. I had met many visitors in my parents' home, and I often stayed and talked with them. I had never had to say "Sir". It had always seemed to me that adults were tolerable, even decent. Of course, many were slow moving and fat, ugly with their wrinkles and their warts, and ignorant of good games, but most of this was not their fault, I thought. After they had finished the best part of their lives – as children – there just wasn't anything left to do but to become adults. I talked to them as equals.

Schoolteachers were different. They used a more austere set of rules in the classroom. But I didn't have to put up with teachers outside of school. And none of my elementary teachers in St. Kitts had ever asked me to call him "Sir". So, in what category was Father Billington, a stuffy teacher or a new, not-so-nice kind of adult? I had thought he would be like my father or my grandfather because he was in charge, but no.

"Why do I have to call you 'Sir', Sir?"

"Because I'm your Housemaster, your Teacher, and your Chaplain, Christopher. It shows respect. You're in a fine boarding school now, just like in England. That's the way we do things."

"If it's all the same to you, Sir, my friends call me 'Chris'. I prefer 'Chris' to 'Christopher'."

"But I'm your Housemaster, not your friend, Christopher, and don't forget it. 'Chris' is too familiar for me. I shall call you 'Christopher'."

I didn't forget. I took in his ruddy face, which was still smiling, and his blue eyes, which were cold, and said, "As you wish, Sir, but I hope the other boarders will call me 'Chris'." Why was he able to choose his name and not me? The pirate inside seemed very small.

In 1952, the Antigua Grammar School for boys was a long, sprawling, wooden building on the outskirts of the capital (St. John's). I didn't discover the main Hall, the Dining Room, and the classrooms on the ground floor until later, for the Housemaster took me at once to my living quarters on the first floor. Somewhere in the school, there was a classroom with my family name, but on that first day I did not inquire. I arrived as a new boy in the middle of a Saturday, under the beating sun, and my confidence melted away with every step.

The Housemaster took me up creaking wooden stairs and showed me the dormitories. My new home, which he called the junior dorm, was painted white and grey with plain wooden floors that creaked like the stairs. That day, the room was just a place to sleep. It looked rougher, less comfortable than my home. That suited me – a pirate must make do with little on his way to great spoils. Later, it would be full of echoes and memories. I wouldn't be able to look at the metal beds with their solid frames without thinking that it took the combined weight of four boys to threaten the structure, or one determined boy jumping on it repeatedly, several feet into the air. I saw the dormitory bordered an immense and fascinating veranda that ran the length of the building. Windows with hurricane shutters led to it from each room. The windowsill formed a comfortable seat on which, in the coming days, I would sit and polish my shoes. I would learn later that the crucial thing was to be *seen* polishing your shoes. No one could hold you responsible if some vicious tree, or wall, or even the ground, rose up and scuffed them a few minutes later. I would even teach my shoes how to defend themselves against all comers, armouring the tips with little metal studs.

As I looked from the veranda, I could see the playing field just below: the soccer goal posts like masts in a sea of hard-packed brown dirt, the faded green oasis of the cricket pitch waiting for the next season, the vague outline of the 220-yard track forming a perimeter. But what held my eye was the disorderly pastureland beyond all this, with wild acacia thorn bushes and clammy cherry (*cordia obliqua*) trees where small boys like me could – and would – hide for hours.

"Here is Christopher," said Father Billington to the group of boys in my dormitory.

The pirate in me woke up diffidently as I sized up my new friends. Most had English-sounding names. Freckled Dickey from St. Croix, the only boy shorter than me, looked even more nervous than I felt. Brown-skinned Melford from Nevis, several years older, greeted me as if he knew me, and that made me pine for Hog Valley. On the contrary, I did not have a good feeling for Derek and Trevor, brothers who hailed from an old English family and whose father was Warden of Nevis, who smirked down their aquiline noses at me. Maybe our families didn't get along, I thought. Then there was Wes, an athletic acne-sufferer from the US Virgin Islands, twice my size; perversely, his facial affliction gave me instant confidence in him. He could fit right into my pirate crew. I noted wiry Miguel, closest to my age and from St. Thomas. I guessed I could take him in wrestling. And then I greeted burly Trapl, standing quietly in the background, who claimed he was a Czech from Anguilla but was later rumoured to be German. I found it strange none of us was Antiguan – we all came from other Caribbean islands, our parents paying for the reputation of Good British Schooling. But, of course, the Antiguans would be day students, not boarders.

"This is your bed, Christopher," said the Housemaster, as he showed me my corner on that first day. "Every night you must tuck in your mosquito net; every morning you must fold it and make your bed. Wake-up time is 7am; breakfast is at 8; school starts at 9. Lunch is at midday, tea at 4pm, and dinner at 6. Sharp. You must never be late. In the evening, you will do your homework in the Common Room."

I lost track of my fellow boarders while trying to memorise this timetable. The words "late" and "homework" had a bad feel to them.

"There are two showers, one for the senior boarders and the other for juniors like you. Cleanliness is next to godliness. You will bathe twice a day, before breakfast and before dinner. Loud noises and fighting are not allowed in the dorms. My room is at the end of the corridor. You can come and see me anytime you have questions. Understood?"

"Yes, Sir." I shrugged off the two showers per day, but wondered where we would be allowed to fight, if not in the dorms.

That's the way he left me on that first day to unpack my bag: full of hope, because I was at last here, in a new country; ready for excitement; and yet, uncertain, because of all these new rules and faces pulling at me like strings. "Sir", indeed.

The afternoon sailed by. Surrounded by the other boarders, I unpacked my belongings: little piles of khaki short trousers (new), cotton shirts (also new), underpants (not so new), toothbrush (one), bar of soap (just in case), sports shoes (what for?), marbles (twenty-five), pen and ink (it hadn't spilled), my faithful penknife (two blades, one notched by accident), books (*Billy Bunter, Biggles…*), and comics (*Beano* and *Dandy*). I was allocated a cupboard where, for the first time in my life, I had to lock my things up. It all went in except the comics, which were already circulating and difficult to retrieve. I had planned to read them later, in place of a bedtime story.

I told myself it must be like this in England: people in Antigua were just more distant and formal. No one had threatened me, after all. Not really. The books I had read by Richmal Crompton and Enid Blyton were all I knew about English children and their English teachers. I had started *Tom Brown's Schooldays* – more pertinent to boarding schools – but found it a bit dull except for the fights. Maybe an English school set in the Caribbean was not going to be fun after all. The books ought to have prepared me for the rigid, un-Caribbean behaviour of the Housemaster, but it wasn't the same when I was in the middle of it. I had no idea what Tom, William or The Five would have done.

A few glimpses of the school grounds, some halting talk about other islands, a dinner in fits and starts, and the strange day wound to its official end at nine o'clock that evening.

At the time, I still knew next to nothing about the intricate rules and customs that would govern my future survival. I didn't yet realise I was a prisoner; that I would not be allowed to keep the cash I had brought in my suitcase; that the senior boarders had authority over me; that I would have to serve as an altar boy; and that I would be obliged to eat every last scrap of the dreadful school meals.

"All of you to bed now, old and new. And no talking after lights out," the Housemaster said, but there was still an excited murmur of voices.

"Can I read a bit, Sir?"

"Didn't you hear me? You will be punished if I have to come back," were his last words as he strode out of the dormitory. I folded the comics under my pillow.

No sooner had he turned off the electric lights than my imagination turned on. Instead of falling asleep to the sound my brothers' breathing in the next room and my cat's purring on my bed, as I would have done at home, I strained to make out the faint outlines of the other mosquito nets in the dark dorm. My pillow smelled musty, as if it had not been used or aired for several months. There were faint rustlings. Would anyone talk? I vowed I would not be the one to get on the wrong side of the Housemaster.

That first night in Antigua, I felt that the boys around me were strangers. There was no comfort in numbers. I had wanted adventure but now would have liked nothing better than to return home at once.

As I lay in the dark, I longed for my family in St. Kitts.

"Come into our room for a bedtime story," my mother would call. Several of us (those of my siblings not yet asleep) would rush to my parents' side and curl up in their bed to listen.

"A father had two sons. The older was smart and sensible and could cope with any situation, whereas the younger was stupid and could never learn nor understand anything." She began a tale from the Brothers Grimm.

The story ended well, I remembered. The stupid son won a chest of gold and a beautiful princess against all odds. Not so stupid after all. I had loved the title, *A Tale About the Boy Who Went Forth to Learn What Fear Was*. I admired his bravery. So did my brothers, and I liked the feeling that we had all shared in this adventure, that we had travelled in our minds together. Afterwards, we could evoke our favourite tales with just a few key words, "pennies... spots... photography".

"Now let me wish you goodnight," said my mother (or my father if it was his turn) and we were each tucked into our beds and kissed. This being the tropics, "tucking in" was never more than one thin sheet, but it felt just as snug as a thick quilt in winter would feel years later. How easy it was to sleep when you knew you were loved.

And so, back to my present predicament. A dreadful thought entered my mind. I needed my parents. But this was not normal. People should need *me*, not the other way around. I saw no contradiction in this. How could I be bold and fly my pirate's flag if I needed someone, depended on them? But I *did* need them, and right then. And there was worse. It was impossible – I couldn't have them. What was it my mother had said? "Your Dad and I will miss you." Unfortunately, I now knew what she meant. I missed them terribly. But these were incapacitating thoughts. It would be embarrassing to break down and cry – this was a crime for which I could be made to walk the plank.

I could see myself all clad in black with a red sash around my head, a knife between my teeth, menacing an enemy ship.

"We surrender," they said. "Take our gold."

"I want to go back home," I mouthed, and dropped my knife into the sea. Suddenly, I yearned for the warm sands of Conaree or Frigate Bay, my island home; yearned to be just a little boy again, not a pirate; yearned to have my parents close by, the sea washing gently and securely at my feet.

The pressure of these thoughts forced me outwards, back into the dormitory.

I heard a snuffling from the far side of the room.

"That's Dickey," I thought, "poor little fellow, he's younger than I am and can't take it." Then, right next to me, more soft noises floated into my ears.

"Why, that's Miguel, but he can't be crying. Surely not! He's my age, after all." But he was whimpering.

I was glad to be tougher and vastly superior. But I asked myself why Miguel, whom I already took as a potential friend, should be so sad. All of a sudden, Miguel and Dickey were more like brothers than strangers.

"Maybe he loves his mother and father a lot. Now they're so far away. Like mine. It'll be months before we go home again. Every night they used to give him a goodnight kiss. Just like mine did. And maybe he has little brothers, who are already asleep like mine are. But he can't hear them breathing. Neither can I. Poor Miguel. Poor me."

And so, by sentimental contamination, I understood why Miguel was crying, and I had no other response than to cry, too. I was sure if neither of us had started crying that night, the contagion would not have spread. Maybe there were only two of us, maybe more. Maybe it continued for ten minutes, thirty, or even an hour. It was hard to know when the snuffling mutated into snoring and a gurgling silence I was part of.

In the days to come, each one of us would find some way to react to this loss of home. Some would suck a finger at nights. Others would wet their beds. Of the two defence mechanisms, finger-sucking was the more damaging, because it can deform the front teeth, as it did mine.

Bed-wetting was rife, though. It took me a few weeks to understand why some of my roommates made up their beds first thing in the morning. I could always get my shower ahead of them, while they were folding their blankets. I would fold mine later. One day, Father Billington came in to inspect and pulled off all those tightly-tucked-in blankets.

"It smells to high heaven!" he said, exposing a ripe yellow colour on several formerly white sheets.

"Boys!" he continued. He threw the blankets back, and called Dickey and Miguel into his office to explain that their families wouldn't be pleased to pay for extra laundry charges. He warned them peeing in bed was a punishable offence.

But then, on the night I arrived in Antigua, these defences hadn't yet been built. I couldn't stop loving my parents, and acceptance of my homesickness was way beyond me. Enough that I was vulnerable and it hurt so much, I who had thought myself so bold and strong, deprived of my warm cushion of family intimacy. This was the first sharp cut into my soft outer shell. And I had some accounts to settle, lights out or not. I didn't care any more.

I had to tell Miguel what a softy he was, and how he had made me so unhappy. His tears had tipped the balance at the worst possible moment.

"Miguel! You awake?"

"No, I'm not. What you think? Just shut up, Chris."

"It's your fault," I told him. "You were crying. Thinking of your brothers, I suppose. Well, you set all of us off – so just keep it to yourself."

"Don't shit on me, man. You've got it wrong."

I sat up and peered into the darkness separating our two beds. "How do you mean?"

"There's no way I could 'set all of you off'. I was fine, and if it hadn't been for *you* I would have been asleep by now. You're the one who started mewling, crybaby. I don't have any brothers, by the way."

I could not reply, because I had betrayed my fleet. Me, the softy. Me, the first to cry. How could I have sunk so low? Eventually, one hopeful thought came to me, like a goldfish moving in a dark pool. It wasn't much, but it was all the comfort I had. Tomorrow was Sunday, and I would write my first jokey letter home to my mother and father. That way, this astonishing pain would dissipate in my ink, flowing back to my family.

Beyond my childish angst, there was change. A knowledge of loss was growing deep inside me like a baby pearl, growing not just that day but far into the future, giving meaning to the contours of a life that had been obscured by the confusion of small everyday pleasures and acts of selfishness. Like the view from the plane, new perspectives were opening. Truth comes through suffering: there is no light without darkness, and the deeper the dark the more I could appreciate the home I had left.

I turned over on my stomach so that my cheeks could dry on the pillow and sucked my thumb until dreams of a tall-masted frigate with its bold skull-and-crossbones rocked me to sleep. William Kidd! William Kidd!

Juniors

Many problems began in the Dining Room of my new boarding school. One of them was the food. At nine years, I expected the Antigua Grammar School kitchen would be like my mother's, full of home-made hams, sweet drinks, and coconut ice creams. Sometimes I pictured myself as a pirate, surviving on courage and scraps of bully beef. Other times, I'd dream of servants piling my plate with roast chicken, or hot spicy fish, and mounds of soft white rice and yams. Had this culinary fantasy come true, it might even have cured the homesickness I was struggling with.

Instead, as I prepared for dinner a few days after arrival, I felt cheated. The food was awful.

This judgement came from the somewhat-pampered son of a middleclass Caribbean small-island family. I thought it natural that my father, as a respected lawyer, had a key role in the sugar-producing establishment of his island and my mother, after dabbling in journalism and kindergarten teaching, had the security of an accounting job. I was used to a comfortable life, and separation from my warm home back in St. Kitts had opened an unexpected fissure in me.

The people whom I met at the school were unsettling. I naturally trusted strangers, the way I trusted my family, with the possible exception of a few adults like the Reverend Mother in the Convent School I had attended who had frightened me, and the doctor who had removed my tonsils saying it wouldn't hurt. Now I had the Housemaster to bother about as well, and perhaps others. None of my friends at home lied to me, as far as I knew, so the notion of deception was exceptional to my life before boarding school; betrayal was something that happened between governments and during wars. An eldest child, I had little experience of boys older than myself.

I waited for the next meal outside the Dining Room with a group of seniors whom I hadn't talked to before.

"You're the new junior, aren't you?" one asked me.

The Housemaster had told me on arrival I was a "junior", and this word had seemed to carry reassuring status. But now, it began to sink in that I had received an identity tag of little-known implications. I had other tags: "Kittitian", "Anglican", and "Scholarship Boy". A junior was simply part of the boarding house community, I supposed, younger and smaller than a senior, but deserving of fair treatment.

On one side of the hallway, I saw a set of stairs leading to the floor above and to several imposing doors.

"What's up there?" I asked the senior next to me.

"Headmaster's office. That's where you'll get caned."

I laughed at his humour, and then inquired what the strange plaque was on the other side of the hallway: "Semper Virens", which meant nothing to me.

"School motto – Latin. That's not about you – it's about the bugs in the school meals: 'Always Flourishing'."

They certainly knew how to joke around here, I thought. Quite English. That was what I had liked about coming to the school. I didn't share my father's reasons for entering – education, family tradition, and discipline. But I had read stories of English boarding schools and thought the whole idea of being a "sort of" English schoolboy out here in the Caribbean was amusing, exotic, and romantic.

I considered my tropical surroundings to be uninspiring. The hot sun, the blue sea, the white sands, the coconut trees, and the cane fields: it was all stubbornly *there*, all year long, never going away, and perfectly boring. I could be a touch more enthusiastic about my Caribbean island assets if something actually happened, but just *being* tropical day after day wasn't enough for me. I would have considered foreigners quite silly to pine for these places as vacation spots.

Besides, it was too hot in the Caribbean, and shady places were hard to find. What excited me were those fascinating grey skies I read about, the deliciously cool weather in Europe, castles and rivers, Arcadian forests, green fields speckled with sheep, boys in uniform, prefects and school prizes, capers and comradeship, and more cool weather – a lot more. In short, the model of English boarding school and country life that our imagination had inherited from the Mother Country in her dusty colonies.

The dinner gong rang at last, and we walked into the Dining Hall, with its airy windows, long wooden table, and worn benches. I looked uncertainly at the table and moved towards the end furthest away from the Housemaster.

"Juniors! This end, please, where I can see you," Father Billington called us to order. So the label "junior" already carried that small constraint – I couldn't sit where I liked. I had found Father Billington – the Housemaster – disturbing on my arrival a few days before, when he had insisted I call him "Sir", and every time I looked at his ruddy face at the head of the table, the feeling came back.

We stood while the Housemaster intoned the opening grace, "For this, the food we are about to receive, may the Lord make us truly grateful…" during which time we folded our hands and wondered if the Lord was going to succeed in giving us a good meal this time.

I sat at the table next to the Housemaster and near to Miguel, Dickey, and the other juniors of my size, and waited for the next event. She turned out to be an enormously fat black cook, balancing several plates of soup on a tray. She wore a soiled white apron, and with her hair tied in a curly black bun she might have graced any of the Caribbean homes I had been in, except that, as she cooked for twenty people three times a day, she knew her power, and she took no nonsense from us. She had several assistants in her enormous, grimy kitchen, about which I would lose all curiosity after I had seen and eaten what came out of it.

The mixture in my soup plate was a greasy yellow, enriched with lumps of orange matter trailing untidy filaments, rumoured to be pumpkin. The odour was sickly sweet. To be fair, I was not used to soups, and today I have nothing against pumpkins, but right then, it seemed an abomination, insipid enough to compromise my utopian dreams of boarding school life. I took in as little as possible of it, in small mouthfuls, and I watched the other juniors confront the slop. After a few sips, two of them put down their spoons in defeat.

"New boys! Food is not to be wasted, you will eat *all* your soup."

At home, I had heard my mother lecture half-heartedly about the starving children on the other side of the world who would be happy to have my meal, but the Housemaster's order was much more definitive – a new bar on this prison I could feel building up around me. I must have been mistaken, but when I glanced up at the cook's assistant removing the empty soup plates, I could have sworn some of the seniors' dishes were still half full. Perhaps *they* didn't have to worry about the starving children?

I could not tell what the meat was in the main course, just that my table knife was scarcely up to cutting it. If only I had access to the grindstone in my father's workshop – but this brought back feelings of home I had been trying to avoid. Better to fight with the soggy and tasteless boiled Irish potatoes that were doubtless the oldest and cheapest the cook could buy.

White potatoes – black cook: I accepted the skin colours around the dining table, but another observer might have found them unusual for the Caribbean. The Housemaster was a white English priest; half of the boarders would pass for white; and the rest – including myself – ranged from light brown to dark brown; whereas the island population outside of the boarding school was 90% at the darker end of the spectrum. We were indeed mimicking the English boarding school scene – from elitist social selection all the way down to the poor food.

During the dessert – a brown, stodgy, fruitless pudding – the finishing-up of the meal became a mouthful-by-mouthful ordeal. The Housemaster used that occasion to "improve our characters". He forbade us to talk until we had cleared our final platter.

"I will not dismiss you until you have eaten everything," he said.

"Your parents have paid for you to be properly fed." So, we juniors suffered under the double insult of poor food and the obligation to stuff ourselves with what we did not like. No one else could leave the table either, and the seniors did not take kindly to the juniors (little wimps) detaining them from their activities.

I thought of that heavy wooden table as a battlefield, with opposing armies at each end: the Housemaster against the seniors, and us – the juniors – caught in the middle. Whereas the Housemaster saw and heard everything that happened near him, the seniors could whisper to each other undetected. If they wanted to attract a junior's attention, they would use a cascade of elbow jabs down the line of boys. Movements of head or hand could transmit even blunter messages, once a particular junior's attention had been secured. Many threats and grimaces came and went under the Housemaster's nose. But things were all right as long as the seniors stopped at looks.

As the weeks went by, the seniors invented a power game. The juniors often finished their meals slowly. The dinner table brought back intimate feelings of home and family, and the food did not improve as the days went by. So, the small boys, myself included, lingered over their plates without much appetite. The Housemaster had to make sure we ate enough, and the resulting delays made the seniors impatient. After a period of mounting tension, they took us aside in their dormitory.

"You bloody juniors are so slow that we will have to shake you up. You've been warned," said Trevor.

Not all meals were as bad as the first few days, and maybe the warning did cause us to eat faster. I had by now understood that "junior" meant (among other things) "must obey senior" and that no one could protect me from them. Even the Housemaster said we were under the seniors' authority when he wasn't around.

"And don't you ever write home to your parents to say nasty things about us," Derek told me. "There'll be the devil to pay if anyone makes a fuss." That was the way it had always been between seniors and juniors, and I would be a junior for three years.

Nonetheless, it was a shock when, in the latter half of my first term, the seniors unveiled their new plan to us.

"We've had enough. You've been warned to eat faster and it hasn't worked. From now on, whoever finishes last at meals wins a prize."

He waited to see which chump would take the bait.

"What prize?" I asked.

"Three cuffs!" he said and proceeded to demonstrate on me with stinging blows from the palm of his hand on the back of my head. I was so surprised I forgot to cry.

"That was just a friendly demonstration," Trevor said.

From then on, things got worse for us juniors. In addition to being forced to eat by the Housemaster and terrorised by the seniors, an unholy competition to avoid being cuffed grew like a weed between us. I recall that the seniors' first victim was Dickey.

That day, he finished his meal last. Trevor whispered to Derek, who held up a finger. He nudged Melford, who nudged Trapl, until the signal reached Dickey. The victim looked down the table and saw Derek's finger crooked at him. The Housemaster saw nothing. Afterwards, we watched nervously as the seniors took Dickey into their dorm. We could barely hear the cuffs, but he ran out crying. No one noticed but us juniors, because Dickey was a crybaby anyway. They won't catch me, I thought, and sure enough the next day it was Miguel's turn. But they *did* catch me eventually, and I received five cuffs, one from each senior. It felt midway between hairs being torn out and scalp being scraped; I couldn't hide my tears, and only then did I feel real sympathy for the other juniors. But it was a passive sympathy: there was no way to help each other.

As our eating speed increased a little, not only did we have to cut down on talking, we had to spy on each other – even among friends – to anticipate our relative finishing position. If Dickey had finished his main course but not his bread, then maybe I could take longer on my dessert. If Miguel was having trouble with his soup (globular pumpkin or watery peas), then there was no imminent danger.

The seniors were well pleased with their cuffing campaign. Sometimes our punishment would come right after lunch, sometimes in the evening. During vacations from school, I would breathe a sigh of relief, and eat what I wanted at the speed I wanted. But I never mentioned the cuffing to my parents, and as soon as the next term began, the seniors would be at it again.

The one junior never to be cuffed was Trapl. Something about his Czech upbringing made him wolf down his food at an astonishing speed. He was the tallest of the juniors and strongly built. His parents had sent him to the Antigua Grammar School, I thought, to improve his English. In reality, he was not so much inarticulate as private, not outgoing. Our community of juniors was generally welcoming – there were so many menaces from elsewhere. Yet, Trapl was different; not able to communicate well with him we had left him out of our games. His immunity to cuffing irked us.

If I thought things were bad in the Dining Room that was because I didn't know how much worse they could get. In my second term, they increased the penalty. Derek would hold up two fingers instead of one. We ate even faster. I learned which foods I could swallow without chewing (not many). Some juniors, like Dickey, hid themselves in a toilet after a meal to be noisily ill. But the returns were diminishing: extra cuffs couldn't squeeze much more out of us, or into us. How remarkable that the Housemaster got no inkling of what was going on.

He seemed pleased we were gobbling our food with energy, and attributed it to his influence.

I began to see the Antiguan school in less romantic terms and questioned why my parents had sent me there. Perhaps I had been considered a tough nut to discipline, or a nut that needed to be made tougher, or perhaps boarding school had only become affordable to them because of that stupid scholarship I had won, or perhaps I was just an experiment.

I cheered up a little when, late in 1952, a ready-made friend, little Felix, joined us at the boarding school. He came from St. Kitts and I knew his family. We'd played together at home, but here at school he seemed too small to be an ally. I wondered if he would survive. The seniors added a new twist to their game. Derek, Trevor, Melford, and the others would no longer administer the cuffs themselves (it had become hard work) but would delegate them to Trapl – the junior who had never been last. They knew we didn't get along with him, and thought it fun to set him against the rest of us. Trapl lapped up their encouragement to brutality like a large, enthusiastic gorilla.

The effect was dramatic. I had accepted the tyranny of seniors cuffing me, but the humiliation of one of our own doing it was too much. We thought of Trapl as a torturer in a concentration camp. He was much stronger than us and he cuffed us harder than the seniors did. Maybe it was our own fault for having been unfriendly; now he was just paying us back; but payment with interest. My fury at the traitor was more intense than at his masters. Since he had the approval of the seniors, Trapl was now the happiest boarder in the dorm. There was debate as to whether, despite his age, he should become a senior.

I said to Derek, "You can't make Trapl a senior. He's in a lower class than me, and I'm smarter, so he must be a junior."

"Conceited are you? Well, you haven't understood a thing. In this school, 'junior' has nothing to do with brains. It means slow, feeble, knobbly-kneed, runty, snotty-nosed, pathetically homesick, undisciplined, tattling, bedwetting, cowardly, unworthy: a kid living in the junior dorm. Senior means savvy, tough, adult: like us in the senior dorm."

I would note later on that "thieving" was not on the senior's blacklist of traits – a practice they endorsed heartily, looting food and belongings from us.

"But isn't there an age limit for juniors? Trapl's too young!"

"Wrong again. Sometimes it happens at twelve, but *we* decide who comes into our dorm. So forget about rules, little mister cheeky."

Trapl *did* move into the senior dorm for a few days and then – mysteriously – we returned from classes one afternoon to find all his stuff returned untidily on a vacant bed in our dorm. Frowning under his bushy blonde eyebrows, he refused to explain his demotion, but it was rumoured the seniors were embarrassed to find out just how poor he was in his schoolwork.

There was no cease-fire; he continued to cuff us for eating too slowly, and I resented him even more for having almost been a senior. I was receptive when one of our oppressors took me aside a few weeks later and watered the seeds of rebellion.

"You know Chris, this cuffing business is out of control. We seniors no longer care about your eating speed." It was true that the last to finish a meal was now sometimes a senior.

"Why do you put up with Trapl?" Trevor asked with a grin.

"Put up with him? *You* tell him to punish us!"

"That's old stuff. Can't you see Trapl is doing it all on his own now?"

"I hate him."

"Why don't you stop him then?"

"He's too big."

"How much bigger?" Trevor stood in front of me, a head taller.

"Twice as big."

"You may be too dumb for this."

"Well, bigger… "

"And your friends – the other juniors?"

"They hate him too."

"You could all attack him at once, then."

"We're never together. You select just one of us for cuffing, and keep the rest of us out of your dorm."

"Well, since you're becoming smarter, we can make an exception. Why don't you do it like this…"

Trevor's plan was that Felix (now the smallest junior) would be persuaded to dawdle over his meal and finish last. Trevor would give the usual signal to Trapl to cuff him for slowness. My friends and I would hide in the senior dorm until Trapl entered. At a signal, we would jump him.

"Just decide beforehand who is going to do what. For instance, one of you might hold him down while the others punch."

"But, afterwards, what if he picks on me while my friends are not there?"

"You might get a little hurt. But you could always gang up again and get revenge, couldn't you? Strength respects strength."

I conferred with Felix and Miguel in secret, on the playground.

"OK, we gonna mash him up good," said Miguel, my height but thinner. He seemed to have forgotten our own "mash-ups".

"Maybe stop him," said Felix, the smallest.

So we agreed to try. Being the heaviest of our trio of rebels, I was chosen to hold Trapl down with an arm lock around his neck. If we

116

cooperated as a group, we might achieve things – good or bad – that were otherwise unobtainable. The seniors played their part of the set-up down to the letter. Threats were heard in the corridors that today was "a big day" and that no one should make the seniors late after lunch. Felix duly lingered over his pudding, although we were afraid he might get cold feet and eat too fast because of the menacing looks Trapl gave him. Finally, Derek gave him a royal four fingers – meaning four cuffs were coming his way. During our homework period, we provoked Trapl for good measure.

"You don't touch Felix! He eats as fast as he can."

"Shut you. I got a job."

"Big bully!"

"I'll cuff you all!"

Trevor intervened opportunely, and declared that Trapl could hit us, too, for all he cared. Now we had the best of excuses for being at Felix's side.

Trapl hadn't been "authorised" to cuff us for several days. He had taken to finding other excuses for bullying, independent of the meals. He considered himself the boss of the junior dorm, and, at that moment, he looked pink with anticipation.

In the senior dorm, he ordered us to line up for our cuffs, Felix first, neck bent. Trapl placed himself behind to strike with his big right hand. Trevor, Derek, and Melford sat on a bed to look on, while Miguel and I tensed ourselves. Our signal for action was for Felix to hit back. It almost didn't happen, but at last, Felix flailed nervously at Trapl, the way you might pat a tiger.

Trapl was surprised when we jumped him. For several minutes, it looked perilous, as he clenched his fists and eyed us dancing around him. Then I gripped him from behind. He tried to shake me off. I felt my grip loosening and called on the others. If he could pick us off one by one, it would be all over. I heard Trevor echo my call for help.

It was Miguel's role to move in at this point and punch Trapl. To his surprise, Trapl could still fight, even with me on his back, and he punched Miguel in the chest. Miguel went crazy. A constrained Trapl was not supposed to fight back. Instead of punching, he now kicked at Trapl. Like the rest of us, Miguel had hammered pointy studs around the edges of his leather shoes; the metal gashed Trapl's knee. This disabled even the huge Czech. The pain diverted his attention, which allowed me to improve my stranglehold. I was able to pull him onto a bed on top of me and it was soon – big as he was – a one-sided affair. Face up and pinioned, Trapl was exposed to any blow from above. By chance, Felix was his nearest executioner. He raised his fist as though to strike, and Trapl closed his eyes. Felix could have struck repeatedly. No doubt, had Miguel been in the striker's position he would have seriously bloodied Trapl. But Felix didn't. Hitting people without an imperative was not his sort of pleasure – that was just one of the differences between Miguel and him. Underneath Trapl, I couldn't care less about this subtlety. A ton of rib-rocking, elbow-digging weight lay between good philosophy and me. But then Trapl became still. He had had enough, and what really undermined him was the knowledge the seniors were not going to support him. Shooting his hand up, he surrendered, and the seniors applauded.

Surrender is always accepted, although it may call for conditions. "Promise you will never cuff any of us again," I ordered. It was the revenge of the little people.

"I promise," he agreed.

We let him go, and exulted all the way back to our dorm. We had had a glimpse of our power – the force of collective action. Yet, we still didn't grasp how easily the seniors could manipulate younger minds – we thought Trapl was just stupid. It couldn't happen to us.

"Did we fight well?" I asked Trevor.

"Yes – I won my bet with Derek."

"You bet on us?"

He laughed and clapped me on the shoulder.

Trapl was red-faced and quiet for a day after this incident. The surprising result – the unseen benefit – was that it brought him closer to us. Since he wasn't a threat anymore, we questioned him about the seniors.

"I only done it because they made me," he said.

He confided how they had tricked him. If he did their bidding, they would give him biscuits from their tea rations – Trapl was always hungry. He would shine their shoes and run errands to earn more food. So, cuffing us seemed like just another service. He seemed eager to reveal all this, to talk to us at last. We accepted Trapl's return with some difficulty. Gradually, despite his size, he became just another junior. Perhaps unintentionally, the seniors had solved our relational problem. Felix and I felt a new confidence.

After leaving school, Trapl would become an excellent US Marine, where his strong physique and blind adherence to authority would stand him in good stead. I imagined he would never question orders, whatever dirty job he was given. I wondered though, in later years, when he was on duty in a far away country, if he would ever let himself be ambushed by three under-sized brown-skinned natives, and what he would do.

As for Miguel, alias Ratta, he boasted he had made the winning kick, and belittled Felix for not having drawn blood. Ignoring this difference in style, I figured I now had two friends I could count on. We formed an exclusive club to which a new member could only be admitted if he successfully picked someone's pocket. And we became more skilled at using our three-pointed metal set squares for knife throwing than for geometry. Juniors began to take heart. The cuffing of slow eaters had stopped: that was good. *We* had made it happen: that was better.

I never saw a senior get caught or punished for anything at dinner. Yet, I knew they were guilty of countless brutalities towards us. The only explanation I could find was in their place at the table; the Housemaster wanted them at the far end on the pretext the younger boys needed to be under his wing. They could joke and plot without being overheard – distance was everything. It didn't occur to me they were also cleverer.

Although I should have become used to it by my second year, the boarding house food seemed worse than ever. Healthy perhaps, but far from the spicy delights our families would prepare for us during the school holidays. Ah! For the pig trotters in souse, the baked yams and eddoes, the salt fish and fried plantains, the peppery black pudding intestines stuffed with rice; but this was home fare. Instead, there were days when the school cook would excel at concocting particularly unappetising dishes: impenetrable slices of mutton, unsalted rice with all the grains fused together in a gooey mass, and soggy fungi balls (a cornmeal-based dish, also known as "foofoo", not to be compared with the Jamaican dumpling).

"Ah, Chris, it's that day again. I suppose we will have meat cakes. You like them, don't you?" Derek asked me, smiling as we walked towards the Dining Room.

"Well, not specially."

The worst meal was on Thursday. At the beginning of each week, we would be served with fresh meat – overcooked beef or mutton – and a few days later, we would have suspicious-looking meat cakes. Friday was fish day, so Thursday was the cook's last chance to get rid of stuff.

"Don't blame you, considering…"

"Why do they taste so bad?"

"It's leftover meat from Monday and Tuesday, didn't you realise?"

"My mother makes good leftovers."

"Well, trouble is, these have gone rotten by now. No refrigerator, you see. Cook tries to disguise it by putting onions and spices in, but she can't fool me. I hate those onions: they make good food better but with bad food it works in reverse."

"Rotten? Surely it's still good to eat?"

"Rotten. A few days ago, Trevor found worms crawling out of his meat cake. I call that rotten."

"Worms?"

"Yes, worms – slimy, creeping things – or would you prefer maggots? The cook has to make do. She isn't allowed to buy fresh meat until the next week. I never eat the meat cakes if I can help it."

"What do you do? Father Brown makes me finish everything on my plate."

Father Billington had retired to England, replaced by Father Brown from Nevis, strict but fair. Less dreaded than his predecessor, more modern in his approach to our welfare – Father Brown was nonetheless the guardian of proper behaviour.

"It's easy – I just wrap the cakes up in my napkin and slip them into my pocket. Or else I feed them to the dog. That way my pocket doesn't get dirty."

"Cleo? You feed them to Cleo?"

"Haven't you noticed how fat she is? Trevor and I feed her meat cakes and other stuff every week. Good garbage bin."

Cleo was a white-and-black mongrel a little like the rest of us: undersized but with strong survival instincts.

"But how, for certain Father Brown would see … "

"Nah, nah, he's not nearly quick enough. Couldn't stop a football with the goalposts two feet apart. Bet you could do it, easy. Not scared, are you?"

At lunchtime, we had meat cakes, with onions. I gagged immediately at the sight and acrid smell. I had eaten them before, but now I *knew* they contained worms. I made it through the hors d'oeuvre of sardines on lettuce, but when the main course was served, I turned my eyes away from the scabby brown objects quivering on a pile of peas in my plate. Whatever composed the crust, it looked tough enough to keep a horde of crawling things inside. I felt sick. Unable to eat those meat cakes, I began to plan. I sat two seats away from the Housemaster – uncomfortably close.

First, I sidled the cakes over to the right hand edge of my plate, clear of the peas and gravy, easy to grab. Next, I figured out where the dog was. There – under the table – not far away. Then, I clicked my fingers softly to attract the animal. Sure enough, the dumb beast came and put its head on my knee. Time for action. I put down my knife and fork, as if I were going to take my glass and drink. I grabbed a meat cake in my right hand and began lowering it towards the dog's mouth. Must be licking its greedy lips. Last check, I glanced up at Father Brown to see if the coast was clear. He was looking straight at me.

I had never believed in that hoary expression "time stood still" until I came to that moment, with the meat cake wet in my hand, ten inches over my plate, dripping yellow liquid onto my lonely peas. I walked through my options. Should I continue the downward path to the dog's mouth, ignoring the threat? I had been caned before, and at least the worms would be gone. Or perhaps I could open my hand, drop the cake discreetly, and hope it would land on the floor – where Cleo would find it – and not on my trousers. Then I could claim to have been startled – an accident. Or should I gently return the cake to my plate as if I had been admiring it? But Father Brown would still notice and I could already feel the shame of failure. How many worms was I holding in my hand? Were they thoroughly cooked, or still wriggling? In my accelerated time frame, the fate of the worms became important. I would have to rely on their cooperation, for there was only one way left to keep my self-esteem. Quick, straight into my mouth with the worm-riddled thing.

I swallowed it in three or four bites, not pausing to taste.

"Have you forgotten your table manners, Christopher? Why are you eating with your fingers?"

"Sorry, Sir, I was just so hungry I didn't think."

"It is delicious, isn't it? Good onions. Come on, finish up with your knife and fork now."

I don't know how my face appeared to Father Brown, but it felt volcanic to me, hot and red. To my surprise, he left the matter there. My attempt at deceiving him had failed miserably, but he seemed to think it was funny. A roll of the dice. Was I unlucky he caught me in the act, or lucky that I saw him looking at me before I compromised myself completely with the dog? I was certainly clumsy, and no amount of practice would embolden me to try this trick again.

The dog rubbed mournfully against my leg, under the table. Stupid animal, I thought, there'll be no meat for you now. Not unless you get close to Derek and Trevor who can feed you more skilfully than I can. No shortage of filthy meat cakes at their end of the table.

So, it was with something of a surprise when I dared to glance up that I saw them swallowing their food – including the last of their delicately browned meat cakes – with apparent gusto. Could they have been served a portion without worms? They didn't see me looking at them, so absorbed were they in some private joke that made them laugh over and over again.

It seemed there was no lack of these adrenalin moments when one of us would be spotlighted in some forbidden act, like an insect squirming in a taxidermist's grasp, with only a split second to decide how we wanted to be transfixed. From the meat cake then, in my hand at the dining table, to Felix's predicament, there was only a few month's interval.

"See what I've got?" he asked me before a meal.

He handed me a smooth wooden object, heavier than I had guessed, and intricately carved in a light-coloured candlewood or cedar. Not just a head and a duct, but contours of taught skin and slightly arced. When I realised what it was, I almost dropped the phallus.

"Who made it?"

"That's a secret, but I can get you one if you want. Mine was a gift but you can buy them for six pence."

It looked a lot trickier to make than the spinning tops I turned on my father's lathe. But I wouldn't dare buy one – it could get me into a lot of trouble if discovered. Everything to do with sex was taboo in our boarding school. There were no sex education classes, hardly a whisper of the facts of human reproduction in biology courses (no drawings). We were not allowed to meet girls except for formal and supervised square dances at the Girls' High School on some Saturday afternoons. So officially, we knew nothing about sex: not its vocabulary, not its function, and certainly not its dysfunction. Of course, this just meant we learned everything from the underground network. We knew – or thought we did – what adults were up to at night, although we found their distinctions between making love and loving very confusing. Since we had no pornographic literature, our eroticism expressed itself in bawdy poems, some from well-known English writers, which were memorised and circulated from mouth to ear.

Whereas most of Wordsworth's and Shakespeare's ditties have gone down the memory drain, some popular classroom lines from those times still float in my head.

In Latin class, we would mumble:

Amo amas, I loved a lass,
And she was tall and slender,
Amas amat, I laid her flat,
And tickled her feminine gender.

And in History, since the islands were still British colonies:

Down by the river where the green grass grows,
I met a girl without any clothes.
I gave her a shilling,
And she was willing.
I gave her a crown and she lay down.
I gave her a thwack and she opened her crack,
And there I planted my Union Jack.

All very well at the back of a classroom where we wouldn't be caught, but in the dining table world of prayers and decorum, Felix's exotica would best remain discreet.

So, it was a pity that the seniors saw us.

"Ho, ho, that's cute!" Melford said as we moved towards the Dining Room. I hurriedly gave the trophy back to its owner, but the damage had been done. They knew where it was. I sat next to Melford and nearly opposite Felix who appeared distracted from the start. By blanking out his face, he seemed to be trying to disappear from the room.

"Pass it over, Felix," was how it began.

Melford muttered his command across the table, and I shook my head vigorously, hoping my friend would understand. Any concession to Melford and the other seniors would surely be fatal. Damn it! Why couldn't he leave my friend alone?

Melford smiled and said more loudly, "I would like it, Felix. I'll take good care of it."

Normally the least menacing of the seniors, he now insisted that "it" be passed across the table to him. Melford was a head taller than Felix and used to getting his way with juniors, especially those he considered "friends". He raised his voice by degrees, insisting on a handover of the organ. He feigned ignoring any looks the Housemaster might be giving them. In fact, as I checked, the Housemaster's attention was elsewhere, on Dickey, who was not eating properly. Daunted by Melford's persistence, and ignoring my advice, Felix passed the penis across the table concealed behind his arm. It was close to his flesh colour. From Felix's point of view, that should have been the end of it. Melford could admire the penis, and then pocket it for future return.

But that was not Melford's plan. Instead, the seniors began to pass it to each other under the cover of their napkins. Every few minutes it would change hands and the person who received this mysterious object would get a shock. Their nervous head movements made us juniors aware something untoward was happening, but Father Brown was now busy remonstrating with Miguel on his poor Latin results.

For the seniors, passing the penis was an improved version of the game of musical chairs. Movement was the point; no one wished to be caught with the thing. Then the music stopped.

One of the seniors, in search of an additional thrill, dropped the penis next to Melford's plate. He expected Melford to quickly conceal it. Unfortunately, the artful cylinder rolled to the middle of the table, out of easy reach. Like a snake striking, Melford leaned forward with a long hand and placed the penis in full view on Felix's half-empty bread plate. We always had four pieces of rubbery white bread to mop up our soup or gravy. Now, there was a penis sandwich. Felix, concentrating on his food, saw nothing. Seconds passed. I hissed at him and caused him to look up. There it was, man's pride showing off on his plate. The object transfixed us all.

Father Brown had missed Melford's quick movement, but now he spotted the object at a distance.

His gaze alighted on Felix, but he said nothing. Silence fell on the table. Surreptitiously, we juniors glanced at the penis in front of Felix, but mostly we studied our plates. Melford was a smiling sphinx. Felix sat immobile, mortified.

This was his moment of choice, and I shared it with him from across the table. How long had I held the meat cake in my hand a few months earlier in my moment of paralysis? Two seconds, maybe five? Felix simply did nothing for minutes on end. The silence squeezed me until I felt suffocated, with only the clink of knives and forks for relief. Then came little gurgles of water in nervous throats, and soft sounds of napkins wiping sweaty faces.

Up to that point, Felix had remained immobile, hands fixed at his sides, scowling at some middle point on the table as if he saw something particularly nasty there, certainly not looking at the phallus on his plate. My own anguish rose for my friend, and I wanted him to move, to do something, to pick up the damned penis and hide it. That way, he would be less exposed, and the rest of us would be freed. Of course, it was Melford's doing, this crisis, but we had all touched the penis, and shared in a collective sexual curiosity.

But Felix did nothing, and neither did the Housemaster. Did he approve, or was he devising an even more severe punishment than usual? I worried for my friend. But it seemed to me after a while that the fear on Felix's face was replaced by determination. I suspected he would not move at all, and the meal would end like that. So stupid! Why prolong his torture? But perhaps he was comforted by the silence, the lack of talk. The seniors were never silent, always chatting. Right then, they were manifestly not laughing the way they had when I was caught with the meat cake in my hand. The punishment Felix was taking on himself was a constraint on them, too. Whether Melford and the other seniors understood it or not, it was a way of saying, "See what you did to me? I'm not afraid to suffer if it shows up your cruelty for once." But what good could come of such an extravagant gesture?

The tension only dissipated when Father Brown asked us to stand for the closing grace, "Oh Lord, for what we have received…"

What could we do against these seniors who were always one step ahead? They cuffed us with their dirty hands; they flicked us with their wet towels; they set us against each other; they stole our books, sweets, and postage stamps. They were cunning. And they laughed at us. Was this the romantic English boarding school life I had idolized?

After the meal, Father Brown called Felix to his office. He wanted to know the origin of the penis and why Felix had brought it to table. The

124

rest of us were sure Felix would be caned, but afterwards Felix told me he had been let off. No one else was questioned.

"Did you tell him Melford put it on your plate?"

"Once I had admitted it was mine, he didn't want to know."

"And Melford himself, what did he say?"

"Not much – I think he was sorry – but I'm the fool to have trusted him."

Father Brown didn't give Felix a long lecture or a sex education talk – that was not part of our school system – but he insisted the wooden penis was neither a proper ornament for the table, nor a collector's item.

"He asked me to get rid of it," Felix said.

"Why don't you resell it?"

"Can't – I've promised to destroy it."

"Well, what about burning it? I could help you."

"I've got a better idea, thanks."

He didn't say any more, but the next day he told me he had cut up the penis with his penknife.

"How long did it take?"

"Doesn't matter, maybe an hour. What was carved with care should be un-carved with patience."

"But – an hour?"

"Look – it depends on what you're thinking. I would ask myself why a friend like Melford would betray me like that, and I'd chip a bit of wood off. Then I'd think of the seniors and all the lies they've told us, and I would chip off another bit. Then I'd think of the school food and I'd chip off two bits. Then I'd think of the school itself, and the Housemaster, and keep on chipping. Often, I'd go back to Melford. Maybe it's funny, but I never ran out of bad things to chip off. I felt I was learning something from each cut. It didn't seem like a long time.

"You should try it – whittling away at your enemies is very relaxing."

Fighting Spirit

Looking back at that time as a boarder, I have tried to separate the forces that engulfed me – the bullies that thrived on us, the ritual fighting, the weighty family heritage, and the canings – especially the canings – each exerting its pressure on my first year. I often think of the fighting. It started with my grandfather's words before I left home in St. Kitts for the school in Antigua: "You must behave with honour in your new school."

My mother and father were always going on about my behaviour – and now my grandfather was about to pitch in. He was probably going to tell me God doesn't like little boys who shout and scrap; that I'd better reform.

"I know, Grandpop, I know. I promise to be good in Antigua."

"Honour is more than good behaviour. I don't think you understand. Here – I've written down my advice to you. Read it now, and keep it with you." He handed me a folded sheet of white paper.

On it he'd carefully printed out four words, "Never shirk a fight."

I smiled at him, surprised. Freedom to fight! Enthusiastically, I thought about fighting: the fun of wrestling, throttling, squeezing, punching, and kicking; but no pinching and biting – that was girl stuff.

I saw images of my grandfather's action-packed youth in Guyana before he became a priest, and his fighter pilot son Beezie before the enemy got him. Of course he approved of fighting. Then I wondered if I might look soft and pampered. In any case, this advice was the real thing – better than hours of talking with my parents. I knew from them I had to study hard to earn a living; that life at boarding school might not be as easy as at home. But I wasn't sure *how* to face the world. My grandfather evidently thought I was not pugnacious enough. If others pushed me over an imaginary red line, would I cave in or strike back? Did things like pride and honour mean as much to me as pain and fear?

I had wrestled with my friends in St. Kitts – Michael, Rolly, William, Carl, Caedmon, and others. But I had never fought in anger, nor challenged a stranger. How would it be at a boarding school? I would be tested, of that I was sure. I treasured my grandfather's advice.

In Antigua, I wore a new school uniform – blue shirt, khaki trousers, and a spindly tie with the school colours that often doubled as a handkerchief. I kept my grandfather's note in my shirt pocket for as long as I could. As time went by, the note grew increasingly illegible and the advice became obscure. Eventually, I forgot to remove the note from my shirt and it went to the laundry and dissolved. But something of it remained in a corner of my mind.

I got into my first fight through playing soccer. There I was on the playing field, excitedly and clumsily pursuing a leather football. Left to roam in a neighbouring wild pasture, local farmers' cattle and donkeys often strayed into our playing area. Cows are what they are, and they showed their gratitude for the grass they ate by leaving large offerings of greenish-brown cowpats. Depending on its freshness, the dung might be wet and gooey, or dry and hard enough to be used as a missile.

It was after tea, at four o'clock, when a dozen other boys joined us junior boarders. With me was Dickey from St. Croix, the youngest in the group. I had my misgivings about playing with him because when things didn't go his way he would say, "I quit!" or "Go jump in a lake!" and leave in a huff. We couldn't avoid including strapping Trapl, big and bulky, as his name would imply. The dining room cuffing battles hadn't yet taken place, but I didn't count him as a friend. He talked little, and when embarrassed – which was often – would turn brick red under his shock of sandy hair. I'd heard English was not his mother tongue. I couldn't conceive of anyone not being born speaking English; I had never heard a foreign language, unless one counts Creole English, or pidgin, which, my father gave me to understand, was just bad English. Since I could not relate to Trapl, I hoped he wouldn't be on my team. I did have a boarder friend beside me. It was Miguel; he was the boy who had been less homesick than I on arrival; he would be my future ally against Trapl. We were the same age, in the same class, and had developed the same mistrust for the devious seniors, the secretive Matron, the bullies, and the whining school dog. He was browner than I was, with curly black ringlets of hair, and looked thin and wiry where I was round. Something about the boniness of his face made the seniors call him "Ratta", a nickname he detested. We had different home islands: he was from the US Virgin Islands; I was from St. Kitts. So, he had a President and I had a King – no big deal, especially on a soccer field. We persuaded the Sports Master to lend us a ball, and two teams were chosen. After the draw, I found myself assigned to the right wing.

"So be it," I thought. I was a slow runner, and since the ball tended to stay in centre field, I imagined I would have an easy time away from the action. I fancied I could kick the ball as well as any, but when suddenly I gained possession of it, I was confused. School soccer was a new sport for me.

In truth, I must have looked like a turtle that doesn't know which side to poke his head out – the crazy ball was hardly under my control, and I had no chance of kicking it as far as the goal. Then, several inconsiderate defenders converged on me.

"Think," I said to myself, but the formula didn't produce any effect. The defenders blocked my path. I had trouble keeping the ball near my feet and away from my adversaries. I lost it entirely and skittered sideways to avoid being stampeded by the mass of players. Before I had time to congratulate myself on at least having touched the ball, it bounced back from between the legs of attackers and defenders alike. And once more, it was – improbably – in my possession, with just one close adversary. At first, I didn't recognise him. Then I saw it was my new friend Miguel.

What a pity he was on the opposing team! And that he moved so fast. I made a face at him so he would recognise me.

That pause while I looked up was just long enough for Miguel to tackle me. I tried to step aside, but one foot refused to move fast enough and got caught in Miguel's. I stumbled. The ball escaped. So did my foot. I fell.

"Well chosen, Christopher!" I thought. There I was in the cow's second-best gift to man after milk, fresh today. A shout went up, and the players crowded round to see the fun. They were all laughing at me. Caked with muck, I had selected the only large and smelly pile of dung within a hundred feet.

Even tiny Dickey, the playmate I considered too babyish, was cackling away. Nearby, Trapl's face split in a large grin. He'd had it in for me anyway. Several other classmates, usually faithful, now stood arms akimbo, laughing.

Because from where I crouched, it wasn't funny. I didn't know what to do. I had never planned to be "King of the Dung" like this, the crown – so to speak – sitting wetly and reeking on my head. I searched for Miguel – the cause of my indignity – to see if he had been splashed. No, he was unsplattered, bent double, and laughing at me, his best friend! I imagined my grandfather's stern face. Friendship be damned!

"Miguel, you'll pay for this!"

He sniggered, "Cow shit, cow shit!"

"I'll fight you."

He gave me a mean-eyed look. "You'll get the worst."

"After dinner, then."

He hesitated, and for a second I feared he would refuse. But when he saw the others' eyes on him, he said, "OK, dung-dung!"

Cleaning up took some time, but later that evening hostilities were engaged. The other juniors understood my challenge. Not that they took sides – the primitive mystique of school fighting is that injustice is settled by the purifying power of violence: whoever won – by definition – would be right. This was how we resolved imponderable issues. Challenge – combat – witnesses: like the European duelling system.

Since fighting was forbidden in the dorms, we gathered in the wide corridor nearby, where we had our lockers and washbasins. A senior took up position at the end of the hall, near the toilets, from where he could see the Housemaster's office. If Father Billington approached, he would warn us. This was not done out of charity, but because the seniors might be punished for not keeping the peace.

"You pushed me in cow shit! On purpose! Then you laughed – I'll make you sorry!"

"Not my fault. You slip and fall on you own. Don't touch me or I'll bust you up!"

My anger purred like a small electric motor, only partly under control. "This fight might be fun, after all," I thought.

I grabbed Miguel by the shoulders, threw a sweaty arm round his neck, and clenched his shirt in my hand, gripping the cotton fabric so he couldn't escape. I absorbed the punches in my ribs from his bony knuckles. He'd have preferred more boxing, being lighter and faster, but I didn't give him that opportunity.

"Hit him, Miguel!"

"Squeeze him, Chris!"

We each had our fans, stamping and clapping.

I wanted to get Miguel on the floor, so I hooked my foot behind his, but he wouldn't fall, he moved away, pulling me with him. We bumped hard into a locker. There was no other way down but to take the fall myself, holding to neck and waist, going down backward, and damn! – that wood was hard on my bum. He came down on top of me, and I had to roll quickly before he recovered, then someone was shouting – maybe Dickey? – but I was on top then, my elbow and forearm across his throat like the Lone Ranger. It didn't seem to work. "Push harder, it won't kill him," I thought. Spitting, crying. "Come on, say it!" Scared now he might break like eggshell china, my grip tightened, but he hung on, brown liquid eyes bulging, face no longer chocolate but apple-ruddy, glaring at me, so I pushed harder and thought, "I must force the end."

"Say you surrender, Miguel! Say you sorry, and you'll never put me in shit again."

"I surrender."

Two little words. He preferred to surrender rather than to say he was sorry, but I was indifferent. My first victory was such a gratifying present that I discarded its terms like superfluous wrapping paper. It mattered to Miguel, though. He wasn't sorry. Of course, it *did* help that I had picked on someone lighter than myself for my first fight. Later, I wondered what I would have done if he hadn't surrendered but lost consciousness. Most of my junior school fights would end with a wrestling contest, partly because we were not trained in fisticuffs, and partly from a hidden desire not to *really* hurt our opponent. A fight was theatre, but only to a certain extent. Miguel had surrendered: a standard protocol. We arose, dusted ourselves off, checking for splinters from the rough floor, and then shook hands. If that last ceremony didn't take place, a return match was probable in a few days' time.

Because of this fight, a new pecking order was established in the dorm: Trapl was first; big and hulking, he outweighed me by at least ten pounds, and I was solidly built, tending to plumpness. Now, I was next, outranking Miguel, and then the others.

By the next morning, though, I was ashamed of this fight. What's life without pals? Where was the honour I had gained? Could I make it up to Miguel in the coming days?

I imagined my grandfather's spirit pointing its finger at me. "Be long-suffering with your friends. Never fight with them, even if they betray you. That's not what I meant by shirking."

Maybe Miguel had a grandfather like mine, because after some days he seemed to understand my lapse. Next time we played soccer, he insisted on being on the same team as me. We never fought again. We would quarrel sometimes, of course. But I felt a comrade in him, ready to undertake wild projects for the fun of it. He accepted the opportunities for daring that I offered, but he would never forget the humiliation of our fight, and would get his revenge one day.

I often thought of my grandfather's message, and especially a year later, when I fought with a boy in my class named Benjamin. He was my height and somewhat heavier, so this time I had no advantage. We fought because I disliked the so-and-so. He had jostled me in the Hall and called me a "conceited ass". This was my red line, again. Although he undoubtedly had some justification for the first half of his thesis, the comparison with a donkey didn't suit me, and insulting me like that in front of witnesses left me no choice – duelling codes haven't changed in a century. He wasn't a boarder, so I had to challenge him during a break period or after classes. We set the fight for late afternoon in front of the school. As the hour approached, I regretted my provocation. What if he pasted me? Was this really a red line to be defended? But backing down is worse than anything.

There was a patch of well-worn earth and grass I knew well, under the flamboyant trees in front of the school. The ground was embedded with pretty red-and-black jumbie beads from nearby vines, and we spun tops on the smooth places. During the holidays, I made my own pear-shaped tops on my father's workshop lathe, out of tough guava wood with a sharpened nail in the middle. The purpose of the top game was to launch your toy as hard as possible from a wound-up cord in order to punch a hole into your opponent's top, or even split it. Benjamin and I were human spinning tops trying to punch holes in each other.

We took up what we thought was fighting posture inside a ring of boys, not just from my class, but also many others looking on for fun. As I clenched my fists, I remembered with a sinking feeling that the school Masters would not intervene, not outside the school building. They were themselves products of the trial-by-violence system; they believed boys should work out their anger on their own. I was a prisoner of my challenge and would have to take my lumps. The Masters would only step in if things got out of hand.

After the customary exchange of battle cries and insults, it seemed the ground came up and grabbed me without warning. Benjamin had thrown me down, was locked onto me, and we were rolling and spinning. I couldn't get on top of him, and while astride me he couldn't get his elbow into my neck because I had learned the trick of keeping my chin on my chest. I tasted grass. I bit dirt and spat out a jumbie bead. Flipped over, back to the earth and soil all over me, I bent my knees and hooked my feet around his upper body. This broke his lock, but he was too fast to pin down. It worked once, and then we were again in a stalemate for long seconds with him on top, grabbing, slapping, and pushing. I felt overpowered; even the blue sky above seemed against me. As our energy flagged, we heard the crowd, "Get him Benjy, mash him up," egging us on.

"Hold on, Chris, knock him off," yelped my boarding house clan, rooting for one of its own.

Clutching schoolbags, jumping and shouting, our classmates were having a whale of a time. Some had taken off their ties and were starting little mock battles of their own, but most were cheering. We provided good entertainment.

Another roll, and I found an opening allowing me to get my right arm around Benjamin's head from behind. It was more difficult for him to protect his neck from that angle. I squeezed and squeezed. Somewhat to my surprise, Benjamin croaked, "Surrender," before I had even suggested any such thing.

It had taken us about fifteen minutes. I staggered upright, and found I was trembling all over.

Something fierce in me said, "You've won!"

Something more sceptical said, "It was costly."

I had many sore spots. Both of us had torn, dirty clothes. It hadn't felt like this in previous skirmishes – perhaps I was no longer feigning the fight.

Had I purged the red line madness – the compulsion to fight at the smallest slight? Certainly, I felt my friends' respect. Was this honour and freedom? Savouring victory, I imagined my grandfather's voice.

He chided me, "Well? Satisfied? Was there sufficient reason to lose your temper? At least you stuck to your guns. But this is as good as it gets. It's downhill from here on."

He might have added I had been quite lucky that day not to swallow or chew the jumbie bead, or rosary pea, one of the most beautiful seeds on earth but containing enough of the poisonous protein abrin per bead to be fatal.

A few weeks later, I saw another kind of fight. A large group of pupils had gathered outside my classroom and voices were rising.

"Who's fighting?" I asked.

"It's Govia and Spencer – really big stuff."

I pushed my way to the front before it got too packed, thinking that Govia and Spencer never fought. They were big, strong-muscled, no-nonsense boys who walked many miles each day to and from the school. There they were in front of me, squaring off.

There were no melodramatics; there was no theatre; the antagonists did not pull their punches; they did not seek to wrestle. The crowd of onlookers sucked in its breath. There was the dull thudding of bone against bone as the combatants hit each other in the chest and head. Defence was ignored. Their faces were puffed and grim but still intact. As I watched, Govia smashed Spencer in the mouth, making it all red. Reeling back, then recovering, Spencer hooked into the middle of Govia's face and changed the topography of his nose. They began bleeding profusely, something I had never seen before, not this close, and not from people I knew. "Why doesn't one of them surrender?" I thought. But it was not an option. Spencer stumbled backward and a wave of unease dilated the circle of entranced boys. Something dangerous was in the air. An eerie calm prevailed, the boys weren't cheering as they usually did. Both fighters now had ripening black eyes. Burst lips clenched, they voiced little grunts, and what might have been sobs, still pounding, thudding, thumping. Limitless.

Then came a much louder shout, a megaphone-level sound, and a torrent of sweaty classmates jostled me to the side.

"Stop, this instant! Now!" The powerful bodies of Mr Barnes, the Sports Master, and Mr Shorey, the Assistant Headmaster, forged through the crowd and ripped Govia and Spencer apart. They must have been observing from a distance. We hated interference, but – this time – breathed a sigh of relief. The fight was ended.

Afterwards, there remained something intoxicating about the violence: a crowd gestalt, as if a veil had been lifted on an unknown but potent part of the universe. I had not fought, but I had participated nonetheless, by looking on. "Maybe honour can only be saved by blood," I thought. My grandfather was silent, but I felt his eyes on me.

Why did this bloody fight seem so different from my encounter with Benjamin? I could have learned from the jumbie beads and the evil within them. The poison in them causes red blood cells to clump together and the result is unstoppable. As for violence, there is no treatment but avoidance.

Wondering about "real" fighting, I needed the make-believe sort more and more. One day soon after, when I was eleven, I struggled with a classmate named Weekes, half in jest. There had been no formal challenge and – fortunately for me – no onlookers. On the ground once again, I stared up at my opponent trying to pin my arms down.

"Got you," he said, smiling.

I laughed, "Oh no, you don't," and used a trick I had seen in a comic book.

I grabbed Weekes' mouth in a pincer movement, squeezing his cheeks between thumb and forefinger, hard. There was a sucking sound and my fingers met in the middle. I felt triumphant. Then his eyes awoke in surprise, he let go, and blood gushed out of his mouth onto my chest. He spat, and ejected four teeth. I jumped up and apologised. He said nothing and ran home.

I was petrified. Never before had my actions caused so much damage. My apology sounded ridiculous after destroying his teeth. If I had disliked him, I might have felt better about it. But Weekes wasn't an enemy – there was no particular reason for our scrimmage. He did not return to school for days. Maybe he had rotten teeth, I thought, but I wasn't reassured. I was responsible for someone who would be missing four molars for the rest of his life; that was where violence led. I lived in fear his family would complain to the Housemaster, and indeed, I would have no excuse.

When he returned, we avoided each other. He didn't open his mouth, and I never played with him again.

Where were the "good" fights, I began to wonder, those I could win and be applauded for unequivocally as a hero; or those I could lose spectacularly, to be lamented as a victim? What sort of trap was fighting getting me into? I thought of what my grandfather would say, no longer sure I understood his advice.

That red challenge line receded into the distance. I began to wear my honour more lightly. In my mind's eye, I looked up at my grandfather.

"Did you really mean me to fight?"

"Of course, you have to learn to give and take blows, physical and mental; to defend yourself; to stand up for what you think is right. It's indispensable. But I was more concerned with the temptation of shirking than the virtue of fighting."

"What about the violence? I could get to like it."

"I'm talking about the need for courage. Do you think fighting is only with fists?"

"But, at least, explain to me about Weekes. I didn't mean to hurt him."

"When you fight, you must answer for every blow you strike."

I tried another tack, "Maybe the teeth I squeezed out were just milk teeth, and maybe he'll get others."

I could see my grandfather shaking his walnut face at me, tortoiseshell eyeglasses slipping down his nose, "Not everything grows back."

Classroom Legacy

Another thing that happened before I left for Antigua in 1952 was my father explaining why he was sending me there and why I should be proud. At age nine, I was impatient. I welcomed the idea of novelty and adventure, unaware of the protective cocoon in which I had lived up to then. Of course, I had been panicked at first over the idea of leaving home for boarding school, but I had let myself be persuaded. Change seemed the most natural thing in the world. Fathers, however, like to justify themselves. Only a day earlier my mother had entreated me to write home regularly, and when, somehow, she had tricked me into agreeing to this, my father, the initiator of the boarding school project, became just as demanding.

It was lunchtime, with my family seated around the oval dining table overlooking the veranda and the port of Basseterre. I was engaged in cutting up bite-sized pieces of sweet potato. As I talked with my father, my objective was to keep the white grains of rice in my plate from sticking to the yellow vegetable – I liked my flavours separate. Things should not be mixed up. "So, are you sending me away because I need more discipline?"

"Not *just* that, Chris." He smiled. "It's a good, British-type system, for one thing. They'll like your way of speaking proper English. But, for another reason, we have old family ties with the Antigua Grammar School. You'll find there's a classroom named after us – the VANIER room."

I felt a burst of pride. "Is that because you went there, Dad?"

"No, that's not why. My parents lived in Antigua for some time, and I did go there, together with my brothers Jack and Beezie; even your mother studied Latin there. But the classroom I'm talking about is in memory of Beezie, not the rest of us."

I didn't know much about my Uncle Beezie, except that he was no longer alive and his real name had been Eugene Dunlop.

"Why was he nicknamed 'Beezie'?"

"Well, your Grandpop thought Eugene was a mischievous little devil, so one day he took to calling him 'Beelzebub'," my father answered. "The name stuck, and was shortened to 'Beezie'."

"It's funny a Minister of the Church should have a son nicknamed after Satan."

You can think about that when you sit in his classroom."

Trapped by my own word "funny", I wasn't sure whether my father meant I would find the classroom peculiar, ha-ha, or church-like. Sometimes I couldn't get a straight answer out of him. That was the way of lawyers. But I had to know whether his brother was a real devil or something else.

"Why is the classroom 'in memory' of him? Why isn't *your* name there? What did Uncle Beezie do?"

"He died the year you were born, in the second world war – shot down flying for the Royal Canadian Air Force."

"And I'm going to this school because of him?"

"Yes, in a roundabout way. I hope he'll inspire you."

I had finished my vegetables, and all that was left on my plate was the spicy chicken drumstick I had been saving up.

I figured I could now discard my father's other reasons. Excitedly, I began adopting the fighter pilot image as my own. With a classroom carrying my name and a hero to talk about, I imagined I would be famous and respected from the day I arrived. Then I remembered Beezie was dead. How very careless. He couldn't have been a good pilot to be killed like that. I would have preferred him to be alive and able to tell his story. On the other hand, suppose it wasn't his fault? Maybe he *was* an ace after all, only the victim of an accident. I decided to be wary of Beezie. If I let myself be too inspired by him, my future could well be that of a second-rate pilot who gets devoured in some future war.

I consumed my chicken leg with gusto, and I decided I preferred pirates to pilots. Though, I figured I would keep the pilot in reserve. The uncle I had never met continued to fascinate me, despite his reprehensible absence. My other uncle – Jack – was ordinary. He had not left the Caribbean during the war, neither to study nor to fight. My father and Beezie had been plunged into the European conflict zone.

That same day, on our living room wall, I admired an old portrait of Beezie, crisp and handsome in his pilot's uniform. Two neat wings were stitched onto his left breast, just above where I imagined his bold heart to be beating. He looked very much alive, even in faded sepia, not at all like a ghost. Maybe there was some courage to be learned from him. At least I could find out whether he had been a good or bad pilot – why he had died. Shortly after, I left for Antigua.

Several days after my arrival at the Grammar School, I began hunting for Beezie's classroom. No one seemed to have heard of it. Finally, an older boarder told me where to go. It was a separate little building on the south side of the school grounds, partly hidden in a hollow, close to the wild bush.

It stood in the sun, its clapboard shingles painted white and beginning to flake. The heat hammered down on my head and there was a shimmer in the midday air. I would find out later – at first hand – that classrooms like this, filled with battered wooden desks and chairs, could hold up to thirty perspiring students.

The boys I saw all seemed much bigger than I was.

"Is this the VANIER classroom?" I asked a black student lounging near the door.

"No, we is Fourth Form."

"Someone told me the classroom called VANIER was near here."

"You heard wrong. Scram, kid."

"On the door," I said, "isn't there any name?"

"No, I done told you, this is Fourth Form."

I saw some lettering above the door. "What's this?"

"Nothing, man." He looked at the small wooden plate with fading black letters painted on a white background that his greater height allowed him to interpret better than I could. "You mean the sign up there?" Some surprise registered.

"Says VANIER (he pronounced it 'One Ear'), but nobody calls it that. Is the Fourth Form. Some buildings have funny names. Why you want to find our classroom, anyway? Someone you know here?"

"Well, my name is Vanier. This was my uncle's school."

"Oh?" he said, without much interest. "You new, you said. Well, you not be in this class for another three years. If you move up, that is. Teachers won't move you up jus' because a classroom have you name.

"You have to be smart to move up, and you don't look it. Nobody call this classroom One Ear any more, if they ever did. Another thing – if I was you, I wouldn't go round saying you was related to One Ear, whoever he be. We don't like fussing with the dead people and such. Bring bad luck."

"Never mind, thanks," I said. What a disappointment my Uncle Beezie was! No one here knew or cared about him. Not only was boasting about him out of the question, the very mention of his name could make me look foolish. Of course, the boy I talked to was right: this building should be known as the Fourth Form, and not the VANIER classroom. Beezie didn't seem to be inspiring anyone. I would be wise to stick to my pirates.

I blamed Beezie for his disappearance and put off thoughts of investigating him, thinking that at least my father had come home from England and married my mother, even if he didn't have his own classroom. On my next vacation home, I asked my mother what she knew about Beezie. What useful thing had Beezie done?

I had to follow my mother around the busy kitchen to keep up the conversation. Lunch was a serious affair. The servant was chopping up breadfruit and boiling yams. My mother had just finished putting pungent green herbs and red peppers on the fish. Now she took out a breadboard.

"Beezie! What a loss," she said, "I loved him dearly."

"You knew him before you got married?"

"Yes, very well. I spent most of my school weekends with him and Ralph at the Vanier Rectory in Antigua. Officially, it was their sister

Dorothy who invited me – we were classmates and good friends at the Girls' High School. But really, I went there to be with the boys."

"What was he like?" I asked, intrigued at her connivance with my Aunt D.

"Charming, full of fun, and a good dancer – much better than your father."

"But Dad doesn't like dancing."

"Yes, that's right," she said, "he doesn't." I couldn't remember seeing my father on a dance floor, which was a bit of an oddity in the music-crazy Caribbean. "He's flat-footed and tone deaf to begin with. Do you know, I almost chose Beezie instead of your father on account of that?"

She was teasing, I felt, but it upset me nevertheless. Was this revenge for all the times when I would side with my father in a discussion? I was suddenly jealous of Beezie on my father's account.

My mother was kneading raisins into something gooey for a cake. I smelt the syrupy, alcoholic odour of the preserved fruit but refused to let it calm me. Ignoring my ill-disguised discomfort, she continued, "Yes, Beezie was a superior dancer, with a real sense of rhythm. He was nearer my age, too; Ralph is five years older than me."

She glanced up from her preparation and offered me a spoon covered with sweet dough.

"Don't pout like that, Chris – your bushy eyebrows make you look ferocious!"

I licked the spoon. "Why did you choose Dad, then?"

"Not really sure. Your father was more serious and I needed that, too. And he proposed first, that was what did it. Beezie took lots of chances on other things, but your father took a chance on me."

My relief was superficial. I was not about to forgive this embarrassing uncle for intruding in affairs I held sacred. I made two resolutions. First, I would never court the same girl as my brother. Second, I would never learn to dance, or else I would study the technique and become so expert no girl could ever call me flat-footed and tone-deaf. Then I remembered the quest my mother had sidetracked me from and continued, "But how did Beezie become a pilot?"

My mother went back to recall her days at the Vanier Rectory in Antigua. She told me my grandfather's car had constantly needed repairs, like most Caribbean vehicles in the 1930s. Beezie was clever with it. Together with my father, they did all the maintenance. Ralph was persistent, and better at scholarly things, but Beezie was a mechanical wizard. Three years after my father left to study Law, Beezie left to study Engineering. My father depended on a gift from a family benefactor. Beezie saved up his money, but it wasn't enough. He borrowed the rest from my grandfather, and gained entrance to McGill University in Montreal. His engineering career was cut short almost at once, since Canada entered the War in 1941, a few months after he arrived.

"He continued writing to us after he joined the Air Force, and even during his active service," said my mother.

She said Beezie had trained both in Canada and in Britain. He earned his wings, then sent letters home in family-coded language because he wasn't allowed to discuss the whereabouts of air force strikes. Ethiopia became "a visit to Rasta Land", and desert warfare was "like Jack's cigarettes" (Camels). Turkey was "stuffing and gravy" and Greece was "elbows have it" – the censorship was quite light.

My mother wrote back to him regularly: he learned of my birth in June of 1942 and sent a gift – a little book.

"A storybook?"

"No, about education."

This seemed boring, and, in any case, by now my mother had lost the book. In September of 1942, my grandfather received a letter from the Air Force telling him his son was missing in combat, presumed dead.

"Grandpop must have been upset."

"More than upset – he was heartbroken and furious with them."

"Why furious?"

My mother gave me a dark look. "Well, he didn't agree to any of it, you see. But you'd better ask him about it yourself." She turned back to her cooking.

I had to pry things out of Grandpop; even twelve years after the events, he was not happy to talk about the great quarrel he had had with his son Beezie. It was best for me to question him after lunch, when he would sit on his veranda with an old pipe. I would settle beside him on a canvas reclining chair, or – better still – swing in the hammock, bare feet just touching the floor.

I pieced it together like this. As an Anglican priest, Grandpop was poor, but he had managed to help Beezie with the necessary money for his studies. He was shocked when Beezie told him he wanted to sign up with the Canadian forces.

The quarrel started, my grandfather told me, when Beezie wrote to him, "I have to volunteer."

"You mustn't think I'm a pacifist," my grandfather explained to me. I didn't doubt this, remembering how he had encouraged me to defend myself at school.

He replied to Beezie, "This is not your fight, son. This is between Britain, Germany, and the other European countries. A just combat is one thing, but your honour is not concerned here. Stay out of this war. We helped you to go to Canada to study, not to throw your life away."

"But," I protested, "he said he *had* to volunteer, Grandpop. Didn't they put you in jail if you refused?"

"He couldn't be conscripted," said Grandpop. "He was a West Indian born in Nevis, not a Canadian citizen. People only ought to fight for their own homes and countries."

"You mean he would have had to fight for Nevis if it had been attacked, and me today for St. Kitts?"

"Except that St. Kitts and Nevis are not countries, just poor little British colonies."

"What about Britain? Shouldn't we fight for Britain, the Mother Country?"

"No, we colonials are not full British citizens. They let us in and out of England for the moment – they even stamp our passports British – but they have never treated us as equals in peacetime. Look at the poverty in our islands! So why should they call on us in wartime?"

It would be many years before I understood the prescient nature of my grandfather's remark about nationality. Being British would be redefined. Starting from the Commonwealth Immigrants Act of 1962, and especially with the United Kingdom Immigration Act of 1971, a distinction would be made between Commonwealth citizens and British subjects. Curiously, I would qualify for the latter category – only just – because of the notion of patriality, within two generations of descent from my Cockney grandmother, but my children would not qualify. Neither my grandfather, nor my father, nor Beezie would have qualified as latter-day British by birth.

"But didn't you want to help them? What if the Nazis had won?"

"Beezie said something like that. He wrote to me, 'I will be fighting for your future. My entire class at McGill University has volunteered.' "

What would I do if my whole class volunteered for something?

"I wrote back to him," said Grandpop, "I said, 'Don't confuse culture and kin. We are wedded to the English culture – we have no other – but in the Caribbean we are not *kin* with them. Neither with England, nor with Canada. Not enough to shed our blood for a war we didn't start and which won't affect our islands.' But Beezie replied, 'Before this war is over, the entire Commonwealth will be involved.' "

"I must confess something to you, Chris," said Grandpop. "Quite apart from considerations of Britain and the Commonwealth, I didn't want to lose my son. I felt it in my bones Beezie would be killed. And I was right. But I struggled with him in vain."

"But Grandpop, I heard that German submarines came and sank ships in the Caribbean. Didn't we have to fight back then?"

"Yes, we lost about three hundred ships in the year of your birth alone, mostly oil from Trinidad, bauxite from British Guyana, and sugar from the rest of the islands – supplies for Britain. Eventually, we formed a Caribbean Regiment, some of whom went to England. But it never saw combat. Beezie did. Hardly anyone in the entire colonial Caribbean died for Britain except Beezie."

My grandfather was, of course, exaggerating Beezie's uniqueness, though he was not so far wrong. I learned later that possibly 10,000 West Indians travelled to and enlisted in the British Army, but they were mostly used as radio operators, motor mechanics, and cooks. The Caribbean Regiment – reluctantly formed – of some 1,200 volunteers was sent to Italy in 1944, then Egypt, but, in effect, it was never engaged in front line fighting. Inadequately trained, it was disbanded in 1946. In 1944, the *British Times* estimated that perhaps 236 Caribbean volunteers might have died in Europe. There were social and political reasons for this under-utilisation of Caribbean troops. The British army was not keen on a coloured contingent, not even in a time of dire need, more for clannish than for racial motives. Beezie wrote home from RAF quarters in England that he felt less welcomed by the officers there than in Canada. And the Caribbean was a "disturbed zone" at the start of the war with a history of general strikes and riots that had spread out contagiously from my birth island of St. Kitts in 1936 to infect the whole region. Following these disorders, the Moyne Commission of 1939 had condemned British colonial mismanagement of her Caribbean islands and the miserable condition of the cane workers. Its report was kept secret until 1945. In this context, the negative impact of heavy Caribbean war casualties would have added oil to the smouldering fires of anti-colonialism. It was – correctly – estimated that the Germans would have used the Moyne report as propaganda (on 9th August 1939 they proposed: "We with our Fascist Vigour and our Nazi Energy could make [the islands] rich and valuable"). No thanks.

Grandpop told me he had disagreed with his son, and had ordered him not to join up. Beezie refused. The link between father and son was broken. They never settled this difference. Beezie became a pilot in the Royal Canadian Air Force. I thought my grandfather was right. What business did Beezie have volunteering for someone else's war? I added another resolution to my list: I would never volunteer, and I would never do military service – anywhere.

Grandpop pointed to his wall where he had pinned up pictures from *Time* magazine of Gandhi and Churchill side by side. "It's hard to choose between these two," he said, "one is preaching non-violent action, the other advocating 'fighting on the beaches'. Neither lacked courage, but Beezie chose the wrong one." My grandfather was always joking – even in the pulpit – but not when he talked about Beezie.

That vacation, one other thing I found out from my grandfather was that Beezie was born in 1916. Since he died in 1942, it meant he had lived only twenty-six years. When I returned to Antigua for the next term, the knowledge my grandfather was not reconciled with his son's sacrifice erased any remaining enthusiasm I had for my pilot uncle. I respected my grandfather, and the more I thought about what he had said, the more I felt Beezie was a dangerous fool. Suppose my father had done the same thing – volunteered for the British Army while studying Law in London? He would have got himself killed too, I imagined. And where would that have left me? Most likely not born. Or would my mother have married someone else? Suppose I had been born with kinky black hair or straight blond hair. Or without my birthmark? Would it still be me? Would I think the same? I was happy my father had stayed out of the war.

I stored all this knowledge of Beezie away, and then forgot it; he became a lost cause in my mental archives. But not entirely forgotten. Every now and again, something came up. I couldn't help noticing my Second Form and Third Form classrooms were dedicated – if one cared to read the faded lettering – to the Hutton and Branch families, respectively. Now what had they done to merit this? "First world war dead," I was told.

When at last I was promoted to the Fourth Form, at thirteen, my turn came to study in the Vanier classroom. The first day of class, I carried my exercise books into the room without even glancing at the name above the door. That day we had English, which I liked, Latin, which I tolerated, and Religious Knowledge, which was new and strange.

The second day, my friend Luke asked me, "You anything to do with this classroom? It's got you name, One Ear."

Startled, I looked at the letters carved in black over the door. I was now tall enough to read them: "VANIER", it said. No date, no explanation was offered. I had by then lost all sense of its mystery. I had almost forgotten it existed.

"I suppose so," I said. "He was my uncle who died in second world war."

Luke's brown eyes opened a little wider. No one else in our class had lost family during the war. We sat down, and he looked at me over the scarred cover of my desk – maybe the same desk Beezie had used a generation before. "That be very brave. You must be sad. All you know him well?"

"No, really, I don't know about him. I never met him. I think he was a pilot, but I don't know much. He died when I was born. A foolish thing to do, going off to the war like that."

Embarrassed, I didn't want to talk about it. I slammed the cover down on my books and pencils. I had no good feeling for this uncle who hadn't even been smart enough to come back from the war to tell his own story.

"What do you have to tell us about your family, Vanier?" This time the summons came from my History teacher, who – for once – showed interest in something Caribbean. I had to stand up and repeat what I had told Luke: that he was my uncle, that he had been killed in the war, and that I didn't see any point in it.

"Be proud," he said, "your uncle sacrificed himself for the rest of us. He was a hero." The class applauded, happy to make noise at my expense. I should have been pleased. Instead, I went red in the face. A hero indeed! I preferred my father any day.

I wanted to be rude, but held my peace because I couldn't explain why I didn't like my uncle. I even felt guilty on his account, as if it were my fault he had volunteered. For a moment, I wanted someone to punish *me*, since Beezie was beyond reach. The teacher should have made me write lines, one thousand times, "I will not be cannon-fodder." Rather than die for nothing in a foreign country's army, I won't leave the Caribbean at all, I thought; at least we don't have wars here.

I knew nothing about the centuries of violence in the region, and nothing of the terror that reigned in Haiti, Santo Domingo, Cuba, and other paradise islands in the 1950s. I would certainly not be taught about these things in the school in Antigua.

After a week, no one mentioned the name above the door again. The last time I was aware I was in my uncle's classroom, we were reading from the New Testament. We came to the night of the Last Supper, when Saint Peter is thrice interrogated and denies any knowledge of Christ.

"No, really, I don't know about him."

However, there was nothing Christ-like about Beezie in my mind – more of a crazy prankster, I thought. That was all I learned about him at school.

Many years on, I was grown up, most of my life choices made, Beezie twice buried as a loser. One day, I found his 1941 flight-training log while rummaging through old papers in the family home. The Canadians had given it to my grandfather and it had passed on to my father. Was there anything more for me to discover about him? Curious, I picked it up and showed it to my father. The log trembled in his wrinkled hands – for he was no longer young – while he talked about it to me. It was a matter-of-fact exercise book, listing the hours of flying, the type of aircraft, and the exams passed with credit. The sparse comments indicated Beezie was of good pilot quality, and his trainers judged him a bit insubordinate, but a future leader. At first I was only mildly interested in the log's contents, my real objective being therapeutic: to cheer my father up. But that faded writing had the effect of a slow-acting drug, working its way into my system. Insubordinate? I liked that. Talented? Why did my uncle waste his lifeblood in the Air Force, then? I studied my father's face as he looked at these mementos. Beneath the grey hair and lined jowls, something lurked. I was alone with him for a week. At his age, he needed a lot of looking after, and I had wanted to give my mother a rest.

"He never told me how he felt towards Beezie," I thought. He dumped the classroom on me, and I had been left to pick up scraps of information about Beezie from my mother and grandfather. Now, huddled in his armchair he told me more: "When Beezie's training in Canada was done, his group of pilots integrated into the RAF in Britain. After several other campaigns, Beezie became part of Montgomery's first offensive at El Alamein. He piloted a Bristol Beaufighter."

"What sort of plane was it?" I asked.

"Ah, the damned Beaufighter," said my father. "It was a heavily armed, long distance, twin-engine fighter often used for attacking submarines and land targets. Certainly, the plane's firepower was deadly in combat, but it was terribly unstable if hit by shells. It was a death trap. Few pilots ever bailed out successfully once they started going down."

"What happened?"

"Beezie completed exactly four missions before dying."

"Only four?" I found this shocking.

"Yes, and it was an above-average performance in the circumstances. His Beaufighter crashed in the Mediterranean, just off the Egyptian coast. He didn't have a chance. Many of his pilot friends died in the same way."

Despite these heavy losses, I knew Montgomery had defeated Rommel one month later.

"What happened to you during that time, Dad?" The question popped out. I was supposed to know the answer: my father had no choice – he graduated and returned home as soon as he could. I patted him on the shoulder.

"I kept out of trouble in London in order to finish my studies. They wanted me for the army, but I managed to avoid all that, because I wasn't British. Once, the police arrested me as a spy. I had gone for a bicycle ride around the countryside, taking photos: a foreigner, clad in a suspicious raincoat. I had the devil of a job proving I was a bona fide Commonwealth Law student. When I finished my Bar exams, at the peak of the war, it was next to impossible to get a sea passage to anywhere. But I had to go home. I escaped bombed-out London by asserting diplomatic privilege to return to Antigua. The 'privilege' was a letter I had persuaded a friend in the Antiguan civil service to write on my behalf saying I was needed. In fact, the only person who needed me in Antigua was your mother. I often thought about Beezie."

Astonished, I closed the dusty flight log. I saw how much this story affected my father – relations between two brothers I had not understood. I had imagined the ties between them were so much weaker than the way I loved my own brothers.

It was upsetting. I had scorned Beezie for his foolish sacrifice. Why didn't my father feel the same way? He, after all, had not volunteered. In addition, he didn't seem at all ashamed at having survived.

My father paused, and I dug for enlightenment. I found he and Beezie had been close, sharing dreams, girlfriends, pranks, and – above all – laughter. They were constant brotherly companions until my father left Antigua to study Law in 1938. I pictured the parting.

"I'll be back in four years – I won't fail. Don't you want to study Law?"

"No thanks, too many books and too little oil and metal. I'm going to be an engineer."

"An engineer? I'm jealous! But I promised Elsie's father I'd become a lawyer. Motors and electricity, eh? Remember how we wired up that toilet seat?"

"How *you* wired it up – you wanted to see Elsie run out naked!"

"Me? I certainly didn't set up the generator… Anyway, mind you keep out of trouble while I'm away. See you in London, perhaps."

But Beezie chose Canada for his studies instead of England. With the flight log still in my hand, a thought occurred to me. The records I had just looked at ended in Canada, but there must have been another flight log for his active duty in England. What had happened there?

"Dad, I think you studied in London from 1938 to 1941?"

"That sounds right."

"Well, Beezie went to Canada in 1941, but didn't he complete his training in Britain later on that year? If both of you were there at the same time, you must have met."

"So we did – I thought you knew that."

"No, I didn't. What did you say to each other?"

"As I recall, Beezie had a day's permission from his military base, and he came down to the outskirts of London. The old man, your Grandpop, had written and ordered me to see Beezie. 'You can't let him go,' he'd said. 'Persuade him to drop out!' So, I had his letter with me."

"What did Beezie say to it?"

"Well, I didn't show it to him right off. He was so cheery that we spent the first hour exchanging jokes about life in cold England – how blue our extremities could get. Then I asked him what it was like to fly a mission, what did he think of up there in the heavens. Beezie told me, 'First, I have to synchronise with the controls; later, I often find myself dreaming of blue skies, crystal seas, and golden beaches. And sometimes of you and Elsie.' "

"Go on."

"Then I told him I had a letter from Daddy with a message for him. 'I can guess what it is,' said Beezie, 'but you won't try to dissuade me from flying, will you, Ralph?' Caught in the middle, I remember I said, 'No,' but then I can't recall what else we talked about."

I got nothing more out of my father that day, and I wondered why he had kept so quiet about these things. He must have wished to share this aching loss with someone over the years. Then I recalled my grandfather had his own private anger, and that my father's other brother, Jack, was not part of the Ralph-Beezie bonding. My mother would have come closest to understanding. She loved Beezie, too. But, of course, she had a different stake in Ralph's future. Not for her the man-to-man complicity, the fascination with machinery; her dreams were of romance and children, and it had to be one brother or the other. So Ralph could not truly talk to anyone about Beezie, about the things they had done, the things they meant to do, the things he would now have to do alone, or not at all. By the time his own children were old enough, many years would have gone by, and besides how could *they* possibly understand Beezie's death in a peacetime world? And so, I came full circle. He left that task to the classroom in Antigua, to try to explain itself to me, to "inspire" me, to tell me what the name over the door meant.

I thought of my father with Beezie: Ralph, serious and sometimes witty; the younger Beezie, witty, playful, and only occasionally serious. Insubordinate. I asked myself why a carefree man like that would go to war, and why the dice should roll against him. Why are there no encores to his story? The audience has dispersed, and there's not even a gravestone, just a name in the Register of war dead at St. Paul's Cathedral in London, and that lonely little classroom in Antigua, soon to be demolished, I suppose.

My father kept it all inside him, his love and grief, an enormous grey creature behind a locked door in his heart. And sometimes, the essence of Beezie would take control, and my father would be much more witty and gay than serious. He lived the life his brother would have wanted him to.

I discovered why I had not liked Beezie when I was at school in Antigua. If Beezie was brave then my father, whom I treasured, was a coward. But now I could admit that neither my father nor my uncle was perfect; that choices like theirs were not binary; and that what one brother did might not contradict the other's course of action.

A few years later, my father passed away, quietly joining his deceased brother in a place where I could not follow. I should have stopped thinking about it, but something still nagged me about Beezie. After all I had learned I kept on struggling to fit him into a framework, like some sort of protein from my family past that continued to shape my life, an uncle whom I had never met. I wanted another opinion.

So, over a glass of wine, I asked an older friend, "You were there in Europe during the second world war, weren't you?"

"Yes, I was ten."

"So you remember how people felt? The bombings, the killing, the fear?"

"And the bravery, the treachery, the hatred..." he said.

"I've been thinking about those days. You may be able to help me."

"Go ahead."

"Once there were two brothers in a poor country, both clever and ambitious, both dating the same girl. In order to earn a living, they both went abroad to study, but in different countries: one to England, the other to Canada. Then the war broke out.

"There was pressure on each brother to volunteer for the armed forces of his host country. The older didn't volunteer, the younger did. The older completed his studies, returned home, and married his girlfriend. The younger joined the air force and was killed."

"What's your point?"

"Well, which brother did the right thing? Whom should I respect more? Was it cowardly not to volunteer? Was it foolhardy to volunteer?"

Maybe I didn't have to feel guilty about my father's choice. So what if he had been scared? I would have done the same thing myself – honoured my word to a fiancée, and incidentally saved my skin. My father didn't have to be perfect for me to love him. Still, I had failed him in one way. Beezie was hardly an inspiration to me. The best I could feel was sorrow. I no longer had any animosity towards my uncle, but I continued to think he was foolhardy to volunteer – I couldn't call him heroic, nor recommend his course of action. What a waste.

"You knew these brothers?"

"One was my father, the other my uncle."

"Do you have a choice? You must approve more of your father, the one who didn't volunteer and lived to marry your mother."

"Forget about me. Tell me which brother *you* respect more."

"Stupid question which only merits an obvious answer. Both brothers were right. The brother who went home had unfinished tasks – he was right. The brother who went to war had done all he had to do on earth."

But it wasn't obvious to me. "So, I'm an unfinished task?"

My friend eyed me speculatively. "Well, in a manner of speaking."

"Suppose I don't accept your manifest destiny idea? This business of having 'done all he had to do on earth' is too religious for me. What about craziness, irresponsibility, derring-do, or just naiveté as an explanation for the younger brother's behaviour?"

"You won't like it. Without faith, you may have to consider the wartime pilot died needlessly."

I did not reply at once. Perhaps I had faith, but not his kind.

"Is there nothing to justify his death? And don't tell me about El Alamein and how necessary the sacrifices were. Winning a war is the big design of the leaders. But what about the little scheme of things: my family, me? Where's the sense?"

"Well, did the pilot at least know about your birth? You claimed he once dated your mother."

"Yes, he knew of me three months before he died. Had time to send my mother a present."

"Anything of interest?"

"Rather prosaic, just a small blue book about how to bring up children. It's lost now. Newfangled ideas about not spanking, always telling them the truth, reading them bedtime stories, and investing in their schooling and development. It's all taken for granted these days, but it was new for the Caribbean at the time."

"And did your mother take the advice seriously? Did she use the book?"

"Yes, very much so."

"Then it wasn't all lost."

From Caribs to Cats

My earliest awareness of social conflict was at the age of ten. I returned home from my boarding school for summer vacation to find my island in turmoil. Suddenly, everyone was talking about "voting". English expatriates, plantation owners, and now even working class people – browns, blacks, whites, Lebanese and East Indian immigrants – all now had a voice, except the forgotten Amerindians.

It was 1952, and the far-away British Government called it "granting the people of St. Kitts universal suffrage", for prior to this, only "men of substance", meaning the wealthiest 5% of the population – the mostly white planters, rich merchants, and professional people – could elect the local Legislature. My father, as a lawyer, was one of the privileged.

He looked at me worriedly and said, "Don't stay out after dark. This is a big change for the island, and I don't know where it will lead. I hope there won't be any fighting."

I had no knowledge of the new St. Kitts constitution – or any constitution. I was blissfully uncaring of the event's political importance, but I could not ignore the noise of the mammoth public meetings at Warner Park, when the new black constituency stomped its feet and shook the ground from under the old order.

Bradshaw's worker's party would win the first open elections based on the new rules by 10,528 votes to 482, this matching closely the colour ratio in the population. He was the man of the moment, a hammer to pound concessions from the planters and the British. Messages scrawled in chalk on the Labour Union's notice board said, "Whitey out, black man in!"

"What does it mean to vote? Why the fuss?" I asked.

"It gives people the power to change the world they live in," my father said, "for better or worse, starting with their leaders. You can vote about anything, from land ownership to wars; the majority wins, hopefully without violence; that's democracy. But – damn it – most of the new voters have no education: everyone shares the power."

I thought of my grandfather and was upset, but not about the lack of education. "Everyone? What about the Caribs, then? Shouldn't they have a vote?"

"Christopher, you know very well there aren't any more Caribs in St. Kitts. I've driven you past Bloody Point several times."

I had been interested in the Caribs ever since I learned that my great-grandmother on my father's side was born in the jungles of Guyana, but – barring a trip of my father's to the Kaitur Falls – my immediate family had not visited that country since my grandfather's departure. I had never seen a Carib, but there was a hint of one when I looked in the mirror, and also in my father's light brown skin, straight black hair, and slightly bulbous nose. I pictured the coastal road of St. Kitts between Basseterre and Old Road Town, crossing the stone bridge that was Bloody Point, where the British and French defeated the Caribs long ago, the crevasse under the bridge overgrown with wild guinea grasses. Even if my father hadn't told me it was a sinister place, I might have guessed. I had once asked to get out of the car and walk around. There was no monument or tombstone at the time. The Amerindians, who had come to the island long before Columbus, had conveniently vanished into history.

"And what about children, am I allowed to vote?"

"Not until you are twenty-one."

This stripped the democratic process of any immediacy for me. I felt in addition that the Caribs would disapprove of today's foreign occupiers, whether white or black. After all, the island was once theirs.

So, I concentrated on the more personal issue of adopting a new kitten, my last cat having disappeared when we moved house. A genetic fairy godmother had engraved a long, sinuous birthmark on my left leg resembling a sleeping cat. Superstitious Caribbean folks said my mother had been influenced by this animal during her pregnancy. My parents made me a cat owner from my earliest days – brown, black, white, or tabby – with a sort of annual renewal guarantee.

The beauty of cats and Caribs coalesced in my imagination. Both were part of my vision of liberty: naked, fearing no enemies, asking no permissions, wandering where they willed, taking from the land what they needed, endowed with a secret language, and understanding the spirits in a way I could only guess at. Information about the Caribs was hard to come by – no one cares for history's losers – but from my grandfather's stories, I pictured them as handsome brown hunters with long, black hair who migrated about a thousand years ago from the Orinoco river basin in Venezuela up the chain of islands from Trinidad to my island and beyond.

My grandfather also told me that they were superb fishermen in their sturdy canoes, and canny growers of manioc and tobacco. They conquered the preceding (more sluggish) Indian cultures that they were related to – notably Arawaks, or Tainos – as they moved through the islands. They are said to have killed the Arawak men and taken their women but I couldn't imagine myself speaking Carib to a wife who only understood Arawak. I would also have disliked having to pierce my lips and nostrils with the bones of my enemies as they did. But I sensed a daring and paganism in them that only my cats seemed to reflect, and in homage, I made bows out of springy tamarind, and arrows from smooth grass shafts, and practised sending the missiles zipping into soft blocks of bagasse on our front lawn.

Unlike dogs, most cats were allowed to roam freely in St. Kitts, which accounted for their short lifespan. My cats would leap onto walls, prowl from our garden to the next, and hunt most of the night. Sometimes they would fail to come back, perishing in combat.

I tried to tell my cats how dangerous it was out there, but they knew I wouldn't stop their marauding. That fierce independence, that utter disregard for safety and convention, that sensuous relation to everything vital – sun, sex, air, food, the palm of my hand – that terrible contrast of cruel claws hidden by the softest fur, this animal that owes nothing to anyone, and whose affection can only be given, not commanded, this animal I envied.

I owned a succession of these cats over the years, all of whom disappeared into the night, but that year of the island's first vote, I particularly remember Simba, short for Simba Numa Leo Bagheera Vanier, which I engraved on his collar, still with me today. He arrived as a kitten but grew rapidly into a hunting animal. One day he was a cuddly, playful ball of black fur, responsible for the tiny red scratches on the back of my hands, the next he was bringing dead birds and lizards onto the veranda. I compared his hunting skills to those of the Indians with their six-foot bows and bone-tipped arrows, his silent footfalls with their forest lore. The nights when he didn't prowl, he would sleep at the foot of my bed, purring with delight if I poked him with my toe. He had bright green eyes, and his adult fur was coarse, as if nature had privileged body armour over caresses.

Unfortunately, Simba developed a taste for pigeons, and raided my brother Peter's pigeon coop, killing all four of his precious birds.

"Chris, you must tell Peter how sorry you are about his pigeons!" my mother said.

I was cross. Sure, it was my cat, but I couldn't be expected to track it everywhere. That was the whole point about cats – they didn't follow orders, and they didn't know the meaning of "someone else's property". I gave Simba a few smacks and he ran off yowling and sulking – not that I thought this would do the slightest good, but justice had to be seen to be done.

Peter was furious, and there was some talk of retribution, of pulling the crazy pussy's claws. "It's not fair! Why couldn't you control your cat?"

"He has to hunt! He's like the Caribs!" I protested.

"You should know the word 'Carib' has the same Spanish root as 'cannibal'," my father said. "They were cruel. They killed settlers and ate them. That's why Sir Thomas Warner's troops struck at Bloody Point."

My father was only reflecting popular opinion. Kittitians couldn't imagine a world in which the Caribs had kept control of the islands and pushed the English and French back into the hungry sea. We, the beneficiaries of those long-gone battles, sought justification. Maybe if he had been a lawyer for the defence, my father would have said that the Caribs had a right to their land. And maybe, if there had been a civil rights lawyer to persuade him, Governor Warner might have left some Caribs alive, whose descendants could join in the popular vote today.

I defended Simba's interests as best I could, pointing out that predators and pigeons in a garden like ours were not compatible, and Simba had been there first. My arguments were feeble, but fortunately, brotherly bonds were strong. Feelings gradually calmed down, and Peter gave up keeping pigeons.

My inner sentiments were darker than I revealed. The sweet violence of the chase, the absence of prudence in pursuit of prey, and the lack of fear: it seemed *natural* to me that combat should occur and that the strongest should win. After all, I thought bitterly, that was what had happened to the Caribs. The European colonists desired their land, fought them for it, and exterminated them.

My heroes, the Caribs, fought back as well as they could and were only vanquished by superior armament, disease, and treachery. I read that their population in the islands dropped from several hundred thousand, when Columbus arrived in 1492, to a few hundred, in 1903. I was proud that the Carib fighters were intransigent – the last of them in Grenada jumped to their death from the cliffs rather than surrender, at a site now named Sauters. The Caribs in Dominica, where my mother was born, were broken at a village renamed Massacre.

"Try and train your cat," my father said. "Teach it not to poach."

My warnings could not have been very convincing, because Simba became the scourge of all manner of smaller beasts. His name seemed to inspire him, and he would leap through my window, land on my back while I was sleeping, and dig his claws in. Through the pain, I felt communion with the wild and feral world. Then he would arch his back and stretch. Here was a creature of a different moral order, doing savage things with all impunity. My affection and admiration knew no bounds.

After the passing of the pigeons, Simba's exploits didn't bother the family. Indeed, they were pleased to dispense with mousetraps during that period, and a little thinning out of the lizard population didn't seem like a bad idea either. Simba fed well and always seemed to come out on top of combats with his peer group. He avoided dogs. I would look at him basking in the sun; body and paws folded like the artwork on my leg.

One morning, Simba simply didn't appear. Our neighbour, Frank King, phoned my father a few hours later, inquiring as to whether we owned a black cat.

"Yes, my son has a cat like that," my father said. "Anything the matter?"

Our neighbour said that he had been losing poultry every night to some wild animal, so he had stayed up until nearly dawn and "caught the bastard in the act". The marauder came over the fence, and he "let him have it" with his shotgun at close range. "There's not much left," he said, "only pieces of black fur and a collar."

My father apologised and agreed to explain it to me, the cat owner.

"Tell him I had to do it," our neighbour said, and he warned he would shoot again if his hens were attacked.

It was a stormy session when my parents reported this conversation to me. "Let him have it," the hen owner had said. The words lingered in my mind, the explosive "t" sounds calling up the shots in the night.

Although he did not rejoice openly, the ex-pigeon raiser in the house took the news much more calmly than I did.

That day, I oscillated between crying and raging. Finally, I shook my fist in the air at my parents, our neighbour, and the world in general. I stamped my feet and shouted, "He won't get away with this! If he thinks he has the right to shoot my cat, then I have the right to shoot him. Vengeance. His hours are counted, as of now." Simba would have been proud of me, and so would the Caribs, whose tribal laws called for the immediate and violent punishment of a wrongdoer by the victim.

With that, I fled the living room, down into our orchard garden where a wire fence separated our land from the King's. My parents were uneasy, for I had never shown such anger. I made sure they could hear me repeating, "Let him have it, let him have it." My father must have checked discreetly as to whether I had taken my .22, but the rifle was still in its rack.

Pacing about the garden, I felt waves of hatred of my neighbour lapping over me. I planned for his doom. I justified it. Why hadn't he at least warned me Simba was stealing his hens? Surely, I could have stopped him. The memory of my brother's devastated pigeons came flapping by, but I blew it away. I forgot my theory that combat was inevitable over property rights and that the strongest must win. Mr. King was wrong, I thought. One can't shoot first and ask questions later. He must have suspected it was my cat. Now, it was blood for blood. He had killed Simba, murdered him, "let him have it", and so would get his just deserts.

Eleven years old, I wanted to kill a grown man. That was what I imagined a Carib would have done. I looked at the wire fence in frustration. I turned on my heels and began sneaking back for the gun left in our house. Halfway there, I stopped, and the ridiculousness of my ambitions sank in. Maybe I could continue hating him without doing anything about it. Keep remembering Simba in a dark and savage manner. Preserve a little dignity.

I stayed in the garden for two hours, pacing the cracked brown path and pulling leaves off the guava and citrus trees. Simba had trespassed. But so much in my short tropical life was bleached and boring. Why did the beautiful – the wild and the wanton – have to end? Even as I thought this, I could feel my obsessive linkage between cats and Caribs beginning to unravel. Animals and humans were not the same, and my personal grief was in contradiction with my ideals of noble savagery. Combat was combat. I now found it impossible to identify with the cannibals, as my father had called them. If I couldn't defend Simba, then those Caribs may have deserved their sad fate. The man with the gun always won.

No one came to look for me. I hardly glanced at the King's place anymore. Eventually, I became hungry and walked back up to our house.

Stone-faced, I said, "He's lucky, I couldn't find him. But he'll be punished some day."

My parents had the good grace not to smile in my presence. Shortly after, they gave our home over to the canine race, a much more slavish sort of animal to my way of thinking, but the constant barking noises seemed to please everyone else to the same degree that they irritated me. "At least dogs can't jump fences," my mother said. So, that year, dogs won the vote in my family and cats lost.

It would be a long time before I learned the Caribs' side of it, those so-called man-eaters, long before I understood their possession of the bones of both ancestors and adversaries was a fetish sign of respect, not of cruelty. They had another vision of the spirit world: their life force depended on the bravery of the fallen; to worship the dead, they needed to keep and absorb tokens. The Europeans painted them as evil flesh-eaters to disguise their own genocide and land theft, but anthropophagy was also the poorly hidden precept of the Catholics when partaking in the flesh and blood of Christ.

Then there was that night in 1626, when – as some said – the English and French combined to "defeat" the Caribs at Bloody Point. In reality, they tricked the Caribs into a feast where they intoxicated the entire tribe with alcohol. They assassinated Chief Tegremond, asleep in his hammock (a word the Caribs have bequeathed us, like "tobacco", "canoe", "barbecue", and "hurricane"), and murdered several hundred groggy natives. In this, they fully merited the wrath of the Carib storm god Hunrakan, whose winds would destroy the island time and again in the coming centuries.

The "ownership" of an island or a country by an immigrant group looked ridiculous: would it be the property of European colonists, the enslaved Africans, or the original Amerindians? I could feel the blood of all these immigrants coursing through my veins, but the land belongs to no one. Only our dreams are truly ours.

Wistfully, I said, "This voting business, Dad. Did you say that people can change their leaders and agree on who owns what without fighting?"

He smiled – the elections were now over – and said, "Sometimes."

Wrong about many things in that year of shifting power, I remained faithful to my cats, and I vowed never to own another one. Maybe I could have educated Simba better, but I hadn't wanted to. Now, the creatures I cared for had vanished, and, regretfully, I would have to take my place among the survivors.

Bats in the Rainforest

Mount Misery was alive with dangers, and I felt it delighted in tricking unwary climbers who wandered up its slopes. Few knew the route up to the crater. My father, as Secretary of the planters' Sugar Association, thought he did. On our next expedition, I was determined to swing on a liana. But I had to wait.

The months and years went by quickly and I was fully occupied by my boarding school problems. Islands like Antigua are flat limestone pancakes encrusted with coral reefs with no conceivable danger from magma. It wasn't until I was eleven, and back home in St. Kitts for summer vacation, that I got my next chance to visit the volcano.

By then, in 1954, my brother Peter was eight and ready for his first climb. During that vacation period, my parents made friends with an English architect and his wife, Roland and Irene Brand. He was dapper, fit, and precise; she was too pretty to go unnoticed; both had done weekend climbing in Britain and mistaken it for mountaineering. Our cramped-up capital of St. Kitts – Basseterre – was breaking out of its historic confines in disorderly boils and pimples; Roland had been hired on a mission concerning the growth of the Bird Rock suburb across the bay from our home. Words about poor planning frequently leaked out of his conversation. He told us how quaint and primitive the Caribbean was, and how much it lacked organisation. People lived anywhere, anyhow, rich and poor. Apparently, my town had no building codes or zoning regulations, often-ambiguous property rights, on-and-off electricity, and non-existent public sewers. Telephones were a luxury. This criticism was new and stimulating to me – but Roland's showing off could be irritating.

Roland and Irene had two children about Peter's age, Martin and Robin, and all four Brands wanted to climb our volcano before they returned home. My father agreed to guide the expedition.

My youngest brother, Noel, was only four and to the great dismay of my sister Hazel, aged nine and trying hard to adapt to her situation as an athetoid spastic, my parents asked her to stay home and take care of him. It would be another few years before she asserted her right to brave the mountain. As for me, when I heard the news of our coming climb I remembered the lianas I had not been able to cling to on our earlier expedition. I secretly practised hanging from doorframes and tree branches until I was red in the face and my arms hurt. I thought I could now support my own weight on a swinging vine. Vowing to succeed, I shoved the memory of my sulphur scars out of my mind.

I was a more faithful observer of the forest at this age than on earlier or later trips. Hunting in Nevis and roaming the bushes in Antigua had attuned me to the littoral woodland. Free of physical limitations and full of new and bookish reference points, I drank in the forest images, not understanding environmental things but at least seeing them and learning their names.

We left at dawn, and the Brands followed our car with theirs. We drove along the coastal road from Basseterre for about an hour, passed Bloody Point, Old Road Town, Middle Island, Half Way Tree, Brimstone Hill fortress, Sandy Point, Newton Ground, and finally turned in to Belmont Estate – the starting point for all climbs to the crater. My father had arranged rough transport from there on with the estate manager. For a few shillings, his foreman drove us in a battered jeep up through the cane fields to the volcano's foothills, via a potholed, crevassed, rain-blasted track. They let me ride on the outside of the jeep, at risk from the sharp cane leaves that attacked us at every twist and turn. Thus, we won our first skirmish with the volcano, carried one-third of the way up its body, over a thousand feet, at the modest price of a few sore bottoms. From there on we would walk, scramble, and climb.

No longer the laggard of the expedition, I had more time to succumb to the rainforest's magic. We walked up the beginning incline, past low trees, many bearing fruit I was fond of. I picked guava, sliding my teeth through the lemon-coloured skin to get at the sweet, pink flesh. This was all I had time for, but I noted the other fruit, out of reach: sugar apple – even sweeter than guava, but with black seeds to spit out; cashew nut – tart; soursop – only good as a sugary drink; and mango – lots of mango – ripe overhead and rotting – reeking – underfoot. The timber trees were more difficult to name: eucalyptus, white cedar, trumpet tree, red sweet wood, and candlewood the Jamaicans call snakewood. Then we trudged by larger species: breadfruit, breadnut, bamboo, lignum vitae, marouba, weedee, and calabash. I had seen bowls and ornaments made from the large calabash nut in Caribbean homes but this was the first time I had noticed where the fruit came from, bigger than my two fists, on its parent tree.

"Now is the time to get walking sticks," my father said, "the path gets treacherous after this."

I picked up a length of dried bamboo.

My father showed my staff to Roland and said, "We have to thank the early English colonists for bringing in many new plant varieties to the forest: bamboo, breadfruit, and mango, among others. On the bad side, they decimated our indigenous trees, like mahogany, for their precious wood."

Roland looked back and seemed about to say something but thought better of it.

In the outer skirt of forest, the ground still dry and firm, sunlight penetrated quite easily. This was monkey country, and we could hear them chattering in the distance. I was told they disliked the higher, wetter parts of the forest. I thought the air would be cooler at once, but in the stillness under the trees, it remained sweaty and warm for most of the climb. After another thirty minutes, we entered the dark, cathedral part. The real forest. Fruit trees gave way to giant palms and large ferns, and then to the forest's dominants: boarwood, gumlin trees, carapite, ironwood, mahogany, and fig trees.

From there on, the ground was increasingly damp under my shoes. The trail was covered with dead leaves and moss, and I could see no one had dared it recently. It was easy to slip. We scaled large rocks covered with roots on hands and knees to follow the path, skirted fallen forest trees – over or under. Ferns of all sorts ran riot near our feet – they somehow thrived without sunlight. Orchids made love to their favourite trees, enfolding them with a thousand tender roots and leaves. The monkey voices and the bird chirping faded away and all we could hear was our own footsteps and breathing. I wondered how much longer it would be before we reached the lianas. I could neither see where we had come from in the forest, nor where we were heading.

As the gradient increased, the struggle against gravity was won by dint of sinews and sweat, my whole body feeling a new sensual awareness. I revelled in having left behind the ordinary world. No noisy cars, creaking houses, hot pavements, and no teachers to tell me to do this or do that: there were no reminders of our ant-like existence in dusty towns. I scoffed at my childish ideas of ghosts or jumbies, but I began to think of this strange forest as magic, nevertheless. Or perhaps the forest was not real magic, but at least it made the humdrum disappear – it was the absence of non-magic. Here was proof I could shatter the boredom that sometimes enveloped me – be elsewhere, in a wholly different place. *Anything* might lurk behind those giant trunks, hide high up in those dark branches, or down in those bottomless ravines. These were secret places, and the creatures of my imagination could not be denied existence. Of course, if I were to peer boldly around a tree and find nothing – which I did from time to time – that would be one surprise less. But there were so many others, lying in wait. It was intoxicating to feel my power of invention over this unseen world.

Long ago, the Caribs had roamed these slopes. And more recently, runaway slaves had hidden here, notably Marcus, self-styled King of the Woods in the 1830s, who by some accounts was never captured.

We came to a fork in the trail and my father hesitated; both alternatives led upwards. On the left, was a curving passage around a brown strangler fig with several large roots criss-crossing our way; on the right, the ground rose more steeply and the passage was squeezed between two grey gumlin trees. My father seemed to be looking for something, scanning the trees, and finally chose the right-hand option.

"How did you know where to go?" I asked. "Are we lost?"

"Look," he replied, and pointed with his walking stick at a mark on the trunk of one of the gumlins bordering our route. The mark was old and blackened. Someone had chopped it with a cutlass a long time ago. "This is called trailblazing. We cut through a tree's bark to show where to turn, but the trees repair themselves and the blazes fade away with time." He chopped the marked tree again – a little lower down – with his own cutlass. I liked the solid thunking noise of metal on wood; leaving a mark on the forest for future climbers – two gashes meeting in a V – seemed like a profound ritual. As if it had heard my thoughts, the tree bled. A sweet-smelling white sap oozed out, evoking incense. It seemed the cut tree was not alone, that the forest itself – or the dark presence of my dreams – was responding to us. Roland Brand approached and we dipped our fingers in the sticky gum. The same conviction must have come to both of us: thanks to the blazes, we could not go astray; disorderly nature had been put in its place.

Farther on, there were several forks in the path, and I was now sensitised to my father's search for cuts and bruises on the forest giants. I wondered what would happen to us if all the blazes were rubbed out. But there was no way they could disappear like that. To make quite sure, my father cut a new blaze every time we found a faded one.

Shortly after this, the Brands discovered some blazes ahead, and smiling to each other, the acolytes decided to find the path by themselves. They moved out in front of my father to lead the expedition, and I remember Roland's bright, amused eyes as he cocked his head and glanced back at me.

"Help the younger ones, Christopher," my mother said, and so it became my reluctant duty to push Peter and the Brand children over the difficult bits. I was annoyed. My body had outpaced my social instincts – I was old enough to climb and scramble without help but not wise enough to get pleasure out of assisting my slower comrades. How I would have preferred to scamper after Roland.

At last, we came to the liana-covered stretch of wide path where a precipitous gully dropped away on the right. Someone had been there during the last few weeks after all, because my father didn't have to cut a new liana. He took the thickest available vine, shook it, and then swung on it himself before letting us try. I thought how reassuring it was to have him test the hazards by putting himself at risk. I noticed how he flexed his shoulders after swinging, as if they were stiff.

"Don't let me slip!" I asked any deity who cared to listen, as I pushed myself forward to swing next. I received the liana from my father, hesitated, and lost control. My first jump was so feeble it barely moved me three feet, still over the path, before I swung back. The adults laughed.

"Move well back and jump before you swing," said my father. "Then grab the liana high up and hold on tight."

Piqued, I retreated a few steps with the liana, jumping up it as high as I could. Suddenly there was nothing underneath me, nothing at all, and I could feel my fingers slipping. They stuck and held. Terror or excitement, how could I tell the difference? The trees seemed to rush away as I plummeted outwards.

I fragmented into several boys, each suspended by the liana. "Don't look down," someone had said, but one of the boys' eyes turned downward all on their own, past my toes, giddily down to the hard slope some thirty feet below. Another of the boys was aware of the adults and children looking at him in anticipation. I had centre stage. Yet another boy was resolved to think of nothing but his fingers clamped onto the inch-thick rough brown vine that alone kept him from catastrophe. "Squeeze – more – squeeze until juice comes out of the liana." And the craziest of the boys was thinking that his parents always protected him in dangerous situations: riding his first bike, swimming too far from the shore, keeping his rifle pointed away from others. And now he had a real decision to make. He could hold on or let go and no one could stop him. Frightening as this was, I had the thrill of being in charge of my life as never before. After a profound and lengthy reflection of several milliseconds, I decided not to let go.

I was trembling like a maimed butterfly when I landed – heavily – on the path again. Everyone else swung, even the younger children, and it began to seem much simpler. Yes, it hurt our fingers, it was scary, but we didn't fall.

Roland seemed strangely uninhibited, crying out like Tarzan as he swung out. He was no longer at all dapper and precise – enigmatic was more like it. At one point, he let go of the liana with one hand and continued swinging, looking proud. I envied the ease with which he did this, and for a moment, I forgot he was an adult, in the other camp, so to speak. After a few minutes, we were all doing multiple swings, folding our legs as we neared the path in order to swing out again. I flexed my shoulders as I had seen my father do, to loosen them just in case.

I had conquered this volcano. I could look into its gullies, climb its trees, swing on its lianas, and avoid its poisons; nothing was impossible. The bite it had given me on my thigh years before was avenged. Still, I couldn't hang onto the liana with one hand as Roland had done. Of course, I thought of trying it, but once in flight, nothing, nothing at all, could prise a hand free until I was safely over the path again. In any case, I wasn't ready – I hadn't made up my mind which hand to trust. Maybe on the way back.

We reached the lip of the crater after another hour of hard walking and scrambling, tired and dirty. I hadn't remembered how cold it was up there, with the mist and cloud swirling around us every few minutes. At the summit of the path, the lip forms a narrow, grassy plateau the size of a living room, where numerous volcano explorers have rested and eaten. I remembered the clearing. The remainder of the lip forms an even circle around the crater – more than half a mile in diameter – covered with stunted trees and thick vegetation. The plateau on which we stood was by far the best lookout and the easiest access into the crater. Although the forest has few animals at this altitude, I spied a mongoose hiding in the bushes, perhaps encouraged by a previous climber's food scraps and emboldened to test our generosity. Lunch was nothing if not hearty, with sandwiches, savoury chicken, and sweet potatoes prepared by my mother. The two men had beers; the rest of us drank water.

An outcrop of rock jutting up to the right of this plateau is called "King Christian's Needle". I was puzzled by the origin of the name – there were at least ten Danish monarchs named Christian – but whoever the king in question, he had an extraordinary view of the island. Years later, I learned Denmark was not involved; two St. Kitts climbers christened it in the early twentieth century, Mr King and Mr Christian. Scrambling up the granite sides of the needle was a great trial in itself, but I found handholds and, once up, I could survey the rainforest canopy, back the way we had come from Belmont. Down a steep valley, the undulating forest treetops were so dark that, away in the distance, the sunlit cane fields were bleached more golden-yellow than green. Beyond, even farther, was the drifting blue sea, three thousand feet down from us, a reminder of the world we had escaped from.

I turned around to the crater, but I couldn't judge the distance down – I thought it was between four hundred and seven hundred feet. I wanted to know where the high spot was, the peak of Mount Misery.

"It's over there, but you can't scale it from the north side where we are." My father, who had climbed up beside me, pointed to the far lip and waved his hand higher. "You have to take a different approach road, from the east. It's a tough climb, more dangerous and less rewarding than this one – I've only done it three times."

Full of my mettle, I wanted to know why it was dangerous.

"Because of the microclimate," he explained.

My father told us it was windy up near the peak and the mountain was almost bald in places, very slippery with nothing to hold on to.

"They call it 'elfin' or 'cloud' forest. It's made of moss and some twisted, low mahogany trees. Climbers have had accidents up there. I'll take you up some day when you are older."

"Elfin forest" spoke to my imagination – what sort of enchantments were to be found there? The words tumbled into my mind and evoked not botany but mischievous green-clad creatures with pointed ears and quivers full of sharp arrows at the ready. I should go there, a place where even adults acknowledged the primacy of fantasy over hot grubby pavements. Nevertheless, I had the curious feeling this trip would not happen. Though I would often think about it in the future, and several times tried to set up an expedition to the peak, with or without my father, the elfin forest would remain a dream.

The time came for the crater descent. Rubbing my hand on my sulphur scars of five years earlier, I was determined not to make the same mistake twice. I needed no help to clamber down; at the price of a few scrapes and bruises, I was there as quickly as the adults, once again inside the volcano. In fact, I outpaced my father and stood panting at the bottom, hands on my hips, watching him descend the last few feet. However, this time the sulphur and steam vents were not active and I failed to find the place with the yellow-and-brown rocks. Not that I would have dared to take any souvenirs, of course. Roland and Irene were impressed and enthusiastic. I saw them looking back and forth, wide-eyed. There was a deep silence, no birds, and no insects, just the eternal magma waiting far beneath our feet.

I looked away from the others, across the caldera, to the volcano surrounding me, and inhaled the acrid sulphur tang. I was at the bottom of a giant cup, or rather a funnel, with an upper lip about 1100 yards in diameter and its steep green walls looming 200 yards high. About a half of the funnel's circumference was coloured dark green with thick trees and vines, like those I had just climbed down; another quarter, near the brown acidic lake, was rockier and unscalable; the last quarter sloped more gently, covered with low, lime-green scrub: the trees had been crushed by a rock slide.

The real danger of being in the crater for any length of time came from earth tremors – there were many, and of varying intensity – and not from the remote possibility of an eruption. Following a survey by a US geological team, there would one day be an evacuation plan for the entire north-eastern half of St. Kitts if Mount Misery were to blow. At least Basseterre would be safe, the report would say, unless of course the Nevis volcano, so close, should blow at the same time.

In later years, I would look back at these innocent moments in the volcano – forbidden to most future visitors because of increased tremors – and speculate on the original inhabitants of the island. When Caribs walked these same paths, they surely perceived the powers and perils of the volcano. I had seen pictures of their religious icons, the three-pointed zemis – sea, forest, and volcano – carved out of shells, stones or clay. It was an ideal spot for sacrifices.

After a moment of daydreaming, my eleven-year-old self started thinking of the lianas again, wanting to get back to them as soon as possible and do some more swinging. I wondered whether it would be better to swing with my right hand or my left. Of course, I was right-handed, but maybe my left hand was more rested because I used it less.

First, we had to overcome the strenuous climb back up to the crater's lip. The only children who had been allowed down were Peter and I, my mother having agreed to stay at the top with the young Brands. Following my father and brother, I started up the same rough traces I had come down, on the north-western side of the crater. The first steep bit had some convenient vines and even a few lengths of real rope left behind by previous climbers.

Roland looked at my father and asked, "Mind if we do something a bit more challenging?" I couldn't be sure, but it sounded aggressive to me. He pointed to an opening between the trees about thirty feet away. "I'll bet we can get to the top before the rest of you by this other path."

My father looked concerned. "I wouldn't advise it, Roland. I don't know that path and these trails can be treacherous."

"Nonsense, Ralph, you can see it goes up parallel to your trail. Don't worry, we've already climbed much higher than this on Ben Nevis in Scotland."

"Well, watch where you're going. We'll wait for you, if need be."

"See you at the top, Ralph," Roland said with a laugh, as he and Irene took off.

Although Ben Nevis was higher than our crater lip at 4408 feet compared with about 2900, the wide, easy path leading up to it presented few real difficulties.

I was puzzled by Roland's attitude. Why should a stranger to the volcano want to use a route my father advised against? Yet, another part of me understood the strange excitement in Roland. The ordinary, the routine, the path everyone else took could not be accepted, not that day in the ancient green forest.

Once at the top, all of us – my parents, two Vanier children, and two Brand children – sat on the plateau and waited for the two adult Brands to arrive. And waited. After a good forty minutes, with quite a few stories and jokes bandied around, my parents seemed to shift into second gear – worried – and started calling out for the missing adults.

"Hoo-hoo, where are you?"

But there was no answer. Voices carried strangely in the rainforest: sometimes you could hear them from far away if there was a convenient green channel, a sound corridor, but often people in a nearby ravine were cut off. I stuck my hands in my pockets, bored and getting tired. What did the adults think they were playing at? It was past four, and I wanted to go back down to the jeep. We still had time to steal some cane, or at least argue about it. And surely, we could swing on the lianas a second time. I had chosen my right hand as stronger for swinging on. My father stood up and announced he was going to find the two missing Brands. He told us that even a slightly different starting path from the bottom of the crater might have brought them up hundreds of feet away in the dense rim vegetation. Their previous experience of climbing would be of little use. I was proud of him, but wished he would hurry up.

A few minutes after his departure, we heard a crashing sound and a yell. My mother looked alarmed, alone in charge of a brood of four. We couldn't tell from whom the yell had come. Maybe I shouldn't have wished for my father to hurry up. What if he had fallen because of me? We helped shout in chorus and, shortly, there were answering echoes. One was my father, saying he was all right, just a little fall. The other cries, much fainter, were from the Brands. Locating them was one thing; getting all the parties back together was another. Like the Old Mc Donald's farm song, it was a "Hoo-hoo here, a hoo-hoo there, and a hoo-hoo everywhere." My father was right: Roland and Irene had reached the rim of the crater two hundred feet away and couldn't get through the vegetation. Progress was agonisingly slow. With no cleared path, the forest was almost impenetrable. At least, thanks to my father, they now knew which direction to scramble in, but it took more than an hour for them to reach us. My father intercepted them and they returned together. Roland and Irene looked puffed and red in the face. I didn't hear any explanation or apology they might have offered for their misadventure.

My father described how he had slipped from a branch and fallen about ten feet. "I was lucky," he said. "When the branch gave way, all my weight was shifted to my right shoulder, which has been stiff lately. I felt it crack as the arm pulled out of its socket. It hurt like hell. Then I fell and was only stopped when the same dislocated right shoulder hit a big tree. Otherwise, I might have dropped a lot farther. My luck was in the angle of impact – the shoulder hit the tree just right and I heard a click as my arm went back into its socket. Now I'm fine. No pain, nothing."

Either from pride or discretion, he would never blame Roland for his misfortune. I couldn't know, there on the slopes of the Mount Misery volcano, but this fall would be one of my father's favourite stories during the next forty-three years until his death. He would be eternally thankful to the mountain for knocking his shoulder back to normal that day. Even when he developed severe arthritis in the same shoulder thirty-five years later, he treasured the experience. Maybe it was his personal victory over the volcano.

Happy to have everyone back, especially my intrepid father, at half past five, I thought we had succeeded in our climb. Though the volcano had tried to separate us, tried to injure my one-and-only father, soon we would be home.

We started back at once, with the adults encouraging the tired children. Gravity helping, the scramble down through the rainforest is quicker than the scramble up, but even fit adults are hard put to do it in much under two hours. We had children with us – including myself. The Caribbean sun starts setting before six o'clock and it's pitch dark about a quarter-hour later, all year round. At six-fifteen, when total blackness enveloped us, we knew we were not even halfway down. Such was our concentration on speed that we went by the liana-swinging platform without noticing it. Afterwards, this seemed incredible to me, how I could miss one of my favourite places in the forest. It may have been because the trees looked so different in the dark. Or it may have been an indication of our deepening worry. Or – just maybe – someone had hidden it from us. Today, you would be advised never to climb Mount Misery without a good flashlight. We'd taken none. But we had matches, and when the path blacked out, my father and Roland lit torches made with the bits of paper we had packed the food in.

Proceeding slowly, we reached the first fork in the path. One way led up, the other down. I couldn't see any of the blazes my father had used earlier. Neither could anyone else, so we took the downward path. Five minutes later, it came to a dead end. We backtracked and went the other way. Sure enough, it went up for a short stretch and then turned down. We couldn't trust the apparent direction, I thought. But the dark trees, the forest canopy above, and our flickering torchlight made it impossible to detect blazes, so we had to guess. Did the blazes still exist? I could hardly see my shoes, and I realised we had no way back home. We began to run out of paper. When we came to the next fork in the path, Roland offered to take the torch and explore ahead. My father and mother politely refused the offer.

We stopped, and the adults discussed our situation. We were lost in the dark, said one. We were not lost because we were still on the path, said another. We had light, but it was soon going to run out. We were getting cold. We had fire, but most of the twigs around us were damp. We had four children falling asleep and we might have to stay up here all night. We could explore, but it would be easy to fall and break a leg in the dark – a thousand crooked roots and slippery rocks were waiting to oblige. Maybe the estate owner would send out a team to look for us. My parents put on a brave face, but Irene looked scared. Roland was grim, as if he were blaming himself for something. The forest looked so much more menacing at night. I guessed this would not be treasured as one of his best-planned days. Finally, we decided to stay put and wait for help. Meantime, we could concentrate on making a real fire.

This suited me, though I clearly didn't have any say. With the last of the paper, we were able to dry out some dead fern leaves to start the fire. I was detailed with two others to collect some bigger branches. I had to stay within twenty feet of the dim light, and all I could find were disgustingly damp logs. On some of them, I was sure I felt woodworms crawling out onto my hands. However, the paper dried the ferns, and the ferns dried the smaller branches, and just when our matches were almost finished the logs caught. The worms will roast, I thought. Then we sat and waited. I doubted a search team would come. Who had ever heard of anyone getting lost on a small island like St. Kitts, much less being found again? I was more thrilled than scared at the idea of a night in the wilds. But I was probably the only one in the party who felt that way. And I still preferred to keep close to the fire. It was a pity, though, that we had nothing left to eat. Time went by. My mother wrapped the three younger children in sweaters – I had to give up mine – and they fell asleep on the backpacks in the flickering firelight. My father and Roland kept watch; no one knew quite what to expect from the night-time rainforest.

My mother first saw the strange shadows flying above our heads. Bats. They circled from tree to tree, disturbed by our fire. She screamed. To my delight, this woke everyone up, and we spent the next ten minutes driving the intruders away with shouts and stones.

"Dracula will come next," I announced, hopefully.

"Shush!" my mother said, looking at the younger children's round eyes.

"They suck your blood while you're asleep," I continued.

"Stop, Chris! There's no need to be afraid," my father said to the others. "Can you imagine why there are bats in this high forest?" he asked me.

I had little idea – I imagined bats preferred dark, enclosed places like caves and tombs. Why an open forest?

"They are fruit bats," he said. "They live on nectar from large tree flowers and help to pollinate them like the bees do in the fields lower down."

My father shook his head at me, and then turned away to the other children who had their arms clasped around their chests.

"In particular, our friends the bats go for the huge flowers on the calabash tree. These are white and odourless in the day, but at night they give off a sweaty, cheesy smell."

I sniffed hard, but couldn't detect the cheese – only moist vegetation and pungent wood smoke.

Disappointed the forest bats did not suck blood, as self-respecting vampires should, I walked a few steps into the dark and let off steam with some more cries. Instead of sounding fierce, the way I wanted, my voice came out high-pitched, and I shivered a little. I had had enough. The damp night air was rolling down the mountain slopes and it was way past my dinnertime. I was exhausted, and the expedition was becoming unpleasant – no fun at all. I didn't ever want to return to this volcano. I was wrong to imagine I could get the better of it. One last cry for help. To my surprise, Roland joined me, a strong baritone adding to my piping soprano.

An echo came back that shouldn't have been there.

"Quiet! I hear something," my mother said.

Strange voices, cries, confusion filtered through the trees. A gun fired. We stood nervously. Friend or foe? What had the volcano done now? Should we hide? I preferred the bats I had chased away to this unknown element. For a moment, I wished I *were* a bat. Instead of being trapped in this humid and hostile forest, I could wing my way to safety into some dark hidey-hole. Or to some other country, and never come back. I positioned myself close to my father. We saw lights flickering nearby and the adults began hailing.

"It's Ralph Vanier here. Don't shoot!" my father said.

Minutes later, we were surrounded by half a dozen black burly men armed with cutlasses, machetes and the rifle they had used to attract our attention. The search party from the estate had found us. It was almost midnight. We had been lost for more than six hours.

"You all far off the good trail, you know. Without you shout, we not going to find you."

Saved by the bats and my cries, I thought, and I saw Roland looking at me.

This being the Caribbean, as soon as our rescuers were reassured we had no injuries, there was a good deal of laughing at our expense.

"Why you start back down so late?" asked one of our rescuers.

I heard my father say casually two of the party had been delayed on a side trail. No mention was made of Roland's insistence to take this path, much less of his strange and stubborn excitement.

I don't remember seeing the Brands a great deal in the following weeks.

I have no trace of the walk back down to the jeeps, and the bumpy ride between the cane fields, but the taste of the salty, steaming bowl of chicken and vegetable soup that Peter and I enjoyed at Belmont remains. Perhaps the person who was the most upset by this misadventure was my sister Hazel, who had to wait until one o'clock in the morning to find out whether the volcano had eaten her family.

The Cannapult

The primary schools of St. Kitts where we lived did not know how to deal with a spastic like my sister Hazel. They couldn't follow her distorted speech for a start. However, at home in our garden, there was no lack of hard knocks, falls, cuts, or bruises to educate her. Faithful to my father's wishes, I welcomed Hazel into all of our rowdy games and adventures, without regard for the consequences. The goal was to let her live her life to the fullest and prove those experts wrong who had said she was "uneducable". But the consequences were always more than her fair share of hard knocks. Where I had one bruise on my arm, Hazel had two; where my brother Peter scraped his shin, Hazel was deeply cut; where Noel was lightly burned, Hazel was scorched, needing iodine and bandages. My parents usually turned a blind eye. The way she bounced on them, Hazel's knees and elbows seemed to be made of rubber. After a while, she became so expert at falling lightly I stopped looking at her difficulties of balance – which was certainly the way she wanted it.

Perhaps the nearest I came to accidentally killing my sister was in the storming-of-the-fortress game. During school vacations from Antigua I was forever seeking adventure, and one of our pastimes was to chase birds, dogs, lizards, and even ourselves with our slingshots. When I read about the fortifications of ancient cities, and how a city's enemies would attack it with siege engines, throwing boulders over the castle walls with huge catapults, I was determined to make a weapon like this. My modern version would be a cannon plus a catapult, a "cannapult", about ten times as big as our regular slingshots. The explosive version of this weapon would have to wait for later.

In our garden grew a flamboyant tree with a useful fork in its trunk, at head height. We often perched in this comfortable place before we climbed higher. What if I attached enormous strands of rubber to each side of the fork, and tied them to a basket? It would take two hands to draw it back, but what a payload! My father had everything I needed in his workshop, including old inner tubes for car tires. Tubes that could be patched were valuable – we could float on them in the sea – but some were too damaged for that, and from one of these I shaped the muscles of our weapon, several elastic strips one inch wide and three feet long.

Every war has soldiers and victims, and my self-appointed job was to nominate them. A simple choice – the cannapult builders, namely Peter and I, had to be the invading soldiers. All others – Hazel, Noel, and a young visiting friend – would be the innocent victims, defenders of the city. We were only two, and they were numerous, so I judged it fair that they be small and helpless. That's how victims are.

The city's fortifications had to be positioned directly in front of the cannapult, or else, what was the point? We built them out of old tables, cardboard boxes, and a few light wooden planks. I advised the defenders to keep well under cover, as I would be hurling two-pound rocks at them.

The cannapult didn't work at first, because our rubber strips pulled off the tree bark, but we eventually hammered them down with two-inch nails. Then the basket to hold the rocks fell apart, so we fixed it with some tough sacking cloth. Finally, we declared war.

"Fire away!" I said to Peter.

"We're weady!" replied my sister.

Peter and I took turns to knock down the cardboard boxes, while the three defenders hid under the tables, squealing, and throwing marbles. I had thought of providing them with boiling oil to repel us more emphatically, but it was too much trouble to steal the stuff from Mum's kitchen.

Now, was it my fault if Hazel chose to stick her head out of the shelter just when I hurled my best two-pound rock? The rock hit a wooden plank first, and only then rebounded onto Hazel's crown. In my nightmares, I wondered what a full impact would have done. This was no ordinary knock such as Hazel was accustomed to. There was blood everywhere; it even splattered the other two defenders. I sloshed water from the garden hose over her and revealed a big gash that wouldn't stop bleeding. Game over.

"Look what you done," one of the small defenders said.

I glared at him, but lost some of my composure when Hazel said, "It hurth."

I was severely reprimanded for not taking better care of my sister, and no amount of explanation about mediaeval wars and the inherent risks to the defenders could justify me. I took it badly, and even more so when Hazel herself pardoned me, before I could huffily apologise. In a mixture of pride and guilt, I dismantled the cannapult. For the next few days, with Hazel's head still in bandages, we played quietly and grimly at Monopoly and checkers.

My mood only lifted when Hazel jerked her head at me and said: "Leth do thomething more ekthiting. I'm alwight now – nod an inwalid."

So, I decided on rock climbing, and proposed to slither down the cliffs to the sea sixty feet below. I was sure Hazel could do it. Anything was possible during my holidays.

From Sardines to Sodium

There seemed to be no connection between the two parts of my life: home in St. Kitts during my vacation, where I felt confident and loved; and away at the boarding school, an uncertain and sometimes hostile place, where I spent most of the year. Travelling between these places, I moved from a pastoral painting to a battle scene; at each transition, an uncaring master artist would brush me out of one picture and into the other. This feeling of dislocation, of which homesickness was an early manifestation, was reinforced by the growing idea that the things I liked least in Antigua were nonetheless of consequence.

"Why do you have to go to work, Dad? Can't you take us to the beach this morning?" It was the end of my vacation before returning to school in Antigua, a Saturday to boot, and I was pushing my luck. But I wanted to surf in the sea again, to be carried once more by a rippling wave, propelled – weightless and effortless – through my days to some soft, sandy shore.

"We all have to work to eat. You too, Chris. That's why we are sending you to the Antigua Grammar School. So you can study for a good job and be able to feed yourself and your own family some day."

Normally happy to explain things, my father was not receptive at 8am that day. I didn't know and wouldn't have understood that he had several difficult tasks waiting for him in his offices at the sugar factory, forcing him to work on his weekend. Cane production was down and the Labour Union was threatening to strike for higher wages. Again. There was even talk of land reform. Work, work, work. I recall my father being able to play cricket in the garden with us only once over the years, although perhaps the sessions my brothers and I spent with him in the workshop should be counted as a form of amusement. But lathes, drills, hammers and nails couldn't compare with the beach on the last days of vacation.

"Think about your studies and your future." He might as well have added, "for a change."

There it was, out on the table – almost a reproach. No, surely a reproach. And even more stinging for it's being exceptional. My father rarely criticised me for anything except errors in English. For a short time, after he had picked up his heavy briefcase and left, I considered what he had said. I was being sent to school not to goof off, not to have fun, not to learn discipline, not even to develop my mind, but to *do* something in the world, to find a career that would bring in money. If I didn't find a career, one day I might starve. Anyone looking at me would have seen the scowl on my face. "You have a potato in your mouth again, Chris," was the way my mother used to put it.

This was in 1954, I think, though it might have been earlier or later, because this consciousness of something missing, an anxiety about the future, built up slowly from my eleventh to my fourteenth year. The trouble was not that I refused to cooperate but that I had no idea how to implement my father's wishes. Career? What career? What did people do with their lives once they left school? And what did I want to do? It all seemed like a blank wall to me, an obstacle I was being pushed into and couldn't climb over. So, I put my father's remarks to the back of my mind as soon as I decently could and found other distractions, wrestling with my brothers on the lawn. Four days later, I returned to boarding school in Antigua, the unresolved questions still tickling. I should find a career, but how was I going to do it?

Retrospectively, when you have five long years in a classroom to think about your future, it seems shameful and ungrateful if you do not develop an idea of what you want to do in the world. Guilty as charged. Or rather, instead of no idea, I had too many fantastic ideas in mind – magician, swordfighter, pirate, cowboy, gunman, desperado, fighter pilot, President – but nothing practical and achievable such as doctor, lawyer, or accountant. However, the British colonial school system just wasn't training any Zorros, or Robin Hoods, or Henry Morgans. And despite my grandfather's great spiritual influence, combined with my duties as an occasional altar boy for Father Brown, I felt religion was a wait-and-see thing, and not a career option for the moment.

The very idea of a career was difficult for me, as if it were something imperative, yet dependent on adult secrets. If someone had asked me what a good career was, my confusion would have been apparent. On the one hand, there was the apathetic world my friends and I could see – the world of black and brown people sweltering under a hot sun, mostly poor, not complaining, and not getting anywhere. In this world, you could be a civil servant, a store clerk, a sugar factory employee, or – if all else failed – a cane cutter. Then there were the planter and merchant families, who seemed to have no difficulties with making money, or – more relevant – with knowing what they wanted to do with it, but you had to be born into these families. Last, there was the virtual, off-island world coming from books, radio, occasional movies, and from all my parents had told me about England. Sometimes I doubted this world existed, and that there was anything tangible beyond our island shores. It was supposed to be a world populated mostly by white people, who lived in Europe and America. They were the ones who did things, if you could believe it. Civilisation. Medicine. Scholarship. Laws. Armies. The rest of the planet, the un-English places – Asia, Africa, and South America – weren't talked about. I would have to choose between the real world of the Caribbean I knew and the virtual world of my books and of people's travel stories.

Abroad, in that virtual world, was where highly trained people like doctors and lawyers came from. Some of them had been born in the Caribbean, but they had all acquired their wisdom elsewhere. These professions did not motivate me. Who wants to be a lawyer like his father and not be able to play cricket in the garden with his children? There was a whiff of freedom about a place like England, but it also felt unknowable, frightening, out of reach. What was clear for a boy like me was that you needed this thing called a "career" to avoid joining the barefoot brigade and the "limers", those who hung out at Basseterre street corners, eyeing up the girls, smoking, and not doing much of anything else. So, for many of us young people in the early 1950's, a career was defined negatively, by *not* doing whatever it was that the working classes, the idle, and the previous generations had done.

We could feel the ground moving under our feet but had no idea that a full-scale earthquake was about to take place – elections, self-government, nationalisation of the sugar estates, and the shifting of power from white to black hands – that would push us forward and bury our antiquated social structures. None of this was of any use to me, however. I needed my own plans. Feeble as it was, all the inspiration I could get to find a career was through my teachers in Antigua.

And a strange lot they were. Some of them – mostly the English brand – were dedicated to enlightening the culturally disadvantaged brown-skinned little colonials like me. Mr Foote and Father Brown were fountains of knowledge to sip from, if only I were thirsty. Others tried to outdo the Brits, like Mr Blackett, the Latin Master who demanded even higher standards than the UK norms. And then there were the local teachers, who existed – some of them – just to fill gaps in the curriculum. Mr Barnes, my Mathematics teacher, was one of these. But I will come back to him.

I couldn't find any quick solutions – ideas about a career took years to piece together. First, I had to acquire perspective on the school curriculum. The British used the word "form" to describe a school year, or class. The basic secondary school programme was five years. The system assumed a pupil would progress from the First Form at age eleven to the Fifth Form at age fifteen, when he could sit his School Certificate exams. That was the theory, but there were many possible detours. To begin with, promotion from one form to another was far from automatic; some boys stayed three years at the same level. Next, the Antigua Grammar School invented "A" and "B" Forms, as in 4A and 4B, 5A and 5B. The B Form in my school was usually a sidetrack, where the school could park unwelcome guests for a year. Pupils who reached 5A (not all did, by any means) were, in practice, aged at least sixteen, sometimes even eighteen. Having entered the school a year early, I could in theory reach 5A at fourteen. The same subjects were studied in each form, with increasing depth as we approached the Fifth. Thus, I struggled up many tedious subject ladders. There was a Sixth Form after the Fifth Form that students would consider essential today, but in the 1950s it was not, and the School Certificate was a school-leaving exam for many.

The subject I liked more than any other was English, so I conjugated "literature" with "career". It seemed easy. In First Form, we had the same theme to write on after each vacation: "My Holidays". Since the English teacher couldn't be bothered to change his exercise, I followed his lead – as did most of the class – and submitted the same essay each time, with minor changes. As I remember, this is what it looked like after a few cycles:

My Holidays
Being on holiday doesn't prevent you from getting attacked.

"Your money or your life!" shouted the masked man. But no sooner were the words out of his mouth than I put my foot in it. He didn't take kindly to this treatment and tried to bite. Luckily for me, I was wearing leather shoes, so the bite was less than his bark and worse for his shaky teeth than for me. In case you were wondering, his mask only covered his eyes, leaving easy access to his mouth.

"I'll teach you a lesson!" he shouted (again), because I think he only knew how to shout and could not talk politely. But since this was my vacation and I didn't need any more lessons until the next term, I suggested he shut up and go away, taking his big shiny gun with him.

"You talk too much – you are BEGINNING to make me cross – but this will be THE END of you!" he gurgled while chewing my shoe.

I wasn't happy about it, but since I have run out of ink, I thought I should obey.
THE END

From Second Form onwards, however, Father Brown taught this subject, and he was more demanding. He would read the class a story and then ask us to write an essay on that subject for homework. Next English period, the best essays would be read aloud; I got used to hearing my voice. He never repeated a subject, but was inclined to excessively dull themes such as, "A Day on the Beach", or "My Parents", or "Our Home". I made up my mind that whatever the assigned title, my essays would turn into adventure stories. It was my interior landscape. Often, I could use ideas or names from my favourite books. For instance, I hoped one day I would be in a Sax Rohmer adventure:

My Best Friend
One moonlit evening, in company with my best friend Nayland Smith, we saw a gang of masked men scaling the front wall of a Caribbean mansion. The concrete had bits of broken bottle stuck in it but the robbers had shinned up the nearby coconut trees and thrown crocus bags over the glass. Quietly, we circled round to the back gate, which was strangely open. Creeping through the hibiscus flowers, we soon found the leader. He was standing calmly in front of a low, dark house, waiting for his robber crew. He watched his henchmen climbing laboriously over the wall grabbing coconuts on the way and he puffed his pipe contentedly. As he turned his yellow face our way, I saw green eyes like daggers in the dark. It was Fu Manchu.

"You again," he hissed as Nayland and I drew our pistols.

"Don't move!" I ordered.

But as we approached, a robber screamed – he had cut his hand on the jagged glass. A dog began to bark and all the hens flew out of the low house that was their coop with an enormous squawking noise. Never losing his legendary calm, Fu Manchu remarked in a barely audible voice, "No eggs for my omelette tonight, then," before vanishing around a corner.

In the ensuing scuffle, I suffered no injuries but Nayland was cut above his left eye; sometimes it didn't pay to be my friend. We arrested eleven thieves with twenty-one coconuts. The thief with the injured hand had dropped a nut. But there was no trace of the yellow mastermind.

I got top marks for these stories, nine out of ten, or even ten if the handwriting was good enough, which compensated for some deficiencies in my English grammar exercises. Like many children who read a great deal, I thought it pointless – even sacrilegious – to formalise sentence structure. Spelling could be amusing though, and I applied myself to it. My father had told me never to encounter a new word without fighting it, dissecting it, and storing its body parts in a mental glass cabinet.

One day, Father Brown explained rhyming to us. He asked us to compose our first four-line poem. I wrote:

Blue was the sky
As I came by.
Green was the grass
As I sat on my arse.

The effect was more than I had expected. The class broke into loud guffaws, and Father Brown had to wait for silence.

"Well, Christopher, I'm not sure whether to congratulate you or to give you a detention. It all depends on how you spell the last word in your poem."

He paused.

I looked at what I had written and hurriedly replaced "arse" with "ass".

Father Brown smiled. "Well done, then. You can see how important the exact spelling is."

I took my stories home to St. Kitts during the vacations, and my parents would sometimes read them with interest. I began to feel more confident about the career thing. Then, in my fourth year of essay writing, Father Brown changed his approach to my disadvantage. I was thirteen, and the following year would have to sit my Cambridge School Certificate exams. If you failed the English Language exam, you would fail the entire School Certificate, however brilliant the other grades were. At the beginning of the year, he gave us an essay title, "How to open a tin of sardines".

I wrote:

How to Open a Tin of Sardines (1)
I opened the tin of sardines by stamping on it. Just at that moment, the door opened too, and a burly detective walked in.
"Where were you last night?" he asked...

I expected my story to be approved, but to my horror, I was graded zero out of ten. Father Brown read my essay out to the class as a counterexample.

"It's time to move on, Christopher," he said. "You can't always write stories. I want a factual description of opening the tin, and until you can do that, stories are forbidden. All of you will rewrite this essay for the next class."

Rising heroically to the task, my new essay read:

How to Open a Tin of Sardines (2)
First, you take a knife. Then you stick the knife into the tin. You push and push until it cuts the tin. Then you take out the sardines and eat them...

I couldn't think of anything else to say. There was absolutely nothing exciting about a tin of sardines, and how did one open the stupid thing anyway? This second essay earned me three out of ten, one of the worst marks in the class. I was asked to write it a third time, starting with, *"First you find a can opener. Then you place the tin of sardines on a table, right way up."* With this encouragement, I did a little better, eventually scoring five. I wondered why people bothered to eat sardines anyway, since it seemed so difficult to get at them. That whole year, Father Brown mercilessly condemned me to writing factual essays. I was never able to score higher than six. The golden age of stories was over. I began to get the idea that – if done "properly" – writing could be extremely boring.

From time to time, I thought in a more abstract way about writing and what fun it would be to tell stories again. Real stories. To be a writer of books. To keep people up at night and have them laughing at my jokes. There was not much coherence in these thoughts, just bits and pieces, with little that could be dignified as analysis or planning. Yet, I was making up my mind.

No one in my family was a writer. My father was a lawyer. Nothing wrong in that, I supposed. But not a writer, though he seemed proud of his writing. He was always scribbling with his pen, always correcting my pronunciation, but none of it was stories, nothing fun to read. My mother did some journalism – but that wasn't *real* writing. Who wants to read newspapers? Especially with all the nasty comments they made about my father. And anyway, look at all the trouble my mother got into with her articles for the *Trinidad Guardian*! How could she avoid writing about my father? He was always in the news because of his job at the Sugar Association. Isn't it a wife's duty to defend her husband if people say bad things about him? It got worse and worse when there were strikes and political meetings in St. Kitts. Afterwards, people said she wasn't impartial, and the worst part was that the Guardian wouldn't take her articles any more. I never understood why she couldn't say what she wanted. She was right to give it up.

My Uncle Jack wasn't a writer either. I wasn't sure what he did, since the failed Nevis project. He once told me he had invented a new type of floor tiling for barefoot people in public buildings – just like heaven, it was good for their soles. My Aunt Dorothy was married to a judge in Trinidad and was busy raising my obstreperous cousins. No writing from that part of the world. Why didn't my grandfather write books? Maybe God reserved all his energy for sermons. Or maybe all the fun stories were about sinners and their sins. Maybe they liked their sins and he wasn't allowed to say that. Anyway, my doctor, my teachers, my friends, none of them had ever written a book. Not even Lloyd, Rosemary's father. He knew a lot about books and things, just like my father. He was always lending me stuff to read, and sometimes I liked it. I could imagine him writing a book. But he never had, as far as I knew, excepting some historical stuff. In fact, no one in the whole of St. Kitts or Antigua had ever written a book, as far as I knew, at least not a book I would like to read.

So, this must be the secret. Books couldn't be written in the Caribbean, only in far away places like England by Shakespeare or Sax Rohmer. Maybe it was the heat. People got tired and their heads swelled and their blood clotted in the heat. Many times, I didn't feel like doing my homework. You needed cold and snow to write, like they had in England. I couldn't be a writer. Not without winter.

Anyway, maybe it wasn't so great to be a writer. You never heard of writers becoming rich or being elected President or King. Politicians, doctors, lawyers, estate owners, and tourists, all of them were allowed to be rich, but not writers.

Perhaps all the real writers were dead – William Shakespeare, G.A. Henty, Rider Haggard, Zane Grey, and so on. I couldn't think of any living writers, except Dennis Wheatley and Isaac Asimov – my fantasy hideaways from the real world.

There was not much point trying to be a writer. All the interesting books had already been written. The only things left to write were more essays on opening sardine tins. Not my thing, really. But then, what could I do to become successful if writing was not a viable career? The tentative connection between English and my future was broken and my father's expectations continued to gnaw painfully at me.

Languages other than English were out. I wondered what practical use they could possibly have in an English-speaking world. I couldn't imagine myself reading or talking another language when there was so much to read and talk about in English. At least with Latin, things were clear. Latin was dead, the original Romans too, and it served no purpose. It was a purely artificial exercise. We had to succeed in Latin to gain entrance to certain old and distinguished British universities. Fortunately, Father Brown and Mr Blackett were excellent teachers. Encouraged by the carrot of matriculation, I agreed to suffer in Latin.

As for French and Spanish, I wasn't convinced people actually spoke these strange tongues, whatever my schoolmasters pretended. We had no contacts with Spanish-speaking Cuba, even less with nearby French-speaking Guadeloupe. The British school system in the 1950s taught us the Geography and History of Britain and of its Empire. We spent those formative years without learning anything of importance about our own region, the Caribbean.

I decided to drop French as soon as I could, and never – not for an instant – could I have imagined that I would spend most of my adult life working in France, nor that I would have to learn Spanish in Peru. But what, then, about my career? I decided to look at other avenues, none involving foreign languages.

"History is bunk," said Henry Ford, the designer of the first model T car, though for a boy who liked writing, this subject could have been a useful career platform. I didn't take to history, and from ten to fourteen, I didn't know why: it just seemed boring. Perhaps the bloody and tortured past of my own region would have gripped my attention. But why should I care about 1066?

Geography had the same distorted focus as History. At most, we were taught European and British Empire geography, not Caribbean geography.

At university, later on, I wondered whether all this was manipulation politics – the creation of an indigenous elite faithful to Britain, or cultural blindness – assuming that what was good for English children was good for us all.

Whatever the politics behind it, English history and geography as taught to us in Antigua was dull and unappetising. I couldn't digest it. When I was little my mother often said, "Eat up the food on your plate, Chris. Think of the millions of poor Africans and Asians starving whereas you have something."

I should have known it was the same way with education. But I stubbornly insisted on not eating unpalatable fare. Spinach might be all right for Popeye, but for me it was green muck. Thus, one day I would come to regret the little importance I gave to British history and geography.

The long and short of it was nothing I learned in History or Geography seemed to have any bearing on a career. I would not realise until much later that this ruled out all paths to a vocation in economics or politics. So, having lost my past, where could I find a future?

During my first three years in Antigua, I was neither clever at, nor interested by, Mathematics. Not until the Fourth form, at least. When I was thirteen, Mr Barnes was my Mathematics teacher. A popular fellow – once Captain of the school cricket team – he had never passed his own Mathematics Higher School Certificate. We nicknamed him "Stink Bowler". I wasn't sure whether the "stink" was due to his dangerous bouncers or prolific sweating. I learned Arithmetic reasonably well, getting most of my operations right – additions, subtractions, and multiplications, though not divisions – but others in the class were quicker than I was. When we started Geometry, it was mainly drawing, and I was clumsy. My circles were faintly egg-shaped and my parallel lines would meet in a friendly manner long before infinity. I didn't shine, although Mr Barnes seemed to take notice of me when I asked him how to draw a wrong-angled triangle instead of a right one. In Form 4A we started on Algebra. It didn't make much sense to me and I did badly on the tests. We spent weeks on factorisation and then Stink Bowler started us on equations.

"X is the unknown," he said.

I found this disturbing. If something was unknown, why didn't he explain it to us? How could he give us something unknown and expect us to do anything with it? Weren't teachers there to tell us about the *known* before confusing us with the unknown? Stinky wrote on the blackboard. A bewildering variety of "X" symbols and numbers

177

appeared on either side of an equals sign. This was an equation, he said. If both sides were equal, what more could one ask, I wondered. Thus, I got nowhere. Yet, our teacher thought somehow we should be able to *find* the value of the unknown he hadn't shown us. It would pop out of a hat like "X = 5". I had no idea how it got there.

"To move up to Form 5A next year, you must pass in Mathematics," he said, "There's no point going too fast. If you don't understand, a year in Form 5B will do you good."

The night before my qualifying Algebra exam, I picked up my work on equations and tried to find a path through my mental fog. I stared my dog-eared textbook in the snout.

"7X = 14," I read, "and therefore X = 2". I wondered where the author had found the two since it was supposed to be unknown. To get 2 from 7 you would have to subtract 5; there was no 5 apparent. To get 2 from 14 you would have to subtract 12; again, no 12 was available. Anyway, it was better to work with the 7 because the 14 was much bigger - twice as big. I felt a small click. If I divided 14 by 7, I got 2! I had discovered an Unknown. It could be done. The Unknown is cleverly hidden, but I could find it by dividing, multiplying, adding, or subtracting. Or all of them, I supposed. Like the bible: do unto others (the right hand, or Unknown side) as you would wish them to do unto you (the left, or Known side). Excited, I worked out several sample equations that had puzzled me before and went to bed dreaming of a horseback hunt for the Unknown Beast. The next day I found the exam easy.

"Your results were poor – only a few of you scored over 50%," said Stink Bowler to my class. "You don't seem to understand equations. But I had a pleasant surprise. One boy reached 85%. He has failed every previous test, but here in the final Algebra exam he got the top mark. How did you do it, Vanier?"

At the mention of my name, I jumped, "It was the equations, Sir…" and I started to explain about the Unknown.

Mr Barnes interrupted, "You were determined to move up to Form 5A, right?"

"Yes, Sir," I admitted.

"And you finally remembered my lessons?"

I gave up on explaining that even his Algebra could be interesting when an Adventurer captured the mysterious Unknowns.

Unfortunately, despite the pleasant discovery that Mathematics was not beyond my reach, I had never heard of anyone from St. Kitts being employed as a Mathematician. It did not seem to qualify as a career. With so many subjects ruled out, my chances of finding an interesting career were getting smaller and smaller.

Instead of "career", I might have thought, "purpose": what was my purpose in life, and how could I achieve it? But the hard and immediate nature of the Caribbean sunshine forbade putting the question like that. Better to stay in the material here-and-now than to open the gates to existential uncertainty.

I had once gone off track. At thirteen, I read that an unconscious part of me called the brain stem controlled my involuntary bodily activities like breathing, heart contractions, and vomiting. But we could take over some of these functions if we wished, I read. So, I wished, and began, first to notice, then to be obsessed by, the movement of my lungs. I panicked on discovering I could not surrender this usurped power to whatever-it-was that did it normally. Would I spend the rest of my life whistling air up and down my throat? And what if my rebellious alter ego didn't *want* to take back this tedious but frightening task of breathing? If I stopped, that would be the end of me, dead from suffocation. Maybe the whole purpose of life was to do things and not think about them – what a pity I couldn't let well enough alone. Only the thought of my next meal was strong enough to pull me out of paralysis.

One foggy evening in 1953, I imagine an obscure Under-Under-Secretary for Colonial development in the British West Indies, labouring late in his Westminster office.

"Antigua, hmm, sugar production is failing more and more. What will they live on?" he said to himself, as he riffled through a pile of badly typed reports. He paused on the Education Report. During the previous year, 20 young Antiguans had sat their Cambridge School Certificate examinations; only 9 had passed in 5 subjects, gaining the full certificate, although 3 had achieved 7 or 8 subjects.

"Not promising," he muttered, "we must do something to help." Then he noticed an even more distressing statistic. "What, Physics and Chemistry exams are not even offered on the island?"

He puffed on his pipe and reflected, "This won't do; we can't have the successful few all studying Law and becoming future politicians and thorns in our side. Let's give them some Science to get their teeth into."

In a few seconds, insignificant statistics like me had their futures decided. He wrote a letter to the Governor of Antigua and the Chief Education Officer recommending a new Science curriculum in the local Grammar School. Britain would help by sending out teachers and paying part of their salary for the next five years.

"It shouldn't cost us too much," he thought, "lots of our people will jump at the chance of a few years in the sun. They don't know about the mosquitoes."

Thus it was that from First Form to Third Form the school had offered me no science subjects, excepting Botany, but near the end of the year in Third, we were given the option of studying Physics and Chemistry in the Fourth. The new subjects wouldn't fit into the weekly schedule, so we had to decide whether to take Botany and Geography or Physics and Chemistry. The subjects we dropped would be lost forever; there was no possibility of catching up later.

My parents let me decide, although I could sense my father preferred the science subjects. For me, Geography was no loss. It consisted of memorising lists of countries and their capitals, names of mountains, rivers, streams, puddles, and politicians. These last were constantly being liquidated, causing me the trouble of learning new names. I regretted Botany a lot more; it was my only exposure to drawing flowers. We were allowed to colour them and label each part. I had already started a secret project of planting beans in the school garden to see if they grew the way the book said. What tipped the balance in favour of Physics and Chemistry was the name of the teacher: Mrs Imbert.

Mrs Imbert! We had never had a female teacher before, there in arid Antigua. Being a Grammar School for boys didn't exclude that possibility, but the female teachers all had a marked preference for the Antigua Girls' High School. This segregation was another British characteristic. A little over half the class decided, like me, that the combination of new subjects and a female teacher was unbeatable. Too bad for Botany and Geography.

Physics was all about electricity, heat, and light. It seemed like fun (at least, the electricity part) but unfortunately, the British had forgotten to send out the equipment for experiments in this subject. With no amps or volts, I would have to wait a while before trying to electrocute anyone. On the other hand, crates of glass and many mysterious bottles were jostled into the Chemistry Lab.

Mrs Imbert was rewardingly pretty, though, especially her hips. It was a pity the vicious Caribbean sunlight made her sensitive skin erupt in red splotches. These splotches were my first hint that Chemistry had a lot to do with colour. Within the periodic table, I found that the names of the elements had panache: copper, tin, lead, zinc, iron, sulphur … And it was magical the way mineral salts could change from red to blue to colourless. Maybe there was more magic that could change skin colours too? I imagined how much prettier Mrs Imbert would look without her red marks. Perhaps I could select a few of my friends and turn us all white with a potion from a test tube. Or what fun it would be to make Mr Foote, the English Headmaster, as black as Mr Barnes, our Antiguan Sports Master. Would we behave the same way if our colour were changed?

Acids fascinated me. If you stuck your finger in a dish of concentrated sulphuric, nitric, or hydrochloric acid, it would eat your flesh down to the bone. If you drank a cup of acid, it would mean agonising death.

"That's it," I thought, "the real stuff of life."

But close encounters with vitriol were deferred to the next year and we moved on to bases. The name was not promising. Base: ignoble, shameful, pedestrian, dull. For our first experiment, Mrs Imbert opened a bottle filled with grey-brown chunks.

"Pure sodium is white," she said, "my samples are a bit old. We will prepare several lumps and dissolve them in water, making a strong base, sodium hydroxide. Be careful to cut the lumps up small. I need three volunteers."

I was not lucky enough to be chosen, so I watched while the first pea-sized lump was dropped gingerly into a bowl of water. The second volunteer grabbed a much bigger lump of sodium. The pea floated on the water, fizzing gently. We moved closer to look at it. With a flash and a popping noise, it disappeared in a cloud of smoke. The next boy jumped and dropped the chunk he was working on into the bowl – it must have been the size of a large marble. Mrs Imbert, whose face had previously been red-splotched, turned a delicate white, just the way I had imagined she should look.

"Out!" she cried. "Everyone, outside! At once!"

Before we could reach the door, the sodium bowl detonated, and the lab filled with the thunder and lightening of Olympus. I stumbled in joy, and fell down. The class ran and shouted until it was clear that no one had been injured. Nothing so exciting had ever happened to me in a classroom before.

It was not just the noise and smoke. I sensed you could tinker with chemicals and create new substances, change the order of things, the tissue of life itself. No more insipid, paper subjects: Chemistry was the casting of spells and the making of explosions. I would learn how to blow up the walls of my undersized Caribbean world, to fashion another, more attractive one.

At this moment, on the floor, my fate was sealed: I would be a Chemist.

Part 3: Mischief (Antigua, 1953-1956)

The Tamarind Rod

In parallel with all my topsy-turvy thinking about getting a purpose in life, there were darker happenings involving mischief and misunderstandings, and, in particular, a long struggle with the punishment system.

When I entered the Antigua Grammar School as a boarder at age nine, I had never been physically chastised by my parents, and had little knowledge of British school discipline (Enid Blyton's five heroes never mentioned caning), so I displayed a sort of bravado. Unfortunately for me, caning was universal in Caribbean schools. Even girls were caned – and still are in Barbados and Antigua. Evidently, bleeding raises the stakes. But expert caners do not break the victim's skin. The real trauma is inside. How does one live with brutality? Or without it? Most of the pupils in my school had been caned at one time or another, and several were caned on a weekly basis. Those of us who *hadn't* suffered were sometimes portrayed as either spineless or teacher's pets.

But in 1952, I ignored my destiny. From the start, when the school was built in 1884, boys were beaten in proper British style. If you broke the rules and were caught, you would be flogged. Boarders had more than the school authority to contend with – there was fighting among us and we were subjugated by the vicious network of seniors – but school discipline was the ultimate power in our lives. As one climbed up the disobedience ladder, several minor punishments could be meted out by the teachers – detentions, writing lines, expulsion from a class – before things culminated in a visit to the Headmaster's Office. The lesser punishments didn't bother me. I only respected the menace of caning, the real coinage of school discipline.

Detention after school had its positive side – this would spare me from having to participate in school sports, which I disliked.

Writing lines was a commercial operation. Quite regularly, my classmates and I would have to do penance with one hundred lines, featuring classical themes such as: "I must pay attention"; "I must not flick ink on other pupils"; "I must not put glue on chairs"; or "I must not make rude noises in class". Some of us would write lines for others, certain that the Master wouldn't bother to check the handwriting. I invented the Five-Pen Line Writer, which consisted of strapping five pens together so they could work simultaneously and produce five copies of the prescribed sentence in one go. Too many pens made the contraption unstable, but with five, I could write pages of lines quickly, and this earned me some favours from my friends.

As for being sent outside, the dissuasive effect of missing a class was very low.

Only the threat of caning was truly respected. As a new boy, I was initially untouched by the corporal punishment system, and the charmed life I led in my first year convinced me I was immune from caning.

One Friday in my second year, however, I pushed my luck too far. I'd managed to get a place in the back corner of the classroom, and the subject was Geography. The Master was busy up front correcting a pile of our clumsy maps of the Atlantic Ocean and had taken his eye off the class. There were twenty of us, each barricaded behind an old wooden desk, with a bottle of black ink and a thirsty fountain pen waiting for action that was slow in coming. I exchanged jokes with my neighbours in the back row, sharp-nosed Francis from Antigua and moon-faced Jones, and we began chuckling. To get the full flavour we told jokes in our Caribbean dialect. The English language could be spiced up as needed – we just added a dose of "pidgin". Most, but not all of my friends could shift the full gamut from an unrecognisable (to a European) vernacular to (almost) proper English, as the occasion required.

"A Kittitian live next to an Antiguan," I started.

"I don't like this story already," Francis said, sticking out his tongue at me.

"The St. Kitts man had a mango tree. Every day, he watch them mangoes get ripe and sweet. This day, the biggest, the juiciest mango done ripen, but it fall off in the neighbour's yard.

'That's mine,' said the Antiguan as he pick it up to eat.

'Gimme back me mango,' the St. Kitts man says.

'Any thing fall in me yard is mine,' says Mister Antigua.

'You wrong in you head! Is me tree the mango come from.'

'Then you tree trespass in me yard.'

'Tell you now, we going settle this St. Kitts way.'

'How you mean?'

'First, I kick you in the kook-a-looks; then we see how long you stay on the ground. Then, you kick me, an you watch me get up. Whoever quickest get the mango. OK?' "

"I know who going win!" Francis said, and tapped his knuckles on his brown boots.

"The St. Kitts man go and put on he big boots with plenty metal. He run fast, fast and kick the Antiguan right in he balls. Man went down moaning and don't stop crying for forty minutes."

"Then what?"

"Antiguan get up and ask for he turn. He really want kick back.

183

"But St. Kitts man say, 'I change me mind – you can keep the mango, my friend,' and he *gone*!"

Chortles and cackles rippled back and forth.

"You know, if we can't stop, this could become a laughing fit," I said to my neighbour.

Meanwhile, our Geography teacher was telling those nearest to him how fortunate it was the Gulf Stream from the Caribbean warmed up Britain in the winter and cooled it in the summer.

"My turn," said Francis. None of us cared about the temperature in Britain. The next story was about a donkey that could answer questions.

Then I told the story of the man who dug holes just to have them filled in, and Jones told the funeral story where the corpse woke up in the middle of the burial ceremony, and the guffaws grew out of control. We delighted in primitive, violent jokes, and in jokes that had no ending – complete non-sequiturs. It was a way of making fun of adults who thought a joke had to have a point. It was a way of domesticating the violence directed at us.

Without much trying, there it was. We couldn't stop laughing. Hysterical: three of us giggling like idiots.

At this point, the noise level exceeded simple background confusion to become an incipient revolution. The Geography Master became aware of us and demanded quiet. The Gulf Stream had its prerogatives. But we were uncontrollable. To his credit, the Master was not bloodthirsty, and gave us ample leeway.

"All right, you in the back, I've warned you to be quiet.

"Stop the stupidness right now!

"Vanier, Jones, and Francis, stop this instant."

After three warnings, our Master lost his patience and sent us all outside. We sat carefully on the grass to avoid stones or prickles, but our hysteric merriment didn't cease – in fact, we made sure our classmates inside could still hear us laughing. We were so convulsed we didn't hear the Master say, "This has gone too far. The Headmaster will have to deal with you."

Two authorities in the school had the right to cane: the Headmaster and the boarding school Housemaster. Being called to the Office of one of these vested powers after a class "incident" almost certainly meant a caning. The official motive and the precise number of strokes were all that remained to be determined. You had to be told why you were going to be beaten, and given a chance to say your piece. This system was passed on to all of Britain's colonies as a direct legacy of its own schools, where caning was authorised until 1997. In 1953, when I first got the lash, no one doubted its suitability as a disciplinary tool. Which brings us to the use of the tamarind rod.

Good British schools abandoned their primitive birch rods long ago, and imported rattan canes from East Asia. Rattan hurts more than birch, and in expert hands leaves less collateral damage – like precision bombing. Rattan canes make it possible to beat boys with their trousers on and still deliver an awesome payload. The whippiness of the wood is what counts. In the Caribbean, our tamarind rod equivalent has the same qualities as rattan, or better: a hard wood, thin, and swishy. In addition, tamarind canes have several gentle curves and bumps to individualise the welts they leave, like the rifling on a gun barrel marks the personality of a bullet. And since tamarind canes were free, the Headmaster and the Housemaster each had a fine collection of varying weights and lengths.

One special tamarind tree in Antigua was called the "Bethesda Tamarind Tree". In 1952, the year I arrived, the sugar cane cutters broke the back of the planters' organisation after a long strike, right under this tree. It was their last big strike. The workers forced the planters to pay punitive salary raises and the Antiguan sugar industry eventually went bust. There is a price to pay for rebellion.

The Geography Master told us to go to the Headmaster's Office after lunch. It meant the three of us would be sentenced and caned. By then, we had stopped laughing. I wished the Headmaster would get it over at once, but he preferred to have a quiet meal first. To get his strength up, I supposed, and leave his victims-to-be the time to meditate on their wrongdoings. I was the only boarder involved. As I sat down to my own lunch in the Dining Room, it soon got around the table that I was coming up for my first caning.

Being caned on the bottom is not necessarily a big deal. It depends on how you take it. Today in Europe or America, you may be appalled at the idea of teachers enthusiastically beating their pupils into obedience. But in the islands, even now, it is believed there is no gain without pain. And until a decade or two ago, a pupil in Britain was almost as likely to be flogged as one in the Caribbean. Few questioned the appropriateness or morality of corporal punishment.

The symbol of caning was the tamarind tree. Whipping and tamarinds have spiced up human lives for hundreds of years. The brown pulp of the tamarind fruit in one's mouth is violent – acidic – stinging – faintly sweet – making you crave for more until your teeth are on edge. The springy wood excels in making switches for unruly children.

Much advice was forthcoming while I fiddled with my food and waited for my appointment with justice.

"Did you say your parents never spanked you? This will make up for the lost time!"

Some things are better lost, I thought.

"Whatever you do, don't jump. He might miss your bottom and hit you somewhere else."

"You may be lucky. It's your first time. He makes the tougher boys take off their trousers to get lashed on their bare buttocks."

"Melford's weal took weeks to heal."

"I wonder how many strokes you'll get?"

"Wear loose trousers and don't bend over more than you have to. If the cloth is tight against your bum, you'll feel it more."

"Best to be first – he's just warming up and will be more careful."

"Best to be last – he gets tired after caning a dozen."

"Next time, try wearing two pairs of trousers. It might not be noticed. But don't put paper into your back pocket – it changes the sound of the lash and you'll get extra strokes."

It was almost a relief when I got up from the table and approached the nearby Headmaster's Office. I listened in dismay to the whack-whacking noises percolating through the thick doors.

"Next!"

Like a duck waddling towards a cook pot, I entered and found the Headmaster waiting – tall, thin, and supple. He had a balding pink forehead and ears that stuck out alarmingly, filled with big tufts of white, nesting hair. A brown tamarind rod was perched like a bird of prey on his desk.

"I am going to cane you for rowdiness and disobedience. Anything to say for yourself?"

"I just couldn't stop laughing, Sir."

"Well, I have a cure for that. Bend over."

I gripped the top of the wooden chair and inclined my back at the recommended angle. I focused uniquely on my tender patch of rump skin and all the vibrant nerve endings underneath. The sensation was violent – acidic – stinging. Two strokes, that first time.

"I don't want to see you in here again."

Neither does my backside, I thought. But I was wrong, of course: defiance was too sweet.

Red and sobbing, I pushed open the door of the Headmaster's office and staggered down the stairs to hide. That evening at bath time, I showed off the damage to my dorm mates. There were two parallel red welts – he had *not* struck the same place twice. My skin was unbroken. It felt sore for days and eventually turned blue, then yellow. Had I been blacker, there would have been less to exhibit. I was now one of the boys, whether I liked it or not, for a first caning does not reform you – it simply sets you up for others. Before this caning, my constraints had been founded on myth. What did it mean to be beaten? How did it feel? The rumours were terrible, but the truth was almost a relief. Past the initiation, my knowledge of pain became concrete, though I suspected there was worse to come. I knew it wouldn't kill me. My caners were experts, and in their precise hands there was much less bodily risk than having my tonsils or appendix removed by a Caribbean surgeon.

I *tried* to avoid the tamarind rod, but that was not the end of it. It seemed to me sometimes things just went wrong and I was blamed for them. I dropped a rock on the shin of a classmate called Luke and it cut him. We were just playing, but because of the blood, Luke reported it. Two strokes. Half the class failed a simple Latin test from Mr Blackett, I among them. I was awarded another two strokes for poor performance. There was lovely rowdiness in the classroom. The Master asked us to identify the culprits. No one squealed, and my entire class received a further two strokes for loyalty. These incidents occurred before the middle of my third year, and I was actually doing quite well, four tamarind rod canings being less than the average. I thought mainly of how to escape capture, not of rights or wrongs. All authority began to seem suspicious to me: the school, the church, and my parents. I resolved for the second time that I would never, ever, to do military service. I was the youngest in my class and acquired a reputation for insolence. My luck depended on which Master I offended.

I feared Mr Blackett the most, so, of course, he was the one with whom I got in trouble. He was a rotund, irascible, Latin teacher, the same brown Barbadian who had had us caned for poor homework. Short, almost a dwarf, he had a close-cropped black-going-grey stubble of hair. His small stature was contradicted by a booming voice that made me think he must have been a giant in another life, or an ogre. Everyone said he was very clever because not only had he gone to University for a B.A., but also he had passed a Master of Arts degree. Few of our Antiguan teachers had gone to University at all. Later on in life, he would become Dr Blackett. It was a mystery to me at the time that Mr Blackett had buried himself in Antigua instead of teaching in the reputedly superior schools of Barbados he often mentioned. Maybe he had a woman here, we thought – but who could love a tyrant like that? What made him forbidding was not so much his strict class discipline – no one talked in his classes – but his intolerance of errors. He was a hard marker and gave us no credit for trying. He would organise collective canings, as he had done with us, for classes that weren't applying themselves. I didn't understand this. I thought a bad mark was punishment enough. But he found it somehow insulting – even criminal – not to do better. A weird man, I thought.

Being a Senior Master, he would lunch at the Headmaster's table in our Dining Room. One day, I was halfway through my first course when he walked in, late. I looked up and before I had time to stop them, some toadish words flew out of my mouth.

"Excuse me."

And then, "Sir."

The three little words hopped around.

He should apologise for his lateness.

I wondered afterwards why I should have said something so foolish, and why the whole room should have heard me, and how unfair it was to assume I was teaching him manners. But there was nothing to be done. I had insulted him. Since it happened in the Dining Room, it was the duty of my Housemaster to take action. Mr Blackett stopped and stared, first at me and then at Father Brown, until the latter broke the silence.

"Christopher, that's very rude. Leave the table at once and wait in my office. I'm sorry about this lapse, Mr Blackett."

By "waiting in his office", he meant caning, of course. Four strokes this time. I think Father Brown didn't care for Mr Blackett that much, which only made him more diligent. I respected Father Brown, and the whole thing was over before I had time to feel afraid. Before this, the Housemaster had never caned me – I trusted him – but these lashes in his office shattered the peace. He hit me standing up, not bending over, as if he wanted to get it over with as soon as possible. I clenched my fists and cried, or rather I howled, not only because it was twice as much as usual but also because I felt it was so unfair. I hadn't meant to insult Mr Blackett – my words had slipped out.

There was no logic to my feelings – my friends would have agreed I had been rude and deserved a bit of hellfire – but I was discovering that a wounded pride has needs of its own that defy logic.

As I was about to leave his office, Father Brown said to me, "Clean up and come back to see me in twenty minutes time."

Twenty minutes after the caning, I was still red in the face and smarting on my butt. The tears had gone, though.

"Now that you have been punished, Christopher, I want you to do something more. Mr Blackett is a proud and awkward man, and won't forgive you just like that. Not even after four strokes. I suggest you go to his office, tell him you've been caned, and apologise for your rudeness."

I thought he must know best.

I trudged along the corridors to Mr Blackett's office. I decided I didn't much like the idea of confronting him, but it had been an order. I would just as soon have seen him hanged by his stubby neck, but one more indignity might save me from future problems.

I walked back and forth in the corridor, trying to get my nerve up. After several minutes, I knocked on Mr Blackett's door.

"Come in," he barked. "Oh, it's you. What brings you here, Vanier? Have you seen Father Brown yet?"

I noted the hostile use of my family name. Mr Blackett's office was Spartan, void of loose objects, with the exception of two books on his desk so thick and heavy I suspected he used them for weightlifting.

"Yes, Sir, I've been to Father Brown's office, and I've been caned for what I said."

"Then why are you here? I've no time for you." Mr Blackett did not believe in making unnecessary friends.

"I've come to apologise to you, Sir. I'm sorry for my remark. It just slipped out."

He shrugged his massive shoulders and glared at me from the top of his five foot two inches. "Just slipped out, eh? Now tell me the truth! Did Father Brown send you to apologise to me?"

I hesitated, and then decided I had no choice. "Yes, Sir, he did. He suggested I should make amends personally."

"I thought so! Then I can't accept your apology. Understand? You're just carrying out orders. Go away, I won't accept it."

I left his office perplexed. The door slammed behind me. I didn't apologise often, and this was the first time I had heard of someone refusing an apology. I took a dozen steps down the corridor and then stopped. I returned to Mr Blackett's office door and knocked again.

"Yes, who's there? What, you again?"

"I've come back, Sir, and you can see I'm on my own. I'd still like to offer you my apology. It's just me."

"Hmm. Clever are you? I'm still not sure I'll accept. Time will tell. Let's say I won't refuse your apology, this once. I advise you not to speak of this to anyone, above all Father Brown. Go now, and don't cross my path again."

I left Mr Blackett's office, burying this caning deep inside my steel box of injustices. I kept my silence, but the feeling the punishment was unmerited further undermined my respect for the school system. A dark seed grew inside me. If I could not get revenge against authorities like Mr Blackett, I had to find other outlets. This is the problem caning poses to its victim: a piece of your self-respect has been damaged, and to treat the wound a balm of bitterness is more comforting than a suture of strength.

The terms went by. I never got used to the canings, but Mr Blackett's incident was the only four-stroke one, so I rationalised them, once again. Canings were understandable: you broke the school rules – never mind who made them up – you were caught; you were caned. Punishments were like random bricks falling on my head that I should have known well enough to avoid. Rules, that was all – and not being caught.

Maybe the clash with Mr Blackett helped, because during the next six months of my twelfth year of existence (Third Form) I was not caned at all. Or maybe the resentment hidden inside me was just biding its time.

At any rate, during the execution of my next crime, I was highly aware of my choices if not their consequences, though this didn't stop disaster occurring.

It all began at a Saturday Fair in the town of St. John's, which we were allowed to visit on our own. At the Fair, we spent whatever pocket money we had on ice cream, cakes, and sweets – rare delicacies. A few coins went a long way, and we played the stands with games like Darts, Penny-in-the Bucket, and Pin-the-Tail-on-the-Donkey.

On my day of reckoning, Miguel and I had run around all afternoon, and when dusk fell we began working our way home. Night falls like a curtain on the islands, all year round between five-thirty and six-thirty. One moment the dying rays of the sun are painting glorious red, gold and green patterns in the sky, the next it's black on black everywhere, with crickets chirping their pleasure at the cool anonymity of darkness. In 1955, there were not many streetlights in towns like St. John's, and none at all on the back roads, so you had to be able to find your way around. As boarders, we should have had dinner at this time, but knowing we would stuff ourselves at the Fair, Father Brown had excused us from the meal.

The school was on Old Pelham Road, a mile or so from the centre of town, isolated from the nearest dwellings by a few hundred yards. Our route home from the Fair took us along a road bordered by a large concrete drainage canal. I left Miguel and jumped into the canal, quite dry at that time of year, and found myself hidden from the road. A sense of excitement swept over me at this sudden privacy, banishing all fatigue.

"Come and see, Miguel."

I felt like a valiant explorer in a new world. The bottom of the canal was flat, about four feet across with a gutter in the middle. It was five feet deep, but the sides were cambered so getting in and out was easy. Weeds and small bushes grew on the borders, reinforcing the feeling of a forgotten, hidden place. Miguel came down to share the adventure. We couldn't see far in the gloom, but the canal seemed to run parallel to the road. I figured we could take this route right up to the school without being seen, with just a swift crossing of the main road at the end of the journey. A solitary car went by us, lighting up our protective fringe of bushes.

We moved up the canal, creeping and leaping as our fancy took us. By now we were no longer explorers but pirates, and the occasional cars going by were treasure ships on the Spanish Main we had reason to spy on.

My feet kicked an occasional pebble and gravel from the last time the canal had flowed. As we played, it grew darker, but with a quarter moon to see by our secret path was clear enough. It came to me in a flash that the pebbles were musket balls and cannon shot, waiting for us to take the merchant ship's treasure as it lumbered by on its sea of tarmac.

"Let's throw stones at the cars," I said to Miguel. I couldn't see his face, but he sounded surprised.

"Do you really want to do that? Suppose they catch us?" he asked.

But with a strong wind in my sails, I wouldn't take "no" for an answer.

"Of course not," I said, "there's no way to catch us. We'll just run up the canal. Look, we're completely hidden."

"OK," he said, "but you go first."

We picked up handfuls of small pebbles. When the next set of car lights came by, I gave the order, "OK, now, fire!" and we both let fly.

But we hadn't estimated the car's speed properly, nor the distance from the canal to the road. Our stones fell futilely behind the vehicle.

"That's no good," I told Miguel. "We'll have to climb out to see the enemy."

Indeed, the extra risk of being seen was intoxicating, but I didn't say that to Miguel. We filled our pockets with missiles and hauled ourselves up the bank, checking behind for the reassurance that we could escape. For several minutes, no more cars came by, and Miguel began to get skittish.

"Look, maybe we should just go back to school. It's late and…" But right then, a car's lights rounded the bend at the bottom of the road, like sea spray in my eyes, and headed towards us.

Closer and closer it came. We were crouched on the bank, half in, half out, hearts thumping. Just before it got level with us, I gave the signal, "Now!"

I threw my stones and was astonished at the clanging noise they made on the car's metal. I had visions of ships fighting. I never knew whether Miguel scored a hit because I turned at once and dived into the darkness of the canal.

"Come on!" I yelled to my friend.

Screeching tyres, and the car halted. This was not what I had planned. Somehow, I had imagined they might not notice our pebbles, and drive on unconcerned, leaving us with piles of imaginary gold and silver. Why had the car stopped and now gone into reverse? I didn't want to find out and charged up the canal. A hundred yards farther towards safety, I realised Miguel was not following. I couldn't go back for him. I risked a glance over my shoulder and could just see the car with all its lights on, and what seemed like several people standing next to it. Heart somewhere near my shoes, I ran without stopping to the end of the canal. Had there been obstacles I would not have seen them. It occurred to me this pace would have broken all my past performances around the school track.

I crept across the road and made my way into the school building and dorm without being noticed. Where was Miguel? I felt I was in a vacuum, out of contact with the universe, the Lone Ranger waiting for Tonto. I took my shower and changed.

About a half an hour later, a car drove into the school grounds, and shortly after I could hear the voices of several people entering Father Brown's quarters. I forced myself to gather a great pile of homework, and was busy reading in the most remote corner possible of the dorm, when I received a summons to go to Father Brown's room myself. My feet had difficulty carrying me there because of the unusual lump of lead in my stomach.

"This is Christopher," said Father Brown to a serious-looking couple seated near to him. I spied Miguel standing up, silent and shivering as he did in hard times. The man was black and balding, in his 50s, with sparse grey stubbly hair. He was dressed formally in a spotless white shirt and dark trousers. His lips were set in a hard line. Through a large pair of glasses, he stared at me like a doctor examining a strange bug under his microscope. In fact, he *was* a doctor. His wife was buxom, brown-skinned, and somewhat younger, wearing a flowery and expensive dress; she appeared more anxious than critical. I guessed they must have been driving to a party or dinner.

"Christopher, meet Dr and Mrs Tompkins. Miguel tells us you were with him when he threw stones at their car. What do you have to say for yourself?"

So, Miguel had been caught, like a paralysed rabbit in the car lights. Why hadn't he escaped? And he had confessed. They had driven to their home and lectured him until he talked, I learned. We were in for the maximum. I didn't have time to regret that my accomplice was so inept – I was now honour-bound to take my share of the blame.

"It's true, Sir. I was there. But we were just playing at throwing stones. We didn't mean to do any harm." No point mentioning Dr Tompkins' car was a Spanish galleon in disguise and that we were acolytes of Sir Francis Drake.

"You're a ruffian and I'm ashamed of you, Christopher. At least you admit your guilt. Do you realise you might have injured someone?

"Now, you are fortunate about one thing. The car was not damaged, and Dr and Mrs Tompkins have agreed, in view of your age, not to press charges with the police. Of course, their garage will still have to check the car by daylight. But with luck your parents won't have to pay compensation."

This possibility – that my parents might be involved – hadn't occurred to me, and if I could have become a puddle on the floor at that moment, I would have liquefied.

"On the other hand, you and Miguel must now apologise to Dr and Mrs Tompkins."

"Very sorry, Sir. Very sorry, Dr and Mrs Tompkins. Won't do it ever again, promised. Very sorry indeed."

Dr Tompkins asked if he could speak to us.

"Boys, I want you to know, and especially Christopher, that we drove our daughter Darlene home first, because she was upset. She was in our car when you attacked it. She's younger than you are, Christopher, and some of your stones flew through the window next to her face. What would you have to say if you had struck her in the eye? I don't know why you did this. Father Brown tells me you come from good families. Before you do anything so crazy again, just think of one of *your* brothers or sisters getting stoned in the eye."

Miguel remained downcast, but I squirmed and said, "It was just a game, Sir."

Dr Tompkins brought his head close to mine, and said distinctly, "I know what you are thinking, that I'm severe and don't understand what it means to have fun. I can well believe you had some sort of game or dare going on in the dark with your dumb friend here." He glanced at Miguel. "Well, you're not alone in this world – my daughter plays games and likes fun, too. And you were about to spoil all that for her! You don't have a monopoly on games and dreams, young man!"

Shortly after this exchange, Dr and Mrs Tompkins gave us searching glances and left the school.

When the door had closed behind them, Father Brown turned to us again.

"One more thing," he said.

We looked at him expectantly.

"I am going to give you the caning of your lives. I've never been so embarrassed. Six of the best for you."

We knew the rules and had been waiting for a sentence. But six strokes? Miguel and I clustered together for comfort, and our eyes wandered to the corner where Father Brown kept his canes.

"No, don't look there. I'm not going to do it now," he said. "I'm so angry with you I might not be able to control myself. I will not chastise you in anger. It will be tomorrow at midday. You are dismissed."

We left his office and commiserated in the dorm. The news had circulated and the other boarders avoided us as if we were cursed. I didn't care any longer that Miguel had been caught and had given me away. He had betrayed me, but what did it matter – we were fellow-sufferers. That I might have been the cause of Miguel's plight didn't occur to me. It must have occurred to him, because he didn't take part in any further escapades during our time in Antigua. Sleep was not easy for either of us.

The next day, "six of the best" was not easy either. Only the tamarind tree laughed. I had never heard the expression, "This hurts me more than it hurts you," until Father Brown used it. I didn't believe him.

The tamarind rod seared me, right through my khaki trousers, like a branding iron on cattle hide. "One, two" – shame on you – "three, four" – your arse will be sore – "five, six" – tamarind licks. As I left his room, the parallel welts on my bottom were so sharp and angry that one could have played tic-tack-toe on them, had I allowed the engraving of the perpendiculars. This was not like my previous canings.

In the following days, I spent some time hating Father Brown. I didn't understand why he had made us wait for almost twenty-four hours. He said it was for him, because a Priest shouldn't strike a blow in anger. But it made it worse for us to have to wait like that, so maybe this was his real intention.

I also tried to dislike myself – never an easy task. It was the stone-in-the-eye-of-the-girl-who-might-have-been-my-sister idea that got to me, and the astonishing idea that other people had dreams, too. I remembered I had hurt my sister with stones several times during games in St. Kitts, and always regretted it intensely. I must not, could not, be the cause of civilian casualties. I sailed into the rough waters of guilt.

Maybe punishment was not only about being caught or not being caught. I thought I knew the school rules from the tips of my fingers to the skin of my bottom. But here was a new set of rules – an escapade mustn't leave me with the blameable feeling this car stoning had done. Caught or not caught, it seemed I had to consider the other parties. Even the buccaneers had been known to respect hostages and non-combatants.

I thought about the tamarind tree from which Father Brown had cut his rod. Maybe I could burn it down. Or seek atonement. Either way, I had to make a bargain with it. It was neither a question of bending to the nonsensical school rules, nor of forgiving the caners, but of common sense about other people's rights, and my responsibilities. No more attacking licensed Spanish galleons in the night; no more provoking choleric masters; no more idiotic laughing fits in class, to name a few. Self-respect was to be found elsewhere. I thanked the tamarind tree for cutting this small bit of wisdom into the most sensitive part of me.

Of Cane and Crabs

On vacation, free of the tyranny of school life and the increasing obligation to study, my goal was to find activities with a spice of danger. In St. Kitts, I had favourite places. During the 1950s, there was the old quarry near to our home – Harbour View – where I played hide-and-seek among the dark boulders and hunted ground doves – now a maze of lawns and swimming pools called Ocean Terrace Inn. At Conaree Bay, we would swim out to the reef for underwater spear fishing – until one day a stingray scared me off. And then there was the cane chute between Conaree and Barker's Point. We had no ready-made entertainment – neither TV nor video games. A boy had to use his imagination. I plucked little threads from the adult world and wove them into games – games where the rules changed as we progressed and the outcome was never certain.

My father introduced me to the cane chute. Freshly-cut, heavy bundles of cane couldn't be lugged far in the Caribbean heat, even on horseback or donkey back, so the sugar factory owners had built a narrow gauge railway to circle St. Kitts and collect the crop from each estate; it's called the "Sugar Cane Train" – now, a popular tourist attraction. However, the locomotive couldn't reach the hilly fields above Conaree Bay. With such a steep slope, it was cheaper to build a concrete slide and let gravity do the work. Harvest time for cane is called "crop season", from February to July, and for the rest of the year the island is "out of crop". During crop, tons of cane would rocket down the chute at the Conaree depot, accumulating in a heap near the main road until it could be picked up by tractor.

Out of crop, the chute sat unused, and one day my parents drove me there on an outing. My father was fond of giving me sugar-production statistics, and he told us the concrete slide was one foot wide and three hundred feet long. I asked if I could play on it, thinking, "If cane can do it, why not me?"

"Just don't come here during crop," my father said, "it's not allowed."

Afterwards, I would ride out to the place by bicycle, or ask for a lift, bringing my brothers and sometimes friends. I didn't always tell my parents where I was going. The chute hugged the steep hillside until near the bottom, terminating in an elevated exit ramp six foot high. The cane would whiz off the end and pile up in the loading area. We used the middle section of the chute for our sliding games – not too high up because it became scary, not on the exit ramp because we might fall off.

The day I experimented for the first time, I just sat in the chute and pushed off. Nothing much happened; my khaki short trousers were somewhat sweaty and offered high frictional resistance. I pulled with my arms and slid a few feet. It didn't feel comfortable. I climbed out and found my trousers were soiled and torn; the concrete inner surface of the chute was smooth with cane wax in most places, but the remaining pits and cracks could snag clothes.

On my next expedition to the chute, I brought rough burlap sacks for us to sit on. This solved the wear-and-tear problem and was much more comfortable.

"It dozen go wery fasth, tho," complained my sister, Hazel, and my youngest brother, Noel.

"I don't like the sack on my skin," said Peter. "I'm going to sit on cane leaves."

Cane trash has a slippery, waxy surface and we discovered that by using it, or even (in my case) packing a bed of it under a sack, we could approach the sliding speed of the cane stalks. Now we could fly – indeed, fly so fast we soon had speed limit problems. We wore tennis shoes because they were light and helped us to climb slippery places. Now I dug mine in to the sides of the concrete chute to slow down. I braked so violently I pitched out of the chute and fell hard on the slope nearby. After that, our equipment consisted of sacks, cane trash, tough khaki trousers, leather shoes, Band-Aids, and a penknife to peel any leftover cane stalks. The wind whipped by, green cane fields and blue sea shimmered in the distance, the sugary smell of cane trash and dried cane stalks tickled my nose. The speed, the breeze, the hint of danger, all took me to paradise for golden seconds. Just a few rocks to avoid if you stuck your hand out, then I slowed down with my leather-protected feet to stop before I could fall off the delivery section.

Most school vacations, except during crop, I would manage a few visits to the cane chute with my brothers. Eventually, what stopped my sliding game was a geometrical impossibility. At age eleven, my butt would no longer fit into the one-foot-wide concrete canal. But afterwards, whenever I ate cane, I would fondly remember the chute.

The summer after I had ceased going to the chute, I was peeling the green bark off the soft inner fibre of a joint of cane, and I asked my father whether children still played at the Conaree depot. He was in his workshop, preparing frames for his beehives. I leaned on his tool bench and watched him work while I chewed.

He told me the factory had abandoned the chute.

"Safety problems," he added.

Eating a sugary section of pulp, I asked, "What problems? We never had any."

My father looked uncomfortable, and stopped hammering for a minute. "Well, maybe you were lucky. A bad accident occurred a few months ago. I should never have let you play on it."

I chomped more fibrous cane to extract the juice. I had been eating for several minutes and my jaw muscles ached – I was applying almost as much pressure on my gums as the huge steel crushing mills in the factory did on the cane stalks. An accident?

"Wasn't it out of crop then?" I asked.

"Even out of crop that chute was not without risk. I didn't know that when I let you go there. No cane should have been sliding, but a few forgotten stalks at the top got loose," my father said.

I had been to the chute once during crop, seen red flags everywhere, and heard the cane handlers shouting warnings to the workers at the bottom. But this time there would have been no signal.

My father continued, "A maintenance worker was standing directly in line with the chute exit. He didn't see the cane coming. Did you know that those eight-foot stalks, starting from the hilltop attain a speed of a hundred miles an hour at the bottom? It went right through him."

I stopped chewing my cane. The image of the unlucky worker was intolerable. His was a different paradise. I pictured myself, transfixed by a shaft of cane like that, and then rejected the possibility. Who could tell if a game was going to get you into trouble, and would it make a difference to know?

"It was nobody's fault," he said. "Come and help me seal the comb foundation onto these frames."

I sighed. Without risk, most pastimes were so boring.

Away from school, my vacation was not always spent in St. Kitts. During the summer holidays between Third and Fourth Forms in 1954, my grandfather invited me to Barbados where he was then preaching. My parents agreed to let me go, and found someone to accompany me on the plane trip from St. Kitts: "Shorty" Pereira, a fitting name given that, although adult, he was just my twelve-year-old height. Granny and Grandpop met me at the airport and drove me to their vicarage near Bridgetown, the capital.

Grandpop had a rectory car, and in the following days he took me to visit places of interest on the island: Bridgetown markets, churches, and the war memorial; the green, polygonal expanses of waving cane punctuated by neat brown access roads; and the fine, white sand beaches. I went to church with my grandmother and grandfather every Sunday and listened to his thundering sermons.

The island was beautiful, though not yet the tourist Mecca of today. Barbados is about the size of St. Kitts and Antigua combined and much more densely populated. I, however, would remember little of its scenery. From my parochial point of view, whereas its omnipresent cane fields reassured me, Barbados felt too flat; the highest hills were less than one-third of my home mountains in St. Kitts. And just as the island was monotonous, that year, the entire Caribbean region was asleep and awaiting. Nothing seemed to be happening, though unpleasant events were hiding in dark places just outside of our ken: Castro was already growing the beard in which he would brutally wrest Cuba from Batista; Papa Doc and his militia of Tontons Macoutes were sharpening up their machetes, only three years away from their takeover of Haiti.

The crabs are what I remember most, however.

In front of the vicarage was an open, paved area with a big tamarind tree, which Grandpop used to shelter his vehicle from the sun. This entrance was a good place to park wedding cars and funeral hearses, but without them, it felt empty. In the back of the house was an enclosed earth yard with shady mango trees. There were no flowers, the soil was damp, and I disliked the yard until I met my neighbour.

The first morning after my arrival, someone knocked on our kitchen door, and Grandpop announced a friend had come to visit me. He lived just next door.

"What's your name?" I asked the cheerful face, whiter than mine, with a snub nose and a shock of brown hair.

"Chris. What's yours?"

"Chris. How will we tell ourselves apart?"

"Well, how old are you, then?" he asked.

"Twelve. And you?"

"I'm ten. So, that settles it. I'm Big Chris and you can be Little Chris, if you like."

About to protest, I suddenly liked it. My new friend could have his way, even if younger and shorter. Having established our relations, the first – and only – game he wanted to play was catching crabs.

"Crabs?" I asked. "Do you have crabs in your garden?"

"No, I don't have a garden. But I come over to play in your back yard all the time. You have lots of crabs there. Are you afraid of them?"

I laughed, and we dashed out to the yard where Big Chris was happy to show me his secrets. As we walked from corner to corner, every now and again he would point to a hole in the ground. They varied from two inches to six inches across and tunnelled diagonally into the darkness of the earth.

"I don't see any crabs."

He cocked his head at me and pressed a grubby finger against his lips. "Shh!" he said. "They're tricksy."

I stared at him in curiosity. He grabbed my arm and pulled me towards the house. Then he continued in a low voice, "They know we're here, silly. They live underground in those holes and only come up when it's quiet."

"Why do they come up?"

"I think they're looking for food, or maybe they just need to breathe every once in a while. Their burrows go a long way down. It's all connected, like an underground city. Sometimes I dream about it. If you want to see them, we have to go up the veranda steps and keep quiet."

We waited on the ground floor veranda. An old Caribbean saying advises hunters to be patient: "Softly, softly, catchee monkey". Maybe it would work for crabs, too. After about ten minutes, I spied two grey-and-purple-backed crabs sidle out of their burrows. Big Chris knew his territory.

"Well, how do we catch them, then?"

On this point, Big Chris' expertise began to falter. He knew how to find them, and how to chase them, but capturing them was still an unresolved issue – especially trapping them alive. It was up to me to take the game further. I went and asked my grandmother how to catch crabs. She gave me a ball of twine.

"Maybe this will help."

With my penknife, we cut off a few lengths of the twine and put the ends down several of the bigger holes. Nothing happened. We went away. The next day, our trailing strings had either disappeared or been thrown out of the holes. I found out more from Grandpop.

"Don't you know how to tie a noose in a string? Here's how it's done." And he showed me how to make a knot that would slip. I wondered why I hadn't thought of it myself.

"Here's what we'll do," I suggested to Big Chris. "We'll tie a large noose around each hole where we've seen crabs recently. Then we'll take the ends of the strings up to the veranda. We'll lie in wait, and when the crab comes out, we'll pull on the string and the noose will close around the crab. And then haul it in, like fishing in the sea."

As our skill at noose making developed, the game turned in our favour. We would often miss the crab's exit, and it would retreat into its hole or dart away. But once or twice, we caught it at the right moment and pulled it in. Big Chris was ecstatic. We picked up the crabs by the string and put them in an old metal oil drum from which they couldn't climb out. They stared at us with their beady, wide-apart eyes and waved their pincers up and down.

"How do you pick up a crab, Grandpop?"

"Always hold it by its back. That way the claws can't get at you."

Then we discovered that if we made the noose just the right size and placed it in the entrance to the hole, the crab would *have* to walk into it. It would tangle its feet and claws in our string. We needn't even be present.

The next morning, several crabs had come out during the night, got snared in their respective nooses, and pulled part of the string back down into their holes. I called Big Chris as early as I could.

"We've captured at least five of them. All we have to do is pull them out of their holes."

The first three came out, small ones, after a bit of jiggling and joggling of the strings. The fourth string broke, or maybe the crab cut it. The fifth string was in a large hole, and I resolved not to let the giant crab escape. We transferred the morning's catch to the oil drum, and giggled at our helpless prisoners scrambling on top of one another.

"OK, you can do the last one, Little Chris," my friend obliged.

It was not easy. The string gave a bit and then got stuck. I kept on pulling the buried creature, and it came up, inch by inch.

"I can see it," said Big Chris, peering into the dim hole, "go on!"

However, it wouldn't budge any further. I decided to help it along. I put my hand into the hole and pulled at the visible part of the crab. It moved, but not in the way I expected. The big claw seemed to unfold, and in a flash, it had my finger.

"Aiee!" Electricity ran up my hand and I jumped back, bowling over Big Chris. Something had ripped, but the pain didn't stop. I looked at my hand and saw the entire claw, large and sharp and purple, biting into my index finger. But where was the crab? Bits of it were halfway out of the hole. The rest had gone. And the claw wouldn't let go!

I ran to the kitchen where my Granny was, trailed by my anxious fellow crabber, surprise and pain fighting for control of me. After one look, my Granny took a pair of pliers and pried the claw open.

"Ah, you boys!" she said. "Hold still now," and she went for her medicine chest. When my finger was bandaged up and my eyes dried, Grandpop came in and examined the crushed claw.

"Didn't I tell you always to hold it by the back?"

I sniffled.

"Reflexes," he said. "You tore off so much of the crab that it was probably dying. It can't live long with only one claw, anyway. But the claw you took didn't know it was dead, and kept on biting."

The crab shot up in my estimation. I wondered if I would be able to do as well: continue fighting in a hopeless situation.

"Now you know what they can do, are you going to stop hunting crabs?"

I shook my head, and, after a little more crab snaring, we caught quite enough for a meal.

"We can't cook them just yet," said Granny. "Crabs eat anything, garbage, Manchineel, and even little boys' fingers."

She purged them for five days on a diet of fresh vegetables, cornmeal, and fruit, washing them daily. Then she boiled them in salty water until they were red all over.

Big Chris joined us for the crab feast. We had fun cracking open the big claws or "gundies" as we called them. "That's the biter bitten," I said, and Chris licked his lips.

Nelson's Dockyard

I couldn't imagine losing a parent, or a friend, or anyone I knew. I had a mother, a father, two grandparents, two pairs of uncles and aunts, two brothers, one sister, and plenty of cousins: my entire family universe was alive and in good health. Relatives who wanted to expire had had the decency to die before my arrival in the world or were waiting until I was grown up.

The only death that *I* had in some sense experienced was that of King George VI, in February of 1952, during my first year at the Antigua Grammar School. This death, in far off England, reverberated all the way to little Antigua because the new Queen, Elizabeth II, granted us a whole week of vacation. Flags, fireworks, and folklore: what a feast of pageantry and sport that was! In the following years, other, lesser, political figures sometimes passed away and bequeathed us a holiday, so the association between death and festivity was strong for me. They died, we played; there was nothing to worry about.

Visiting dignitaries and old boys of the school – the successful ones, of course – also contributed to our store of unexpected holidays. The Headmaster would introduce the visitor during morning general assembly. I would stand among the rows of uniformed boys, and stare curiously at the well-dressed time traveller on the platform, returned home full of a life's attainments to salute his schooldays' origins. I would listen to his words – strange, manicured, un-Caribbean diction – cajoling us to work hard and succeed in the larger world as he had done. But what we were trying to detect was the moment when he would ask the Headmaster to give us a half-day off. It always happened – our school veterans knew what we wanted. When it came, we would give a heartfelt roar of approval.

Every year the school had a water sports competition. We were divided into four "Houses", each with a colour – red, yellow, blue, and green – in a thoroughly British manner to balance individual achievements with collective House prizes. My fellow boarders and I were all in "School House", colour blue.

Swimming was my favourite competition, because contrary to most other sports, I already had the basic skills. Isn't it surprising that, surrounded by the warmest, most beautiful sea in the world, so many Caribbean small-islanders are afraid to swim? I owed my swimming knowledge to my sister's physiotherapy and my parents' insistence. She couldn't take part in the usual activities that required speed and reflexes. Swimming was gentle, and quite feasible for a child with a mild motor handicap. They found a rare indoor swimming pool in St. Kitts – more like a large bathroom – and paid for lessons for all of their children. Otherwise, I might still have been dog-paddling. At age twelve, I couldn't swim fast – not nearly enough to win a prize. But considering how many boys would not venture into the water at all, my ability to keep afloat, to do the breaststroke, and to dive was enough for me to look forward to the water sports.

The day came, and we were each given a packed lunch consisting of substantial meat and cheese sandwiches and an orange. Mrs McDonald, a friend of the school, mixed an enormous batch of fresh vanilla cream and sent it packed in wood-and-metal ice cream churns surrounded by ice and salt. We were crammed into battered buses with open windows and driven across the hot middle of the island, ignoring Antigua's many sandy beaches, to English Harbour, right in Nelson's Dockyard, where there was no sand at all, just quays and dark blue seawater. This was where our water sports were always held.

I was vaguely aware of the historic importance of the site, where several famous naval officers had been based: Rodney, Hood, Cochrane and, of course, Admiral Lord Nelson. I knew that in 1787 Nelson – he wasn't a Lord then – had married a Nevis girl, Frances Nisbet, and that made him an adopted Caribbean citizen, whatever he did later. The Docks were ideal for supervising distance races, and the colours – brown hills, grey stone, indigo wavelets, and white sails – were astonishingly peaceful.

On that particular sports day, our morning sped by, with 50-, 100-, and 200-yard events – crawl and breaststroke – for all age groups. As expected, I won no points, but my House was leading anyway. In the afternoon, we would have the diving competitions and the relay races. Some of the boarders, like Wes, swam far better than I did. He was gifted with powerful lungs, and came second in the underwater distance race, which was a special individual event, not a part of the House competition, open to all, even staff. Only Mr Barnes, the Sports Master, beat Wes. They plunged into the dark water, disappearing from human ken for up to three minutes, and then emerged like torpedoes forty or fifty yards away. Lunch was, however, the high point of the day.

At midday, the whole school of more than 150 boys and Masters spread out on the grass near the quays, some sitting on boulders or old fortifications, munching and drinking with pleasure; sandwiches were much better than our usual fare.

I looked at the Masters. Father Brown, the English Chaplain, was timid in shorts, and his natural reserve would keep him from swimming; Shaky Jack, our Headmaster – also English – would bathe and love it, not caring how outlandish his floppy, wet ears looked. Mr Barnes was a magnificent black athlete, so much better at teaching swimming and cricket than Algebra and Geometry. The podgy classicist, Mr Blackett, unusually affable, revealed a richly muscled and hairy upper torso – acquired by obsessive weight lifting. Strange adults.

"What do you want to do when you're grown up?" I asked my friend Miguel.

"Maybe I'll be a doctor, or a dentist like my Dad. It must be fun pulling out old teeth, or drilling new ones while the patient squirms."

"Don't count on me to visit you! What about you, Felix?"

"Dunno – whatever I'm good at I suppose, but I'll decide later."

They looked at me.

"Well, I don't know either. Maybe a scientist. Whatever it is, I'd like to come back to the school when I'm famous and give everyone a half holiday."

"You'll have to be *really* famous and *really* old to do that," they laughed.

The future stretched out ahead of us, invitingly. But what stretches can snap.

We had another hour for digestion and a nap in the shade before the events that were scheduled to begin at two o'clock. Somewhere, lying on the grass or sprawled on the cannons, were all the boarders; my other friends; Lester Bird, the future chief minister of Antigua; and many notables-to-be; a sea of brown and black skins relaxing in the sun.

At one-thirty, I saw a crowd forming.

"What's going on, Miguel?

"Must be a fight. Let's take a look."

Like many others on the fringes, Miguel, Felix, and I got up lazily, taking our nearly empty lunch bags with us, and sauntered over to watch the fun. But the fight, if that's what it had been, was over. Someone was on the ground, and several other people, mostly Masters, clustered tightly around him. We couldn't see much, but the crowd was full of whispers.

"What's happened? Did someone get hurt?" I said.

"Is Thomas. He fall in the water."

"No, is not Thomas, is Davis. And he don't fall in. He dived."

"So, what's wrong with practicing for this afternoon?"

"Is not time yet. He just eat he food, now he in trouble."

"Bad trouble," chimed in an older boy. "He a good diver. So he dive, go under deep, and no one think anything. Five minutes come, and we notice he still down there. So we call the Masters, and Mr Barnes and another went in for him. Bring him up from the bottom, not moving. Now they trying to make him breathe again. Taking a while."

That was all we learned for the next half hour, but we could hear noises and see frantic movements from the centre of the crowd. Then an ambulance arrived and a shiver went round as we realised how serious it must be to require doctors. Maybe Davis was still not breathing. Another fifteen minutes, and one of the Masters made an announcement on a megaphone.

"Please do not go back in the water, any of you. Get dressed. One of your friends has had an accident and a medical team is applying artificial respiration and all other means to bring him back. His state is serious but not critical. We have cancelled the rest of the water sports and the buses will return for you shortly."

Of course, I wanted to believe his state was not critical. But by the time our buses left, the word went round that there was no hope.

"He's still alive, isn't he?" I said.

"Maybe, maybe not. I hear he breathing but not conscious."

"I hear they never got him to breathe again."

"But why didn't he come back up?" I asked again. "Did he hit his head on the bottom?"

"They think he eat he sandwich too quick. When he dive, a lump get caught in he throat."

"No, stupid. Who ever hear of sandwich killing you? It was the ice cream. He jump in just after eating a big bowl. He hit the water too hard – belly flop – and throw it up. Then he suck it back in, struggle and panic. You eat any?"

I thought of him struggling near the bottom, unable to breathe, unable to surface. Water and vomit being inhaled instead of air. Suffocating.

Our schoolmate was pronounced dead that night. Disbelief and fear echoed in our heads. For the first time I was frightened of the sea; it was not always warm and welcoming; for I was a land dweller and the depths could be hostile.

I knew little about Davis. I hadn't met his family. I had hardly talked to him. There were no stories about him, which meant he was neither a scholar, nor an athlete nor a miscreant. But I participated in the collective shudder. I had seen him, black and still on the ground – pale in his blackness. His funeral took place two days later.

The whole school was ordered to turn up, in full uniform. We assembled in the grounds, khaki trousers, white shirts, and green school ties all spic and span for the occasion, scuffing the gravel. The sky should be grey, I thought, but it was an uncaring blue and as dispassionately hot as usual. It was a twenty-minute walk to the cathedral in St. Johns, trudging along the cracked roads.

"Miguel," I said as we walked, "this ice cream thing…"

"I didn't have any, remember?"

"Yes, but I did. Two helpings."

"Not my problem. You greedy, man."

"But suppose I had dived…"

"You know we weren't allowed to. Father Brown said one hour for digestion!"

"But suppose someone pushed me…"

"No way. We weren't even near the water!"

"But suppose I had gone near, just to look, and then someone pushed me in…"

"Why you do a stupid thing like that? Anyway, you fall in, you climb out."

"But suppose I couldn't. Suppose I went down deep like Davis, and the ice cream choked me."

"Why it choke you? You didn't take much. Davis must have eaten at least five helpings."

"But maybe my belly smaller than Davis, so…"

"Cut it out, man! If you choke or had problems, you know the person who push you must see and call help."

"But what if he run and not see me down deep, all choke up?"

"Stop that shit, man! Stop, or I punch you! Can't happen to us. I don't eat yucky ice cream. Not us get drowned. Going to be a dentist, like my Dad. No more, right?"

In the church, we didn't look at each other as we cried. But years later these feelings of loss and darkness would remain, even when my memory of the boy's face was obliterated. We got two days holiday, including the day of the funeral.

Breaking out at Night

Instead of sobering me, it was as if my recent, small knowledge of death drove me to confront my fears. I needed to understand this elusive thing, existence. I welcomed situations where I could pit myself against something other than the school authority, private skirmishes with the unknown. That's why I broke out of the boarding house at night.

My fingers hurt. The wooden trellis trembled under my weight as I struggled to find a toehold. It seemed more difficult to descend the framework at night. I hoped I was nearly down and let go. The fall must have been at least four feet, and with a jolt, I found myself horizontal on the hard earth. Climbing trees as a younger child had served some purpose. Nothing broken. I got up, stood cautiously, and took in my surroundings.

Behind me stood the school, the dorm filled with sleeping boarders, hopefully a sleeping Housemaster, and even more hopefully my ex-friend Miguel having guilty dreams. In front of me lay the dark path to something new. At this hour, I should have been asleep in bed, travelling in other worlds. I often read books by Dennis Wheatley until lights out. Mrs Maxwell, the owner of the bookstore where I ordered these stories of the supernatural, would ask whether they scared me. On the contrary, his tales of the astral plane, devil worshippers, succubi, and assorted werewolves would cajole me to sleep. But that was when I was warm in bed: now, outside, those creatures became disquietingly real.

The whole thing had begun with rumours about the seniors breaking out at night. The school rules were rigid: no boarder was allowed outside after 6pm without special permission. The combination of dark and danger caught my spirit.

"Trevor and Derek used to break out at night quite often," my friends said, after the infamous pair of brothers had left the school.

"Whatever for?" I asked. "What's there to do at night? Where did they go?"

"No one knows. Visited girlfriends, perhaps," Miguel said with a shrug. "Anyway, it takes guts."

The problem for me was the modus operandi. "I can't work out how they managed to get past the Housemaster. His room is just opposite the staircase that is the way out."

"And his dog. Don't forget Cleo, that miserable animal prowls around all night," said Miguel.

We created a mystery, and from time to time over the months and years, one or the other of us would acquire more snippets of juicy information to keep it alive.

Melford was reputed to have broken out and been caught drinking beer in a bar miles away by someone who had recognised him. It was said he was caned in secret and forbidden to talk about it. Dougie and Geoffrey were supposed to have broken out just to smoke cigarettes – they never left the school grounds.

Among the seniors, Wes was the first to be authorised to go out on a Saturday night. A family invited him for dinner and – reluctantly – Father Brown agreed he could go if he returned to the dorm by 10:00. Wes was very independent at sixteen and hated the rules. I would have found it ironic if I had known that his future was to be a disciplined Rear Admiral in the US Navy. Other friends invited him, and Saturday night out became quite a regular feature for him, but always with the constraint of a 10 o'clock curfew.

One day, Wes was cross with Father Brown and he complained to anyone who would listen.

"It's downright stupid not letting us have more pocket money," he fumed. "It's ours, isn't it?"

"Well, how much do you need anyway?" I asked. "I'd like to buy more books, but $1 per week is all my parents provided."

"But it's my money!" he exclaimed indignantly. "I worked for it during my last vacation. I should be able to decide what to do with it, and when."

Money, of course, was the key to breaking out – without it, you couldn't do much with your freedom. At twelve, I found the idea of working during vacations to earn school pocket money strange. I had once worked in a grocery store at Christmas – cadging chocolates on the sly – and my father sometimes paid me for odd jobs in his workshop. However, these wages had gone into my savings account, and, unlike Wes, I relied on weekly contributions from my parents to compensate me for the rigours of boarding school life. Wes grew his hair long and took charge of his life – vigorously. I was envious.

He continued, "Anyway, I'll get my revenge. What Father Brown doesn't know is that I ignore his time limit."

My ears opened wide. As in a conch shell, I seemed to hear the murmur of distant, seductive seas.

"But I thought you came back at 10 o'clock!"

A crafty grin. "Coming back at 10 o'clock is just for appearances. I pretend to go to sleep and then, half an hour later, I climb over the veranda railing and stay out as late as I like."

At last, I knew how it was done: scale the side of the building.

"But it's much too high," I objected. "You'd break a leg if you jumped."

I looked doubtfully at Wes' athletic build. After all, my schoolmate had twice won the competition for throwing the cricket ball, and was excellent at long-distance swimming. He was a senior and a head taller than me. Maybe he had a special technique for jumping down twelve feet that I could learn?

Wes smiled. "Come on, haven't you noticed at the end of the veranda there's a small section that has trellis work almost down to the ground?"

Someone had once told me the trellis was supposed to stop the wind blowing along the ground floor corridor.

"It's easy to climb down," said Wes. "No one uses it during the day because it's close to Father Brown's room, but at night, he can't see it. You have to be careful he doesn't hear you, though."

I had passed by the trellis a thousand times without imagining it had any possible place in my life. Now it did. Images of myself swinging light-heartedly down from the veranda to the ground swelled through me; if Wes could do it so could I.

Wes had my entire attention focused on his revelations. He continued: "I've been over the veranda railing at night more times than I can count. And not only on a Saturday. I go when I like. Sometimes I borrow a Vespa scooter and leave it hidden in the bushes. I've been to parties miles away like that. And I've never been caught. Only once did I have a problem. I tie my pyjamas onto the bottom of the trellis. That way, I can change before climbing up, and if I were to be caught in my nightclothes, it would be easier to explain. One night it rained, and I had to sleep naked, but everyone thought I had peed my pyjamas."

Gratified to have discovered how my friend broke out, I didn't know I was just the latest recipient of the holy grail of impenitent Antigua Grammar School boarders. Ever since 1884 when the school was built, over much of the next century boarders had had a tradition of breaking out at night. They passed their secrets on by word of mouth, and it became a rite of passage to see if each generation could live up to the daring of the previous one.

Which explained why the dark bulk of the school building now loomed over my shoulder. I slowly left it behind, and picked my way towards the town of St. John's. The trellis had changed from friend to enemy in the dark. In the daylight, I had been able to see all the handholds, and I knew exactly how far away the ground was, how bad the fall would be if I slipped. At night, I had had to guess. The way into town, too, now seemed foreign and menacing. I couldn't even see the beginning of the path, yet.

I should have had a companion in adventure, of course.

"Hey, Miguel and Felix, anyone interested in breaking out with me next Friday night? I need one of you," I had said.

"To do what?" asked Miguel, before Felix could respond.

I told them my idea.

"What I want is to go to the cinema. All the best movies are shown late at night, especially Friday at 10 o'clock. There's a Western on next week."

It was a few months after Wes had talked to me. I had done my homework and found a worthy target. There was just one cinema in St. John's, perhaps in the whole of Antigua. Father Brown didn't like his charges to go there; it could be the start of a dissolute life. But for us (without TV), a movie was the only peephole we had on the outside world – a Hollywood-tinted world. On the rare occasions when we got permission, it had to be the Saturday children's matinee, the least exciting show of the week.

"OK, I'll go with you," said Miguel.

"Maybe not this time for me," said Felix.

A recruit. I looked with exhilaration at Miguel and gave him the details. Save up our pocket money for the cinema entrance fee. Go to bed as usual at 8:30. Keep underclothes on, shirt and trousers nearby. Stay quiet in bed – but wide-awake – until 9:00 when Father Brown would turn all the lights out. Wait some more until 9:30 when Father Brown himself would go to sleep. Get up quietly. Get dressed, except for shoes. Roll up our pillow in bed, under the blanket, under the mosquito net. It was Caribbean camouflage – just like the little Brits in their school stories. Climb over the veranda railing and down the trellis. Stroll into town to reach the cinema by 10:00. Stay incognito. Enjoy the movie. Return to the dorm after the film, well past midnight. Sweet dreams.

For the first time, I began to appreciate the orderly, step-by-step approach to things. It reminded me of Father Brown's essays on how to open a tin of sardines. Annoyingly, I also remembered that none of my factual essays had ever been graded higher than six out of ten. I hoped my breakout scheme would be more foolproof than that.

"Why do we have to walk into town without shoes?" Miguel asked.

"Didn't I say you put them on again after climbing down?"

"No. And are you sure to find the way at night?"

I inflated my chest. "Of course!"

"Aren't you scared of being caught?" Felix said.

"Impossible! Can't you see I have it all planned?" I didn't tell them what I was scared of, because I hadn't formulated it properly yet.

It all went like clockwork until that penultimate phase of departure. I had been lying tensely in bed, proudly checking the luminous dial of my watch every five minutes, ignorant that this type of radioactive display was bathing me in alpha particles. When the pale green second hand ticked over the 9:30 mark, I eased myself out of bed. Miguel seemed asleep so I pulled up a part of his mosquito net and shook him.

"Time to go."

"Huh? No, no, it's too damned dark. You forgot about the moon!"

"Moon? What moon?" I said. "I can't control the moon. So what if there's no moon! We have to go."

"Well, I'm not going!" he raised his voice.

I recoiled and cursed him silently for sabotaging my plans. "Can't trust Ratta," I thought, remembering the fight we had had years before, and the time he had caused me to be caned by giving himself up after our canal escapade. I considered getting back into bed, but my anger made me continue dressing. I would do it on my own.

So there I was, walking into town, companionless. It was forbiddingly dark with only the stars to guide my way. The cinema was about two miles distant, half of the way on a narrow, winding footpath and the rest by public road.

I crossed the school's front lawns, avoiding the gravelly driveway for fear of noise, although it caught the starlight so reassuringly, and I looked for the start of the path. I came to a dark grove of shack-shack trees and thorny acacia, but couldn't find my way. Damn! We used this shortcut so often in the bright sunlight of Saturday morning. Where had it gone? I looked back at the sombre mass of the school and saw no lights anywhere in the huge prison-like building. Good. I looked forward at the bushes hissing in a light breeze and saw no features. Bad. Apart from the poisonous acacia spines, might there be nefarious people lurking nearby? Or even spirits pretending to be nefarious people? I could hear night insects chanting sinister incantations but I couldn't turn back now, so I wandered frantically in circles until I found an opening and charged in blindly.

I scratched myself repeatedly on the thorns, but I didn't stop running. I knew in my head there were no such things as ghosts or werewolves, but might there not be mad dogs or murderers? I was never sure whether I was on the path, I just ran where the bushes snagged me least, and my heart only slowed when the paved road surged into view. I walked in the middle. It was dark even there in the open, but I could now see the lights of the town in the distance. I was fifteen minutes late to the cinema.

Then came my next test. I expected to be challenged as I offered my money.

I feared the cashier would say, "You young to be out late, no? Don't I know you from the boarding school?"

"Oh no, it's not late for us. I'm a senior in Fourth Form, and we're allowed out to the cinema," I would reply. Surely, I looked bright enough to be in Fourth.

Then I would smile confidently and walk in.

I held out my hand with the ticket money, and a frowsy, gum-chewing, brown woman took it without even looking at me.

"Film done started."

It was a disconcerting disrespect for my fantasies.

The John Wayne western filled my head with gunshots, and I held on to that as I filed out afterwards alongside the other spectators and headed back to the dormitory. On the path, I galloped my cinematic horse all the way, blanking out the brooding night. As I climbed painfully up the trellis to the dorm veranda, every little creak and crack of the wood seemed like the Indians were chasing me. Then there was a raucous noise I identified as a banshee, until the "Hee-haw, hee-haw" began to sound more like braying than wailing, and I knew it for an ass. That must have been when I cut my fingers climbing up the rough wood, although I didn't feel the torn skin until next morning when I washed. I hauled myself onto the veranda and breathed deeply. Before I slipped back under my mosquito net and punched my rolled up pillow out of the way, I had persuaded myself that survival was everything; no night monsters had molested me. I focused on the scorn I was going to pour over Miguel the next day.

He pretended at first it had never happened, that I hadn't broken out but had fallen asleep. Luckily, I had kept the stub of my cinema ticket, and I could display my cut finger. When we were out of earshot from the other boarders, Felix came to me and said, "Next time, you can count me in."

Next time was two weeks later, sufficient time for us to save up the pocket money to buy another cinema ticket. I made sure for the second breakout that the moon would not desert me. I went over the revised plan with Felix, told him we should practice climbing up and down the trellis, because it wasn't as easy at night as in daylight. After one or two inconclusive tries, he looked uneasy.

"You're not afraid of ghosts, are you?" I said.

"'Course not, just of getting myself killed."

Next morning he told me, "I have a better idea, Chris. I don't want to break my neck falling off the veranda in the dark. I think we should go quietly down the stairs."

"But the main door is locked. I checked it. And Wes told me he always went over the veranda."

"Wes is Wes – he has long arms, remember? I have a solution for getting out from the ground floor."

"Yes?"

"There's a classroom under Father Brown's quarters that has windows which open out onto the playing field. Burglar bars protect all of the windows, but I've found a damaged one. There's a bar missing, and the bars next to it can be bent. I'm sure we can wriggle through. Then all we have to do is leave the wooden outer shutter unhooked, so we can come back the same way."

Felix was thinner than I was, and I wondered whether I could wriggle through a gap just his size. We did our best: using our feet, we enlarged the gap somewhat, but the iron resisted us, not bending as far as I would have liked. It would have to do.

"Better test it," said Felix, but just then, a group of inquisitive boys approached, and we moved away.

"Don't worry, I can do it," I decided, "but what about the dog?"

"Cleo knows me. She won't bark. She's a housedog, anyway. Never learned to bark properly."

I looked up at the dusty wooden ceiling and said, "This room is right under Father Brown's bed."

"No matter – he sleeps soundly, takes medicines or wine or something at night."

I still didn't like it – wriggling through bars was not as romantic as Tarzan-style climbing – so I insisted we leave the school by way of the trellis.

"OK," he said at last, "but I'm not climbing back up it."

I remembered the donkey and agreed to return through the classroom window.

We were tempted to discuss our plans with Miguel, but finally said nothing to him. There was no telling how he might use the information – we'd have time enough to boast afterwards.

That night, despite my prior experience, both Felix and I slipped on the last few feet of the trellis, and fell. He put on his shoes slowly, as if to show it was my fault, but soon the moon and the cool breeze cheered us up.

How reassuring it was to walk through that dark grove of bushes in good company! With more light, it was amazingly easy to find the path. This time, the cinema featured a detective film, although later I thought it should have been Houdini's great escape. We were on time. Outside the cinema, I suggested Felix stay back while I bought the tickets. Wasted ingenuity – the cashier again ignored the two young boys who passed in front of her. As long as they could pay...

However, Felix nudged me as we entered. "Look behind you."

I turned and saw a dirty, grey-haired man in a black shirt studying us and smiling. I stared back at him and he crooked his finger at me. Felix pulled my arm and we hurried into the cinema. The strange man sat at the back, so we scuttled to find seats in the front row. After the showing, we waited until the room was empty before leaving.

On the return journey, I thought Felix was being awkward. Even with the full moon, I preferred to walk in the middle of the smooth paved road. The thought had come to me that maybe Dracula preferred the shadows to the open. Felix, on the other hand, insisted on skulking from tree to tree on the bushy borders of the road, on an irregular trail covered with roots and stones. I was about to ask why he didn't join me on the paving, when he cried, "Jump!" and two bright headlights burst around a bend and drove straight at me. I found myself in the roadside ditch, breathing hard. The driver didn't even slow.

"They can't see us," Felix said. "Better stay on the side."

More cars passed by, and we both hugged the side path all the way home.

Back at the school, I was not at first sorry to have the classroom window to climb through rather than the trellis to scale. The wind had blown the outer shutter in, and we had to pry it open to get to the bars. Felix slipped through the gap first, and then I wondered whether we had found the right window. Even with a missing bar and our attempts at enlargement, the gap now seemed very narrow. I felt like a runaway animal giving up my freedom to return to my cage. I poked my left arm and shoulder through the hole, and then my head, but the rest of my body wouldn't follow. I instantly regretted not having tested my wriggling earlier on in the day.

"Come on!" Felix whispered from inside, preoccupied with something I couldn't see.

I gave a good shove and felt cloth rip. "OK, I can't do it," I thought, "I'll have to go back out and climb the trellis after all." But I couldn't – I was stuck. As panic gripped me, the dog Cleo started barking. Now I knew what Felix had been doing in the dark – trying to calm Cleo. But she had escaped from him.

"Keep still!" Felix whispered to me.

This was, in fact, my only option. "Yip? Yip?" The idiotic, treacherous beast.

"You said she wouldn't bark!"

"Yip! Yip!" came again, as Felix searched for Cleo.

"Calm down, Cleo." He patted her gingerly.

"Yip! Yip!" She was louder this time.

Desperately, I shoved in, shoved out, and felt I was scraping the ribs off my internal organs. Nothing gave. It was the dog's spittle in my face – licking me, a dog lover would have said – that provoked my best effort. Buttons popped off my shirt and I collapsed onto the classroom floor. I bumped my head against a desk and it fell over with a crash. That's when I heard Father Brown cough in his bedroom above us and knew the worst was about to happen.

We froze, all three of us, and suffered with Father Brown through his bronchial spasms. Quickly, my amazement surfaced. Why was Cleo so silent after barking her head off? I could see little in the shuttered classroom, but Felix seemed huddled over. Was he throttling the dog? It might deserve that fate, but what would we do with the body? Five minutes, maybe eight or nine – an eternity – we held still. It was agonising: surely, Father Brown had heard the desk fall and the dog bark and would soon come down the stairs to punish us? This was what breaking out led to. Then my sight adjusted to the room and I saw Felix was now holding Cleo's collar. I heard a soft, slurping noise. No barks.

"She likes sweets," Felix whispered.

I had never suspected him of harbouring sweets in his pocket, or else, greedy as I was, I would have asked for one. I wondered whether it was mint or toffee. Just as well he had saved it for Cleo, though. My reverie was ended by another whisper from Felix.

"Listen – he's not coughing any more – he's snoring!"

We were free, and neither the creaking of the stairs as we went up to our dorm nor the obsequious pitter-pattering of the dog's paws behind us could take that away.

As we undressed, Felix said, "I'm ready to go out again, now that you can get through the bars."

"OK – soon," I replied.

The next morning I dressed early and before breakfast, I searched the classroom under Father Brown's study. The windows were open but the janitor hadn't swept yet. I sighed with relief when I found two of my shirt buttons near the bars. It had seemed vital to find them, even if there was little risk of being incriminated. I would ask Matron to sew them back on and my moment of panic would become more acceptable. I wanted to remember that the real problems of breaking out had nothing to do with the supernatural. The gap in the bars in front of me looked so small – I couldn't imagine how I had squeezed through. I used a chair and levered it open another inch. "There were no ghosts out there," I thought, "I was scared for nothing." Then I remembered the speeding car and the smirking man at the cinema. It seemed unnecessary to break out a third time. Wes' generation needed the stimulus of danger every week. I didn't like conformity to the curfew any more than he did, but a new perception allowed me to save face. It was as slavish to break out repetitively as it was to obey the school rules mindlessly. I knew I could face the night and my devils if needed, and that was enough for the moment, for I felt a more critical test in the distance. There would be other cage bars to escape from. Beyond the boarding school, I sensed the larger constraints of my islands – smothering me – and knew absolutely my time would come to get free.

No one learned of these escapades, and I might have kept the secret forever, but in my last term in Antigua, almost two years later, a young boarder would ask me, "Did you ever break out of the dorm at night? Miguel says you tried and failed."

I can see myself: reticent at first, I would have checked no one else was listening.

"Don't believe him," I said. "He's just jealous. I did it – several times," my indignation giving way to a sense of déjà vu.

"Before me, there was Wes, but you didn't know him. And before Wes there were..." I stopped – right then, I thought, he needed geography more than history.

I told him about the possible veranda gambit and the exit from the classroom under the Housemaster's study, if the bars were still bent.

"Which is easier?" he asked.

I studied his skinny build.

"The stairs and the dog." I did not want to be responsible for a broken limb.

"How can I keep the dog quiet, then?"

"That's for you to work out. It's your adventure now."

I put my hand firmly on his shoulder. "By the way, do you believe in jumbies?"

Truth will Out

In my fourth year of boarding school in Antigua, I didn't set out to be dishonest; my intention was quite the opposite. With a fiery priest for a grandfather and a rigorous barrister for a father, honesty in all things was the only game in town. Yet, at the Antigua Grammar School in 1955, I was forced to think again about cheating.

It started one evening in the senior dorm with Michael. He was sitting on his bed in his underwear with Melford next to him. A sweaty smell of conspiracy floated through the warm air.

"Chris, come over here. Melford and I want you."

I was at last a senior, but the smallest of the seniors at age thirteen and a half. Michael was tall and good at athletics; Melford excelled at cricket; I had never attained the school standard in any sport, except once, age ten, for shot-put. These two loomed over me.

Right then, I was more concerned about my coming exams than anything else. Near the end of my Fourth Form year, everyone said I would be promoted. But to what? There were two Fifth Forms, 5A and 5B. Form 5A was a qualification year in the secondary school cycle, after which some students stopped studying. Most boys were age sixteen in 5A, some older. It was the class in which Antiguan youth sat the Cambridge Overseas School Certificate. Far-away examiners in their frosty English rooms would decide the future of sun-baked brown-and-black-skinned students for whom "cold" meant 25°C. We needed to pass this exam in five subjects to be eligible for further studies. For those who continued, there would be several years' hard work in Sixth Form before possible university entrance – to universities as foreign and distant as the examiners. Most boarders planned to leave Antigua after 5A and continue their studies elsewhere. Boarding school was supposed to take the rough edges off us, not necessarily to provide the finishing touches.

And then there was 5B, the class for slower students, those who weren't quite ready for the rigours of Cambridge exams, and needed another year of preparation. We called 5B the "Remove". I didn't want to go to the Remove. It was filled with hulking bullies of up to nineteen who had little interest in studying. A few made it to 5A a year or two later, the rest dropped out without qualification. In Fourth Form, we had been told that, in view of the increased number of students, only those with the best end-of-the-year exam results could go to 5A.

"Look, Chris, what we have to tell you is top secret."

I said nothing.

"You can keep a secret, can't you?" inquired Melford.

I nodded. "What's it all about?"

Michael leaned closer and said, "It's about the French exams."

"Oh," I said. "I've just had my French Grammar results. Not good – 20%. I hope I do better in the next exam." I had not – at the time – accepted that real people spoke French, and I refused to concentrate on its obscure, un-English grammar. Latin seemed just as pointless, but threats and canings from Mr Blackett had convinced me to apply myself to that subject, whereas the French master just whined.

We were allowed to sit for a maximum of eight subjects in 5A – more might explode our small brains, not to mention the school timetable. In the Fourth, I was already studying nine: English Language, English Literature, Latin, Mathematics, Chemistry, Physics, History, RK, and French. I would have to discontinue at least one. RK was Religious Knowledge and I didn't think Father Brown would approve of my stopping that. I liked the science subjects and although I thought History was dull, I was under family pressure to keep it.

"I'm going to drop French next year, if I can."

"Well, we're all in that boat," said Melford. He and Michael were not in the same Fourth Form as me, but we were sitting the same end-of-year exams.

"You won't move up if you don't pass French," said Michael. I couldn't tell if he was lying or not. "But Melford and I know a way to get better marks on the second paper."

"How's that?" I was curious, but suspected nothing. "Want to revise together? I can't help much, you know. The next paper is Translation from French to English, and I never get good marks. Sorry I can't help." Maybe they would leave me alone.

Michael put his two meaty hands on my shoulders. I wondered if he had skipped his evening shower.

"Chris, what if we could see the French text beforehand? It would be easy if we had time to study it and get our vocabulary right."

"But we can't."

"Yes, we can." Michael's muddy-brown eyes stared into mine. "Melford here had a lucky break today. He went to the Headmaster's office for 'a small disciplinary matter', and he saw where the Head – Shaky Jack – put the French paper. You know, he checks the final exams in each subject. It's in an unlocked drawer of his desk."

Eyebrows rising, I said, "No one would dare take it out of his drawer. After all, that would be cheating."

"I would," said Michael. Melford's face cracked into a big smile – the sort that he usually reserved for scoring a boundary in cricket. "Look at it this way, Chris," Michael continued, "none of us will survive if we don't see the paper in advance. Melford and I have low marks in several subjects. We both failed the French Grammar, with 35% and 39%. We want to move up to 5A. If you don't help us, we're all done for."

"I can't!" I blurted out.

The enormity of what they were asking began to sink in. I was petrified. I had no desire to get involved but what would these two do to me if I refused? Had I promised to keep their secret? In a small dorm with all three of us taking this exam, I realised they hadn't had much choice – I would have found out anyway. My best hope was not to have to *do* anything except keep my mouth shut. I looked at Michael and wished I could stare him down and persuade him to drop the crazy project, but hypnosis was beyond me.

"Look, let me think about this. I won't rat on you. But, honestly, I don't want to see that French paper. I'm not going on with French. Maybe I can fail it and still move up. Or maybe I'll be lucky. Anyway, I'm sure I'd be of no help. You seem to have it all worked out."

"No, Chris, we *do* need you. And first off, you need us. You're too young for 5A unless your grades are exceptional. You must pass in French.

"Now, here's our plan. Melford knows which drawer the exam paper is in, because he saw Shaky Jack put it there. But the drawer might be locked after all. I have a key that should fit. If not, I know a lot about locks. So, I'm the one who'll go into his office. Melford will be outside the door with a torch."

"What about me?"

"We need you in the middle of the corridor, at the door between the dorms and the Housemaster's rooms. You'll be the advance guard. If Father Brown comes along that corridor, you have to warn us."

"And how'll I do that?" I imagined myself shouting in a small whisper.

"You'll have a torch, like Melford. Shine it down the corridor, on, off, on. That way we'll have time to lock up and escape."

They needed me, and I couldn't find a way out. They even had torches. Despite misgivings I began to get excited by the adventure and said, "Well, are you sure that's all I'll have to do? Remember, I don't want to see the paper." Visions of great honour came to me: I would be the student who sacrificed himself for his desperate classmates without making any personal profit.

"As you like. Just be our eyes in the corridor, and don't let anyone else know about this. Not anyone, hear? Especially not your friends in the junior dorm."

There was enough hardness in Michael's smile to make me uncomfortable. Melford, normally placid, looked at me in the same way. I was well and truly compromised. These two could get nasty if betrayed. But, if push came to shove, it was Father Brown, the Housemaster, I feared the most. His blue eyes always seemed to see right through me.

"When?"

"Tomorrow, after the Sunday night dinner. Too many people are around today, and Shaky Jack won't be back tomorrow. The exam's on Monday, but we'll only need an hour or two with our dictionaries to translate the French."

Sunday night I was standing in the corridor, sporting an innocent look, imagining I was a spy, my pocket weighted down by the torch. I leaned against the door that separated the two long stretches of corridor. On one side were the lockers, the dorms, and the washbasins. Quiet at night, this was the passage where I had once fought noisily with Miguel. Life had been simple then, I thought, punching the air – just win or lose. Now I was at sea – a stormy sea – for I could lose in three different ways: desert my companions and I'd be clobbered; get caught in the act and I'd be caned; pilfer the paper successfully and I'd be tarred with the same moral brush as Michael and Melford.

Farther on, there were some stairs, and around a corner, toilets, showers, and Father Brown's quarters. It was surprising how much he could hear from the dorms. From where I stood, there was a low hum of voices coming from the juniors, almost masked by the night-time chirping of crickets. From time to time, a higher-pitched voice would say, "Quit that!" or a pencil would fall with a clatter.

I held the door halfway open.

On the other side, there was darkness. The Matron's room was inhabited, but she was so scared of thunder and lightning or overgrown boys that she never put her head out at night, whatever she heard. Beyond were empty offices, among them Mr Blackett's. At the end, about forty yards away, was the evening's El Dorado: Shaky Jack's office, with its cruel memories of past canings.

Every now and again, I would close the door, then open it, and stare into the darkness towards where I thought Michael and Melford were. I was getting anxious. Why were they taking so long? They had said five minutes and it had been at least fifteen. I could hear nothing and see nothing. But I smelt something.

I was close to my own locker. These lockers were private and no one knew what I had inside mine. Right then, I detected the aroma of Mango Rum. A week before I had had a narrow escape, showing how you could never tell when Father Brown was listening.

Wes had explained to me how to make what he called "Jungle Juice".

"It's applied Chemistry, Chris. You'll find it fun."

I did. You pulped a fruit like a mango or a pineapple, added tap water and sugar, and stoppered it up tightly in a glass bottle. Like magic, it would ferment (even without yeast) and turn into alcohol and other stuff. Maybe we could drink it or sell it. I had never tasted alcohol, except for the sweet wine at school mass, but I had seen my father drink rum. I'd left the bottle to stew for at least a month, and it was so well hidden I'd forgotten about it.

Last weekend I had opened my locker door when Wes was nearby. He asked, "How's your Jungle Juice coming?"

"Don't know," I said, and pulled the bottle out from the back of the locker.

It looked impressive, with several shades of yellow liquid and a large head of frothy green stuff on top. Wes said it was just getting to the alcohol stage.

"But I thought I told you to open it every ten days and let off the excess pressure?"

"I forgot, but I'll do it tomorrow."

I must have jolted the bottle as I put it back down, because there was a loud bang as the cork popped out and a fountain of would-be-Mango-Rum sprayed all over my locker and the floor nearby.

Amid the confusion, Father Brown's voice cut through the aromatic fog, all the way from his office, "What's going on out there? I'm trying to work."

Wes had the presence of mind of an experienced illicit distiller.

"Nothing, Father, I dropped some books."

"Well, pick them up more quietly then." Father Brown stayed in his room and continued marking homework.

Wes had laughed and told me not to start things I couldn't finish. He and I then spent a half-hour clearing up the brew, sponging the greeny-brown mass off the locker walls and out of my sports shoes. Once, I felt compelled to lick my fingers, but regretted it. The resemblance to jello was misleading; it tasted slimy and bitter. The sickly sweet odour never quite disappeared, and even then, on that night of French skulduggery, it could make me slightly queasy.

Was it the smell of Mango Rum remnants, or was it something else, I wondered? A light flashed at me from the dark, on, off, on. I started; this was not planned; I was the one who was supposed to signal in case of trouble. I squinted past the beam to see it was Melford, coming back to talk to me.

"Don't panic. This is taking longer than we expected because the drawer really is locked," he whispered. "Michael can't open it with his key. So we're searching everywhere for Shaky Jack's set. We think he leaves it somewhere in the office. It won't be long now."

He turned back into the darkness, leaving me nervous.

I had worried like this in the dark on other occasions, hoping not to be caught by Father Brown. Misdeeds seemed to generate these moments of tense waiting. But cheating was surely a different category of offence; no one would believe I had been forced into it.

It did seem long, but after another ten minutes, they found the keys in a first-aid medicine chest. The key to the medicine chest itself was on top of it. The desk drawer opened smoothly, they told me later. The envelope with the exam paper was not sealed. Once it was hidden in Michael's shirt, he and Melford seemed almost unhurried, sauntering up the corridor and flashing their light on and off at me. I eased the door shut behind them and said, "Shh!" We were soon huddled in a corner of the dorm, and I breathed a sigh of relief.

"Now we have to copy it quickly before I go back," said Michael.

"Go back?" I yelped.

"Of course. Didn't you realise we'd have to put the paper back? It must go into the same exam envelope, in the same drawer, locked in the same way as before. And the keys must go back in the medicine chest. Or else Shaky Jack will know something's wrong."

I hadn't thought of this – maybe I would never make Master Spy Grade. We now had another chance to be caught and expelled. We couldn't laugh away an exam paper in our hands.

Michael reproduced the exam at high speed. We sneaked back with trepidation to our former positions, but this time it went quickly, and, back in the dorm ten minutes later, they started work translating the copied French.

"OK, it's over for me," I said. "Don't say anything out loud. Let me alone now." I moved to the opposite corner of the senior dorm, which we had to ourselves that evening. I felt proud to have survived this dangerous burglary; I held myself hardly guilty at all.

French was not the only exam I had to prepare for; on Monday, I would also sit Religious Knowledge and History. While Michael and Melford were seductively rustling the pages of their French-English dictionary, I was studying the New Testament, wondering what the apostles thought about cheating. I found nothing to clarify my situation. I was blissfully unaware of Dr Samuel Johnson's remark: "I hope I shall never be deterred from detecting what I think a cheat, by the menaces of a ruffian."

What did run through my mind was the title of a book I had recently been given, "*Gamesmanship or, the Art of Winning Games without actually Cheating*." Was this what I was doing: winning a game against my thuggish companions while trying to keep my hands clean?

Finally, after at least an hour, Michael broke my determined and euphoric isolation by saying, "That's it, done. This is the English version. Now, we have to memorise it." I put away my bible and picked up a history book about the Victorian era without enthusiasm.

Luckily, we were allowed to stay up late before end-of-year exams. They got to work memorising, and were finished in half an hour.

Looking across the dorm, Michael growled at me, "OK, Chris, thanks for your help. We're going to hide the paper now, and destroy it later. There's only one copy. Sure you don't want to admire it, just for a second?"

Suddenly curious, I felt tempted by the rare object. What harm could a glimpse do? "Just for a second, then." At most, I would pick up one or two useful words. It was a unique occasion, after all.

Michael's handwriting was neat; the translation held on a single page, which took me thirty seconds to scan. A funny thing happened. Each word chalked itself on a blackboard in my mind. I had memorised the page in one go. I don't have a photographic memory, and I've never been able to reproduce this effect, however hard I try. Was it total recall after one reading? The other two had spent an hour translating and thirty minutes memorising.

"A gift of the gods," I thought. "Or maybe Beelzebub's curse."

This miracle came at the worst possible moment. At first pleased with my prowess, it hit me that now I was the boy who knew too much. My excitement turned cold. Contrary to my best intentions, I was now heading for a perfect score.

I put on my pyjamas and set myself the goal of *not* getting a high mark. The French Master would never believe it if a language dunce like me who had only scored 20% in Grammar suddenly scored 100% in Translation. But I couldn't very well let myself get zero either. That would be equally strange. So how much should I get? The overall passing grade was 40% and both papers had the same weight. So, I needed 60% on the Translation to give me that passing 40% average. Would it be too much? Could I jump from 20% on one paper to 60% on the other? I didn't know, but I decided to try.

In my head, as I lay in bed, I looked for several French words I probably wouldn't have known. The French text was about a meal. I substituted plausible errors: "*rendez-vous*" became surrender, "*verre*" a worm, "*couteau*" a cake, and "*boisson*" a fish. When I thought I had changed the menu enough, I stopped. I could always leave a few blanks at the last minute. Now I had two blackboards in my head, the perfect one and the 60% one.

The next morning, that butterfly-in-the-stomach feeling became a booby flapping its wings in my guts. I sat down at my desk in class and waited for the exam to start. Michael and Melford took the exam in another room. I had seen them with a group of their friends but, with so much to hide, we didn't greet each other.

The French exam paper floated onto my desk. It was indeed Michael's translation. One final difficulty faced me. My work was too quick. Fifteen minutes before time, I had finished writing my 60% text. This was not my usual style. I busied myself scratching out words and rewriting them until the last minute and then handed my paper in.

The French Master – his name has perished from my memory – glanced at me.

"How was it?"

"Well, not perfect, but a bit better than the Grammar exam, I think, Sir."

"Hmm. Let's hope so for your sake, Vanier." He was not happy about my casual attitude towards French. It seemed that if I dropped it next year, it would fall on his toe. I hoped he would pounce on my errors and not think too much about the rest.

Actually, I scored 62%. The marks in French were announced early; to my horror, Michael and Melford scored 96% and 92% respectively, coming first and second in the exam. They looked exultant. I was certain they would be found out, and hoped they wouldn't tell on me. But they weren't detected. As for myself, I reasoned that it must be quite common – in the Caribbean and elsewhere – to benefit from the ill-gotten gains of someone else's crime. But was the foot soldier any less guilty than the planners? At least this was just an Antigua exam, I thought. Even in cheating, a colonial hierarchy existed: it was less reprehensible to diddle a local French teacher than far-away-but-distinguished English examiners. Woe to him who ends up doing both.

Months later, I learned that Michael and Melford had done more – they had sold some of the information to other students a few minutes before the exam.

At the end of most terms, we left on vacation without knowing all our marks. The school would send a written report to our parents a week later. But the end of the year was special. We needed to know the outcome. We had to meet with the Housemaster or Shaky Jack to discover what Form we would be in for the next year, and what he thought of us in general. That year, I was summoned to Father Brown's office by both of them.

Shaky Jack began, "Christopher, Father Brown and I have a special decision to announce to you."

I looked at his face to see if this was good or bad news, but I couldn't tell. He was quite serious. I knew I had done wrong, but I couldn't see my way out. It would do no good to put the blame on the other two. It might even be a relief to have everything cleared up and tell the truth. I clasped my damp palms behind my back and wondered if Peter Pan's crew had felt like this when they walked the plank.

"Normally, at your young age, you would have to go into 5B, and that's what I had planned. But your exam results were better than hoped for, especially the Algebra and the French. Exceptionally, you will be promoted to Form 5A."

At the end of the gangplank, I turned around and walked back to the ship, safe again.

"For the Algebra, your Mathematics teacher thinks you were lucky or inspired, which may or may not happen again. On the other hand, concerning your pass in French after a miserable first paper, your teacher thinks that you have no inspiration, so it could only have been hard work. Father Brown says you studied late the night before; he heard voices. A boy who can work hard and catch up on his weak points deserves a chance. Congratulations."

At last, Shaky Jack allowed himself to smile. So did I.

After Shaky Jack had gone, Father Brown looked hard at me.

"Between us, take the Headmaster's verdict with a grain of salt. I don't need your surprise exam results to know you can study hard when you want to. I would have put you in 5A, whatever your grades, because I wouldn't want someone upright like you under the bad influence of Michael and Melford and the others who will be in the Remove."

Altar Boys

They have their exits and their entrances, those who matter. I've learned to watch the exits – they're more revealing. Some of us prefer first impressions to anchor our attitudes, and that's not to be disdained. But think of the importance that Yitzhak Rabin or Abraham Lincoln assumed *after* assassination. It shouldn't be this way, but sometimes at such tragic moments we understand some essential aspect of courage or virtue in the victim. When they disappear, we finally see what mattered most to them, and to us, and what they were struggling for, which in turn can illuminate all the dusty corridors of our previous acquaintanceship. We may have thought them foolish – we learn they were brave. We may have judged them cold – we discover they had passion. We may have thought them truthful, but that was always going to be naïve. Like a jumble of string, to untangle a life you have to start with its end.

When I knew him, I hardly paid attention to the "Ralph" in Ralph H. Brown – the same forename as my Dad – because we always addressed him as "Father Brown". Perhaps this conferred on him some parental responsibilities over me. "Ralph" is also *my* middle name, which ties the three of us together. As for the "H", he never used it, so I surmised it stood for something too embarrassing to disclose, like "Horace", "Humphrey", or "Humbert".

I first met Father Brown in the days of our Hog Valley farm, in Nevis, in 1950. The one thing missing during those epic holidays in the island hills was a good book to read. In St. Kitts, I could borrow from the Basseterre public library. The Nevis Charlestown library, which I joined, was much smaller, and was far away from Hog Valley. I craved adventure and fantasy stories of all sorts and my supply always ran out in Nevis. On Sundays, my parents would take us to an Anglican parish church, run by a young English priest who had immigrated to the island a few years earlier, after the war. He had a thin, ascetic look, contradicted by a smiling Clark Gable face with that characteristic dimple in the middle of his chin. He was roughly the age of my mother, born during the first world war. On one such occasion, my parents mentioned my interest in reading and the lack of good books.

"I have just the thing for your son," said Father Brown. "One of my friends in England has written a marvellous series of stories for children. His name is C.S. Lewis and his stories are about a country called Narnia."

At this point, I was not optimistic – nah-nah yourself – what would a strange English priest know about interesting stories?

However, he invited us into his parish rectory, and reached down a book from his well-stocked shelves called *The Lion, The Witch, and The*

Wardrobe. I brightened: with a Witch in the title, the story couldn't be all bad.

"Before I lend you this book, I'd like you to do me a favour." He took a black leather box out of a drawer, and opened it to reveal a glass lens.

"Please let me take a picture of you." Father Brown turned out to be an excellent amateur photographer, and, over the years, he took many photos of me. My face was shown against the sky, and I was often surprised to find the result even better looking than my self-conceit had imagined.

Those Narnia books opened up my imagination and not only did my mother spend countless hours reading them to us, but also I was occasionally recruited as an assistant reader for my younger brothers.

A few weeks later, Father Brown asked me why I liked the stories.

"Strange lands, and magic happening to children," I said.

"And what didn't you like?"

"Well, the children get old, and it didn't seem right for Aslan to die on the altar. Surely, he could have defeated the evil Queen in some other way? Why did he have to be sacrificed like that?"

"Maybe it's a true story, Christopher. This has happened before in another context, and will happen again."

I understood he was talking about Christ and the Bible.

"Well, I hope that only happens in books. Killing the innocent like that just didn't seem necessary."

"You know, pain and suffering are unavoidable. The victim is not always the loser."

I couldn't agree with this idea. If you have a choice, I thought, suffering is stupid. Who wants to bleed on an altar? I had not known much discomfort in my middleclass Caribbean upbringing, and didn't crave it. However, the conversation continued over many years, off and on, and led to my reading the more intractable works of C.S. Lewis, like *Out of the Silent Planet*. At that time, many years later, I would grasp – and reject – the notion of divine imperatives having ascendancy over our mortal loves and hates. Father Brown liked to throw up philosophical challenges to those who would listen. He cared more about involving us than convincing us. Commitment, like love, was too personal. He never questioned my faith, except to ascertain I said the Lord's Prayer every night, which was just as well.

I came under Father Brown's direct care in 1953, during my second year of boarding school. He had left Nevis to take up the jobs of Housemaster and Chaplain at the Antigua Grammar School.

There was a mystery about Father Brown, if I stopped to think about it. What had pulled this charismatic theology graduate from England to the faraway Caribbean seas – a minor outpost of the disintegrating British Empire? Or what had driven him? He had lived through terrible events in 1942, before leaving Europe. That much I knew, because of the dark look on his face whenever the War was mentioned. I couldn't find out more. Was he atoning for something?

Later, I wondered if he had felt guilt as a non-combatant priest, or if he had been to the front lines and suffered. As far as we boarders at the Antigua Grammar School were aware in 1955, Father Brown hadn't returned home to England since his arrival in the Caribbean. With his white skin, flowing cassock, and vigorous manner of holding his head up, he stuck out among a largely coloured and lethargic population. Yet, the Caribbean became his home. Some boarders said he had a mother in England to whom he wrote regularly, but that was his sole contact. He never returned.

Like Chaplains before him, Father Brown held a private mass most mornings in the small school chapel. There were never more than a handful of worshippers kneeling at the wooden pews, sometimes none. The Anglicans among the boarders were encouraged to be altar boys at these morning services. I was on duty once a week, clad in a white surplice. At first it was intimidating to be an altar boy in that stone-floored chapel, but finally, in exchange for memorising a few prayers, I had my first taste of communion wine from Father Brown's silver goblet.

At times, events would let us glimpse the struggles within Father Brown, like undersea reefs causing vortices on a calm surface. He seemed to care passionately about giving those in his charge the tools of independence and choice, like a good knowledge of English – cared enough to cane the laggards until their blood flowed. I flinched when I saw this ascetic side of him. I could not believe he liked administering severe physical punishment. Caning should have seemed evil to a priest like him. But, he explained to my disgust, he felt the *lack* of caning in some situations to be even more evil. So, he assumed the moral responsibility for it. I might have been sympathetic to the idea, if I had not myself been saved from this "greater evil" on several occasions by a sound thrashing. And, he caned more frequently as time went by, not just for breaking the school rules, but also for scholastic under-achievement, like Mr Blackett did.

I would have been more comfortable if his concern for us had stopped at discipline and class work. One Saturday when I was basking in the absence of school, he called me into his study and said, "Christopher, I've been thinking about your defects. Under cover of humour and other subterfuges, you are a selfish boy. You never go out of your way for anyone, neither helping them with their homework, nor lending them your personal belongings. The word for you is egotist, and you need to change."

There was more, but I didn't take his criticism in and fled to my inner sanctuary. My good opinion of myself took a beating, even more so because I wasn't sure what "egotist" meant, but the sound was bad. It was one of those words at the edge of my reading, not used in Caribbean schoolboy conversations, in the same category as "fascist" and "rapist". The shame I felt at being this horrible egotist was curiously like a caning. What was the harm in looking after myself, if that was his meaning? I hadn't hurt anyone, and I didn't deserve this. Father Brown was a tyrant who persecuted us. He sometimes still peers over my shoulder.

He truly loved his flock, but what was the nature of his love? Maybe the action of caning or reforming his pupils for their own good was easier to control than the more treacherous manifestations of love. This was perhaps his greatest pain. He entered some students' minds and then found he could not stay, must not get too close.

Things came badly undone in 1955 when a new Friar arrived – Friar Smithson – but I didn't believe the rumours about him at first. As far as I was concerned, the only strange aspect of the Friar was his heavy brown cassock, so different from Father Brown's white one. I heard that the colour was dictated by his Franciscan religious order. Anyway, since his arrival a few weeks earlier, I had had little to do with him; he had come to teach the younger children, the under-elevens. I was thirteen.

"How you mean, 'funny things going on'?" I asked my fellow boarder, Melford, who was often in the forefront of dubious events.

"You going see."

We paused in a corridor near the dormitories. Melford put his hands on his hips and smirked at me. As was often the case when I was excited or concerned, I reverted to my core diction and refused to talk in dialect; my companion hardly noticed – he knew that was the way I was.

"Come on, tell me."

"Well, you know the new boy Tomasso, arrived with Friar Smithson?"

"Yes – he's in the junior dormitory."

"He stay in Friar Smithson's office long, long."

"So what? He has special lessons. I heard he's never done Latin before."

"Not just Latin, boy. Funny things going on."

"Tell me, then! What funny things?"

"You know, touching, feeling up, a lot of sex stuff."

He made a crude circle between thumb and forefinger of one hand and jerked the other forefinger in and out.

"With a boy? Between Friar Smithson and Tomasso?"

"That's what I'm saying…"

"No! Not possible! You forget, he's a priest!"

"Don't say you not warned."

"But you don't understand – a priest or a friar wouldn't bother a little boy like that – it's forbidden."

"We see what we see. The door of that office always closed with the two of them inside."

"How could you see then – it can't be true – have you asked Tomasso?"

"You expect him say yes?"

I didn't know what I expected, but when I approached him, Tomasso turned red and started crying at the first question. Afterwards, he wouldn't talk to me. But I remembered that nine-year-old Tomasso cried easily – he was often teased. He was Spanish and didn't speak much English. I didn't believe the rumour. But the talk went on for days and days. None of the boarders wanted to talk of anything else. I couldn't ignore it.

"You still don't believe about Tomasso and Smithson, then?" Melford said, after dinner.

"No – a priest wouldn't do those things."

"I see them this time man, hand in hand."

"Doesn't mean anything. If they're doing something wrong, why doesn't anyone tell Father Brown?"

"You think he could stop it? All of them priests alike, boy. They don't have no woman, and the pressure just build up. So they all after the little boys."

"You think Father Brown himself would do things like that?"

"I don't have nothing against Father Brown, see? But I tell you, all them single priests the same. Anti-men we call them. Why Father Brown not get married if he normal? He Anglican, he could get wife."

I had never met an anti-man. In our Caribbean culture of the day, this was a bogey word; it meant any sort of sexual deviant, with no possible reprieve; curiously, there was no concept of an anti-woman. I realised the boarder teasing me was right about at least one thing. Anglican priests *can* get married *and* have children. My own grandfather was one of these. I was living proof they could have a family life if they chose to. So how come Father Brown hadn't married?

That evening, when I had finished my Latin sentences homework, I took my draft to Father Brown in his office for corrections. He closed the door behind me. No problems for my first three sentences. Then he saw the fourth, and he marked a red line through the verb. He put his hand on my knee. His flesh felt warm.

"Here, you know better. This verb should be in the past tense. Look it up."

Something in the way I was silent and not looking at him must have registered. Like magic, the hand was no longer on my knee. I had made two more mistakes. The hand didn't come back. He corrected my errors and then dismissed me.

I walked back along the creaking wooden corridor to my Dormitory, confused and scared. Was there anything to the stories? Could the rumours be true? Maybe priests really were after young boys. Maybe I was as much at risk as Tomasso? What should I do? Where was the trust I had had in Father Brown up to that instant? When I thought back, I remembered there was often physical contact with him: a hand on a shoulder, or a tap on a knee. But I had never been bothered before. Closeness was a small part of what I expected from a parent. And my parents had given me into his care. It wasn't as if he kissed his boarders, just a tap on the knee.

Damn Tomasso and Friar Smithson for giving me these doubts, I thought.

I didn't have long to wait for clarity on these questions before events took over. The next day, Father Brown called a general meeting of all the boarders before school started. Everyone was there but Tomasso.

"Boys, a serious matter has come up. A story has been circulating about our new teacher, Friar Smithson. Who has heard the story?"

There were a few nods, but most of us remained prudently rooted to the ground.

"I repeat, who has heard this story?"

A few more heads nodded.

"That's not good enough!" he threw at us. "Who, then, has *not* heard any stories about Friar Smithson? Step forward!"

No one moved.

He lowered his voice. "Now that we have *that* clear, tell me what you think these stories mean."

This took a little longer, but then we started volunteering information. I said, "We think he's been doing improper things with Tomasso, Sir."

Some boys took a guilty look around, like I had, to make quite sure our little roommate was not there.

Stalking towards us, Father Brown hissed, "It's monstrous! You don't know what you are saying! Child molesting – that's its name – is a crime. Do you think this is some game? Don't you see this accusation might land someone in prison? Rightly or wrongly?"

I wished I hadn't been the boy to speak up.

"Have you any idea of the sacrifices a priest makes? Have you any notion what he gives up on the altar of the Lord's will? Can you imagine how a story like this could break a man's life?"

I realised we were all going to be caned.

Father Brown paced back and forth in front of us, bone white with suppressed anger, except for two red spots on his cheeks.

"You should all be caned, every last one of you."

I felt his eyes swivel across me, and I knew I would not be exempted, even though I had not started the rumour, not even wanted to believe it. If only I hadn't made a mistake in that fourth Latin sentence.

"But, exceptionally, I will not cane you, not even those who deserve chastisement the most. None of you will speak of this again. Ever. And especially not to Tomasso or Friar Smithson. If I hear any remark on the subject, all of you – all of you – will be severely punished. Do I make myself clear?"

"Yes, Sir."

"And next time, THINK before you blabber nonsense in the corridors. And if you throw thoughtless stones, expect to be hit yourselves. Go back to your work – this business is now OVER."

We didn't discuss this meeting, not even among ourselves. Not a word.

Tomasso did not come back to the junior dorm, nor did I see him again. We heard Father Brown had found him lodgings in town, paid out of his own pocket. Then he was transferred to another school, on another island. He just disappeared from our lives. We did not see much of Friar Smithson either. Three weeks later, Father Brown announced that the Friar had been recalled to England by his order. I made many more mistakes in Latin, but there was never a hand or even a tap on my knee again.

In 1956, the year I was fourteen, I was admitted to the Fifth Form, and was preparing for my Cambridge School Certificate exams, when I tried to exploit the paternal side of Father Brown. My exams seemed gloriously far away.

We were healthy boys – the school Matron patched up our small cuts, scrapes, and bruises. A dab of iodine and all was fine. However, we discovered that a whiff of illness could get us off from classes. Father Brown worried about our physical welfare. So, my friend Miguel often had a severe stomach ache before a Latin test and brawny Trapl's brain hurt amazingly a few hours before a Mathematics quiz. When Father Brown noticed I had scratched my ankles and shins into sores, the incident was worth a half day of special dressings and ointments. "*I'm ill, again,*" was the name of the game, until after a while, Father Brown got suspicious, and I knew I had to be careful if I wanted to outfox him.

I'd had my little victories, but I also remembered the anger Father Brown had shown in the Friar Smithson affair, and I remembered the many canings he had given me, not least the four strokes for a tiny insult to my Latin Master, and the six strokes for throwing a handful of pebbles at a car. I found him cruel, but paradoxically, despite this major defect in our relations, I was never afraid of him for long. I sensed a compensating tenderness alongside the disciplinarian, close by his

English sense of humour. I remembered that my priestly grandfather accepted violence, and had sometimes tried to spank me.

After dinner one night, I felt nauseous – a rare event for my cast iron stomach.

"I don't feel well," I said to my friends. "Maybe it's the meat cakes again. Should I tell Father Brown?"

They looked at me knowingly and asked if I had any pains, and I didn't, not at first. Everyone knew I had a tough test in History coming up the next day, so they laughed. When a diffuse abdominal pain did develop, I was surprised my body could betray me in this way. What had I done to merit this distressing sensation of my skin being stretched and tender from rib to thigh? But there might have been a chance to get some time off, so I reported the pain to Father Brown.

"Do you know the story of the boy who cried, 'Wolf'?"

That night he gave me a bicarbonate of soda drink and he came early to check on me the next morning. I told him my tummy hurt more – the pain was now quite sharp – and I felt ill, even a little feverish.

He probed my stomach on the left.

"Does it hurt here?"

"Not specially."

Then he gave me a vigorous jab on the right.

"Ouch, yes, it hurts there!"

He hesitated. Then there were more jabs, back and forth, but gentler. After a while, I became confused. I felt pain everywhere below my navel, and he looked at me doubtfully.

He pursed his lips, went back to his office to consult one of his medical books, and returned to order me not to go to class.

While I slouched on my bed, trying but failing to relish my victory, amazed that this new sort of stomach pain could be so impressive, Father Brown used the only telephone in the school, located in the Headmaster's office.

A few minutes later he said to me, "You may have appendicitis. Do you know what that is?"

"No, Father."

"I've called in the school doctor to have a look at you."

The arrival of a doctor was an alarming event. Missing my test should have cheered me up, but for the horrid way my head and stomach were misbehaving. My plan, if I ever had one, was going wrong.

"What's appendicitis, Father?"

"Well, it's something serious, but quite treatable by the doctors today. You may have to go into the hospital for a short stay, if the doctor confirms my suspicions. Try not to worry."

Father Brown was blunt and reassuring.

However, I already knew if people told me not to worry about something, there *was* something to be worried about. I hoped the pain would go away.

Things accelerated after that. The doctor concurred with Father Brown's diagnosis of an inflamed appendix. They planned to operate at once.

"The boy had never heard of the condition before, so he can't be misleading us," I overheard.

Father Brown sent a telegram to my parents, and my father gave his consent for an operation and promised to come to Antigua as soon as he could get a flight; they should not delay surgery, however. When I knew they wanted to operate on me, I began to panic. Why had I started all this? Maybe the pain would go away by itself if they would just let me lie in bed. I mentioned my horror of the time when I'd had my tonsils removed, but I wasn't in a fit state to debate with them.

"Can't the operation wait for my father?"

"No, this is an emergency," the doctor said. "Don't worry, we have a good anaesthetic."

So it was done; the surgeon did his cutting while I slept. I had no nightmares. When I awoke later, I found Father Brown at my bedside.

"I still have pains," I said.

"That's just the stitches waking up. Do you know you were thrice lucky today? First, your unruly appendix was indeed in poor shape, ready to burst. Second, the surgeon couldn't easily find it. You had quite a layer of fat, and the sac wasn't exactly where it should have been, over on the right. But the only consequence is you'll have a somewhat larger scar than usual."

At last – a knife scar like my grandfather's, bringing my collection of combat trophies up to three.

"And third?"

"Well, you are lucky you weren't born twenty years ago. Before the war, appendicitis was often neither diagnosed, nor operated on, in time. A burst appendix – like yours would have done – could cause peritonitis. In this part of the world, lots of boys your age didn't survive."

A pleasant, uncharitable shiver went through me, driving the pain away for a moment. I had chosen a good time to be born. Think of all the unlucky boys a few decades ago: perforating, bursting, and exploding their guts. Whatever else happened to me from now on, I would be a step ahead in the survival game. I would never regret the "good old days" of before the War.

The next day my father came, accompanied by the surgeon and Father Brown.

"What am I going to do without an appendix? Don't I need it for anything?"

"No," said the surgeon, "the appendix is a perfectly useless organ: an appendage that should have withered away eons ago. You'll be fine without one."

"Well, where is the thing, anyway?"

My father turned to the surgeon, who produced a small glass bottle, three inches by one and a half inches. Inside was an amorphous little grey-and-pink sausage, floating in a clear liquid. I felt quite proud.

"Will it go bad?"

"The tissue is preserved in formaldehyde solution and should keep for as long as you want. I'll give the bottle to your father."

"You can take the guilty party back home to show to your grandfather," Father Brown said.

We three Ralphs looked at each other.

"I'm going back home?"

"Yes," said my father, "the surgeon here says you need to convalesce for at least two weeks, and you'll be better off with us at home."

"Then I'll fail my end-of-year exams!"

"Father Brown says you'll be quite alright. There'll still be two months to prepare. He'll help you to catch up."

It turned out I had a lot less than two months to prepare, because I developed a wheeze, attributed to asthma, which I cultivated as long as I could, and succeeded in being pampered in St. Kitts for a whole month. My grandfather – now retired from his priesthood – was indeed interested in my tale of appendicitis. Before I returned to school, he looked at the bottle with the bit-of-me-that-should-have-withered-away-eons-ago.

"Did you thank Father Brown for saving your life, Chris? If he hadn't sent you to the hospital in time – "

"I know, I know, this little sausage might have burst. But the surgeon was the one who operated."

"Nevertheless, you must thank him when you go back to Antigua. A priest like Father Brown spends his life without many earthly thanks. Sacrifice is woven into the cloth. I should know. Think how much he cares for you boys!"

"But he canes us all the time!"

"That's neither here nor there."

I was not at all sure I agreed. "Why didn't he get married and have his own children like you did, then?" I asked.

"I can't answer for him. Each one of us is his own keeper. But I can tell you this. He loves you as if you were his child, but he is honour-bound not to show the slightest favouritism."

He was not preying on us, then. I owed him something. I thought of the photographs he took of me on the school veranda, that he was so proud of – face open, smiling, hair wind-blown – and how he reworked the prints in his small laboratory to remove all the little defects.

I held up the floating appendix. I was still feeling proud of it, though that little bit of flesh had caused me so much pain. I felt an attachment, as if I mustn't lose any part of myself. I hoped that, in the future, even if painful, I could keep within me all my other kinks, deformities, blemishes, imperfections, and assorted defects, without anyone – even Father Brown – trying to remove them.

After sitting my Cambridge School Certificate exams in 1957, I said goodbye to Father Brown. He promised to forward the results to me in St. Kitts as soon as they arrived. I left the Antigua Grammar School forever without a regret. It never occurred to me anyone might regret me.

About a month later, my father brought home a telegram.

"Open it," he said, "it's addressed to you."

I read as follows:

"ENGLISH DISTINCTION MISSED GOOD RESULTS PASSED OTHER SUBJECTS EXCEPT PHYSICS
RALPH BROWN"

So, I had a distinction in English after all. I had had some doubts after the exam. The text to be analysed was a piece by G.K. Chesterton, *The Red Town*, which I had felt at home with. I remembered skipping over the author's political comments and savouring: "Red is the most joyful and dreadful thing in the physical universe…" My doubts began in the grammar section, which seemed boring, and I knew tedious things did not bring out the best in me. Anyway, that subject had turned out all right, I supposed, but I didn't like "Missed good results". What had gone wrong, apart from the Physics?

The next day, I received the second telegram in my life:

"SORRY NOT CLEAR STOP SOMETIMES I DON'T KNOW WHEN TO STOP STOP SHOULD HAVE READ QUOTE ENGLISH DISTINCTION MISSED STOP GOOD RESULTS STOP PASSED OTHER SUBJECTS EXCEPT PHYSICS STOP UNQUOTE
RALPH BROWN"

I could do without the distinction in English, I figured. What did he mean, that he "didn't know when to stop"?

I didn't see Father Brown during the following heady years in St. Kitts, nor before I left the Caribbean. As I climbed up the academic ladder, my attention was always focused on the rung above, not below, so my next contact with Father Brown was nine years later, by letter:

15th January 1967
Dear Father Brown,
Thank you so much for your recent letter. I'm glad my parents gave you my address over here. The work is hard, but exciting. I see you don't approve of computers!
It's not what you think, really. I've not given up the challenging pencil-and-paper arithmetic you remember so well – I still have to do that. Solving engineering equations always requires some paperwork. And I use a slide rule extensively, if you know what that is (think of logarithms drawn to scale). But the computer is for problems I couldn't calculate in weeks or months. It's a mind-extender, not a sign of intellectual failure or cheating. You might even like programming yourself if you had the opportunity!
And yes, I do think back to my schooldays in Antigua from time to time. I'm here thanks to you. I've made many sacrifices to become a scientist, but it all began in Antigua. My parents said you are now Headmaster of the school; that must be a lot of extra work. I hope they appreciate it! Please keep well.
Love and best wishes to you,
Christopher

I wrote to him once or twice after that, and then was caught up in other activities and lost track of his situation and all sorts of things from my past. But in 1976, my parents sent me news of Father Brown. Age had forced him to give up his teaching job; he was semi-retired in a quiet village parish on the coast of Antigua called Falmouth. A terrible thing had happened.

Impressions surged through me: Nevis, Aslan, Antigua, the secret war trauma, my canings, the painful incident of Friar Smithson, undetected crimes and escapades, my appendicitis, my pain, his pain, the struggle for my own world, his mysterious mix of brutality and compassion, and the thoughtless way I had forgotten the priest. I dropped my parents' letter and stared into a void. I felt my cowardice. I didn't want to think of my friend and mentor suffering, but the very lack of detail forced my imagination into overdrive. I could hear his aggressors' words and smell his fear.

On the night they came to his rectory, they didn't have guns. Those would not be needed for a frail priest. Just a gentle knock on his door after dinner. He had been praying, or perhaps reading by the glow of a candle. And he opened the door. He always let people in. Then they pushed past him, too quickly. If only they had been robbers. Two smooth faces, hard muscles, and a smell of sweat.

He knew, right from the start, what they were there for. But there was nowhere to escape, so he sat on his chair, cold lipped.

"Have you come to be altar boys?"

He had been semi-retired in his village on the coast, but still socially active, not just the caretaker of the parish church. Then the first wave of hard drugs had come in, bringing its cortège of violence. Smugglers bought off customs officers and governments. An admirer of C.S. Lewis and his Narnia tales, he saw what was happening – the evil White Queen assuming power – and fought it from his pulpit. He denounced the cocaine traffic. He used his telescope to spot the smugglers' launches. Unfortunately, he'd named names.

It had come to this: a charismatic theology graduate from England who emigrated to a faraway outpost of Empire in the Caribbean, a gifted teacher who inspired generations of West Indian students, a courageous priest who had looked like Clark Gable when younger, an ascetic who had given up family and country, was now too feeble to defend himself.

The leader began, "Old man, you damn good preacher. Plenty people listen what you say. So, why you preach about what not concern you?"

Father Brown waited for more.

Then the intruders offered a packet of white powder to their accuser.

"Look, good Columbian stuff, smell it, eat it, then at least you can't tell no more lies. Lot more where this come from, if you like."

Father Brown slapped the powder away and allowed himself to be inflamed, one precious, useless moment, with anger against them and their kind. Face bloodless, lips quivering, he still showed a bit of Clark Gable.

But when he saw the knife flick, sharp and bright, he stopped shouting, fascinated by the blade that looked like a serpent in the candlelight. Later, when they had finished their business, they would take three candlesticks, to make it look like a burglary-and-struggle crime.

"Take care, Father. You got a big mouth for an old man. You talk bad about my boss in church. That's no way to preach. He give the people what they want."

"It's an ugly thing to give some people what they want."

"That's what I mean, old man! You don't have respect. Look at me. I got respect for my boss. We is his altar boys. Respect for you, too. But, my boss so good, to so many, it hurt me to hear you talk. You must get some feeling for him, and done with the lies you been preaching. You can't call his name in vain."

The leader picked up a silver candlestick, admiringly. He put one hand on the priest's shoulder in a friendly fashion, and perhaps, I think, Father Brown forgave him.

Not one of Father Brown's myriad of pupils was there on that night in 1976, but we all took his brutal snuffing out as a personal sorrow. From far away, I wondered if I had been wrong about the futility of sacrifice.

I had two fathers, three if I counted my grandfather.

Part 4: Experiments (St. Kitts, 1957-1959)

Willpower

Changing schools can be as challenging as changing countries, and I did both. In 1957, I transferred from flat and arid Antigua, garlanded with its coral beaches, where I had been a boarder, to fertile St. Kitts, crowned with its lush mountains, where my family lived. I didn't know what to expect. I had it on good authority that the St. Kitts Grammar School didn't cane boys in the Sixth Form. This was good news, if true, but surely not sufficient motivation for continuing my studies. I was there because my father wanted me there, and he wanted me there because he thought I could win a scholarship. On the bright side, I was looking forward to being a Prefect, whose job was to maintain the system of authority over the younger boys. Prefects had their own study room and privileges. I was tired of being bullied and wanted to be on the winning team. But I feared disappointing my father in my studies.

I soon found this freedom from physical punishment *did* indeed apply to me, even though, at fourteen, I was a very young Sixth Former, and I let out the breath of fear I had been holding for the last five years in Antigua. It's odd how the absence of a physical threat can change your whole relationship with an institution. I discovered I could be friendly with my teachers, although in doing so, I somehow respected them less.

I now lived with my parents and two brothers at the far end of Wigley Avenue, overlooking the spectacular bay of Basseterre. My sister Hazel had left home for special education in England two years before; she was handicapped and got family priority. I didn't envy her the trials of being a boarder, especially in a country as cold as I heard England was.

On my second day in Sixth Form, I walked in the morning sun to my new school. The day before, my father had driven me. On foot, it took ten minutes along Wigley Avenue and then Jones' Hill. "Wigley" was an old sugar plantation family name, and the road sloped down, but the origin of "Jones" was a mystery to me. I sweated going up the steep hill, wishing I were whizzing down it. A quarter mile beyond the hilltop, the dilapidated school buildings – which pre-dated the present concrete sprawl north of Warner Park – made the Antigua school I had just left seem quite imposing. Before me were creaky, wooden, single-level structures with corrugated metal roofs and jalousies for ventilation. I saw an open playing field that was all dirt – no trees or grass – and placed right next to a poor "village" zone of the town. The rum shop doors of the village were gaping, and the kerbside gutters were never sluiced out, except by storms. Scrawny hens and mangy dogs ambled across upper Wigley Avenue, avoiding the empty-eyed, bedraggled villagers squatting on the sidewalk.

When I drove a car later on, I would come to think of that stretch of road as a place of despair and mild menace, to be driven by a little quicker than elsewhere, but in 1957, on my second day, it just seemed quaint and somewhat smelly, my road to school. I didn't question why so many around me were unwashed and listless whereas I was freshly bathed and eager to learn. The world was like that. But at some deep level, all those young people like me lucky enough to have obtained a secondary education were dreaming: how to escape from this place?

A tall tamarind-brown youth I didn't recognise approached me in the schoolyard.

"Hey, you with the funny glasses! Where you from?" I was briefly sorry I had chosen the largest eyepieces that my parents would agree to.

During a confusing first day, I had learned the names of my classmates: Clive, Welby, Louis, Kaye, Nizzie, Nasals, and Sammy. They were all from St. Kitts and seemed to know each other. I tried to place the unknown older youth who now questioned me, but failed. Maybe he belonged to the upper Sixth.

"Hear you come from Antigua?"

"I attended Fifth Form there."

"So, how come you're here? Why not stay on for the Sixth in Antigua?" Given the rundown state of the St. Kitts school buildings, I had been asking this question myself.

"I got tired of Antigua. And, I heard this was better."

"Right, man, we're *much* better! Your Head was Foot, right?"

I laughed. "You mean Shaky Jack, that's what we called him."

"Well, as you can see, man, we don't have any British teachers like him around, hardly any non-Kittitians. I trust you've met our rare off-islander, our Chemistry wizard, Mr Blackman? No one's found a better name for him yet."

I laughed again, and as we got talking, inevitably, the conversation drifted to what would be on our minds for the whole time in Sixth Form: the Leeward Islands Scholarship.

"Is it true that St. Kitts has won the scholarship three times in a row?"

Instead of replying, he crossed his arms on his chest and raised his eyebrows at me. "You think you can win it?"

"I intend to try."

"Lee said you looked ambitious. You talk like a dictionary! And yes, the Leeward Islands Scholarship is going to stay in St. Kitts. But why should we allow *you* in here? We don't need foreigners."

For a dreadful moment, I thought he might be an authority, not a student. "Allow me? How's that? Look, Sir, I was born here in St. Kitts, just like you."

Abruptly, he broke out laughing and pointed to a small building next to my classroom. "Just joking! Come around and meet the Prefects, including the *next* scholarship winner."

Not realising I was being favoured (in fact, interviewed), I followed my host, who confided, "For your information, I studied here in St. Kitts, but I was born in Antigua."

So, we were symmetrical from the start, me a Kittitian who had gone to Antigua, and he an Antiguan who had come to St. Kitts. But while my birthplace would never be a political issue, he would one day be ignored for the highest office because of his.

We entered a bare room – almost a shed – that the Prefects called their own. Two large wooden tables dominated, each of them etched and inked with a lifetime of scholastic passion. As I settled into one of the eight shaky chairs, I began to associate names with the three faces around me, all at least four years older. The most outgoing, the one who had asked me where I came from, the intermediary, was Fitzroy Bryant; lean, and sporting a loosely-trimmed stubble on his chin that made me jealous; it would be another five years before I could shave.

His friend, stocky and very black, had prominent lips and an upturn to his face. He seemed to be looking down at everyone, which was curious because he was quite short. This slightly arrogant look (which I would try to copy in future years) belonged to Lee Moore, the one who had thought I looked ambitious. I was cocky about my English, but would find out that his was as good as mine, and his Kittitian island speech was more expressive, whether we called it "dialect", "pidgin", or "Creole".

I met another tall, peanut-coloured young man, in casual clothes, the only one of us not clad in the school uniform. This seemed to indicate a more adult status; he took his feet off the table as we entered and relaxed on a chair. He was Billy Herbert, soon off to study Law in England. Where Fitzroy was all sharp angles, Billy was smooth and urbane. Where Lee was a trifle aggressive but frank, Billy was reassuring but opaque.

Of course, I couldn't see myself, but imagined they looked down on me as young, brown-skinned, and chubby. I was unusually short of words because I didn't know whether they approved my presence or not. But my new friends put me at ease quickly because they were proud of the school and eager to groom new talent.

"Billy, this is Chris Vanier," Fitzroy introduced us, "a bright young spark just arrived from Antigua. You know, he's Ralph Vanier's son."

I wasn't sure what pleased me most, to be called a "bright young spark", or to be recognised as a notable lawyer's son.

"Our fathers work together in the Sugar Association. What are you hoping to do with your studies?" asked Billy.

"I haven't chosen yet." I paused, not knowing what to say to these students who seemed so much wiser than me, but sensing an ally in Billy. I was aware that I would have to discard some of my Antiguan exam subjects, but my father had told me not to decide too quickly. "Could you tell me more about the scholarship?"

"It's about a hell of a lot of hard work. The British Government gives out just one scholarship per year to the whole of the Leeward Islands – St. Kitts, Nevis, Anguilla, Antigua, and Montserrat. It's based on the results of the Cambridge Higher School Certificate.

"You can forget about Anguilla, though," he continued, shaking his head, "the Valley secondary school has no 6th Form, so they've never had a candidate. How many subjects did you pass in your School Cert?"

In later years, I thought of these exams as "A-levels" and "O-levels". In reality, these "A and O" terms (and likewise "GCE") were only introduced when the exams were reorganised later on, and for the Caribbean in the late 1950s it was "Higher School Cert" and "School Cert", exams that still exist in other parts of the Commonwealth.

"Seven."

"A good start. And what are your best subjects?"

I hadn't given this much thought, but I knew I wanted to be a scientist. "Chemistry and Literature," I answered, "and perhaps Mathematics."

"Hmm," mused Billy. "A bad combo. Literature usually goes with History, Geography or Latin."

"No, I don't want those."

"If you're serious about trying for the scholarship, you'll have to take a fourth subject. Candidates who succeed in four subjects are favoured over candidates with only three, although no one really knows how the scholarship committee picks the winner."

On this cardinal point, there would always be secrets. The Cambridge examining board and the colonial education office made recommendations, but it was up to the island governments to jointly make the final choice.

"What's it to be?" continued Billy.

"Physics, then."

"Majority science, eh? No scientist has yet won the scholarship – you would be the first."

Fitzroy interrupted, "You know, someone with distinctions in two or three subjects would probably beat a competitor who just had passes in four."

"Don't confuse the man," Lee said. "In the Caribbean, we can't count on distinctions – maybe one at the most. We live in an outpost of the British Empire – not close enough to their teaching system to achieve our best. The name of the game for us is survival – a good pass in each subject."

Lee sensed the existence of a privileged Public School education in Britain without being able to clearly identify it. At the time, it was fortunate for me and other scholarship contenders that we didn't have to compete head-on with our British counterparts.

I drank in my new friends' advice, accepting Lee's lecturing tone, but feeling a bit confused. I had assumed all I had to do was take a few exams in St. Kitts to win a scholarship and secure a university place. No sweat. What would these boys say if they knew I had failed Physics at O-level?

"Chris, this is vital. The competition is tough. The work is tough. Figure that if you want to win the scholarship and get into university, you have to be *first* among forty candidates from the Leewards. You need to study, late at night and many hours per day; you'll have to bust your arse working."

Forty competitors? It seemed more than tough to me. Fitzroy had called me a bright student, but there had always been subjects I didn't like. I had never been overall first in my class in Antigua. Studying for long periods was not fun. How could I ever beat thirty-nine others?

Lee must have noticed I looked discouraged. "Tell him about the possibility of repeating, Billy. He's quite young."

"There is an age limit," Billy said, "but within this you can try for the scholarship as many times as you like. The oldest you can be is eighteen, so many students have only one chance."

"It's true – St. Kitts has had three successive winners: Hodge, Simmonds, and Richardson. Our Headmaster is very protective, and our students help each other. Billy missed it two years ago," Lee said, "but he's going to study Law in London, anyway. Richardson beat me last year. But I have a second chance – I'm going to win it this year."

Fitzroy looked at me. "I'm jealous," he said. "If you're only fourteen now, you can have *three* tries at the scholarship!"

This gave me some hope, until I realised that three tries would mean spending four years in Sixth Form: one year in 6B, three in 6A – a long time. What if I had bad luck on my third try?

"Isn't there any other way to go to university?" I said. "You said Billy is going anyway."

They laughed. "Sure," Fitzroy said, "you could pay your own way. Is your Dad rich?" They laughed again.

I had no idea what a university education cost. In fact, outside of my weekly pocket money, I knew little of financial matters. But I felt from their laughter my father couldn't afford anything like that, even if he had a good job, especially as he was already paying for my sister abroad; almost no one's family could afford a university education in the small islands at the time.

"It's a tough, tough world," Billy said. "No scholarship, no university. Unless you have a fairy godmother, like me." I never found out how Billy financed his studies.

"Actually," Fitzroy said, "there might be another way. I'm twenty and no longer eligible for the scholarship. That's why I'm working as a teacher. If I save up my pay for a few years, I might be able to get to London with a little cash left over for tuition fees. They say you can find jobs over there to pay for your lodgings."

I was surprised to discover Fitzroy was already teaching, but the future would show me just how eager this Caribbean school was to use its ex-Sixth Formers to transmit their knowledge. I would teach there myself one day.

The reality was both worse and better than any of us knew at the time. On a St. Kitts salary, it would be impossible to save up for a complete British university education, let alone one in America. But in a few years, the Caribbean islands would begin to emerge from their educational dark ages. Within a decade, there would be several other grants and scholarships to go to Britain or Canada, and the regional university of Jamaica would one day make a huge difference. Once on a foreign campus – if you could obtain a visa – help was available for the needy. And Fitzroy was right: poor students could work on campus to pay their way. But there would only ever be one Leeward Islands Scholarship, and I needed it.

The future lay ahead of us, endless, and – despite the difficulties – singing a siren's song.

That first conversation was a lot to digest, but there were others in the weeks to come. I learned I could not join the Prefects in their duties until my second year in the Sixth Form, but that I was often welcome in their room as a scholarship candidate. Billy was sometimes present, although no longer at school.

"So, that's what you advise me to do," I said to the three of them a month later, "try again and again for the scholarship, hoping I get better each year?"

"Not just hoping," Fitzroy said, "but making it happen."

I objected, "No one can be sure of winning against thirty-nine-odd competitors."

"The number doesn't matter," Lee said. "First, of the forty, how many really count? Perhaps ten. Second, and most important, it's all a question of willpower! I don't mean only the scholarship. Look at this beaten-up, poverty-stricken, second-rate world around you! Nothing's happening. Nothing's moving in these islands, Britain's forgotten colonies. But it doesn't have to be this way."

He gestured with a stubby finger at the lone picture – the Queen – on the otherwise bare wooden walls of the Prefects' room. "The glory of

England, the end of slavery, and the fairness of the rich: all bollocks! Yet, our ideas, rules, and regulations still come from Britain. But what about us: our thinking, our will, and our projects?" Lee's eyes reminded me of my grandfather, the priest, as he said, "Our willpower can change the way the world works. We can impose our own views."

"But slavery is over – that was a century ago!" I reacted against his fervour.

"You think so, do you? Then why are all the black workers so poor? Have you ever seen a black plantation owner? Beware of popular ideas."

While I was trying to think of an answer, he continued, "It's because of the land. Without popular land ownership, the people can't improve their lot."

Then Lee laughed and clapped me on the shoulder, "Don't pay attention to me – Billy here doesn't agree with my ideas, and Fitzroy changes his mind every day. Let's go back to the question of studying. Billy once mentioned busting our arses with work. It has a literal sense. Tell him about our experiment, Fitzroy."

"What experiment?" I asked. This might be my key to success.

Billy winked at me as Fitzroy began with a sheepish smile, "Look, I'm not sure you can use this. It's just to show the power of mind over matter – an idea of Billy's, actually. How many times do you go to the toilet each day?"

"Twice, I think," I said, taken aback.

"Some go once, some three times," Fitzroy said. "But isn't it a waste of time?"

I couldn't see where he was going. "But you have to excrete, don't you?"

"Well, we decided to test this commonly accepted knowledge and use our willpower to change the way our bodies work. We did something original. To put it bluntly, we stopped shitting."

"What? That's impossible!"

"No more impossible than beating thirty-nine other scholarship competitors. Lee and I stopped shitting for three whole weeks. By sheer willpower. That was the point."

"Pissing was allowed," Lee said.

"I don't believe you! Three weeks?"

I looked at Billy, who seemed more serious than the other two. "Yes, it's true," he nodded.

"You did it too?"

"Do I look crazy, man? No, I just counted the days."

This willpower thing was definitely not my style. I thought of denying myself a bowel movement, repeatedly. No way. "I still can't see how it's possible. You would explode or something."

More chuckles.

"OK, I'll help you out," Fitzroy said. "Even terrific willpower can do with a little assistance. We did some research first and decided not to eat any bulky foods; no vegetables, potatoes, rice, or bread. Instead, we ate concentrated bits of protein: corned beef, salt fish, and boxed cheese. We avoided fruit, but took lots of sugar: honey, condensed milk, and sweets. And plenty of liquids."

"It was hard for the first week," Lee said. "But the sphincter is a powerful muscle, and we willed it to keep everything in. During the second and third weeks we mainly had to put up with stomach cramps and nausea."

Awestruck, I heard Billy say, "Tell him what happened after that."

"Well, it doesn't change anything," Fitzroy said. "It worked."

"What happened to you?"

"After three weeks, I have to admit I didn't feel well. Otherwise, I might have done a fourth week. But both of us had to be taken to hospital and treated with laxatives and enemas. It cost us two days out of school."

"Sounds horrible!"

"Their intestines were almost welded together," Billy said. "They didn't know when to stop and only just avoided surgery."

"I'm not saying those two days were pleasant," Fitzroy said. "But see, it proves my point. It was an original plan. We did something everyone else thought impossible. It may have been risky. But with willpower we did it."

I was impressed, but didn't think my low tolerance for pain would get me very far in this game. But was that true? With the number of canings I had received in Antigua, my acceptance of pain must be reasonably high. It was more my reluctance to deny myself something I craved: to study instead of reading comics, to stay awake when I was sleepy, not to eat when I was hungry, and, of course, to stop my bowels from moving when they asked to do so. And then there was daydreaming – I spent a lot of time in fantasy worlds. Later, I would be thankful that, in addition to my other temptations not to work, I didn't have to contend with TV.

"I called it 'The Great Shit Fast'," Billy said.

"You can apply it to anything," Fitzroy said. "Willpower, that's what the Caribbean needs."

"Nuclear fission of the human spirit," Lee said.

Suddenly, it was all a bit too much. I was the scientist – what did they know of atoms? They were smiling at me as if this scatological story made them superior. They could see I didn't even like to use the common word for faeces.

"Well, maybe I believe you, now. But why call your experiment an exercise in willpower? I don't see the power in it. I just see artificial constipation!"

Billy laughed more than the others. "He has you there, doesn't he? And he might have said masochism."

It did not occur to me to analyse the roles of my three mentors. I was impressed by the doers, those who had risked their health to show willpower, and less aware that Billy may have been the real mastermind.

"No, he's not right," Fitzroy said. "Willpower it is. To call it just artificial would deny our courage and creativity. Words matter. I'll choose my own epitaph, thank you!"

Regardless, I didn't think I could apply his willpower formula to studying. A person was gifted enough to win a scholarship, or he wasn't, and no amount of self-delusion could change that. A little hard work wouldn't go amiss, I figured, but sound-and-fury wasn't my style. Comforted by the idea that I had always been able to do well in my exams with an hour of work the evening before, I felt there were more amusing ways to use my time than to study obsessively. No fasting for me. With reasonable luck and three tries, I could win. But maybe there was something in Fitzroy's creativity and Lee's distrust of popular ideas. As for Lee's politics, my head swirled with contradictory thoughts. My new companions had gone farther along the road to personal freedom than I had. This was admirable. Was I too scornful of their bizarre tactics? Did I feel an undercurrent of hostility to my father's role as a lawyer for the sugar industry? My boarding school had taught me how to "break out" of an institution's confining rules, so I was pro-revolution, in principle. But whose revolution? Which icons to defy, and how much risk to accept before the revolutionary became simply a damn fool?

Abruptly, it occurred to me that Fitzroy's emphasis on the use of language might affect me directly. I was now sure of my subjects: Chemistry, Mathematics, Physics, and – above all – Literature. "Which forms will you teach?" I said.

"Lower school for now. But next year I will be in charge of English and Advanced Literature in 6A. You'll be in my class, and I'm afraid you'll have to call me 'Mr Bryant'."

"As long as it's not 'Sir'."

"Outside of the classroom," he said, "my friends call me Bug."

Those were happy days, when everything seemed possible to those three confident faces. But, years later, my new friends would not remain friends with each other. Billy would be opposed in politics to Lee and Fitzroy. I couldn't know then how much I overestimated my own talents and underestimated their extraordinary willpower, which would take the three of them to riches and fame. Fitzroy would one day have a school named after him, the Clarence Fitzroy Bryant College, and he would become Minister of Labour in a future St. Kitts government. Lee would be a gifted orator, winning the British Inter-University Debating Competition two years in a row. He would take a theology degree along with law; become a QC and Attorney General, and, briefly, Premier of St. Kitts some twenty years later. Billy, another gifted lawyer, would be chief strategist of the Opposition anti-Labour party, and become quite rich, more so than the others. He would be the St. Kitts delegate to the UN, though never making it to elective office. Success was hard earned; equilibrium easily lost. Just as the earlier willpower experiment ended in a painful purge, so things would turn sour for the three of them one day: they would all disappear tragically in mid-life, consumed by their ardour. Going against the flow of things is not without danger. One would reputedly die of AIDS, another of an alcohol-damaged liver like my grandfather Cecil Rawle, and the third would disappear at sea with his close family in June of 1994, likely assassinated. In the Greek temple of Delphi it is written, "Nothing to excess."

Despite the seeds, in 1957 these events were far away. My intellectual relations with Fitzroy were just beginning, and I was in strong disagreement with the willpower idea and the whole notion of grinding competition. I needed to find a path of my own, a continuation of my efforts at independence begun in Antigua. And, as before, paths leading into uncharted territory carried uncharted risks. I was not interested in politics, nor in religion, nor in physical effort, nor yet in sex, but I was convinced there must be other, more magical countries to dwell in. I was not going to listen to my well meaning, if ambitious, friends, nor to my well-meaning, if intrusive, parents. I had only one true guide: from my earliest awakening with *The Wind in The Willows* and *Narnia* – books.

Mosquito Bites

It was the wet season and I liked the way weather disturbed the world. In the early morning, sometime between five and seven o'clock, pellets of warm Caribbean rain would trouble our slumbers, pounding on the roofs and verandas. The downpour would stop just in time to let us get to school dry, avoiding the glistening grass on the roadside and the pools on the pavement.

"Empty all the buckets, tin cans, and oil drums," my father said to the gardener. "We don't want to breed insects."

Sometimes the rain returned at midday, grey clouds sweeping in from the sea with force and majesty. Then I would watch from the classroom windows. I craved novelty, anything to liberate me from the claustrophobia of my school studies. During that first year in Sixth Form, 1957, I was an introspective teenager, and both family and friends seemed to be expecting impossible dedication and hard work on my part to do well in my examinations. At least a storm had the power to stop things. I loved the suspension of everyday concerns, just listening to the drumbeats of the rain and the screaming of the wind. Let the battle begin. No one could clean, or shop, or cook, or study under those conditions. I wished I had the disruptive energy of a storm; the aftermath was not my concern.

On Saturday, we had no school; and on that particular wet Saturday morning, when there was a respite from the rain, it was a time for reading. I went to the public library where I had been borrowing since I'd found my first books, years before. I liked to prowl the shelves. Each week I was allowed to take two books, and I had exhausted the Basseterre library's modest stock of fantasy literature. This meant everything from fairy tales to science fiction, even the difficult works of Poe. I had digested everything available by Dennis Wheatley and H.P. Lovecraft. That rainy season, I had to make do with historical dramas like those of G.A. Henty. Once, I had discovered a cruel and intriguing novel about slavery in the American South by Kyle Onstott, only for adults. A black man called Mandingo was boiled alive because he had made the plantation mistress pregnant (on invitation).

I had already found a Zane Grey, and needed one more book to fill my quota. Wandering through the aisles, I slid my hand along the spines of the books as I read their titles. I stopped at a new-looking, green-backed book with no title showing. I pulled it out and read *Hypnotism for Beginners* on the front cover. On the inside was the Table of Contents:

History of a little-known science
But does it really work?
Famous Hypnotists

Hypnotism on the stage
The medical uses of the art
Who can be hypnotised?
How a trance works
Ending the trance
Dangers and warnings
Modern applications

I checked the library card attached to the flyleaf and saw that only two people had borrowed it before me. The absence of other readers was a beacon – as if the book were intended for me alone. I hoped no one would stop me from taking it. At the time, I equated hypnotism with witchcraft, and I had heard that some such books were forbidden to under-eighteen readers. But the librarian who stamped my card didn't bat an eyelid; hypnotism or hopscotch – it was all the same to her.

On the way home, skipping along the still-wet streets of Basseterre, past the shuttered windows and darkened shops, the midday heat now baking the steamy pavements with a smell like a clothes iron on moist cotton, I clutched my discovery to my chest. Books, like this one, could have unusual things concealed between their innocent covers. It was only ink sprinkled on paper, but like the rainwater disappearing down the city drains, I wanted to be swallowed up in the words, to visit places where no one else had gone before. How drab were the activities of my classmates with their politics, sports, and servile school studies. How pointless were their boasts of burning midnight oil, as if anyone could think clearly after 9 pm, and as if quantities of dull facts could equal the spell of the unknown. *I* had found this book. Neither my parents nor my teachers had talked of hypnotism, and as far as I knew there were no confessed hypnotists in St. Kitts although there were several supposed voodoo priests and obeah women. The little I knew about hypnotism came from cinematographic references like John Barrymore in *Svengali*. Yet, if I believed even the chapter headings in this book, hypnotism was real. You could control people – if it were true. But I doubted someone could really be persuaded to fall asleep and do everything the hypnotist asked of him or her. Could the tone-deaf Trilby in du Maurier's novel become a singing star?

Now that I was able to go to the cinema more often, I remembered *The Climax*, where an insane Boris Karloff does just the opposite to Svengali: he hypnotises a talented young singer into losing her voice. Then there was the Chinese touch, where Myrna Loy stares into her victims' eyes in *The Mask of Fu Manchu* and launches them against Nayland Smith. And there was the film – *The Woman in Green* – about Sherlock Holmes, who escapes from the beautiful hypnotist Lydia Marlow and Professor Moriarty. Most recently, in 1956, I had seen *The She Creature*, where Dr

Lombardi regresses the lovely Andrea into prehistoric life by hypnotism, so that her ectoplasmic incarnation can murder his enemies in grisly ways. Movies were just make-believe, but now... Now I had a book.

From the comfort of my bed, with the storm clouds still playing hide-and-seek outside, I propped my head on a pillow and flipped the pages of the first chapters. It had spells and gestures. I caressed the smooth green cover. The breeze from the rain cooled my bare arms and legs, helping me to think. I read greedily. The first thing to discover was the role of the hypnotist and his subject. I already knew who the hypnotist would be. Next, I had to find someone to hypnotise. Some people, the book said, were quite resistant to suggestion – poor subjects. Most were susceptible, even those who thought themselves immune. I had to distinguish who was who. The book said little habits like a love of chocolates could be a sign.

My mouth watered. Chocolates! I could just see a Milky Way bar, soft and melting in my hands, or a box of brown delights wrapped in foil. Yes, I loved chocolates, so maybe *I* could be easily hypnotised. But wait a minute. I hadn't eaten any chocolates recently. None since last Christmas, surely. Chocolates were expensive in St. Kitts. Because of their scarcity, nothing was really proven here. There was no mention in the book of local treats like guava cheese or coconut sugar cakes, which I often consumed, so my sweet tooth didn't count as susceptibility. Maybe I could resist a hypnotic attack, after all. I searched for other indications of suggestibility. "People who are fond of daydreaming are only a step away from a trance," I read. There was no escaping this time. Daydreaming was my favourite pastime. How else could I get to be King of the Universe in less than five minutes?

So, I was probably suggestible. Self-hypnosis would be a good way to prove or disprove the existence of this art. I would send myself to sleep, do something extraordinary, and then... How would I wake up? I worried about this, seeing myself asleep for weeks and weeks, surrounded by parents and doctors trying to wake me, in vain. How would I eat? Equating poison and hypnosis, I thought that Sleeping Beauty had set a bad precedent – lying comatose for a hundred years before a stranger embraced her. As I wasn't sure I could trust girls, this was far too dangerous. Who would kiss me? I had better hypnotise someone else. In addition, just suppose that hypnosis drove a person crazy, or something. You never knew with magic. I decided to hypnotise my younger brother.

"Hey, Peter, I have a new game for us."

He was doing his homework in the study as usual. Unlike my own last-minute tendencies, he liked to finish everything to do with school early on Saturday before anything else came along.

"Just a minute, I'm almost done with my Arithmetic."

"Now or never!"

My youngest brother, Noel, saw an opportunity. "Can I play your game instead of Peter?"

"Later – you cry too much – I want Peter."

I pushed Noel out of the study and locked the door with Peter and me inside. I could experiment on others later, but Peter had an air of concentration that went beyond chocolates and daydreams. I closed the metal-framed glass windows both on the seaward side and the mango tree side of the study. The grey skies had brought some wind, and the chapter on trances said the room must be very quiet, not even any buzzing flies or mosquitoes.

I smiled at Peter and waved the green book. "This is going to be fun," I said, "but no one else can play, it's a two-person game."

"What's it all about? Hide and seek?"

"No – mental powers." I waved the book again. "And story-telling. It's a game called hypnotism."

"Powers?"

"In this game, you can become even smarter than usual. It's a sort of test. Think you can do it?"

"I'll try. How does it work?"

"Well, you have to sit in this chair while I stand up in front of you. Then I tell you a story and you have to pay attention. There you go, sit still. Do just as I say. It's not difficult. At the end of the story, you'll be smarter than you were before. Or else we'll have a good laugh."

"Will it be as good as the other stories you tell?"

"Better."

"Do I have to tell *you* a story afterwards? I can't think of one right now."

"Don't worry about that. Don't worry about anything. Just listen."

From there on, the book said I had to control the cadence of my voice. I liked acting, and often scared my brothers with ghost stories – I had been chosen for our end-of-term school play. So, just in case things went wrong, I'd prepared certain props.

"Listen and relax. Don't talk anymore. Just listen and relax. All you can hear is the sound of waves and my voice. The sound of my voice and waves."

In fact, with the windows closed, I couldn't hear the sea anymore, but the book said that the idea of soft, repetitive sounds was soothing.

I held up my first prop – a stone wrapped in silver paper and suspended by a string; I guided it into a pendular motion.

"Look at this, and nothing else. You don't see the room, you don't see me, only the stone." I swung it back and forth, to and fro.

"You're perfectly relaxed now and feeling so comfortable you are a little sleepy. Let that comfortable, sleepy feeling move from your toes up your feet and through your legs."

Peter stared at the stone and his leg twitched.

"...through your legs and up into your tummy and your back. That sleepy feeling is so pleasant, you can't resist it. You don't want to resist."

I opened my eyes as wide as possible and moved my gaze up his body. Hopefully, this wouldn't affect his urinary control.

"It is creeping up your chest now – a warm, sleepy feeling. You are comfortable. Now the sleepy feeling is moving down your arms and all the way to your hands and fingers. You can feel nothing in your arms – they are floating – just sleepiness. Now your neck and head and eyes are sleepy. You are sleepy all over, all over, every bit of you, and it's so pleasant, so-o-o pleasant."

I tried to get it right. Lots of repetition, the book had said, and make the subject aware of his whole body. I kept the silvery stone in motion and stressed the key words.

"*Now* you are really going to sleep. A very *deep* sleep. The *deepest* and most *relaxing* of sleeps. Now you are *really* going to sleep. Now you are really going to *sleep*. When you are asleep, you will be com*pletely* relaxed. You will *feel* nothing. You will *hear* nothing but my voice. You *will* hear my voice. It's the *only* thing you will hear. And you will *obey* my voice. That's what you *want* to do. *Obey* my voice. Whatever I ask, you will do. Your only wish is to *obey* my voice. When I next say, '*Sleep now, Peter,*' you will start this very *deep* and pleasant sleep. You will not wake up until I tell you, '*Wake up now, Peter.*' You will *obey* my voice in all things and not wake up until I tell you.

"*Sleep now, Peter.*"

At last, I could stop swinging the damned stone.

I paused and looked at him, squeezing my hands together. The book had used the words "glassy eyed". If Peter were truly in a trance, he should be glassy eyed. He didn't look like that to me. His eyes were wide open, as brown as usual, and staring straight ahead. But perhaps I hadn't told him what to look at when I removed the stone? I stepped two feet to the right. Peter didn't budge. Then I moved back to the left. His head was immobile, just drooping slightly.

Uncanny, his eyes weren't following me. So that's what "glassy eyed" meant. But how did he know? Peter was clever to have thought of it. Not good enough to fool *me*, though. Two could play at that game, and I knew he was not really asleep.

"OK," I intoned, "you are now sound asleep, and you will reply to my questions."

I said this in a solemn voice, though part of me wanted to laugh.

"What is your name?"

Start from the basics, said the book, and establish contact with the subject.

"Peter."

"Be more formal, please. Say, 'My name is Peter'."

I had to make it clear who was the boss. Also, this was the recommended book dialogue. All the subjects said, "My name is…" No shortcuts.

"How old are you?"

"I'm eleven years old."

How could he be so composed? His voice was not quite normal – just a little slower. Or was that my imagination?

"What class are you in at school?"

"I'm in Second Form."

"Who am I?"

"You're my big brother, Chris."

"How old am I?"

"You're fifteen."

"What date is it?"

"It's Saturday, nineteenth of September, 1957."

It was all too simple. He could easily fake it. Of course, he knew the answers. I had to ask him something to prove he was in a trance. Maybe I could have given him one of my own Mathematics homework problems. But no, he'd not had any calculus yet. The book said the subject in a trance could do things better than in real life, but only if there was a basis.

"What are we doing?"

"We're playing a game called Hypnotism."

"What do you have to do?"

"I have to obey everything you tell me to do."

This was getting me nowhere. I decided to increase the stakes. According to the book, a subject in a trance could sustain unusual muscular efforts.

"Stand up. Hold your arms straight out in front of you. Palms up. They are very light. You do not feel any weight. You can hold them like that forever."

I had to give it to Peter; he was playing this game perfectly. Without moving his head or any other part of his body, he projected his two arms horizontally and held them there.

But now, I had him. I had tried this muscular test myself. After three minutes of holding your arms out, it really hurts; my arms would begin to tremble shortly afterwards. I looked at my watch. Two minutes, and Peter was still rock steady. He didn't know what was in store for him. Three minutes, and no change. Pretty good for a young kid. Funny, I wouldn't have thought he could do it for as long as me. But then, his arms were lighter. And he was wearing short sleeves. Perhaps I'd been in a heavy shirt the last time I tested myself. Not sure. Now this was *really* peculiar. He'd been holding his arms out steady for five minutes and I couldn't see any trembling! What the hell was going on? It must be a trick.

At eight minutes, I was furious. How dare he make fun of me! I knew he was cheating somehow. I circled around him twice, looking for head or eyeball movements: nothing. No trembling either. I was forced to use my last resort to reveal his hoax. This would break him down. I searched for the handkerchief I had carefully prepared beforehand, hoping the metal in it was properly sterilised. I had been unable to find my mother's disinfectant and had cauterised the points with a lighted match, but they looked black and unhealthy afterwards, so I had in the end washed them with soap and water.

I hid the two sharp pins behind my back as I approached Peter.

"Close your eyes and continue holding your arms out. You will feel no pain."

He closed his eyes. This would really teach him a lesson. He had been holding his arms out for more than ten minutes, which was clearly impossible. I chose his left arm because, after all, he was my brother and I didn't want to handicap his writing arm. Gripping the first pin between my thumb and forefinger like a dart, I pricked it lightly into the flesh of the inside forearm. I was expecting an exclamation, but it didn't come; the arm just sagged slightly in reaction. That was the last straw. I jabbed the second pin firmly in, perhaps a half-inch. No reaction. The two pins stood defiantly in his flesh.

Anger vanished, and a cold shiver of delight ran down my spine. My feet felt unsteady. Wild thoughts cascaded. It was true! Hypnotism worked and I had succeeded. We could go on stage – it was real magic. Peter would accept pain, do whatever I said, and perform beyond his normal limits: I had created a superman. Or a monster. Then abruptly I lost all my enthusiasm. I had not thought success would be like this. The room was silent: an absence of sea, wind, and booby's cries. But I was still there, and so was my subject. Peter's eyes were closed; his arms were still horizontal and no longer moving, with the two pins standing tall like sentinels. He was no longer my brother, but a stranger. I was frightened.

Without thinking, I pulled out the pins and hid them in the handkerchief.

"You may lower your arms now and sit down."

He lowered them. I was losing control: I shouldn't have given him the option with "may". Then, not missing a step, he sat down in the chair with his eyes still closed. I had to cover my tracks – no one must find out.

"You will not remember any of this. When you wake up, you will think we have been playing a game that didn't work. You fell asleep in the middle of my boring story. You will forget everything I ordered you to do. Never in your life will you remember this, unless I tell you, '*Peter, remember the hypnotism*'."

Who could tell, I might need this memory one day.

"Soon you will wake up. After I give you the command, you will open your eyes and yawn."

I looked at him sitting motionless in the chair, eyes closed. If I had asked him to bite off his finger, or smash his fist through the glass window, or strangle the dog, he would have done it. I couldn't accept that sort of responsibility.

"*Wake up now, Peter.*"

Peter opened his eyes and yawned. Then he rubbed his shoulders and his arms.

"Ouch, I'm stiff. Must have been asleep. Sorry, Chris."

I walked over to him and held his left arm up to the light. Two bright red spots were visible.

"Better put something on these. I'll have to find the disinfectant," I said. "Mosquito bites."

Thus, the humble mosquito became my scapegoat for a deeper disquiet. Of course, I resisted this fear of unwanted responsibility; a general needs foot soldiers. Some weeks later, I had my brother Noel stretched out in a trance – rigid as a board between two chairs – but I was scared to sit on him, and broke the trance instead. Then I persuaded Noel's friend Mostyn – also in a trance – that he was a dog, and it was fun to hear him bark and scramble around on hands and feet, but after making him eat Purina dog biscuits, I couldn't get him to spit them out. The better my control worked, the uneasier I felt. So I retired as a sixteen-year-old hypnotist – perhaps the only one in St. Kitts – and looked for other voyages of discovery.

The Usual Poisons

I may have found the idea of toxins by chance, or it may have been a conscious desire for risk, or it may have been the link with Chemistry – the subject whose excitement had lured me into science. At any rate, this research promised to be hazardous, allowing me to explore the perimeter of my security.

My frustration had increased with the soporific Caribbean island community around me, but this did not lead me to devote myself to slavish school studies. The scholarship I should have been working for receded into the distance. I wanted something else – a cup that no one else had drunk from. Although I attended classes regularly and made friends I often thought my real life was elsewhere.

Once again, a book from the St. Kitts public library triggered my project. I passed over *Prestidigitation*, thinking my father was too expert at conjuring tricks, and *Chiromancy*, because my mother still read palms at parties, and settled for a diversion no one in the family appeared to have tried, *The Book of Poisons*. Chance encounters with books had more influence on me than people.

Hypnosis, my previous fascination, might be considered a quaint fantasy or even a branch of medicine, but there was no way poisoning could be judged respectable. And that was something I craved: the unorthodox, the disreputable, and the untrodden path. I wanted to see the true nature of the world. The more I read and explored, the more I felt adults were deliberately or unconsciously concealing this world from me. There were rules out there, stores of knowledge, ways of behaving and of gaining power over others – ideas that I was not supposed to possess until later, if ever. I even thought I knew why: it was because these ideas might upset the established order. The adults, my teachers, and the newspapers might all be lying to me. The Church thing, the do-good thing, the study-hard thing, the democracy thing, the crime-does-not-pay thing, how could I believe any of it? As for my family, I was fiercely loyal; this was one value I did not put up for auction. And my parents' open-mindedness encouraged my research. That didn't mean I could believe *everything* they said – they were adults, too.

It was like diving. Once, at Nelson's Dockyard, I had been afraid of the deep, dark waters, but no longer. To find my place, I would have to leave the land, with its solidity, and plunge into the sea, with its mysteries. I needed that hidden knowledge, and what started as curiosity became obsessive. Right then, with the book in my hand, I thought a study of poisons, with its suggestion of desire and death, was a good hunt to pursue. What was their role in society, and could I use them? I didn't at the outset fancy myself as a poisoner of others – but what about stray dogs? – and I scorned the possibility I might seriously harm myself. The power bestowed by the possession of poisons enticed me on, like having my finger on the trigger of a loaded gun. Thirty years later, my library book might have been entitled *The World of Drugs,* featuring Caribbean cannabis and Columbian crack.

The first thing I learned was that poisons were everywhere around me, even in tea and coffee. But these were common beverages! The coffee my parents drank contained a drug called caffeine. This drug was habit-forming, a concept that didn't apply to Deadly Nightshade and other strong poisons; one dose of these would suffice. Caffeine was not at first taste a poison, but a stimulant. However, taken in large doses over a period of time it was accused of producing palpitations, stomach ulcers, sleeplessness, weak bones, premature births, and even strokes. Of course, this might just be adverse propaganda.

Tea, that oh-so-British institution, contained an identical stimulant called theine, three cups of tea having about the same effect as one strong coffee. I quarrelled with my Uncle Jack about this. He dismissed my chemical wisdom and claimed tea had no caffeine until I showed him the contrary in my book. I thought he might have boxed me if I had been his son. Uncle Jack had left school after Fifth Form, not because he was unintelligent but because he hadn't seen the point to further studies.

I decided two things: I mustn't assume adults welcomed the truth; and since Uncle Jack was a tea drinker, I would become a coffee drinker.

I hated my first coffee. We had the imported, instant kind, with no spoil date indicated. The beans were not grown locally in 1958 in the Leeward Islands, and the canned powder tasted to me like carbonised toast and bitter aloes. I could only drink it with three spoonfuls of sugar and lots of milk. It was not a success, because it *did* give me palpitations and had no favourable effect on my studies. I fainted one early morning after a large dose. To compensate for this unfavourable beginning, I began in the following days to experiment with other "social poisons", though the adults preferred to call them pleasures. And after caffeine, why not nicotine?

My book indicated smoking would kill you only very slowly by rotting your lungs, so I was game. It was supposed to give the user a kick. I had to try it, believing I could stop long before the rot set in. Inhaling the smoke into your lungs did the main damage; my book suggested pipe smokers who didn't inhale could get a similar kick with a lot less risk. Out of the last set of Christmas crackers, I had acquired a small plastic pipe with a tiny wooden bowl, which seemed quite serviceable. My parents didn't smoke, although my mother would occasionally offer a cigarette to a visitor.

It confused me that she offered poison to her friends. I would have preferred to get rid of my enemies first. But perhaps my mother didn't realise she was killing them? It couldn't be so bad. I felt impelled to taste this poison myself.

I didn't know where my mother hid her guest cigarettes, so I couldn't steal them. Instead, I mustered some hard-earned pocket money one Saturday morning, and set off to buy some. I opted against a grocery store because word would get back to my parents. Everyone knew everyone on our small island.

I didn't have far to go to find a rum-and-tobacco shop. No place was far in Basseterre. In twenty sweaty minutes, I could have walked boldly across the town, from the cane fields and abandoned sugar mill at Buckleys Estate, along Cayon Street; past the quiet Springfield cemetery; across the ghauts, Westbourne and College; by St. Georges' dark and imposing belfry; pausing at the busy intersection with Victoria Road; and right along Pond Road to the east until the bare Frigate Bay hills came into sight, and more cane fields, still more.

The town had its well-defined respectable areas: the historic centre around the Circus and Pall Mall Square, where the lawyers and large stores did business and the wealthiest merchants lived; the Fortlands, an affluent residential area overlooking the sea to the west, where my family had just moved; the sugar factory and Taylor's Range area of newer houses to the north; and the beginnings of the Bird Rock development to the east, a middle-income zone that would shelter a quarter of Basseterre's population by the end on the century. In-between these havens, on either side of the central business area, were the poor zones – casually built shacks of garishly painted cement, cheap wood, or even bits of oil drums that also made steel band pans.

I found what I was looking for in the Irish Town slum on the west, just off Central Street where my parents' first home had been. It was in an alley, visible by the rusty signpost advertising its cigarettes. I had never entered this sort of place before: dingy, dark, smelling of perspiration and liquor. My parents had told us to be careful of rum shops; they said – perhaps in jest – children could disappear inside. I felt tense, but reasoned nothing could happen to me in broad daylight. I asked for two cigarettes from the wizened black shopkeeper.

"Sorry, only sell packs, Mister." He had both elbows planted on the soiled wooden counter and was examining me. I didn't believe him, but he stared me down.

"One pack, please."

Another client, who might have been a cane cutter, was leaning on the counter with a glass of rum, head turned away from me. There was a grey cloth around his forehead and he wore heavy sandals made of car-tire rubber from which his grimy toenails protruded.

"Filter or not?"

"The cheaper."

The cane cutter grunted.

"No filter is ninety cents." The shopkeeper placed a crumpled box of Camels on the counter. I paid, grabbed it, and ran, scanning outside to ensure no one I knew had seen me.

At home, I checked I really had twenty unfiltered cigarettes. In the privacy of my bedroom, I cut a cigarette in four quarters and split open one of them. I picked up the brown strings of tobacco and smelled their peculiar earthy tang. This, at last, was a poison in my hand. I jiggled it and squeezed it as if some magic essence could seep into me. Then I took out my Christmas-cracker pipe and packed the precious fibres into its bowl; it just fit. I struggled to light it with a match, coughing each time I drew on the stem. It took three matches before I got the hang of drawing the smoke into my mouth, then puffing it out. It tasted foul and peppery, like burned feathers, so I wanted to share it with my younger brothers, and in a short while all three were coughing: nine-year-old Noel, twelve-year-old Peter, and I. Between us, we were able to finish the entire quarter cigarette. We were immensely proud. There was a nauseous sensation, but it didn't last long, and the excitement of the forbidden brought us back to my pipe the next weekend – when we could hide from my parents – and the next, each time consuming a quarter cigarette. Smoke rings were on the agenda, but never achieved. After each session, I hid the pipe and the remaining nineteen-and-a-bit cigarettes in an ultra-secret place – the back of my mahogany desk drawer, behind my Shakespeare textbook. On the fourth weekend, while I was sitting at this desk, my mother entered the room without knocking and smiled like a Cheshire cat.

"Oh, Chris, your room smelt so awful that I opened your desk and found this." She held up my pipe and the cigarette pack. So much for my ultra-secrets.

"Mum, how could you – "

"I can't believe you've actually been smoking with it," she said, dangling the pipe between two fingers.

Expecting the worst, I said, "I just wanted to see what it was like - "

"It's so cute! And you bought these cheap, unfiltered cigarettes?"

"Well, the filter is no use in a pipe..."

She looked at the pipe again and laughed. I saw it was a toy to her and that her teenage son looked ridiculous smoking a toy with his door locked.

"Your father and I don't mind if you want to smoke in moderation, but you shouldn't encourage your brothers at their age, with their immature lungs. And for goodness' sake – let me buy you some quality cigarettes next time."

I would have preferred her to be angry. I burned with embarrassment, turned away, and said, "There won't be a next time."

"What do you want to do with these?" She gestured at the untidy heap of nineteen-and-a-quarter unfiltered cigarettes.

"I don't want them, you can have them."

She picked up the cigarettes and handed me the pipe.

"A souvenir." I heard laughter as she left my room.

I was furious. Instead of discovering the secrets and lies of the adult world, my cigarette experiment had backfired and my own secrets had been exposed.

In later years, I understood the conditioning that my parents had imposed on me. To my shame, my mother told the story of my pipe to several of her friends. I had pro forma liberty to smoke or experiment, but I would be laughed at if I persisted. If pride was a sin, then I was surely condemned. There was nothing to rebel against, so the scientific and rational part of me gained control. Whether or not cigarettes caused lung cancer – and it was not so clear at the time – I would just let the rest of the world, the non-scientists, those who asked no questions, do the destructive testing.

My parents' thinking was that choice had to be individual – dictating and punishing were ineffective – which was a natural extension of my mother's soft-discipline ideas. Understanding a psychological mechanism does not annul it: I would never, ever, smoke again. At the time, I had to count smoking as my second failure in studying poisons. It was no comfort to me that my mother's "little trick" would protect me from tobacco addiction. I was searching for something transformative, a mastery of the world, and didn't realise that she had given it to me. All I could see was the humiliation.

The end of smoking was not enough to stop me reading my poisons book. I could still borrow it for a few weeks, and I found the next chapter on alcohol just as intriguing. Quite as habit-forming as nicotine, it said, but with more immediate – and pleasant – effects. You got drunk. You felt free. Excessively used, the book insisted alcohol was a poison, but people really went for this one.

I thought of the glass of rum my father drank in the evening, and the rum punches the adults adored at parties. And whisky and gin like Humphrey Bogart. Even beer – which, in 1958, was imported, but would soon (1960) be produced locally as Carib Beer – contained alcohol. However, still smarting from the smoking incident, I had second thoughts. One aspect worried me – the loss of control that came with inebriation. Alcohol made you silly. I might be made fun of, yet again. Poisons that were stimulants like caffeine might have a place in my life, if I could get used to the bitter taste, but how could I afford to lose what little mental powers I had, even for a few hours? It didn't seem glamorous to have your brains gently curdled.

My next decision came soon after I passed my driver's test. I was now sixteen. I had been unenthusiastic about learning to drive – why bother when my parents could take us everywhere? Anyway, I liked my bicycle, and I had none of the fascination for cars that my contemporaries did. But my parents had bulldozed me into getting my licence; then they obliged me to help those who couldn't legally drive. My friend Rolly Uddenberg would hold a parentally approved, Saturday-night party in the Hermitage estate house where he had recently started working. No adults would be present. Uppermost in my mind was how to behave at this party – my first such. It could be a liberating new step or a huge fiasco. I would have to drive my friends Willy John and Jenny to the party, and above all bring them back safely at midnight. Willy John was the white, English, factory manager's son, and Jenny was the daughter of a planter family.

In the choice of my friends, I was not concerned with class or colour, accepting whatever cards were dealt me. Rolly's family was white, but lived modestly in the centre of town, not on a rich sugar cane estate. Had I been attuned to people's wealth, Rolly's situation would have stuck out – there were few middle-income whites on the island at the time, most were well-off. Still, it was a matter of definition – to be white or not. Almost all Caribbean families had some black or brown blood in them if you scratched back a few generations; but provided it didn't show as more than a light suntan, they were white.

At school, my mostly-black and not-well-off friends were intellectual competitors, all vying for the same scholarship. At a gathering like Rolly's, my mostly-white and well-off friends were social competitors, vying for position or friendship, or perhaps not vying for anything, since their future was assured. There was no overlap between the groups – except me. These ambiguities were built into my Caribbean life and any notion of preference was far from my mind. I would not have been moved one way or another if someone had pointed out that there was yet another group of young people my age who had neither schooling nor money, yet who smiled at the sun every day. This was the third world.

Willy knew where the Hermitage house was, so I would in theory be able to find it. But I had not driven much at night. More than a little scared of my responsibility, I promised myself that at this, my first party, I would abstain from drinking.

"Be back home before one o'clock," my father said, "and you're allowed a beer or two."

But it would be none at all, I thought.

"Come on Chris, have some real stuff."

Willy John offered me a glass with a lonely ice cube floating on an inch of brown liquid that might have been rum or whisky. Strange odours wafted to me through the dim light and I heard loud music and voices. I took the glass carefully in my hand as if it were a stinging nettle. Once again, I had my finger on the poison trigger. I swirled the mysterious beverage under my nose and inhaled the liquor fumes. The cold in my fingers was the best part of the experience.

We were on a rough, wooden patio adjoining the estate house. Benches were sprinkled with cushions and two large tables were covered with bottles of beer and imported Mount Gay rum from Barbados, and a huge ice chest with fizzy soda water, ginger ale, Coke, and other soft drinks from the local bottling company. A few plates of crackers and cashew nuts floated on the tables in pools of water condensed from the cold glasses, but real eating was not on the menu. On three sides of the patio, the warm night air walled us in, and on the fourth, an open door led to a simple kitchen, a bathroom, and Rolly's sleeping quarters.

I refused Willy's proffered drink. "No thanks. I have to drive you back, remember?"

I had a valid reason not to drink, but no one respected it. Had I known what surrealism was, that's how I would have described this first party. I heard the conversation picking up decibels and slipping intangibly from normal good humour to strange and high-pitched nonsense. Willy began imitating The Duke of Iron, a naughty calypso singer, chanting: "...*my friend one thing I need from you / is a little tiny piece of the big bamboo*", to the blond girl next to him. There were about a dozen of us, clad in gaudy, short-sleeved shirts, pretending we knew what we were drinking and that we did this often. A few seemed unaffected, but others' character and even appearance evolved with the calypso music until I didn't know them anymore. Eyes widened, mouths slackened, and faces reddened – even the brown ones. There was dancing, which I tried without success, but most of my friends sat, or wandered around like Willy John, glass in hand, continuing his song "*She wanted big bamboo four feet long / Big bamboo so full and strong*." Meanwhile the Mighty Sparrow sang out his own invitation from the gramophone:

"Tell you sister to come down quick,
I have a message for she.
Tell she is Mister Benwood Dick,
The man from Sangre Grande."

It was hard to refuse all the offers of drinks, Sandy Grandy or not, but I was determined to be different. My friends became increasingly inane, and soon only Jenny still looked reasonably sober. I felt happier when I realised I was seeing a poison in action at first hand, without having to pay the entry fee. Eventually, the others stopped pestering me and I could drink straight Cokes or fizzy orange, provided I laughed at their antics. It did not cost me much to acquiesce. I had seen adults drunk like this at my parents' parties, and now my friends were determined to outdo their elders. They were sozzled, and the evening was going well.

It was a small, eccentric decision of mine, not to drink that night. I considered I was not being a snob, just choosing to distance myself from the crowd. I was discovering I disliked parties and hated following any sort of group. And that to deny myself something that I didn't need – alcohol – gave me just as much power as my friends Fitzroy and Lee who had denied themselves a more essential function – excretion – without any painful costs – the purge. I didn't suspect that this seemingly unimportant and temporary choice would remain more or less in force for thirty years until I discovered French wines.

After eleven o'clock, someone cried out, "Lord, who just fall down?"

"Something happen to Willy John."

"Pick him up, man."

"He's just fooling, leave him be."

"Willy, Willy, wake up!"

Willy John's eyes were closed and he was on the floor breathing heavily. Rolly and I got him to sit up, but he couldn't hold up on his feet. Someone turned off the music. Like a rollercoaster cresting, the party mood swung downwards. Willy John couldn't talk, couldn't walk, and looked in bad shape. There were no adults anywhere near; I was one of the oldest. I had to do something.

"We should cool him off. Let's get him under a shower," Rolly said.

We dragged Willy John to the bathroom and stripped off his shirt. Rolly himself wasn't seeing too clearly, so I turned on the tap. There was no hot water. We held Willy under the shower for five minutes, until he began coughing, rolled his eyes at us, and mumbled, "*Only big bamboo pleases one and all…*"

My book of poisons had simply drawn comparisons between drunkenness and drugged states; it had not given remedies. I had no idea whether my friend's condition was serious. But I was worried.

"It's time to go home anyway," I said. "I promised not later than one o'clock."

"You're sure you want one drunk and one half-drunk in your car?" asked Jenny. I felt she was exaggerating her state.

"No problem," I said. "I know the way."

Since there is only one road around the island, I was not asking much of myself, from Hermitage back to Basseterre was straight ahead. Maybe this was why my parents had lent me the car in the first place.

When we left, we put a dry shirt on Willy John and shoved him into the back of my father's Rover, where he collapsed onto the leather seat and fell asleep. There were no other cars on the road. It was a moonless night, the countryside only illuminated by the canopy of tropical stars. I turned the headlamps on full, and drove tensely back to town, keeping to the middle of the road. Trees jumped in and out of sight as the road weaved, and the waves murmured nearby. I was on the alert for goats, dogs, or other animals crossing, with both hands glued to the steering wheel.

The road around the island – all thirty-odd miles, with the Atlantic Ocean on the north-east side and the Caribbean Sea on the south-west – was paved with asphalt, but not very well. It was narrow, with many dangerous bends. Two cars passing in opposite directions were like shy dancing partners – too close for comfort. Finding a half-mile stretch of good road was so unusual that it was a provocation for speeding.

"Remember, you have to stop at the factory first and drop off Willy John," Jenny said. Willy John's family lived in the manager's premises, a mansion near the works. The living quarters had to be close to the factory, but the disadvantage was that when the breeze blew the wrong way it brought a smell of caramel and decaying organic mud from the effluent pool into the bedrooms. As I approached his home that night, I welcomed this obnoxious odour for the first time. My task was nearly accomplished.

"Wake up, wake up, Willy John, we're here! Prod him please, Jenny."

"How are you feeling, Willy?"

No reply.

It was an unusual moment. I had never felt like a parent before, not even when taking care of my brothers; but now I had to get the helpless Willy safely inside. At the same time, I was disgusted by his weakness; what sort of person let this happen to him? I might attend more parties like this, but I couldn't feel empathy with the group.

A few determined prods later, Willy John squirmed and said, "I'm fine. Feeling fine."

Abruptly, he vomited his evening's intake all over the back seat of my father's well-kept car, just a hundred yards away from his front door.

I couldn't say whether I was more concerned for my friend or the car. I slammed on the brakes, and we hauled Willy John off the back seat to the roadside where he continued puking. It seemed he would never stop. Under the factory's street lighting, the world was yellow. Jenny turned up her lips in disgust. Then Willy woke up, again.

"Where am I? What happened? Chris, I feel terrible." His eyes half-opened and his tongue lolled out like a puppy. He was so miserable it was impossible to be cross with him for long.

"You look that way too, Willy. Now, let's clean you up. You're home."

There was an old cloth for engine maintenance in the boot of my father's car. Jenny used this to wipe off Willy John, not caring if it left a few oil marks on his face or shirt. Then we helped him up the stairs to his room, one on either side, as quietly as possible so as not to wake his parents. He fell onto his bed, fully dressed, and didn't move. I took off his shoes and then borrowed a towel and a cup of water from his bathroom. Now we had the Rover to deal with.

I was glad to have Jenny's help, because cleaning the back seat was finicky and disgusting work. I felt queasy several times; the crackers and Cokes in my stomach threatened to mutiny. Finally, it was done: seat, door, and floor; a few bits and pieces had even been projected onto the windscreen.

"Thanks Jenny, now let's get us two survivors home."

I dropped her off at her home, where she lived in a concrete house with a fruit garden. It was already past one o'clock.

"Not a word of this to anyone," I said. I was glad she hadn't drunk too much – one Willy John was enough.

We didn't kiss goodnight: close encounter with girls was another drug I had not taken to yet, and I considered kissing was a serious business. I waited until she was inside her gate before I left. I guessed she would not waken her parents, either.

That left me with the drive through the deserted streets of Basseterre, along the bay road and up to the Fortlands. Empty streets – I was alone, as I had been at the party. But wasn't this better than to be brainless like my drunken friends? The idea comforted me: at least the study of poisons had shown me how the world of parties worked, and how I could find power for myself by abstaining. I parked the car quietly in our garage and climbed out. Then I opened the back door for a last check. Damn! The upholstery still had an unsettling smell. I crept into our house and found some soap, water, and another towel. I couldn't be too careful. It was worth another five minutes of cleaning.

But it took me a half-hour to wash the car again. Two o'clock – an hour later than my promise – I locked up everything, hid the towels, and dropped into bed, trembling slightly.

Next morning, Sunday, I woke up knowing I had a problem. I had witnessed the poison of alcohol in action, and my foreknowledge had given me some leverage over events. But it was not over: there was a different kind of toxin working within me – guilt. Normally, I would have told my parents everything. I enjoyed narrating my adventures, and, after all, my father had a right to know what had happened to his beloved Rover. But I couldn't, because of Willy John. His parents were strict and would be angry to learn their son had been dead drunk at his first all-teens party. I wasn't going to say the mess in the car was due to me either, or anyone else. So, my best plan was to say nothing, though it didn't feel right.

"How did your party go, Chris?" my mother inquired at breakfast.

"Fine, everyone had a great time."

"Did you have any trouble getting back?"

"No, it was easy with Jenny and Willy John to guide me."

"Well, you don't need to tell us the details. That's young people's business," my father said.

"We got home a little later than I promised, Dad, more like two o'clock. I hope you don't mind."

"No matter. Hurry up and finish your egg or we'll be late for church."

In the car, I made sure not to sit where Willy John had been. Still, I couldn't detect any odours from the night before – the car actually smelled cleaner than usual.

All morning, I kept to myself. During the church service, the secret I carried seemed especially heavy. Neither Willy John nor his parents were present at St. Georges Anglican Church. Willy's father, George Warren, had been bitten by religion late in life and it was unusual for him to miss a Sunday mass. I looked at the cold stone, the hard wooden pews, and all the stained glass shim-sham. Surely, it was better to protect a friend at the expense of a little subterfuge?

It was at lunch that a bubble of indecision burst in me. In holding back the truth, I was doing exactly what I detested in adults. At dessert time – roast plantains with a brown sugar topping – I said, "Dad and Mum, there's something I have to tell you."

As usual near the end of the meal, Noel was picking at his food while Peter had finished eating. My parents seemed to be avoiding my eyes. Suddenly, I was on centre stage and scared, but I plodded ahead.

"Last night, at the party, there was some trouble I haven't mentioned."

The whole family looked at me.

"You see, it wasn't his fault really, but Willy John got a bit ill. He mixed his drinks or something."

"So, you had to take care of him?"

I leaned back in my chair and pushed away the empty plate.

"Yes, but that's not all. Of course, I took him home. But despite everything we could do, he was sick all over your car. I'm sorry, Dad. We did clean it up."

"Well, I'm glad you told us, because I've been thinking all morning you should drive over to the factory this afternoon and cheer up Willy John, who's not feeling well."

"You knew?"

"Of course. His father was on the phone to me before church, thanking you for bringing his son home. And I had to have the gardener finish scrubbing the Rover – it was still fruity in the back. But we knew you'd explain things to us – eventually."

The world was always one step ahead of me. Even the overindulgence of my friend was taken as a matter of course – only my reaction had been unknown. Had I learned anything by revealing the truth about Willy? That sort of "truth" was a measure of the normal reciprocal trust between my parents and me, and I took it for granted. What I wanted was The Truth, objective and useful knowledge of my world concerning poisons and power. In this area, my progress was small, I thought.

It would have been easier to struggle against strict parents. Mine wished to make sure I understood the consequences of getting drunk, but if I had one or two beers or an occasional rum punch it would have suited them just fine. My response was to assert myself beyond their desires and continue the sobriety I had started that night – no alcohol would pass my lips for the next three years. Although I had not mastered the polite use of alcohol, and derived no pleasure from my temperance, at least it was more *my* decision than with smoking and I could positively annoy others by refusing their drinks.

Still, this left me without any exciting poison or drug, so I decided to read about more potent chemicals, things that could kill. One day I might have enemies and need to use poison, in attack or defence.

To experiment further, I had to get my hands on a serious poison. Skipping over arsenic and cyanide, which were possibly available in my school chemistry lab but didn't seem romantic enough, Deadly Nightshade was my first choice. I could give the stray dogs a dose or practice on lizards, perhaps. I preferred the sinister sound of Deadly Nightshade to Belladonna and was thrilled its poisonous black berries were so extraordinarily sweet that they had tempted and killed many innocent English children; it seemed the queen of poisons. Unfortunately, it grew mostly in Europe and Asia, so there was no Deadly Nightshade in St. Kitts. It was the same with Foxglove; the mottled flowers with crimson spots, or their succulent nectar, could finish off the unwary. But no Foxglove grew on my island. I scanned the shelves of the Basseterre pharmacy in vain – nothing resembling either of these plants was on sale. Maybe I shouldn't have been surprised; the adults were trying to keep their weapons out of hands like mine.

Then, to my astonishment, on reading further in my book, I found out that poisons were not always poisons – my chosen toxins could be ambiguous in their effects. The two I had picked were normally cultivated not as lethal weapons but for use as *medicines*. Foxglove contained digitalis, and while an overdose could smash the coronary system, smaller doses were useful for regulating heart ailments. I couldn't know it, but my father would need this one day. Deadly Nightshade was also two-faced. It contained a powerful alkaloid called atropine, which in large doses caused loss of voice, convulsions, and death; but in tiny doses was invaluable for dilating the pupil, and maybe I'd had a drop of atropine in my own eyes when I was last tested for glasses.

It was 1958; I was dreaming of dark and magical things, yet many of the practical, medical uses of natural poisons were waiting to be discovered. No one had yet tried low-intensity injections of Botox – botulism is a paralysing poison – to smooth out facial wrinkles and release knotted muscles. Forty years later, this treatment would be essential to stabilising my spastic sister's head and neck movements, and as a beauty treatment for movie stars and politicians.

It began to dawn on me – another contradiction to be sorted out – that most of the bad poisons people feared could actually be good drugs in the hands of doctors. I suspected duality everywhere: the Church as a teacher of love versus the Church as a tool for enslaving primitive peoples; my parents protecting me from a violent world versus the same parents constraining my freedom.

I still wanted to get my hands on a real poison, though, so I contrived a last attempt to extract more information from my father during a family meal; he was always overeager to explain.

"Dad, what are the local poisons in the Caribbean?"

He looked at the pearly black seeds of pawpaw in my plate. "What do you want with poisons? Be thankful that all our fruit is good to eat."

"All? Isn't there anything that makes people on the islands ill?"

"Fish poisoning, sea eggs, mad dogs, nettles… and Manchineel."

"What does Manchineel do?"

"Never go near it. Eating the apples from the tree will give you stomach lesions and kill you," he said, wiggling his fingers, "and if you touch any of the milky sap it will blister and blind you."

My brothers looked up from their plates at the mention of killing, especially Noel.

"But it's all over our beaches, and I've never heard of anyone going blind," I said.

"People know it's evil, that's all. The Caribs used it to poison their arrows. Sailors who sheltered under the Manchineel tree for the night developed oozing sores. Remember any Latin?"

"Dad, I've stopped studying it – it's a useless language."

"Well, the Latin name for Manchineel, *Hippomane mancinella*, means literally 'little apple that makes horses go mad'."

"OK, I won't take my horse near a Manchineel tree."

"You don't have a horse," sniggered Noel, who was now drinking in every word, "not even a cat anymore."

I ignored my little brother, because maybe Manchineel was something I could use. Years later I learned that it, too, had medical virtues (it helped to cure syphilis and tetanus), but at the time, my father made it seem unambiguously life-threatening. Although I supposed him to be in good faith, I couldn't exclude the possibility it might not be as toxic as he thought. I decided to check out this poison for myself.

There were many good beaches for sea bathing in St. Kitts, but not the one to the west of our home in the Fortlands. People scorned this beach, and there was no proper road to it. Only the local fishermen used it, because of its coarse black sand. Even with beaches, the Caribbean had a prejudice scale: white is the best; brown or yellow may be acceptable; but avoid the black sand. My beach was called Lime Kiln Bay, and salt-weathered trees with grey trunks bordered it. They were Manchineel, and their leaves were shiny green, peppered with tiny yellow flowers.

I walked down a steep path bordered by scrub, and at sea level I studied the Manchineel trees from a safe distance. There were several of them, forty or more feet tall, boring deep into the sand. On beaches that were more popular, they would have been cut down – at great risk to the cutlass-wielder who might be sprayed with skin-eating white sap. Or they might have been burned, if it weren't for the release of alkaloid physostigmine smoke – a respiratory killer. With no one to complain, the trees on my beach inhaled peacefully in the sunshine, fruiting little green apples.

The Caribs plunged their arrowheads into these apples before entering combat.

I gazed at the sinister trees and noticed a group of small black boys at the far end of the beach playing under one of them. Barefoot in the sand, they called out and threw missiles at each other. As I approached, I saw one near-naked brat sitting happily on a branch.

"Hey, come down! Don't you know Manchineel can kill you?"

Surprised by my shout, the boy scampered down and ran off to his friends. I went after them. Of course, they wouldn't know anything about poisons, I thought – they probably couldn't read.

"You heard me? Manchineel tree is bad. Don't play there."

They talked among themselves, but I couldn't hear.

The climber advanced, laughing.

"We don't trouble tree, and tree no trouble we," he said, sticking out his tongue.

Something hit my leg. Without thinking, I picked it up from the black sand and found I had a poisonous apple in my hand. I could see the boys grinning. This was my icon of power – another poison in my grasp. I threw it back in disgust, but then they began pelting me with a barrage of the fearsome green fruit. I retreated in confusion, even though I was somewhat bigger than my assailants, terrified of being struck by a fruit leaking deadly juices. They seemed to have no fear of contact.

"Go away, whitey!" they shouted. I pinched the brown skin on my arm to see if it had lightened in colour recently but could find no justification for the jibe.

They didn't pursue me though, and from the top of the hill, I watched them go back to their games, diving into the sea where the black sand made the water unnaturally dark. My father was certainly right and the trees were poisonous, so I couldn't understand how these objectionable kids could survive. Damn them for attacking me when I had only been trying to help. The climber was perched again on his branch, in the bosom of poison. As long as he didn't break the Manchineel bark, he was safe.

As anger permeated me, I had a vision of my antagonist scratching that bark, or nicking it with a toenail, and letting the milky destroyer discover his skin. First it would itch, then the evil sap would infiltrate his dermis and attack his nervous system. I expected him to be paralysed, go blind, frothing and writhing on the bloodstained sand within minutes. Perhaps the sea would soothe the damage. But it would not be enough. I needed an antidote.

Though I waited until dark, to my disappointment I heard no screams. The boys had the power, not I. The next day, I returned the poison book to the library.

I had failed with coffee, cigarettes, alcohol, and now with Manchineel; I did not wish to be a poisoner either of myself or of anyone else. I might have been right about the existence of secrets around me, but what good did arcane knowledge do? I had to find some other way to shake up the world. And what about explosives? It was time for my Chemistry studies to fulfil their promise.

Tinkering with Chemistry

For the thrill seeker, few things are more titillating than making bombs in one's bathtub. The puff of smoke, the rush of fire, and the great boom – fitting rewards for a lengthy preparation. It was not really a bathtub, of course; I carried out my illicit activities everywhere but the bathtub: in the laboratory after hours, in my father's workshop when he was absent, in the study, in my bedroom, in the garden, over the cricket pitch, and even in a cane field. The best and worst part was the element of surprise: what would happen after the boom?

Although it had been the sodium pellet explosion that had ignited my love for Chemistry, solid sodium was not a practical explosive, so in St. Kitts I was mischief waiting to happen until my father gave me the opportunity.

On a small island, people contribute socially however they can, often in areas far removed from their professions. Among his community functions, my father did conjuring shows and organised fireworks displays. While I was back home on vacation in 1954, after the sodium incident, he asked me if I would like to help in his next fireworks event. All of the equipment had been ordered and would soon be ready for installation.

"Will I be lighting things with matches? Yes, I'd love to, Dad."

The event would take place in the middle of the bay road, just in front of the Basseterre Post Office, on a large pier. This solid, many-footed structure was the main sea link between St. Kitts and the neighbouring islands. All one hundred yards of its heavy wooden beams and pylons would be festooned with firework stands for the occasion. It was fitting. This was man's finger poking into the treacherous Caribbean Sea – usually blue and inviting, sometimes destructive with hurricane waves. The fireworks would show, as all explosives do, that man, too, could take control of the world and split the calm night with his fire.

We prepared during the afternoon and the display began after dark, at eight o'clock. The citizens of Basseterre watched from their houses or on Bay Road itself. My role was to carry material, help set up, and then light some pieces at the far end of the pier. My father had no other way of synchronising the display than to rely on four diligent helpers, my brother Peter and me included. We worked with flashlight signals, my father orchestrating everything from the middle of the pier. The pieces were numbered: rockets, roman candles, resounding bombs, and walls of fire; each had a fuse that gave the initiator several seconds to get out of the way. We used special long-burning wands to light the fuses. I was nervous at first to be performing in front of hundreds of onlookers but soon realised the public couldn't see me – we were just dark shadows that scurried from one point to another – and I relaxed in anonymity.

Along the shoreline, the public, too, was invisible on that moonless night, but far from inaudible. The delicate displays of Catherine wheels drew mild applause but the Caribbean temperament is more suited to explosions, the louder the better, and the bombs and rockets drew deep sighs and handclaps of sensual approval. An acrid sulphurous odour – which I knew from our local volcano – smothered the usual smells of salty sea air. The thunder and flashing lights enthralled me and when the noise stopped, the echoes continued in my head.

"What makes them explode?" I inquired the next day.

My father said: "Think of imprisoned oxygen celebrating its freedom. Most of the fireworks are made of some variant of gunpowder. In a bomb, the mixture is adjusted to explode all at once; in the other devices, such as rockets, the powder is modified to make it slower-burning."

"And the colours?"

"That's witchcraft: the manufacturer adds bits of magic – bat's eyes and toad's tongues – to create special effects. It may be your job, one day."

"That's for me. But just what is gunpowder? Is it the same as the powder in your shotgun cartridges?"

"I'm not sure I should tell you about gunpowder."

"I can ask my Chemistry master."

"Well, it's an old formula: carbon, saltpetre, and sulphur. Food for cannons."

"Could I make it?"

"Well, I suppose so, but you must be careful! Lots of local boys mix it – all the little bombs you hear at Christmas are gunpowder."

I knew which bombs he was referring to. During the Christmas and New Year's season, I would buy them by the dozen – bomblets really, two-inch balls of tightly wrapped cloth. There was no fuse. A hard throw against a wall and they would explode with a satisfying whump. Better still, I could launch a bomb with a catapult and make people some distance away jump.

"Where can I get the ingredients?"

My father seemed to regret having been sucked into the conversation.

"A drug store, I would think. Look, if you do this, be extra careful of the mixing and grinding. You'll need a mortar and pestle, which you can find in the workshop, and each ingredient must be ground fine, individually. But when you mix the three constituents together, watch out. Stir rather than grind. Gunpowder makers who grind too hard end up with a few fingers less." He wiggled his right hand for emphasis.

I laughed, wiggling back, "Don't worry, I need my hands to write with."

Thus, I started on the bomb-maker trail, though my first efforts were ludicrous. The Corner Drugstore did sell raw chemicals, but I thought I had heard "salt", and bought sodium chloride. Sulphur was no problem, but they didn't have powdered carbon. The druggist suggested charcoal or antimony, with a knowing wink. I took charcoal. I found my father's pestle, which in fact had belonged to my grandfather, and ground the three ingredients finely, then stirred prudently, but the mix refused to ignite. Then it became clear, by asking around, that saltpetre, the vital oxygen-rich ingredient, was not salt but potassium nitrate. One part of sulphur, two of saltpetre, and three of charcoal.

Focused like a cat on its prey, I began mixing small quantities in the study, scrutinising my fingers before each step. It felt good to have ten of them. Any traces of yellow or black dust were rubbed off on my trousers. I roped in my brother Peter, who was as keen as I was. I needed help, and if I was going to get blasted, I might as well have company. One of us could pick up the loose fingers while the other writhed on the floor. When our first batch of passable gunpowder burned with a pop and a whoosh, we cheered. If I was a wild-eyed explorer of science, Peter was quickly a methodical and devoted helper. In another universe, we might have been the true followers of our grandfather, whose mortar and pestle we were using. I was already teaching science to my younger brother, not suspecting one day I would be paid to do this.

That's when we discovered good bomb making requires skills other than pure Chemistry. I wrapped up some gunpowder in a small brown-paper bag that used to hold sugar, tied off the lump of chemicals with string, and threw it against the nearest available stone wall. Nothing much happened. The bag split open and our precious powder dispersed on the ground.

How perverse. Not only was the stuff apt to steal my fingers when I wasn't looking, but also, when we wanted it to explode, it wouldn't.

We had to find out the secret of our competitors, the local bomb factories. I went downtown to a back-alley store and bought three bombs to analyse. At the time, I didn't know the expression "reverse engineering", but that's what we did. Each bomb was hard-packed, like a dry mango seed. The outer layer was crocus bag (burlap) tied with a heavy string. Inside was a solid ball of waxy paper. I unwrapped the ball – carefully – and found a spoonful of greyish powder, quite like my own mix, and little stones. Not just any stones, but sharp yellow-grey splinters of rock.

"Why are there little stones in bombs, Dad?"

"Ever heard of flint? And sparks from rubbing two flint stones together? Plus, you need weight to throw an object. Try chucking a feather around."

I then discovered that the rocks from which the splinters came, a type of quartz, could be found on some hills and beaches at nearby Frigate Bay.

I wondered whether my father hadn't made bombs himself – he seemed to have all the answers. Although Peter and I kept our activities to out-of-the-way corners of the house, he sometimes surprised us with a visit, but said little. Years later, I was mystified by his laissez-faire approach. Did he have so much trust in me, or did he not expect the coming escalation of risk? Even great fathers sometimes make mistakes.

A few more experiments helped me to master the vital elements. The quartz stones were easy to procure. With thuds and cracks, we hammered large pieces to splinters. On my first test, I used cheap paper from a school notebook to wrap the powder and stones; then I tied it up in crocus. Peter watched as I catapulted it against our test wall. It did explode, but it was only a pop. I found the paper in shreds. We concluded the paper had to be tough, airtight if possible, to seal in the expanding gases. The crocus wrapping was there for mechanical strength. Gases pushing furiously outward – strong paper and crocus resisting – bang!

We made more than a hundred bombs that Christmas, until my pocket money ran out. I even thought of selling them, but it was too much fun getting our own bangs. When he saw our batch size increasing, my father regaled us with more stories about the-boy-who-exploded-his-mixing-bowl-and-lost-two-if-not-three-fingers. But by then, I was convinced I was too clever for such a fate.

In the months following, I was deeply satisfied with my mastery of gunpowder. I washed an empty milk bottle and filled it with the smooth grey stuff – no label. I hid it in my clothes cupboard, behind a pile of socks, where I could take it out and admire it from time to time, or show off to trusted friends. I was a young Guy Fawkes, ready to blow up the world. But the novelty eventually wore off.

A more advanced knowledge of explosives had to wait for three years, until I entered the Sixth Form in St. Kitts; I was then fifteen and determined to be a scientist. One of my early Chemistry preparations concerned ammonium salts. With great delight, I chanced across a text book reference to ammonium iodide: "… this is an explosive substance and not suitable for class experiments." So, of course, I had to try it out.

I was struggling with my first year of A-level Chemistry, especially Inorganic Chemistry. So many unrelated facts to memorise. But the lab sessions were what I preferred – heat, light, and sound – even if my grades didn't show any particular talent. It made things easy that Sixth Formers were given free run of the lab. We could even come back after class hours to finish off experiments. I would often be delegated to borrow the key to the lab and return it to the Masters' office afterwards. In this unsupervised atmosphere, it was easy to run my own projects.

My eye fell on a manufacturing footnote in my Chemistry book: "Ammonium iodide is sensitive. It is formed by adding iodine to a concentrated solution of ammonia. After some gentle evaporation, ammonium iodide crystals appear. While wet, the crystals are stable, but as soon as they dry, the slightest impact will cause them to explode. Even an ant running over a crystal can set it off."

"I've got a good experiment here," I said to Clive Ottley, my classmate, scholarship competitor, and friend. "Now I've done the assignment on ammonium hydroxide, I'm going to make some ammonium iodide."

Clive was a black student from Sandy Point. He shaved his hair very short, a few millimetres at most, as if to say he didn't need any decoration. Some tilt about his firm lips set above a square chin gave him a quiet, quizzical look. He read the footnote, and looked dubious. "Better stick to small quantities," he advised.

Not too small, I thought, but I made less than three cubic centimetres of the stuff. A pleasant surprise – it crystallised with very little warming. My only problem was to stay clear of the pungent ammonia vapours. The result was a purplish mud of ammonium iodide at the bottom of my beaker. I spread some of the goo on the lab desktop to dry. Then I remembered my friend Nizzie and a few others would soon be coming to the lab. How to take advantage of this invasion? I smeared the rest of the stuff on the concrete floor with a large minefield near the door.

"Watch it!" said Clive. "The Master is coming with Nizzie." My classmate had been unable to finish his experiment last session, and had asked for help.

Footsteps sounded outside the lab. Worried, I glanced at the floor. The smeared portion now looked purple. It wouldn't do for the Master to put his foot in it. I ran to the door. At least I could remove the biggest gob before the Master sparked it. It still looked sticky. I took out a pocket-handkerchief and stabbed at it. Crack! A cloud of purple gas shot up and I felt a searing pain in my finger. Then the door opened. Nizzie and two others stepped in. No Chemistry Master. I backed up and let them pass. Sure enough, wherever they put their feet it was snap, crackle and pop.

"Holy shit! What you guys been doing?" With no Master, we could afford to laugh. My friends walked all around the room, stamping on the treated spots, which dried much quicker than I had expected.

I looked surreptitiously at my hand – it wouldn't do to admit I had been hurt in the line of action. My handkerchief was a rich indigo, but to my relief, all my fingers were still in place and operating normally. Only my thumb and index had been burned where I had touched the gob. As a bonus, the hurt area was already disinfected.

A few minutes later, the ammonium iodide remaining on the floor and desktop got so dry it began popping off in the breeze without assistance. Unless it was the ants, which had turned up to fulfil their suicidal destiny.

But something as unstable as ammonium iodide couldn't be used in the projects that were tickling my imagination. What I needed was some way to set off large packets of gunpowder without having to throw them against a wall or to light them within finger distance: in short, a good fuse.

By now, I had taken to actively perusing my Chemistry books for any further reference to explosives, not just waiting for a chance mention in my homework assignments. I don't think I was aware that this caused me to spend many more hours studying formulas than I would otherwise have consented to; my Chemistry grades improved steadily as a consequence. The ammonium iodide formula was Inorganic Chemistry but now I turned to my Organic textbook. When I discovered that all organic chemistry was carbon-based, I recalled the carbon in my gunpowder mix and knew I was going to have fun. We had just met the chemical family of aromatics with benzene, toluene, and the like; a bunch of neurotic carbon and hydrogen atoms gripped in a deathlike embrace. It seemed incestuous: the carbons had no idea which hydrogen they were mating with. But they could be encouraged to marry other species, and even split up, violently.

There was a fascinating follow-up chapter about nitrating aromatic compounds. For a starter, there was nitroglycerine (dynamite). Then, for a main course, I could tangle with trinitrotoluene (TNT). I read the synthesising details with longing, but it seemed a bit difficult even for an earnest apprentice. I was impressed – but not deterred – by the "this is VERY dangerous" comments. Fortunately, I found an easier alternative – tri-nitrocellulose, commonly known as guncotton – in the same chapter. Ordinary cotton was all I needed to provide. The rest was in the lab. Ordinary cotton burns slowly and unreliably. I had to treat it with a mixture of concentrated nitric and sulphuric acids to replace a hydrogen atom with a nitro group. Within the nitro group there would be lots of fun-loving oxygen, just the partygoer needed to make the cotton fibres flammable.

I started with long pieces of cotton twine and a few balls of cotton wool for variety. The most difficult part was mixing the acids; the yellowish-brown, corrosive nitric acid had to be added in small quantities to the colourless sulphuric acid, and not the other way around. I knew what exothermic meant, but now I could feel it, and smell the fumes – the mixture became boiling hot. Into this devil's brew,

I dunked the cotton objects and let them stew for an hour or so. Then I poured off the hot liquid. There was no public sewage system, so the angry acids went hissing down the pipe into the school cesspit to fight with the bacteria. I then rinsed off the cotton in lots of water and dried it using the lab towels and good quality Caribbean sunshine. To my disappointment, the cotton looked much the same as before treatment: I had expected it to change colour, at least to take on a golden tint. But it did seem a little stiffer.

It would have been wise to stop there, because this guncotton worked well. A length of twine burned quickly and reliably, giving a few vital seconds to step clear of whatever device it was attached to. When lit by a match, the balls of cotton disappeared with a satisfying poof, leaving no residue. In this form, it might even serve as a detonator. I should have moved on to the practical applications of guncotton, but a little farther in my Chemistry book, I found the recipe for a superior detonator. It was called mercury fulminate.

A week after I had stockpiled a supply of guncotton, I plunged into the manufacture of this new substance. I chose a late afternoon when all the masters had left and three of us were alone in the lab. Clive and my other classmates were by now used to my eccentric projects, and left me alone, but not without some curiosity.

First, I tracked down our small supply of liquid mercury, stored in a tightly closed jar, without having to pillage a lab thermometer. I jiggled some of the silvery stuff in the palm of one hand – there must have been about five grams, the size of two green peas. No one had told me – perhaps no one on the island knew – that skin contact of that sort could result in mercury poisoning. The potent mercury went into a large flask, to which I added a now-familiar ingredient, thirty-five millilitres of concentrated nitric acid, and stirred with a glass rod. It bubbled a little, but did not dissolve easily. I heated the flask over a Bunsen burner. When it reached boiling point, the mercury disappeared and the brew turned a leaf green. At this stage, according to my plan, I had a highly reactive mixture containing mercury nitrate. Now to add the organic component that would give it muscles. To produce the fulminate, I needed ethyl alcohol. In a beaker, I prepared thirty millilitres of what would have made good rum. The pallid liquid gave off a rummy odour, but didn't look like much. Nothing was said about this part of the synthesis, except to watch out for brown toxic fumes. I leaned over the boiling acid mixture and poured in the alcohol in one go.

Mistake. The alcohol should have been added drop by drop.

There was a loud cracking, splintering noise under my nose, and my vision got a bit confused. I remember seeing the flask in fragments. How was I going to replace it? Then I noticed the Bunsen flame was extinguished: how did that happen? And one of my friends was saying something ridiculous like, "Throw water on him! Quick! Douse him!"

Then I was leaning over a sink and they were spraying me with tap water: face, chest, and legs – all wet.

"What you doing? Why you wetting me?"

"Acid, man, acid all over."

The counter where I had been working was a shambles with pieces of glass everywhere and fuming liquids. I was still clutching the empty beaker of alcohol in my right hand.

"Stop! That's enough – I'm all right, hear – "

"Cool off, cool off." My friends let up, to my relief.

I looked owlishly through my glasses and said, "Thanks, I'm OK."

No flying glass had cut me. My shirt and trousers were soaking wet, but I didn't feel any injuries. I patted my forehead, thumped my chest, and decided I was simply a little shell-shocked. No need to exaggerate the accident. I wasn't sure what had gone wrong, but perhaps I would not repeat this synthesis for mercury fulminate. What did I need a detonator for, anyhow?

We cleaned up the lab, and I left before dark. I trudged down Jones Hill toward our home, in my own way fulminating about my failure. My shirt should have dried by then but it was flapping annoyingly against my chest. I tucked the bottom firmly into my trousers and – without even tearing – half of it came away in my hands. Astonished, I looked down to see I no longer had a shirt, just shreds of cloth. There were large holes in my trousers too.

You don't mess with hot nitric acid and get away with it that easily. My mother would be cross; this meant a new school uniform. Maybe they would dock my pocket money.

I slipped into our house unseen and stripped off what was left of my clothes in the bathroom. What a stupid thing to do. Maybe I had added too much alcohol. Or the acid was too hot. Wonder if any acid went through my shirt?

I approached the mirror to check my skin. A few red marks showed here and there on my chest and neck, but no apparent cuts or burns. For some reason, I couldn't see clearly. I took off my glasses to clean them. They were covered with white specks that didn't wash off. I felt a shiver. The surface was pocked in many places. If I hadn't had that protection, my eyes would have taken a direct hit. This whole Chemistry thing might be too damn risky, I thought, staring at the damaged glasses.

I was a lion tamer on the shadowy stage of a molecular circus. Facing me were organic adventures, like hoops of fire, searing and sizzling, illuminating the dark corners. Beyond, and padding toward me, were the beasts: toothy Oxygen, hairy Hydrogen, snarling Nitrogen, and frisky Carbon. My role was to make them jump through the hoops without being clawed.

I cracked my whip.

During the next few weeks of my school term in 1957, I avoided unauthorised experiments in the school Chemistry lab. Not that I was afraid, or thought I was jinxed, but, after all, I had my basic tools: guncotton and a large supply of gunpowder. The time had come for a more ambitious project, with no confining beakers, flasks, or Bunsen burners. I just needed to apply my precious knowledge about gunpowder and move from research to engineering. I wanted outdoors action, despite the problem this had once caused.

I recalled a few years earlier, in 1955, when I had been designing my first cannon when on vacation from Antigua. It was a logical way for a bomb maker like me to use his powder. My father gave us a free rein in his workshop. First came the sizing – I didn't need a cannon capable of firing five or ten-pound shot. A cannonball consisting of a marble weighing five grams would do the trick. I picked out a few of these from my brother's toys, clear glass with whorls of red and green entrails.

For the body of the cannon, I selected a length of lead pipe with a three-quarter-inch internal bore from my father's workshop. Two feet of this seemed quite enough to me, the first half to be filled with powder and the second serving as a trajectory guide. I capped the powder end with a wooden plug hammered in a good two inches. Then I drilled a one-eighth-inch ignition hole while my brother Peter held the pipe steady. Into this went a short length of guncotton string. I packed the gunpowder into the cannon's mouth, a small bowl of it, and last came the marble, wrapped in toilet paper to make it fit in more snugly. It was definitely tight. We were ready to fire.

The "we" this time included my sister Hazel, and my youngest brother, Noel. Peter, as usual, had been the co-designer, but this would be the first whiff of action for the others. I assembled the firing team on the front lawn under the flamboyant tree. The cannon was anchored on a pile of stones and pointed across the lawn towards our neighbour's wall, coincidentally the same neighbour, Mr King, who had shot my cat Simba years before.

As chief designer, I had the honour of lighting the fuse. I ordered everyone out of the hoped-for path of the missile, positioning myself behind the gun and to the left. I didn't want to shoot anyone by accident. Would a glass marble bounce off clothing, or would it inflict a deep wound? The onlookers stayed on the right, about two yards away.

I lit the fuse. Silence. What was it waiting for? Then came a large bang and a little smoke. Everyone cheered, or almost. My first concern was the projectile, but looking at the target wall, I saw nothing. I discovered the marble a mere five feet away. Why? The cannon! It had split open like a ripe banana. Something had gone wrong with my design. Belatedly, I checked out my siblings. They were all looking curiously at the smashed cannon, except Hazel, who had not cheered. She had been seated closest to the pipe, and as I looked, she appeared to be absorbed in her leg, which was covered in blood.

"Hazel! You've been hurt!"

She groaned rather than replied.

"I felt a thousand little pinpricks – "

"Hold still."

With a not-too-clean handkerchief, I wiped her leg while Peter ran to get some water. When the blood was gone, we saw our sister had no major cuts, but rather several dozen tiny lacerations from the shards of the pipe. We picked out the bits of lead one by one, using our fingers and a moderately clean pair of long-nosed pliers. None was deeply embedded. Then we bathed her leg and disinfected it with iodine. The torn body of the cannon was hidden, but not jettisoned.

"Sorry, Hazel, I didn't know that would happen."

"Oh, ith my fault. I shouldn't have thayed that close."

That evening, my mother spotted Hazel's leg. "What have you done to yourself, dear?"

"Fell on bwickles in the garden while blaying with the boys. They bisinfected ith."

"How thoughtful of them. Do pay attention where you walk, Hazel."

If my brothers and sister were not involved, I usually felt honour-bound to confess everything to my parents. That is, until my late teens when I began to look at girls and felt the need for more privacy. When playing with my siblings, however, the unspoken code was that we didn't tattle on each other. That way, there would be no recriminations, and always another adventure to look forward to. This mutual arrangement to avoid sanctions was part of Caribbean life. People were not litigious and human rights were not on everyone's tongue. When someone got hurt, it was considered bad luck, or even the victim's fault for being careless. I once saw a barefoot boy walk in front of my father's moving car and get knocked down. The boy picked himself up and did not appear to be hurt. Despite, or because of, my father's status as a lawyer, he gave the boy $5, admonished him to "pay attention next time", and sent him packing; there was neither a police report nor a hospital check-up.

The same year, I collided with a car at the bottom of Jones' Hill, cycling at near full speed. Only one of my brakes was working, and the car had stopped transversally in the middle of the road. On impact, I flew over the stationary vehicle and landed in a gutter. I was quite bruised, and my bicycle was crushed into a monocycle. The driver apologised and took me home, where I was put to bed for a few days.

To my knowledge, no other action was taken except to reprimand me for not fixing my brakes.

So I should not have been long deterred by Hazel's injury, which disappeared in any case after a few days with no ill effects except for a tiny set of scars to add to all her other marks of bruising. Hazel fell frequently; it was a consequence of her cerebral palsy.

But this was not sufficient for me to absolve myself. I recalled the hard knocks with catapults and rocks, years before, when I had gashed Hazel's head. I recalled the incident in Antigua where I had been caned for nearly injuring a young girl. I might be leading a charmed life, but my safety record with bystanders was not good. It couldn't be allowed to happen again. What kept me from abandoning explosives and gunpowder in particular, and even Chemistry, was curiosity about the cannon. Why had it failed? I had planned things so carefully. Was it bad luck, or bad design? This mystery allowed me to recover from my fears and keep my milk bottle full of a gunpowder reserve.

That was the past, and now I had other, more dynamic things to do. The cannon had been an immobile thing – only the bullet moved. I wanted a pyrotechnical object that could fly. A rocket.

I regretted not having tested the cannon on a smaller scale before wasting powder on a two-foot version. This time, I planned a series of increasingly larger prototypes. Some aspects were the same as for the cannon – gunpowder and a fuse – but I had to learn what made a rocket fly.

The rockets in my father's fireworks display were made of cardboard, so for our first attempt, Peter and I chose a light five-inch cardboard cylinder – a toilet paper roll. With a loop of wire, I constricted the rear end; the front end was plugged with tape. We strapped this tube to an arrow made from a shaft of wild grass. My guncotton fuse went through a hole at the bottom; I used a reduced quantity of powder. We called it the ZZ1, but it betrayed its proud name by fizzing and burning without taking off.

I thought there was not enough fuel, not enough constriction at the exhaust end, and so I had to be bolder if I wanted it to fly. I found a better cardboard tube for the ZZ2; it was about twelve inches long, and had been used to deliver a calendar. It was the same design, just more cylinder and more powder. To our delight, ZZ2 left the ground. It must have risen more than six feet before succumbing to gravity. I was ready for the big time.

But not in our back garden. After my preceding hot acid fiasco in the lab my status as an experimenter had suffered. I didn't want to be known as the chemist-who-had-his-shirt-burned-off-and-never-touched-explosives-again. My next rocket was meant to be a technical and social triumph. How to up the ante? I thought about the rocket casing. It must be bigger, a lot bigger. I wanted to pack in about five times as much fuel. And it must be strong; obviously, metal was better than cardboard. When I found an old five-battery flashlight in a workshop drawer, I knew I had a winner. The sleek tin casing looked ideal. This time the nose-cone and the spent gas exhaust cone were not left to chance. Peter and I turned them on our father's lathe from blocks of wood. The V-shaped inside of the exhaust was sculpted by hand. In the middle of the nosecone, we left the nail used for holding it in the lathe. Even with the head of the flashlight unscrewed, the casing was bigger than I had thought, and took more than a pound of powder – nearly my entire milk bottle supply.

Then I convened my school friends for a Saturday afternoon's entertainment on the school grounds. One other chemist from the Sixth Form was present – Donald Walwyn. Clive and the others lived out of town and couldn't attend. Donald – tall, brown, and exuberant, with a prominent forehead – checked out our technology with great enthusiasm.

"Think it'll fly?" he asked.

"Of course. This thing has enough fuel to reach the moon. Where should I aim it? I wouldn't like the nosecone to fall on anyone's head. The nail would give them quite a headache."

"Why don't you aim for the cricket pitch? It will have to fly over the Chemistry lab to get there, but I don't think there's a match on this afternoon."

"But Donald, that's almost two hundred yards away."

"I thought you said the moon!"

I oriented the ZZ3 rocket shaft in the direction Donald had suggested, at forty-five degrees. We used some school chairs to hold it steady. Then I looked around at the small crowd and remembered my sister's leg injury. Between my friends and some curious villagers, there must have been about thirty people gathered.

"Everyone move far back," I shouted. "No one closer than ten yards."

I could see young Noel sneaking up to where Peter and I were standing behind the ZZ3; I ordered him back to the ten-yard perimeter. Donald was much farther back than most, about twenty yards, but with a fine, clear view, perpendicular to the flight axis. That was good enough, I thought.

I moved behind the ZZ3 and lit the fuse. Then I recoiled about two yards and wondered whether a pound was not too much gunpowder. There was a hissing noise, and I thought I saw a brilliant orange flash, but the boom of the explosion was so loud it swamped all my senses. The noise smashed into me like Thor coming down from the heavens and I couldn't say how long it lasted. First, I had the immense satisfaction of having destroyed the world; next came the appalling thought that nothing might be left. Transfixed, I grabbed my ears and found myself coughing, bent double. Smoke was everywhere and I imagined I heard shouts, but it was just people with their mouths open, since I couldn't hear a thing for the longest while. Peter was next to me, also clutching his ears. At least he was all right. Some of the onlookers were running away. Others were on the ground. Donald was standing up looking particularly dazed with a hand on his head.

When my hearing returned, Donald's was the first voice I heard.

"Fellows, I think I've been hit."

I went over to him. He was bleeding rivers from the forehead just over the left eye.

"What happened to the rocket?" he asked.

"What happened to your head?"

He pointed to where I had been standing with Peter. There was no rocket, not a trace. The chairs were blackened and overturned.

"Anyone see it fly?" Donald asked.

I shook my head.

"Something went up, but the flash was too bright for me just after the launch."

"Your head, Donald."

"Yes, maybe I'd better do something about it."

He wouldn't take his hand away; but that didn't stop the bleeding, and I thought I caught a glimpse of metal between his fingers.

"Where's the nearest hospital?" I asked.

"I'll take you there," he said, "it's round the corner, a five-minute walk. Are you up to it?"

"But it's you... OK, let's go."

Then, to Peter, "Better take Noel home. I have to go with Donald."

Under the immense pressure of the hot gases from a pound of gunpowder, the thin casing of my ZZ3 rocket had ripped into many pieces. Why was I untouched, close by, whereas at twenty yards my friend Donald was struck? I never learned whether there were other casualties.

At the hospital clinic nearby, a black nurse in a white apron removed the metal fragment from the two-inch gash above Donald's eye. The small, twisted bit of tin lying on the table seemed incapable of doing so much damage.

"Damn lucky, you," she said, "one inch lower and you eye would be gone."

I helped Donald pay several shillings for the copious dressings. It took eight stitches to sew him back up. Still in disbelief, he refused to let me accompany him back to his home. Would he associate the scar with me in the future? I walked back through the school grounds on my way home, full of remorse. I reached the blackened chairs, kicked them, and moved them out of the weather to an open hallway.

Look what I had done now! How could I have been so stupid? Once again, I didn't even know what had gone wrong, only the damage. To start with, a safety perimeter of ten yards was not enough. They should have been fifty yards away. Was there any safe distance from my experiments? Poor Donald. The shrapnel should have hit me, not him. Well, that was the last time I would mess with rockets, cannons, or explosives. No more secret bottle of gunpowder. Chemistry was a mug's game; I was a public danger, to family, friends, and myself. I had burned and almost blinded myself, cut up my sister's leg, and caused Donald this nasty injury. He might not come back to school on Monday. I might never have come back at all. It was time to stop playing with this crazy stuff. Amateur explosives were for fools. Better stick to the straight and narrow path.

While I circled the school grounds, deep in the darkness of my mind, a boy approached me.

"You the one fired the rocket earlier on?"

"Yes, sorry, it was me."

He produced a wooden object from behind his back; his eyes gleamed.

"This yours, then. It fell on the cricket pitch."

It was the nosecone, complete with its nail. Incredibly, it had followed the trajectory I had hoped for, riding on the lifeblood of its parent booster, two hundred yards of impossible freedom. In a flash mirroring the rocket's blast, I knew that I was not going to give up so easily.

That evening, my father said, "The whole of the town is talking about an explosion in our area today. Know anything about it?"

Peter and Noel stared at their dinner plates.

"Well, it's nothing much, Dad, just a rocket that turned out badly. We were playing on the school grounds. The buildings are still standing."

He laughed. "As long as no one got hurt. But you will be careful, won't you?"

"I'm determined to be, Dad."

Donald returned to school on Monday with a bandage and didn't bear me a grudge. We had been partners in the same scientific venture. I let things settle for several weeks while I got on with my studies and the school moved to the other side of town, near Warner Park. The launching site of the ZZ3 was thus abandoned and forgotten. But my ideas were not. Nor was the milk bottle.

I figured out what had happened with the cannon and how to fix it; it always seems simple afterwards. Although I didn't know the term "hoop stress" and wouldn't study pressure in thin-walled tubes for some years, I saw that the lead pipe needed circumferential reinforcing. I built another cannon to the same dimensions and bound the lower part of the barrel tightly with copper wire. The marble was given a little leeway – not wrapped in fine paper – and no one but I was allowed outside the house during testing. It fired perfectly every time, pinging on our neighbour's garden wall forty meters away, opening the door to future exploits by young Noel.

As for the rocket, the problem was similar: the tin casing was far too weak to withstand the hoop stress; thick cardboard was actually stronger. The powder burning also needed to be slowed down in order to merit the name of "fuel". It was more of a grenade than a rocket. But instead of trying a new rocket design, I built what I thought of as an aerial H-bomb.

It was only a dozen years since Hiroshima, and the H-word was still burning its way into our consciousness, even in out-of-the-way places like our little island in the Caribbean. Those born in the mid-1940s like me would be known as the post-atom-bomb generation. One day in 1968, I would attend a lecture by the American anthropologist, Margaret Mead, who would explain that the thinking of my generation was necessarily quite different from those preceding, coloured by the knowledge that man was now capable of destroying himself and his planet by nuclear warfare. At the time, this did not worry me.

My H was for plain hydrogen, and it was not a bomb but a balloon. And who better to help me than an older and wiser Donald? We filled the balloon with hydrogen gas made from zinc and hydrochloric acid. When I tied off the balloon, I introduced into its neck the end of a slow-burning fuse left over from my father's latest fireworks. I wanted our balloon to rise over the school grounds and explode over a precise spot. Tests showed us the length of fuse to cut for a flight of seven minutes. Then we checked the wind direction. It was blowing from the north-east at a fair clip. We had to guess speeds and distances, but at last, we cycled off with the balloon and positioned ourselves a mile upwind from the school. This turned out to be in the middle of a cane field, not far from the sugar factory. I lit the fuse and we let the balloon go. Up and up it went and our future with it. Cycling back to school at high speed, we reached the gates just in time to hear a flat, cracking noise in the sky above our heads, like a big zipper coming undone, exactly where we had intended, high up over the cricket pitch. As we had known, there was a match going on.

Afterwards, Peter could not believe that the H-balloon had exploded directly over the pitch.

"Near enough," I said.

"How could you get the air-speed right?" he protested.

I rubbed my nose speculatively, once for each of the cricket pitches I had targeted.

"That's it? Just lucky? I suggest you don't tell this story to Noel. He's even crazier than you are, Chris."

After the balloon went off, a wild jubilation filled me that I could see reflected on Donald's face. I looked at my past and saw the tortuous transitions from magic to hypnosis to poisons to explosives, always a step more dangerous into the unknown, fearing less the physical perils than the collapse of the mystical into the mundane. Now I knew science could make us rise into the sky if we understood it and willed it. Willpower, always. Now I had the confirmation that earned knowledge did bring power, and that the darkness around us held more mysteries to unravel than I could imagine.

At the end of play, I talked with our school cricket captain. "Did you hear the explosion in the sky?"

"You and Donald have something to do with that?"

"Maybe, maybe not."

"Well, I'm damn glad if you did. You know, we were losing the match. They had only fifty runs to make with six wickets in hand. I was bowling, and I'd been hit – really hit – for six, but that weird crack of thunder in a clear sky threw off their batsmen at a critical moment and they tumbled like ninepins."

Donald and I smiled at each other timidly, not unlike two acolytes about to enter a gigantic cathedral of learning. We buried the ghost of the ZZ3 that day.

Like Father

I thought my objections to the world were unique and, as I adventured down bypaths, I thought that my solutions, too, were unique and personal. But how many others had thought the same, and, in particular, how much was I like my father? My future hung on this question.

I had finished my first year in the Sixth Form with minimum effort and was unjustifiably pleased with myself. I had written two essays that I was proud of, on "Poetry is as much concerned with skyscrapers as with roses", and, "A cynic is a man who knows the price of everything and the value of nothing". I feigned to ignore that the essay-writing paper, called the General Paper, was only an accessory to A-level results. My main exams would be Chemistry, Mathematics, Physics, and Literature. In these subjects, I was not excelling, and my university ambitions looked fragile.

A few years before, in the mid-1950s, a Liverpool manufacturer – Meccano Limited – had stepped up its production of metal erector set toys. The company had been in business since 1901, when Frank Hornby devised a set of metal strips and plates for children to make into models. It had interrupted toy making during the Second World War to manufacture weapons, and again in 1950 when the Korean War caused a metal shortage. But when I reached Sixth Form, British families and their Caribbean emulators could buy large, mysterious boxes full of green and red Meccano pieces for their young builders to fasten together. Like many others at the time, my brothers and I plunged into the construction of miniature mechanical devices, complete with nuts, bolts, brass wheels and gears. Meccano acquired a huge following in Europe and the British colonies like St. Kitts – it was training for future engineers and a paradigm for making a new, clean world. But sometimes the structures would collapse and the wheels fail to turn because I had not put them together properly. That was the way my studies were going.

I remember the day I stopped drifting. It was after school one afternoon in late 1957, when I came home to announce to my parents that Lee Moore had succeeded, that he had just been awarded the Leeward Islands Scholarship – the LIS – for that year and would study Law at King's College, London, and my father took a long drink from his after-work cocktail and replied, "Now it's your turn, Chris."

The family was gathered on the veranda, a long rectangle of green-painted, roofed-over concrete that bordered the front of the house, set on a hill less than two hundred yards from the sea, looking over the bay of Basseterre. The sea in the harbour was getting up, and my brothers Peter and Noel watched the boobies spread their wings and career over the waves, hunting for agitated fish, while my mother was absorbed in a book next to my father. I stood near to them, also looking at the waves, but my father's words made me put down my leather schoolbag and turn to him.

"I'll do what I can, Dad, but it depends on the competition, you know."

He glanced at me, then back at the coming storm, and said, "I know what the effort costs."

As if wishing for something could make it happen. When my school colleagues Lee and Fitzroy had championed willpower to achieve the impossible a year before, I hadn't agreed with the method, but it seemed to have worked for Lee. On the contrary, up to then I'd spent my time on anything esoteric I could find, like hypnotism, or poisons, or explosives, rather than studying.

"Almost thirty years ago," my father continued, "I was in your shoes. I tried to win the same scholarship. I failed."

I stood with my back to the sea and fidgeted. "But you went to school in Antigua! And that was a long time ago!"

I paused, and said, "How come *you* competed for the scholarship?"

"It's for the best student in the Leewards, no matter which island. And it's been offered since the 1920s. I was very disappointed not to win. And worse: my father – your grandfather – couldn't afford to pay for any more schooling on his priest's wages, so I had to go to work."

My mother closed her book and looked up at us.

"Look, you *have* to win that scholarship," my father said.

"Well, suppose I can't – you got to be a lawyer, anyway!"

"Not easily – I began as a school teacher. In my day, a student who had passed his final exams with good school-leaving results could turn around and get a job teaching in his old school."

I was amused to think of my distinguished father with chalk on his fingers in front of twenty rowdy boys. It did not cross my mind that this might also be my fate. And what would it have been like to be a pupil in my father's class?

"It took seven years to get out of that trap and into law school – the Inns of Court – and all because I missed the scholarship. I didn't mind the teaching, if that's what you're thinking, but Cecil Rawle wouldn't allow a humble teacher to marry his daughter. I was nothing in his eyes."

Incredible that my father and mother had depended on a silly scholarship to get married; there must have been other ways. Still, it had bothersome implications for my own studies.

"Where did you get the money? Did you find another grant?"

"There *aren't* any others, and there weren't any then, either. After seven years, I was desperate. I had tried everything, even sitting part of my Bachelor's degree by correspondence. Then a friend of the family lent me money. Your mother said it came from God, and who knows?"

My father didn't often touch us – it wasn't part of our family habits – but now he put his hand on my shoulder and sharpened his voice, which made my brothers turn around.

"Hear me! That exam you are going to take is *very* important. It's your whole life. My dream is for you to win it."

The stakes were rising. I considered the alarming idea that I was being asked to do something my Dad had failed to do. And if *I* failed, not only would I be mucking up my own future but stamping all over his dreams.

Peter and Noel drank in his words. They would have their turn, especially if I didn't deliver. I thought of all the schools I had attended, from kindergarten onwards. Had my father been planning my future for sixteen years? The long perspective was a lot to take in. It could mean that as far back as age four, when he had suggested to my mother to open a play school for me, he was already thinking of the scholarship. It could mean that pushing me into a boarding school in Antigua at ten was not just for discipline, or for family tradition, but explicitly to groom me for the competition. It could cast a new light on his obsession with speaking fancy English. I did see one thing clearly: I mustn't disappoint him. He wanted this for me terribly, maybe more than a new car, a new house… He wanted it too much – something was missing.

"Dad, I don't understand. You are surely the best lawyer in St. Kitts." I was not trying to flatter him. "You said you lost seven years. But your school results should have qualified you for something. Were they that bad?"

If he couldn't get a scholarship, I didn't see how I could possibly do better. Also, if he had lost, someone must have beaten him.

He didn't respond, so I added, "Who was smarter than you?"

"Smarter, I don't know. But win she did."

"She? Who she?"

"Evelyn Tibbets," my mother said, looking up from her book, again.

A light rain swept across the harbour.

"A clever girl," my father continued, "but I had better exam results. Especially in Literature and Mathematics. She came overall second."

"So they should have given the scholarship to you!"

"Politics, Chris. She had the highest A-level grades of any girl since the exams had first been offered in the Leewards. The scholarship committee thought she should be encouraged, that she might even become famous."

"And you? What about you, Dad?"

"They were convinced that sooner or later I would find some other way to continue my studies. To be fair, I don't think they realised my father couldn't support me at school any more. I'll always blame myself for not anticipating a close result and not doing more work."

"But, but, that's so unjust – "

"Don't look so worried; those boy/girl issues can't affect you. These days, the best candidate wins." He looked out over my shoulder at the grey sky. "At least, I hope so."

"It was outside of your control, Ralph!" my mother said.

My father shrugged. "There are other dangers for you in the setup," he said.

"The exam?"

He hesitated. "Yes, because everything depends on one test, a dozen papers spread over a week. Suppose you are taken ill on the day of the exam? The people marking your paper won't care if you've been brilliant all year. Pray for good health."

I saw my whole life hanging on just one or two lucky or unlucky days. I hoped I would be clever enough to beat my classmates, but against the plague…

"You're scaring me, Dad!"

"It's the same for everything. The real trials in life have a tragic background: you blunder at the wrong moment and all is lost, you do it right and you're a hero. No second chances – but if you work hard enough you don't need a second chance."

I wanted to avoid a discussion of hard work. "And did the Antiguan government's plan succeed?" I said, "Did the Tibbets girl become famous?" I had never heard of her.

My mother giggled.

"Not in the way they hoped," my father said. "She did well enough at university, all right, and qualified as a lawyer. But when she came back she got married in two winks of a pretty eye, raised five children, and never worked a day in her life."

I added to my list of lifetime resolutions that, if I were beaten in the scholarship competition, it must not be by a girl. This was hardly an original thought – just an echo of our male-dominated Caribbean culture, where higher education was scarce and girls in a Sixth Form were even scarcer, less than 25% of the class, and considered lucky to get that far. How quaint that idea would seem a few decades later, near the end of the 20th century, when – even in macho Jamaica – girls began to outnumber boys on the university campus. But it remained true that, for most of the century, female winners of the scholarship would be few.

As if on cue, my mother said, "It's not just your father who had bad luck. I, too, tried and failed to win the scholarship. When your father was in England studying law, I sat the Cambridge exams twice. Each time, the ship carrying our exam papers back to England for grading was torpedoed by U-boats. After the second loss, my father said I was cursed."

"Well, tell me, then. If I can't win the scholarship however hard I try, what happens?"

"You try again. I can't fund four children's education abroad – one at the most, and that will have to be Hazel, because she is handicapped." My sister had left for England three years earlier and had just transferred to a Grammar School for disabled students near Coventry.

"I'm cold," my mother said, "let's go in to dinner."

I didn't protest, although I realised a girl – my sister – had already beaten me in my quest for studies in another country. Then I felt frightened and exhilarated: for every scholarship winner there would be a loser, or several, but these were my friends at school, not just names on paper: Clive, Welby, and others. There was going to be intellectual bloodshed among us, and I didn't want the blood to be mine. I thought of my cat Simba crouched for combat, extending his unclipped claws.

That Sunday, my father's parents had lunch with us. My mother had stuffed a chicken with breadcrumbs, and accompanied it with yams, tannias and chayote, or christophene as Kittitians name it. Grandpop was thus present for the second phase of my father's message to me. He wanted to expand on what a scholarship could mean.

After my grandfather had said grace, my father began, "You see all this food on the table, and our house in a good area – it was hard earned. Unless you start off rich, the only way to get ahead is by education, especially in these Caribbean islands. If you want to make money, you have to get a university degree. Otherwise, you end up as a sales clerk or a government stooge. But it's expensive to study abroad. You must get that scholarship, Chris! Sacrifices now will pay you back many times in the future. And anything your mother and I can do to help you win it, we will."

I heard echoes of the willpower theory I had rejected from my classmates, but I was distracted from replying by my grandfather, who had been looking increasingly uncomfortable during this advice.

"Ralph, no! Don't teach the boy to value money above everything else."

"And what should he value more?" asked my mother. Her family had had more resources than my father's, but nevertheless for lack of money she had never gone to university.

"Anything spiritual: love, faith, friendship. Money is the root of all evil, that's what he should learn. It doesn't even matter if he can't go to university, provided his faith in God is strong. Of course, I hope he succeeds, but surely it's more important for him to love people and for people to love him."

For a flirting moment, the loving and being loved back seemed sexy, but then I realised I had never heard my grandfather contradict my father. An uncomfortable silence fell over us. I discovered the background noises of knives and forks. My grandfather and grandmother were getting quite old. He had retired from active duty in the church after a bad fall in his bathtub, an injury to his hip that never healed completely. Two years later, my father would have to build an extension to our home at the Fortlands to lodge them, a kitchen, bathroom, and large bedroom with access to the veranda and the sea view. Their togetherness was so strong that further down the road they would expire almost simultaneously.

I didn't hear what my father replied, but it might have been, "Don't interfere." Abruptly, he left his place at the head of the table to fetch the carving knife. When he returned, my grandfather finished his meal early and asked to be excused from the table; my mother helped my grandparents to a room where they could rest.

What could I make of this? Was my grandfather right to say money was of little importance? To him, I supposed it wasn't. He had subsisted all his life on the minimum the Anglican Church gave him. My mother once said he should have been appointed Bishop in Antigua, but they passed him over because he was coloured. He never showed resentment as far as I could tell. Assigned from parish to parish, I realised he had never owned a house, and never owned a car. Did he own anything? I thought of his books and two or three suits of clothes. He didn't even give out Christmas presents – unless you counted packets of raisins and used paperbacks.

This had never seemed to matter, but the confrontation that day said it did. My father's movements suggested he was cross at my grandfather – or perhaps disappointed was nearer – a truth I'd never seen before. Taking my father's side of the argument was automatic, but there were consequences to be thought out. If the adults got so worked up about it, then I had better make piles of money, I thought, just to be on the safe side. I wouldn't like to have to tell my own son he must stop going to school and work for seven years before fulfilling his ambitions, whatever they were. He would surely have challenges similar to my scholarship, but it mustn't be "all or nothing" like it was for me, just because of money. No doubt in my mind, money was essential. And the scholarship was money.

When I thought about the difficulty of earning money, I didn't include the servant who worked for us and was clearing away the meal. All over the Caribbean and Latin America, domestics were employed for next to nothing, excepting their meals and sometimes their lodging. Even a struggling middle class family had a servant, or *criada*, or *empleada*. At the time, about ten percent of the population in St. Kitts worked as servants, black women with little schooling, who had often started having children at sixteen or younger; the male equivalent was a gardener. I took it all for granted and couldn't imagine that this unregulated work force – at the same time an avatar of the days of slavery and an indispensable economic buffer – would wither away over the next twenty years when more education and new labour laws would raise salaries sufficiently until there was little difference in compensation between a servant and a sales clerk.

There was another problem for me: if my father was right about values, then my grandfather, who opposed him, was wrong. This had never happened before. After the meal, I walked onto our veranda and stared at the warm blue waves rolling onto the sandy shoreline of the harbour, over and over again. You could count on the waves doing their gentle, repetitive roll, unless there was a storm. And even after a storm, the waves returned the next day to their comforting motion. I felt the grandfather I loved and respected had lost this enduring power. He who had helped to tide me over so many rocky places in my earlier schooldays, from tree climbing, to fights, to being an altar boy, was shorn of influence in his old age and would no longer be able to guide. Grandfather, father, and then myself: the effects of our life choices persist, for better or worse, into the following generations, like the wind shaping a succession of waves and each wave pulling its successor behind it. Still out at sea, the currents gripped me, and I was what I was because of all of them. But sooner or later, the oldest wave reaches the shore and breaks with a crash or a murmur. This, then, was melancholy – the ineluctable fading of my grandfather's wisdom that had been so dear to me.

The next day in the upper Sixth Form (6A), I had several occasions to think of my end-of-year exams and the scholarship – still four months off. First, we had two hours of Literature, usually an inspiring class. I liked the Shakespearian aperçus. From *Henry IV*, I noted: "*Rebellion lay in his way, and he found it,*" which suited me just fine – a quiet disagreement with the world to put in my pocket.

We would have one exam paper on Shakespeare's plays (including a tragedy and a comedy), and another on the Romantic poets. But that morning we were preparing for a third exam called Literary Criticism. In order to analyse other people's work, we were encouraged to write our own poems.

"Christopher, could you honour us with your poem?" asked Fitzroy Bryant.

Poetry was easier to swallow in doses from Wordsworth or Keats than to spit out in gobbets of our own invention. Take this business of rhythm – it could get clumsy. I had experimented with different beats in my poem and wondered whether I was about to become a laughing stock. I opened my essay book and stood, reading to the rest of the grinning Sixth Formers, ignoring Fitzroy's sarcasm:

Caribbean Night
Loud are the crickets in my yard
The night has come and it's time to sing
But where is he, the man on guard?
So silent under the tamarind.
The sun has gone its lonely way
I am really so ready to sleep
If only I could have my say
I wish I could still the peep-peep-peep.

There was mild applause after I had finished.

"So," said Fitzroy, "awkward! A poor choice, eight and nine syllables. I don't like your iambic tetrameter, though '_The sun has gone its lonely way_' is not bad. But you evidently think 'sing' rhymes with 'tamarind'?"

"Well – "

"And by the way, crickets don't make a peeping noise – that's chickens. You don't know fowl, man? Crickets chirp, like, 'Aiee, aiee, aiee'!" When Fitzroy smiled he showed his long, sharp teeth.

"Not one of your best, Christopher. Better avoid the poetry composition question in the exam." So, I would keep my poems for myself.

Next, we had an hour of Chemistry lab. My adventures with explosives had given me a taste for mixing and heating, but I knew I was weak in the measuring league. The exercise that day was to titrate oxalic acid against a standard base. Suspiciously, I measured the clear base into a conical flask with a glass pipette, made it up to a hundred millilitres with distilled water, and added the colour indicator. Was this going to work?

"What colour is it supposed to turn, Clive?" I said.

"Chinese yellow – if you're lucky."

Clive was more methodical than I, and had already started titrating.

I poured the oxalic acid solution into the burette, and noted the starting level. I turned the tiny glass tap. Drop by drop the acid fell into my basic solution. It produced no colour change. I looked over at Clive, and saw he had finished. A straw-like liquid smirked at me from his flask. More drips fell from my burette and still I saw no colour change. It was close to lunchtime when I decided to fiddle with my tap. Suddenly, it came loose. A flood of oxalic acid rushed to meet its enemy in unseemly haste. Before I could stop it, my solution had reached its yellow transformation point and gone way beyond it into deep orange. To my disgust, I had overshot.

The bell rang, and Mr Blackman looked around the lab sternly. Only Clive had got a result. "OK, pack up, boys. Those who haven't finished can come back after school or do a calculation instead. In the real practical exam, you would have had less time."

That afternoon we had Mathematics, and, as if the morning's events had not been discouraging enough, I couldn't solve my equations. My algebra was so-so (not having progressed much since my days in Antigua), the class in differential calculus was puzzling, and coordinate geometry was boring – all those monotonous lines and inhibited circles forever trying to intersect, and me having to find the point to it all. Today we had Applied Mathematics, with the mechanics of falling bodies. My mood was not good, and I began to develop a grudge against gravity.

What a nuisance it was, I thought, when things accelerated! It was so much easier to compute distances at constant speed. In my problem, I had to find the speed of a ball projected upwards against gravity when it reached a certain height. It seemed I would have to calculate a square root, which I wasn't too sure about; besides, it was the square root of something negative. I knew I'd made an error and I didn't hand in my paper.

The day kept on drifting down, and ended with Mr Ribeiro's class. Louvered glass windows on two walls made the Physics lab bright, illuminating my own ignorance.

"Why do things float, Christopher? Like a piece of wood on water?"

I fingered my lab stool as if the polished pine could give me inspiration. "I don't know, Sir, it just means it's lighter."

"But what does lighter mean? Why doesn't wood sink in water?"

The lab bench in front of me was covered with tough, grey plastic; I scratched at it with my nails and said, "Well, it can't – "

"Did you read the chapter on Archimedes' Principle?"

"I thought it was for next week."

"Read it tonight, then. And next time you have a tub bath, think of the liquid you displace."

"I only take showers, Sir."

He looked at me disapprovingly, and for a moment I thought I'd gone too far.

"Well, let's see if your shower works, Christopher. Consider an ice cube (density 0.9 gm/cm^3) floating in a glass of rum (density of ethyl alcohol 0.79 gm/cm^3), which is showered with water at 30°C weighing 0.996 gm/cm^3. Assume that the rum cocktail is a 10% mixture, and calculate the visible fraction of ice." My classmates were all smiles until he added, "The rest of you can try it, too."

I hadn't got anywhere when Clive announced the answer was 7.35%, thus confirming my opinion that the entire world was against me. I might have been comforted to know that one day I would do research on the boundary layer between melting ice and water, but at the moment I was ready to agree with another *Henry IV* quotation: *"Doomsday is near; die all, die merrily."*

I knew I had to study more. There was no alternative. With several months still to go before the exam, maybe I could make up the lost ground. I didn't have to be perfect, just better than the others. How much was I studying, anyway? I came home at 5pm, if I could get out of sports, and if I didn't have to stay on in the Chemistry lab. Then I worked until dinner at 6pm; after dinner was more difficult – starting at seven or seven-thirty, my concentration would flag soon after eight. Unless I read a novel, of course, in which case I could stay awake until ten. So, I was studying less than two hours per day. Occasionally I would work during a free period, provided I didn't chat in the Prefects' room.

It seemed I was sleeping too much. I forced myself to read a textbook between eight and nine at night: anything – Shakespeare, Mathematics, or Chemistry. It didn't work – at 9pm I would still be on the same page as at 8pm and my pencil would probably have fallen on the floor.

During the morning break at school next day, I tidied up my books quickly and cornered my fellow Sixth Formers before they could leave the classroom. The first two would not be sitting the scholarship exam until the following year.

"Nasals, how much time you spend studying?" I asked.

The boy with the squashed nose looked up from his desk. "A lot, a lot, man. I like stuffing all night. Start at midnight and stuff my head until sun come up." "Stuffing" was our Caribbean term for studying, or rather, cramming.

Frightening. Even for such a desirable scholarship, I couldn't bust a gut or cram my brains, or suffer any such mutilation. Besides, Nasals' grades were curiously unimpressive.

"What about you, Nizzie?"

"Coffee, man, coffee. That's the secret. You need good blood pumping in your veins. So, drink lots of coffee. Or take pills."

I was already starting to use coffee in small quantities, but it made me nervous. I didn't want to hear about the pills.

Next, I questioned those who would be sitting the exam that year.

"Kaye, what about you? Do you work all night? How do you keep awake?"

"Not all night. Keeping awake is a problem. I go for a short walk with my dog whenever I feel sleepy. That works."

I didn't feel like walking, and especially not with a barking dog.

"And how late does that make it?"

"Well, my dog needs to sleep by ten o'clock," she said.

"And you, Welby?"

"What's all the excitement about hours of studying? Bother about nothing. It's not how much you study, but *when* you study. I never do anything until the night before an exam. Waste of time. Then I read my book quickly so it'll be there in my brain the next morning."

I already knew the fallacy in this approach, because it had been my own: it didn't work when the textbook was more than an inch thick.

"I know you're going to ask me next, Chris," Clive said. "I don't have any tricks – I just use all the time available: a little before school, a little at lunchtime, and a little each evening. And the weekends, of course."

"The weekends? You study during the weekends?"

I looked at Clive in amazement. It hadn't occurred to me to give up playing games and reading comics during the weekend.

My studies started improving after discovering I could work on weekends. I accepted that my body needed sleep after a day at school, and went to bed at 8pm I started waking up at 5am and drinking coffee. I had paved the way for this, months before, when studying poisons. Sometimes it made me dizzy; once, I fainted. But I didn't give up. And I used my weekend time. I kept track of my daily and weekly study hours on a scoreboard.

There were complications, though. At about this age, I began having intense sexual urges. I discovered what made my clock tick and indulged myself. It didn't help my concentration that I had to express my feelings several times a day. In the beginning, there wasn't even a girl on my mind – that sort of advanced fantasy would require further training. As I was recording my hours, I recorded these episodes also. When I reached ten ejaculations per day I decided to apply some restraint. Pleasure had to be earned; each indulgence required at least one hour of study; and this gradually gave me some control. So many things turned around willpower.

But, auto-satisfaction or not, there was still a quality problem in my studying: would I remember what I had read? The breakthrough occurred during a Chemistry class.

"I know industrial organic chemistry is new for you boys, so don't be discouraged by your marks," Mr Blackman said, waving our papers at us. We had done an exam on the manufacture of benzene. I wasn't expecting much, but I remembered my guncotton experiment. I looked at the graded paper he had returned to me. Five and a half out of ten; and, scribbled at the bottom, "Shows promise." What? Which promise?

"You'll see that most of you got half marks. You don't know the details well enough. Not yet. I gave Christopher an extra half-mark, however. I think he has the makings of a Chemist."

He turned to me. "Your description shows you understand, or could understand, the benzene process. I think you are going to do well."

This was a bolt of lightning. If any three things determined my future career, they were: Mrs Imbert's exploding sodium pellet, the ZZ3 rocket that turned into a grenade, and Woodie Blackman's generous half-mark on that Chemistry quiz. Detail, he had said, and the next week we would have a quiz on toluene. Once home, I went straight to my textbook and read the two dense pages on this new compound, the next member of the aromatic family. Some of the words poured right out of my head onto the floor; I could feel it. So, I closed my book and walked from my bedroom into the – fortunately – empty kitchen, repeating the words about toluene that had stuck. There were less of them than I had hoped for. Then I went back to the book and saw the gaps. Then I closed the book and repeated, over and over. I didn't stop until I had the text memorised, even the most obscure formulae. It took the whole afternoon, without any of my habitual breaks in concentration. Read, test, read, test... And having memorised the words, it became a story, and it made sense. My grade on the toluene quiz was nine out of ten. But, as I patted myself on the back, I noticed how thick that Chemistry book was – a lot was still left to read.

As the exams approached, my other work began pulling together, too, and I dreamed of the scholarship most nights. The dream always began with an official saying, "We have the pleasure of announcing that..." but there were many ceremonial variations of the award. It always stopped with the award – I had no idea what came next.

In Literature class, I was invited to play Falstaff in the annual school play. Fitzroy didn't think it would be a waste of time, since we were studying *Henry IV* and *V*, anyway. I rolled around the battlefield of Agincourt with a pillow over my stomach and learned most of the play by heart. In Organic Chemistry, I became unbeatable. In Applied Mathematics, I discovered equations could have physical meaning beyond the numbers. If the argument of a square root turned out to be negative, then it meant that some physical situation was impossible. It couldn't happen – the ball would never reach that height. Only in Physics did I still have disagreements with Archimedes, Huygens, Wheatstone and the like. But at least I was able to build an electromagnet in my father's workshop. I used it to ring a buzzer until everyone became annoyed. Overall, I was so confident in my cleverness I began anticipating my father's satisfaction after my victory.

The 1958 Cambridge A-level exams came and went. For my General Paper, I chose to write on, "Science is the source of all human progress", a point of view I contested. I cited the example of nuclear fission, which could be used for good or for evil. Science is neutral; politics decides the issues. My papers went well, with the sad exception of Physics. It took two months for our unseen judges at the Cambridge Overseas Examinations Board to send us back our results, and the stress of waiting for them was greater than that of taking the exams. When at last we received our grades, Clive and I hurried to the Prefect's room and compared marks paper by paper – a whole school career compressed into a few numbers. This room, with its uncompromising bare white walls and concrete floor, had always seemed a good place for mathematics and rationality. It had been clear for some time that we two were the leading St. Kitts contestants for the scholarship.

The papers were graded from one to nine, the lowest being the best in the eyes of the British examiners (1 and 2 were distinctions, 3 to 5 were passes, and 6 to 9 were failures). Each subject had three papers, marked separately. I had three distinctions: General Paper, Organic Chemistry, and Shakespeare. Clive had none. Overall, my Chemistry grade was better than his, and my Literature grade was superior to his Geography. But his Mathematics result was better than mine and my Physics was distinctly worse than his History. He had not failed any individual papers – I couldn't say the same of my practical Physics. Overall, Clive had been more consistent, though some of my papers had high grades. Only the scholarship committee could decide.

Clive reached across the table and said, "Chris, let's shake hands on this. I don't know which one of us will win, but no hard feelings either way, please."

I was happy he had said that, for I was already feeling guilty about winning. Certainly, the committee would choose the candidate with more distinctions.

"No hard feelings, Clive, ever. Let the best man win."

I shook his hand, and this was significant, because touching other people's flesh was not a common thing for me.

"What are you going to do if it's you?" I asked.

"I have it all planned out – medicine at the new University of the West Indies in Jamaica. What about you?"

The question took me by surprise. I had been so concentrated on winning the scholarship I had imagined everything after to be simple.

"I haven't thought that far yet – maybe I could do Chemistry in Jamaica on the same campus as you."

Clive smiled, then he spoke slowly, "But only one of us can go."

That evening I showed my A-level grades – and Clive's – to my father. He was sitting on the veranda as usual for that time of day. I told him I was fairly confident of winning. He examined the sheet of paper carefully and then returned it to me, saying, "You've done well, son."

I started a discussion of which university I would like to go to, but he stopped me. "It's a bit early. We'll wait for the committee to make its decision. There's many a slip twixt the cup and the lip."

It made sense, but still I needed to talk about Jamaica. "But, Dad – "

Not unkindly, he cut me off. "Not now, Chris. Believe me, it really is premature. Things are much more complicated than you can imagine."

I had thought he would be pleased, very pleased, but I was still sure of victory so the joy of success was only being deferred. Maybe he was preoccupied by his honey business: two hives had recently swarmed, and now it seemed many other queen bees were too old. I would soon show him, I thought, that he was being too prudent about me. I would satisfy his dream and mine simultaneously.

However, the exam committee took another month to make up its mind, by which time the summer was over and we had returned to the Sixth Form for a third year. We took regular classes and pretended to study, but in fact, Clive and I – both repeat scholarship contenders, not to mention those unknown students in Antigua, Nevis, and Montserrat – twiddled our thumbs, waiting for our fate to be decided. We were not synchronised with the university admissions cycle: one way or another the winner would not be able to enter before September 1959.

"Boys, would you please go to the Headmaster's office."

The scholarship winner was about to be announced.

The Headmaster's office had the biggest metal desk in the school and I marvelled he could keep it neat. All his papers were in orderly filing cabinets. On one wall there was a map of the Caribbean and on the other a map of Europe. I remembered playing mental games about the order of viewing these maps. Should one first look at the Caribbean, our birthplace, and then the lure of Europe, where we might go to study; or look first at the European powers that had birthed the sombre past of the islands, and then the Caribbean itself, where those who willed might create a new future?

"I have been informed by the scholarship committee," said the Headmaster, "that the decision was particularly difficult this year. Several of you had good results, but there were three candidates to separate, two from St. Kitts and one from Antigua. The winner is Clive Ottley. I am authorised to say that Christopher Vanier was the runner up. I want you all to congratulate Clive, and…"

I was stunned, so much so that I had difficulty afterwards distinguishing the roles of my mentors, Mr Blackman and Mr Ribeiro. How could they ignore my distinctions, all my long hours of work? Clive had won after all, despite my sacrificed weekends. I felt my eyes bulge and my mouth drop open; I balled my hands at my sides in a vain attempt to stop the room spinning. This couldn't be fair. And how was I going to explain it to my father? I couldn't imagine his reaction. Cross – maybe he would be cross. I would prefer that. What I didn't want was for him to look sad. Then I cringed at what would come next. I could not accept the humiliation of trying again. And had my father known I would not win?

As the Headmaster's voice ceased its rambling, I shook Clive's hand, but didn't look at him because I wanted to hide my red eyes. He held the warm contact longer than I had intended. Unknown to me, Mr Blackman had already driven out to his home that morning and informed his family privately.

I was moving towards the door with the others when I caught the sharp sound of my name.

"...Christopher, stop a minute!" Mr Ribeiro waited until the others had left, and then he took me into his office.

"Now, you must be generous, Christopher."

Me, generous? Not in a pig's eye.

"I wouldn't like this to spoil your friendship with Clive, and I know it won't. You both have to spend at least one more year in the school, and we are counting on you, as Prefects and teachers to stand as examples of fair play and generosity. Clive is going to teach, and you, I presume, are going to re-take the exam."

"I haven't decided yet."

"Yes, you have. You're going to decide it right now."

I said nothing.

"Let me tell you something you mustn't repeat. Not even to your father."

This scared me. Not the keeping of a secret from my father – I had learned to do that – but what did the Headmaster have to confide in me that was so personal?

"Chris, given your age, you have three possible attempts at the scholarship. You must accept that Clive won. And don't listen to anyone who says the contrary! Although you were a close second, Clive's overall results were better. The Antigua student was definitely third. Now, be glad that Clive will be going to university and St. Kitts has won the scholarship again. Next year may be yours. OK?"

I thought of our handshake, and felt myself relaxing. It would be all right if I could direct my disappointment elsewhere than towards Clive.

"OK, Sir, I'll try." He ushered me out of the door.

But there was still my father to deal with.

I walked slowly to the back of the school where I had chained my recently acquired, motor-assisted bicycle. Its gasoline engine was tiny, and the assistance it gave proportionately so, but I loved it. On the flat and level, it carried me along at a respectable putt-putting pace. On steep hills it cut down on the pedalling effort I needed to make, though, if I faltered, my motor and I would stall together. Not the least of its attractions was the sense of danger it conveyed. The extra weight of the motor wore out the rear tire prematurely and could cause sudden decompression and a bad fall if not detected. The clutch cable was temperamental, and the unshielded exhaust pipe and muffler often singed the hairs off my leg.

That day, with the scholarship results still spinning in my head, I took a long route home, and practiced spitting at the lampposts as I cycled by. I missed more than half of them and took to wondering whether this would be my success rate in future scholarship exams. And if I couldn't hit my targets, was it the fault of my aim, or the wind, or the quality of my phlegm?

I cycled up Victoria Road instead of down, then through the Greenlands residential area with its improved version of the gaudy concrete shantytown houses, which was all a young person could hope for if he didn't get an education. I passed the lonely Springfield cemetery where they buried winners and losers alike, and then I bordered the splendid Governor's mansion, where I had once shot ground doves with my BB gun when Rosemary's father Lloyd had been acting island Administrator. That was where the scholarship and a good degree could get you, I thought. As I approached the treacherous Jones' Hill leading down to my home, I worked the motor up to full speed. It was a rash thing to do, given the near escape I'd had two years earlier with a car on the crossing at the bottom of the hill, but my brakes were in good shape and I felt – what the heck – I'd already had my share of bad luck for the day and nothing more could hurt me. I tinkled the bell on my handlebars continuously, as if it would make a difference to any traffic ahead, and I scowled at the rich houses with high walls as I hurtled past. I knew the owners had inherited their wealth and thought they had never come close to winning a scholarship. It was not a moment when I could be fair. I didn't suspect I would one day go to the same college as a Wigley had. I pushed away the fact I lived on the same street and my father's house was almost as large, with a better view. The rushing air cooled my cheeks, and the feeling of control over my souped-up bicycle gave me confidence to face my father. I knew I had to win that scholarship next year, and if it couldn't be then, it would be later. There was no car at the crossing so I coasted home.

"…but I just wasn't good enough, Dad. Almost, but not quite."

My father was not looking at me this time, but staring out at the late afternoon sea and the sky, places where we all took solace. Sensing something unusual, my mother came out to join us.

"I suspected this would happen."

This was going to be harder than I had thought. "I'm sorry I failed you, Dad. I really will do better next year."

"You were bound to fail. It's Bradshaw."

Bradshaw? What did he mean? Then I realised he was referring to the Chief Minister of our St. Kitts Government, his long-time adversary.

"Not content to be boss of St. Kitts and Finance Minister of the West Indies Federation, he has taken revenge on me."

Surprised, I soon saw my father's point of view was plausible. The plantocracy had been crushed in St. Kitts; all power was now in the hands of the ex-trade-unionists, the island's first black government. But the plantations were still privately owned – land reform was down the road a while – and dislike of the planters' representatives, among them my father, ran deep. Whatever the scholarship committee called itself, even with other islands' representatives on it, the last word on the winner would have to be approved by Bradshaw. QED.

I did not understand my father's antipathy to Bradshaw at the time, but he had his reasons that would amply be born out in the future. About ten years later, in the troubled period 1967-1969, my father would have a real tale to tell. Although his Labour opponents thought him a conservative, he saw himself as a quiet revolutionary; he would never use dynamite to tear down a building, just knock out the keystone and see the structure crumble under its own weight. When things were bad for all manner of English-oriented Caribbean citizens, and worse for friends of the plantocracy, and rumours of violence began to circulate, he tiptoed. The Labour government was nervous and vindictive. Without being summoned, he surrendered to the police the shotgun that had given him so much pleasure hunting doves and pigeons, his precision rifle that had won him the island marksman's prize at the factory shooting range and in inter-island competitions, and even my boyhood .22 rifle (in my absence). This only made the authorities more suspicious. The possession of such objects could land you in jail or have you deported on charges of treason. My father had been shocked when several of his friends had been imprisoned and was under no illusion his brown skin would exempt him from Bradshaw's malice.

He had been as open and respectful of the law as possible but, nevertheless, one day a police patrol stopped his jeep on the way to the beach. He was alone.

"Good morning officer, how can I help you?"

"Get out you car, Sir."

"Of course. What is it that you want?" he articulated precisely.

"Just stay with me men."

The police proceeded to open the small trunk of the vehicle, search behind the seats, and poke the motor area with truncheons for a good fifteen minutes. Finally, a sweating lieutenant crawled out from under the jeep and waved his hands negatively to his superior officer. My father had been standing as casually as he could between two policemen who were pretending not to restrain him.

In disgust, the officer said to him, "Where you got you gun, then? We know you got something hiding."

"I don't have any guns, officer."

The police packed up and started to leave.

"Wait, officer! I do have a weapon!"

My father was quickly surrounded.

"What weapon? Where?"

My father put his hand slowly and carefully into his pocket and gave the officer a slim object. "It's loaded and very dangerous," he said.

His interrogator grabbed it, face crinkling in puzzlement at the writing pen.

Years later, I understood the military precision of that pen. In 1972, Bradshaw would nationalise the St. Kitts sugar estates and the factory over the vehement opposition of the planters. Britain, and the sugar manufacturer Tate and Lyle, would quietly acquiesce, on condition that the operation be capitalistic rather than Marxist, and that the planters be properly compensated. Bradshaw would then enact legislation that expropriated the owners for a fraction of the land's market value; his offer was ten million $US. The planters would give up their lands to the labour government administration but refuse the proposed level of payment. My father would spend the last ten years of his career writing legal briefs and negotiating for the planters. After a change in government, and thanks to hundreds of pages of written argument, the planters were awarded twice the original figure.

So, yes, even in 1958, it was plausible I had been denied the scholarship because of political prejudice. Plausible, but false, according to Mr Ribeiro.

"Why didn't you tell me this before I sat the exam, Dad?"

"No point discouraging you. And if there had been a big difference in grades between you and the others in your favour, who knows?"

Maybe my father grasped more than Mr Ribeiro. I couldn't tell who was right. I remembered hearing Mr Ribeiro was a government supporter. On the island, everyone knew which way his neighbour voted. It was a pity I couldn't discuss with my parents what the Headmaster had told me; but one way or another, I had lost the scholarship, and I began regretting all the weekends I had invested.

"It's no use trying next year, then? The same thing will happen?"

My father paused, searching for a balanced reply.

My mother reacted to this upsetting exchange, countering my father's momentary pessimism, "No, no, you must try again. If you try, there's always a chance…"

We were still out on the veranda, our green garden of coconut, lime, mango, and pawpaw trees now covered with shadows, the sea hissing its evening lament, when I had a revelation: contrary to what I had often thought, although finances were important, the scholarship wasn't primarily about money. My father's real anguish – the unsaid thing I could now see – was seeping through to me. To win the scholarship, to be the *best*, was a goal of the spirit, non-material in essence. It could compensate for a lifetime spent in a backwater culture, at odds with the new labour politics, looked down on by the Mother Country, so unattainably far away from her little colony. My father was a freemason, and the pride of a craftsman in the quality of his work was one of his deepest values. I felt his keening disappointment of thirty years before, and again that day; it was hard to be *nearly* good enough. He couldn't accept that honest efforts were lost. To deserve his love I had to win. A painful harmony gripped us. I wanted what he wanted. I had the same awkward aptitudes for science and literature that he had. Maybe he'd once been as lazy as I was, too. The exact explanation of my failure didn't matter. "Not good enough" was the reality. Maybe I had worked hard for a few months, but the comparative of "hard" was "harder". I had the answer to my question about family destiny, though I couldn't come to terms with it at once. Through and through, I was like my father. And the cards fate was dealing me, to almost but not quite succeed, were unmistakeably like the hand he had been dealt in his youth. The only remaining unknown was: were there any jokers in the pack?

Part 5: Scholarship (St. Kitts, 1959-1961)

Lincoln and us

Writing the essay: May 1959

Early one Saturday morning, with the Caribbean sun romping into my bedroom, I sat down to write an essay about a famous man. I'd had a breakfast of eggs and bacon, and through my open window I could see central Basseterre waking up. Along Bank Street there were bicycles carrying dusty people from the country, occasional cars idling by, a cart filled with breadfruit and guineps pulled by a silent hawker, and a slow flow of women of all colours doing their weekend shopping before the morning got too hot. Near the Circus monument, a few layabouts were picking their teeth. No one was in a hurry.

I was determined not to like the man I had to write about, and I can be stubborn. In addition to being famous, he was American, and foreign countries were not at that moment in my good books – not unless it was England. He was a dead, white, political leader, long gone: nothing to do with me. I translated my annoyance and frustration into words. Not even for $25 was I prepared to give the man any unearned credit. Thus, I began:

"Lincoln was not a god. Lincoln was not even a demigod; he was a man like us."

Then, since I had already scuppered any hope of winning a prize, why not throw some more punches? Ugly? Uneducated? I went for the jugular.

"He was not a rich man, nor a handsome man, nor a well-educated man, nor a man for whom Providence had made the path of life a rosy stroll."

Not quite as aggressive as I had intended, the negations still made it pleasingly sly. However, some American readers might take lack of riches as a good start. In St. Kitts, we didn't entertain any romantic ideas about poverty. From the little I knew about the man, I considered him lucky. Not lucky in the sense of his personal life, of course, but historically lucky for the fame that settled on his shoulders. Was Lincoln's prestige relevant in other times, to other countries, or wasn't it more likely to be a fortuitous accident, due to his assassination? Then, I signalled that he was born in an obscure place called Nolin Creek, Kentucky, and made it clear on whose behalf I was writing:

"...people who have never seen America, people who will never see America, and people who do not wish to see America."

I chose as the title for my essay, "Lincoln and us".

Before the essay: April 1959
I had been in a bad mood for several weeks, from the day my parents said they were going on long leave. Again. We were in the living room of our home, Harbour View, talking about their trip, and I protested by crossing my arms and grimacing as much as I thought I could get away with.

"How long is long?"

My mother was calm and reasonable.

"Three months, Chris, just like before."

"But why do you have to go to England in the middle of my exam year? You know I must win the Leeward Islands Scholarship this time."

"Your sister in England needs us more than you do: she has a school crisis. We can't help you in your work – you're always telling us that."

"Well, I won't stay with Granny and Grandpop. He'll try and preach at me."

I had mixed memories of staying with my grandparents: there was much affection, but my grandfather, Canon John George Vanier, seemed to think the road from hell to heaven was paved with good sermons, or physical persuasion if needed.

"We don't want you fighting with Grandpop, so you'll be with your godmother, Elaine."

Elaine played the organ in church, which was a doubtful starting point for me. However, she wouldn't scold or bully me. Some found her tone acid, but to me her sense of humour simply had a wicked flavour. When I was very young, she would take me to visit the cemetery, where we had serious discussions about fairies and foxes.

Belief and disbelief were deformable, sometimes overlapping, structures in my young mind, like coconut trees bending and weaving in the storm of events. I wanted desperately to believe in fairies but knew deep down I was most unlikely to encounter one anywhere nearby. Wily foxes were a substitute: they were just as scarce on my tropical island as fairies but it seemed they were alive and well in some far-off countries. Enchantment yielded before the mundane.

"OK, but you never take me with you. Hazel is the only one to have been to England."

From my mother's look, I could see that going to special English schools for spastics, as Hazel had done, and being separated from your family for years on end, was not her idea of privilege.

"You'll see, those three months will fly by like lightning, and you'll have all your time to study. Nothing will disturb you."

And so I was comfortably installed in Elaine's elegant house in central Basseterre, on Bank Street, near the Circus crossroads and its brown Berkeley clock tower (now green). My brothers had to lodge with my grandparents on Victoria Road and listen to grandfatherly homilies. A few days after my parents had left, the disturbance that wasn't supposed to happen showed its face. At the St. Kitts Grammar School, Fitzroy Bryant, our English Master, assembled the Sixth Form for a special announcement.

"Today, I have major news for you, about an essay competition." He took off the dark glasses he wore everywhere, sat on the teacher's desk, and read to us from an official-looking letter. It had a portrait of a bearded man in the top left corner and an enormous scrawl of a signature at the bottom; on his desk, there was an envelope and more papers. The letter was from the United States Information Agency.

I had never heard of the USIA. American influence in the islands was much weaker than it is today. Fitzroy said the competition was all to do with a "sesquicentennial celebration" – whatever that was. As part of this celebration, the USIA wanted us to write a commemorative essay about one of their Presidents.

"Sesquicentenary," said Fitzroy, "means this year, 1959, will be one hundred and fifty years since the birth of Abraham Lincoln; by deduction, you Mathematics scholars can see he was born in 1809. That's whom you have to write about."

"Do we have a choice? Can't we write some other sort of essay for the Americans?" I asked.

"No," he said, "they want a Lincoln essay."

As I wasn't taking History, I found this infuriating; I could think of lots more interesting subjects. How about "Human freedom is impossible", or "The mind: your own business", or even something provocative from Keats like:

"Love in a hut, with water and a crust,
Is – Love forgive us! – cinders, ashes, dust."

I insisted, "Is this homework, Mr Bryant, or can we just skip it?"

"I haven't mentioned the prizes," he said. He leaned forward and spoke carefully, weighing me up, the way a judge looks when about to sentence a miscreant.

"No, you – in particular – can't skip it. Not after your distinction in the essay paper last year. I will dispense a few students from wasting their time, if they request it," and he looked at Nizzie, who picked at his fingernails, preferring biology to books. Then he turned back to me,

"But not you, lazybones. Each school will judge its students and select the best essay. The writer of this essay will receive a prize of twenty-five American dollars."

That, at least, was something. Even if I didn't want to waste my time with History, what wouldn't I give for $25? It would be enough for several books, a pile of comics, and goodness knows what else. Pocket money for six months. And I had no doubt I could write the best essay in the school.

"And there will be a committee to judge the best essay from the island. The writer's school will receive a statue of Lincoln – we hope to win this – and the successful essayist will be able to meet the other island winners, and ..."

I didn't follow the last bit too well, since it obviously didn't concern me. Even if I won the school competition, which – on second thoughts – was not entirely certain, there were three other island schools competing and any government committee would probably vote against me, just as they had for the Leeward Islands Scholarship exam the year before. Beyond that, it seemed the Americans were mostly interested in the Caribbean regional winner, whom they would invite to the United States to visit Lincoln monuments. Well, they could keep their thirty-day-tour of monuments, I thought, as I cycled back to Elaine's house that afternoon.

But I was hooked – I wanted my $25. I agreed to write an essay, even though it wasn't compulsory and wouldn't help me in my Cambridge exams. It was more work. When I sat down to write, I realised I was going to have to read a fat history book, Herndon's *Life of Lincoln*, plus other stuff; a lot of work, and all of it difficult. There I was, wasting my time studying History for the Americans, when I had my own exams to prepare for. That's why I was so disgruntled, and disliked the man from the start.

Writing the essay: Later in May 1959
Three days had gone by since my first lines on Lincoln. I had placed my desk close to the window, where I could look out on the streets of Basseterre and catch any available breeze. It was midday, the sun hot enough to turn asphalt to jelly. Right below me, Losada's general merchandise store would soon be closing for lunch. High noon for Lincoln, I reckoned. Now I dipped my pen into my inkpot, and pressed on the rubber plunger so that it filled up with cool, black ink. I hoped it would give me cool, black thoughts, full of pessimism. I had read a few chapters of Herndon and wasn't the slightest bit more sympathetic towards Abe. In case the Americans or someone gullible ever read this $25 essay, I wanted to show them why it was a mistake to over-praise

the man. He was just in the right place at the right time, and that, by itself, didn't prove he had any talent. I put pen to paper:

> *"If he had not been elected President of the United States, he would have been doomed to obscurity."*

That's dotting the i's and crossing the t's, I thought, even if it seemed obvious. An official title like "President" didn't give him the right to bully Caribbean youngsters into writing praises for him. It wasn't as if he were a scientist, or a writer, or something intellectual. One critic even admitted how apathetic he was before becoming President:

> *"...it was not until the Kansas-Nebraska bill, allowing the spread of slavery, was passed in May 1854, that Lincoln, as one biographer says, awoke from his 'civic slumber'."*

Slumbering in his backwoods – that's the way he was. Of course, he *did* win his subsequent debates, but that even happened to *me*, sometimes. I finished the paragraph just as Elaine called me to lunch.

After the essay: June-July 1959
"I'm sorry to disappoint you." It was mid-June and I had just had a despondent seventeenth birthday, the first one without my parents. And there was Fitzroy, who had summoned me to the Headmaster's office and was now nonchalantly pacing and smirking at me from behind his dark glasses. Mr Ribeiro, on the contrary, looked quite solemn sitting behind his desk. I realised my essay must have annoyed someone and that I would not get a prize – it served me right for not being more diplomatic. Perhaps I should have allowed Lincoln demigod status after all.

"Your friends say you don't care whether you win the Lincoln prize or not. You don't even like the man. So this is a sort of punishment."

"I didn't mean to be rude to anyone – "

"But you were. Your essay was quite offensive, like a good soccer striker, or a dangerous fast bowler." He held up a fist and made a face. "You disturbed the judges so much with your candour they have decided to award you the St. Kitts prize."

A shock ran through me, as I fell headfirst into their trap. My body tensed into a panic reaction. I remember jerking both feet into a wider stance and flinging my hands chest-high as if to ward off the devil. Which way to run? The top prize! I had conceit in abundance, but had not expected victory at the island level. And the way they looked at me meant I had a chance to go further.

311

Mr Ribeiro grinned for the first time. "You must understand we can't announce this officially until the Lincoln essay committee in Trinidad has approved everything and decided on the regional winner. But we wanted to be first to tell you that you've at least won the school and island prizes."

The adrenalin currents changed direction. I began to relax, as shock transformed into delight, in the satisfaction of knowing my hours of work would be recompensed. In the days that followed, this was only tempered by the unpleasant delay until I could get my hands on the $25. I wrote to my parents in England telling them of the unexpected events, but I knew they wouldn't get my letter for three or more weeks.

"I thought you would win it and beat those other no-good schools," Elaine said that evening, she who had not read a word I had written, but had kindly refilled my inkbottle several times. "And it's not over, mark my words."

She made me wonder about the winners from the other islands, like Jamaica, Barbados, and Trinidad. Doubtless, they had been full of praise for Lincoln, and equally doubtless, the Trinidad committee, consisting of Caribbean personalities and USIA representatives, would pick one of them.

Two weeks later, I was summoned once more to the Headmaster's Office about my essay. The morning assembly was just over, and I had been busy with my Prefect's duties, scolding younger pupils for making noise. I entered the room, determined they would not dupe me again, but Mr Ribeiro and Fitzroy seemed much too excited for that. Fitzroy shut the door and the air gathered electricity.

"Sit down, Christopher, sit down," Mr Ribeiro said. "We have a problem. As we hoped, you've been awarded the regional Lincoln prize, including the one-month tour of America."

I was ready. "It's not a problem for me. I think I can find the time to go."

"But how?" Mr Ribeiro brandished a telegram, appearing more excited than I had ever seen him, hair on end. "You're under eighteen and your parents are away!"

"When will they be back?" Fitzroy asked.

"I'm not sure, another month or so, I think."

"Impossible! We have to reply now. Where are they?"

"Maybe in Scotland, maybe England. They're looking after my sister. I write to an address in Bayswater."

This must have been the wrong answer, because I had the impression my teachers wanted to tear out clumps of their hair. The regional prize was a huge event – America and the big Caribbean islands were waiting to entertain the winning essayist – but its control seemed to be escaping from us. Telephone contact with the UK was all but impossible from St. Kitts. At the thought of losing this grand opportunity, I began to want it.

"Look, you said you would accept the tour. I know your father well enough to think *he* won't refuse. I'll send the committee a telegram in loco parentis accepting the award. Then I'll ask the British authorities to contact your parents urgently. Do you have a passport?"

I didn't. Neither did I own a suitcase, nor the clothes necessary for a one-month tour. When my parents were informed, they would have to cut their holiday short and return to St. Kitts prematurely. I wasn't sure they'd be pleased, although Elaine was elated. After all, I hadn't planned to win this competition, and in a way, it was Lincoln's fault.

A week later, they rushed breathless into the house after a long plane trip from who knows where. Usually avid for the story of their holidays, I was now focused on my own departure.

"You must go to Macy's in New York to shop for clothes," my mother said.

"I've got $25," I volunteered.

She laughed, "We'll give you whatever money we've got left over from England."

"Thank goodness you were on your own when you wrote the essay," my father said, setting down their bags. "Your own copyright – no interference possible. Not a bad chap, by the way, this Lincoln fellow of yours."

Two days and a plane flight later, I was in the middle of a cocktail party in Trinidad at the US Embassy. I struggled to digest the opulence of the large rooms filled with green plants and brown guests, the tables spread with spicy things to eat and drink. I now had more proof that giving someone an official title like "President" artificially magnifies his public image without adding to his real value. My essay on Lincoln was not – at least initially – intended to be taken seriously. It was illogical that all these people should crowd round me because I'd been given the label of "Regional Essay Winner". I was no different from yesterday. I was supposed to be superbly knowledgeable about Lincoln and endowed with keen historical sensitivity, when in reality my knowledge was limited to three weeks' study in the evenings of two books and several USIA pamphlets. I had always intended to criticise the man rather than praise him; hadn't they read what I had written? I found myself lucky to be a winner without intending it.

A red-lipped Trinidadian woman accosted me; she smelled of something pleasantly musky, and I judged she was about twice my age. She wanted to know about my emotional attachments.

"I don't have a girlfriend, if that's what you mean."

"Really? What do you think of women, then?"

"I'm too young to have an opinion."

She laughed. "Well, what do you think of Lincoln and women, then?"

Not sure what I was getting myself into, I said, "Do you mean Lincoln's affair with Ann Rutlege? Seems he had a nervous breakdown after that – as much mental torture as the whole Civil War, I've read. But he still fought the war against the South. I'm sure women had a positive role somewhere, though his wife was crazy, too."

This should have been the end to our conversation, but it intrigued her even more. So much so that I had difficulty escaping, and was relieved when my USIA escort and protector intervened. Hal T. Cupps was a sandy-haired, fit-looking American in his late thirties. I never discovered what his other duties were in the USIA. Maybe an information agency was not there to give out information but to collect it. In short, I suspected him of being a spy.

Hal steered me through the crowd and said, "Chris, here's someone I'm sure you want to meet. It's Hart Edwards, the essay winner from Trinidad."

I shook hands with a handsome black youth about a year older than myself. "All of this is an accident," I said, "I just wanted the cash."

"You don't have to apologise," Hart said, "I read your essay – you took a risk and it paid off. I was too prosaic." He had written a more classical and laudatory essay, centred on the economics of the Civil War.

We drifted away from the other guests to discuss how strange it was to write an essay about long-vanished Americans. What about our own urgent issues of beating England at cricket, choosing the next calypso king, and saving the West Indies Federation? Astonishing, on the other hand, how generous the Yanks were to organise parties like this, to pay our plane fares island-to-island, not to mention my coming US trip.

I discovered we had the same hopes and fears about our Cambridge exams – too few scholarships for too many students – and how to pay for university if we didn't win a scholarship? I felt something positive was emerging from this essay – I was meeting my student peers from around the Caribbean, and the attraction of this far exceeded that of my limited circle of friends in St. Kitts. I would meet other island Lincoln Scholars in the course of my travels – including Dennis Edmonds of Jamaica and Tony Williams of Barbados. These were bonds to be preserved. More – I felt I could rely on the judgement of these friends because they were from outside.

"Sorry you other island winners can't come. I promise to keep in touch."

The next day I read my essay in public to a room packed with officials, teachers, and reporters. I supposed they were curious to discover how a small-island composition could be chosen in preference to essays from the bigger and richer school systems in Barbados, Jamaica, and Trinidad. I might have been nervous if I hadn't kept in mind that it hadn't been my intention to win the regional competition in the first place. If the judges had been masochistic enough to choose an essay some called "pungent", I had nothing to feel embarrassed about. The annoying thing about that essay reading was the playback. They recorded my voice, which was a first for me, and when I heard it, I didn't like it. I wrote and told my parents I sounded too high-pitched and girlish, and why hadn't they warned me. But it was too late to change.

Next stop, New York. Flying out of Trinidad from Piarco Airport I was leaving my native Caribbean for the first time. Like a rabbit that has slipped through the bars of his cage into a vegetable garden, I didn't know what to nibble next. Everything was huge, everything was motorised, and everything was strange. I gaped at the skyscrapers and the madly rushing people, I gawped at the madder cars, learned the expression "traffic jam", and boggled at the incredible stores where clothes were ready-made in all sizes instead of being sewn at home, until with Hal's help the St. Kitts schoolboy was attired in shirts, trousers, and suits fit for the occasion. In my mind, I burned the clothes I had come with.

And then, without transition, there was Washington. It was uncomfortable in the US capital in August, and I complained to Hal, still my escort, that it felt hotter than St. Kitts.

"It's the humidity," he said, "it's not really hotter, but it's less easy to perspire."

I remembered with a pang the sweetness of the constant sea breeze on the small islands, and how most Caribbean homes didn't need electric fans because they had been built to catch this breeze. Fortunately, the USIA headquarters and the US Senate had something new for me: air-conditioning. The cold air stimulated me for the meetings with Kentucky Senator John Sherman Cooper, and USIA director Sergeant Child. My self-confidence returned.

What marked me was not the presentations but my visit to the White House. We were allowed to jump the line of visitors, and lo and behold, I found myself in the office of the Vice-President of the United States. As Nixon was away visiting Russia, I was allowed to sit in his chair, behind his massive oak desk, and have my picture taken, with my newly acquired bust of Lincoln's head perched on the glass and leather top. In the photo, I tried to look like a Vice-President, grave and concerned about the state of the world. Inside, I was chuffed: this was a lot grander than the prize I had casually set out to win. Only much later would I revert to thinking how inconsequential a title and its trappings could be. There is no guarantee that it will make any difference at all one hundred and fifty years after your birth. "Cinders, ashes, dust".

Writing the essay: Still later in May 1959

After working spasmodically for a week on the essay, I had to come to grips with the slavery issue. This required more tedious reading. After school, I put my thoughts on paper. It is a terrible time to do anything, between five and six o'clock in the tropical afternoon. The day is lost before the night is born. That is why the British invented tea parties and Caribbean people drink before-dinner rum to excess. It was always the low point of my day, and that hour of dislocation flowed into my thoughts on Lincoln. This man was forcing me to think of a nasty past.

I had heard Lincoln was the great emancipator, but his actions didn't look that great to me. It's opportunistic to start a war on one issue and then claim another justification later on. Lincoln's attitude to slavery in 1854 looked like a politician searching for a topic to set him apart. He didn't belong to the abolitionists, whom he considered dangerous extremists. When he began to oppose slavery, he wasn't breaking new ground – the British Parliament had already passed an emancipation act and the French had voted their second abolition-of-slavery law in 1848.

Of course, the British act of 1834 only freed black children under six, and kept the majority of Kittitian slaves in a forced "apprenticeship" until 1838, and even after there was no solution for most ex-slaves on the small islands except to emigrate or return to plantation labour under contract. It was freedom nonetheless, just a few hundred miles from the hopelessness of Dixie.

Lincoln was, at that point, happy to let the South do its slavery thing unimpeded, and too bad for the victims. He seemed convinced the evil institution would collapse under its own weight.

The South, however, wanted not only to keep but also to extend the slavery system. Having drawn his yellow line, Lincoln was forced into war in 1861 when the South seceded from the Union. But it was clear to me that the main issue in the Civil War was the break-up of the Union – not the abolition of slavery:

> "...as Professor Randall said, Lincoln fused the cause of the Union with the cause of freedom. In January 1863, he declared all rebel slaves free – following in the wake of British freedom lovers."

Quite clever: fight to save the Union and then claim the war was for the poor blacks.

I was forced to admit that – whatever his dominant motives – Lincoln had to pay the enormous cost of four years of war and 600,000 lives to break the South's back, and that without those sacrifices, who knows how long slavery would have remained hanging over our heads? But I had to remind the starry-eyed Lincoln lovers as to who benefited whom:

"Lincoln in his glory is likewise indebted to the Negro race, the poor and the downtrodden for his inspiration, because the major part of his eminence arises from his defence of them, and only through them did he fulfil his aspirations, as declared to the people of Sangamon County 'of being truly esteemed by my fellowmen'."

After the essay: August 1959

Now I had finished with the official receptions in Washington, my escort Hal Cupps took me all over America to visit Lincoln shrines and other phenomena. Among the non-Lincoln events, I asked to see a fun fair. Hal took me to Coney Island, where I could stop being a solemn little Caribbean ambassador for a few hours and enjoy sliding, spinning, falling, and shouting. Fortunately, after five years of boarding-school food, I had a rock-solid stomach. To my amusement, Hal's military training was insufficient and he became ill after just two rides. I think he was supposed to stick close to me for security, but he agreed to make an exception when I requested three more hurtles into the sky with the Big Dipper. Then he refused to spin round like a squeezed orange in a wheel called the Cyclone. As for the Devil's Drop and the 200-foot parachute jump, I could only regret his absence and keep the thrills to myself. Afterwards, Hal refused to eat anything, while I stuffed myself with hotdogs.

Back in Washington, I was invited to appear on TV – a programme called *Teentalk*. Television was not available in St. Kitts and it fascinated me. I didn't see much difference between looking *at* a programme and being *on* a programme. I learned better. After a few formalities about Lincoln, the interviewer dived into questions about dating. I had to correct his language. We "went out with girls" in Basseterre, but we didn't "date". The newspapers took it as a remark on my sex life, "Vanier, a serious student, says dating is not in his vocabulary and he knows nothing about it." This was reprinted in Ebony, and months later I received letters from girls in the US and Trinidad who wanted to clarify the question with me.

At around this point in my trip, an official – whose face I immediately forgot – asked me if I wanted to study in the United States. Without hesitation, I declined the offer, explaining that I was happy in the British educational system. I did not say what some of my Caribbean classmates thought: that most US universities were only good for those who failed to get into England. Instead, I praised the few I had heard of, like MIT and Stanford, and explained that our British exams were preparatory for another kind of higher education, more Newtonian. Fortunately, no one asked me to explain.

Looking back, maybe the "essay champion aura" had gone to my head to make me so confident I would win the Leeward Islands Scholarship.

Since I had begun my essay by disdaining Lincoln and America, I was being stubborn. It occurred to me later that turning down a proposition – even vague – for university studies in America was not a clever move for a financially limited student like me. I didn't tell my parents or my friends I had done anything like this. But, as they say, it takes seven years to change a mulish man's mind, and it would be almost that long before I did eventually accept a scholarship to graduate school in the land of Lincoln.

The slavery issue in my essay made me wonder about its repercussions in the America of 1959. Had the great emancipator done a proper job, even unintentionally? As I walked their clean streets, looked at their black-and-white television, and sat in their colourful hotel rooms, I tried to understand the Americans' attitude towards race. I wanted to know if America was a good place to live for the descendants of the slaves.

Of course, I wasn't qualified to answer such a big question; for a start, I lacked most of the information. I was unaware that a certain Martin Luther King, fresh from his Ph.D. in 1954, was leading a growing civil rights movement, although even in the Caribbean I had heard about Little Rock and school segregation in the Southern states. I didn't know how many black people were in prison, and the Ku Klux Klan was an unreal sort of bogeyman for me, its masked members like Tolkien's trolls.

Not only did I want to know how Lincoln's anti-slavery measures had worked out a hundred years later, but also I had in the back of my mind the quaint notion that the Caribbean islands might have things to teach America about racial harmony. I was seventeen; history was not my subject; and the bloody bygone days of the Caribbean were not my concern. Our past was so ignominious we did our best always to look forward, or sideways.

America was a huge, proud, complicated country I was trying to keep at arm's length. Questions about colour had looked simpler on my small island. For everything essential – schooling, legal rights, and political power – I felt that Kittitians in 1959 enjoyed multiracial peace. We had no riots, no shootings, no bussing problems – no buses either. In a country 95% coloured, our strife was minimal, and our bust-ups were mostly non-racial, despite some fallout from the plantation era. At this first level, citizens used their rights to go anywhere in the island, mingle as they pleased, and elect the government of their choice. That was my world. Naturally enough, in 1959 our St. Kitts government was all black, with no planter representatives. Or rather, we had a *coloured* government, because the Caribbean didn't shrink from terms like coloured, Negro, mulatto, quadroon, and octoroon. "Black" had not yet taken on its socially coded meaning. "Black power" would have reminded me of energy from coal, and I would have expected to find "Black Panthers" in a zoo. In our home-brewed Caribbean physics, black was a primary colour, not the absence of light, and not an all-encompassing Afro-American ethnic origin. The people of the islands worked, played, and loved together, irrespective of skin colour; education, class, and money were the social differentiators.

I felt that coloured skin was a gift from mixed black-and-white unions. Back in 1630, Sir Thomas Warner – the founder of St. Kitts as the British "mother" colony – fathered a child with a Carib slave from Dominica. "Indian" Warner, as the child was called, grew up in Sir Thomas' household. A dangerous person, that first cross-cultural citizen, because he mastered both worlds: English tools, books, and weapons; and also the language, ferocity and animistic beliefs of his tribe. He became leader of the Dominican Caribs and pushed them to independence from the British and the French until his English half-brother betrayed and killed him. Sir Thomas and his English progeny didn't stop with that first mixed union, especially after African slaves were imported, because my school was filled with a kaleidoscope of coloured Warners. I was myself a product of diverse ethnic origins.

Yet, acceptance of different skins wasn't the end of the story, as we could have told the Americans. We were not colour-blind in the Caribbean; on the contrary, we were profoundly colour-conscious. Skins don't just go away. No way could a black man be mistaken for a white man, or vice versa. In the USIA documentation, I read some pie-in-the-sky American stuff saying we were all equal, all the same under the skin. Equal opportunities: yes. But – all the same? Not for us in the Caribbean. No way for the whites to run faster or box better than the blacks or the coloureds.

Caribbean people, it seemed to me, had colour bestowed on them at birth in a thousand nuances: pitch black, off-black, dark, dark brown, walnut brown, shoe polish brown, coconut husk brown, light brown, honey coloured, golden, pollen yellow, fair skinned, tanned, very fair skinned, conch shell pink, off-white, unwashed white, lily white; a whole rainbow sequence. And according to how many generations back the miscegenation went, we could have straight hair or tight curly hair, flat African noses or pointy European ones, slit Carib eyes or round ones, without taking into account East Indian and Asian traits. As soon as a Caribbean baby enters the world, or an adult enters a crowded room, he or she is classified by his skin tone. We are experts. If being colour-conscious in this manner is racist, then we of the Caribbean are more racist among our black-brown-white selves than other countries, but without the antagonism.

I had never felt my colour to be a handicap, or even thought much about it, but this annoying Lincoln fellow was forcing me to do so.

There was no escaping that a fair-skinned heritage was an advantage in life, like a well-off family or a good education. But it was no more than that, an advantage among others. If you were born poor, dark-skinned and disabled, you had three strikes against you. If you had an education and spoke well, you could afford to be quite dark. If you had good features and dressed well, you could marry up the social ladder, no matter what your colour. If you had money, you took on the colour of your riches; if you had none but could make people laugh, they would never let you starve. Your colour mattered, but what you did with it mattered even more. We had taken the Victorian class system and overlaid it with our local colour indicators. And the indicators of our islands were not the same as the rest of the world. Years later, a well-travelled Kittitian friend would look at his tanned skin and explain it to me this way:

"My friend, in St. Kitts they call me white; when I'm in London, they think I'm brown; but when I visit America they call me black. I feel like a chameleon."

On second thoughts, our Caribbean racial harmony, or perhaps transitory non-belligerence, was not pertinent to America. As long as *they* didn't have a coloured government, we couldn't compare social systems. And in that August of 1959, someone in the USIA must have realised how odd it would appear for me to meet only white senators, congressional representatives, guides, and museum curators. As if I'd ask, "Where are the coloured Americans?" So, first, an impromptu visit was organised to the United Nations, where I met Dr Ralph Bunche. What interested me about this man was that he had been born into a poor coloured family in Detroit; his grandparents had known the last years of Southern slavery; his parents died when he was twelve; yet, he graduated valedictorian from the University of California and went on to Harvard Graduate School.

The forty-floor UN building was the tallest I had ever visited (my Empire State building tour was yet to come), and Dr Bunche could have impressed me just by his lofty executive office on the 38th. But when I found myself facing an articulate coloured Nobel Peace Prize winner, I was happy that at least some people of my sort did achieve the highest ranks. If this was Lincoln's heritage, it was good. In addition, the man was charming to me. I had met so many adults who were either ignorant or talked down to me. I enjoyed every minute with Dr Bunche. Perhaps he was talking down, but it was too subtle for me. From the start, he used my language. "What form are you in?" not "What grade or class are you in?" He also had a son of my age. I knew too little of geopolitics to understand his mission, so we talked about opportunities in America and air conditioners. This had become an obsession. I wanted to know how the UN cooled the air in such a large building when nothing was air conditioned in Basseterre.

The other gesture the USIA made was to have me meet a "typical middle class coloured family" in Chicago. By comparison with St. Kitts, they seemed rich. They took me in their open-topped car for a cruise near the lakeside, where I marvelled at the six-lane highways. I thought ruefully of the pitted and potholed asphalt main road around St. Kitts; at least it was better than Nevis.

"Hey, with all this Lincoln stuff, you think he did good like?" At times, I couldn't follow my host's language.

"Well, he wasn't my President, but your family seems well off."

"You ain't seen our brothers down south, pal. Hell of a place to be right now, the South."

I was curious, but my escort Hal redirected the conversation to the impressive Chicago skyline. I could see and hear anything, provided it reflected the "right" America.

My last image of the great emancipator's heritage was at Santa Claus Land, Indiana. The governor and his family were host to Hal and me for a day. I usually avoided being linked to girls – who knew what the folks back home might say? There, I was photographed with Santa himself and the governor's pretty daughter. It was a happy day, but looking at the picture afterwards, I had the strange impression that all the governors, daughters, and Santa Clauses everywhere in America were white. I sorted out the myths of Lincoln from what I had seen, but I couldn't tell which was the real America: Dr Ralph Bunche, the Chicago boy, or the governor's daughter. I thought maybe my question as to whether America was a good place for blacks to live was wrong. No synthesis was possible: the country was like an enormous collection of islands, each speaking a different racial and social language.

The end of the essay: May 1959

After dinner one night late in May, I finished my essay. My window was now full of quiet darkness; the sparse street lamps did little to spread light in this part of town. And it was a sombre time for Lincoln. I'd had to read even more to get to this point, and this reading confirmed my suspicion that Lincoln's fame was overrated – presiding over America after the costly Civil War would not have been popular, if he had survived to do this. On the freedom and slavery issues, he emerged better than expected. Maybe he rode the public mood, but still, he got results. And then just at the end of the Civil War, in 1865, he was assassinated. I read most of James Bishop's *The Day Lincoln Died* in one sitting. Lincoln went to the theatre to see *An American Cousin*, and was shot in the back of the head with a derringer. I felt for the man; his loss was dramatic and unacceptable. It made me reassess everything he had done – debates with Douglas, increasing opposition to slavery, his slow rise to power, the difficult decision for a man of peace to go to war, pity for the war dead, his freeing of the slaves, then his fanatical assassination by Boothe. Simultaneously, I won and lost my struggle to criticise the man. My essay was a victory for objectivity, because he *was* lucky in the timing of his misfortune, and his status depended on that accident of martyrdom. Had he died quietly of old age, I wouldn't be writing this essay about him.

> *"Lincoln's death was his final guarantee to immortality. He could make no more mistakes – what he might have done was limitless – and he was a martyr to democracy. His philosophy and ideals together with the tremendous drama and pathos of his extinction in the prime of his career lifted him above Illinois, above America, to the Valhalla which only the few can achieve."*

But at this point in writing, I lost my neutrality. I could feel him dying in that theatre with the assassin's bullet embedded in his skull. His tragedy touched me. Lucky, artificial, or not, his achievement became part of me, and it was not true that one hundred and fifty years had made him irrelevant. The man's reputation was advantaged by his dramatic exit from life; but I had been fortunate to make his acquaintance, even from books. I ended my essay:

> *"He believed with Wordsworth, that other great humanitarian, that God did not intend even the meanest and plainest of people to exist divorced from good, or from equal opportunities for good. His creed of freedom and human rights embraces everyone, everywhere, as friends, and equals, and perhaps his greatest eulogy has come from Edwin Stanton in the words 'Now he belongs to the ages'."*

After the essay: August 1959
Towards the end of my thirty days in America, I visited Old Ford's Theatre, the site of Lincoln's assassination. Mr Fenton, the guide, described the manner in which President Lincoln was carried across the street on Friday, 14th April 1865, to the house where he died the next morning.

I thought of his wife, who (according to some books) maybe loved him less than he would have liked, and of the millions who did love him more than he hoped.

If he "belonged to the ages" then a little bit of him belonged to me, I thought. The bit I wanted to keep was not of the civil war leader – this being a matter for Americans – but Lincoln's humour and his wish for all people to be free.

Before I left Washington to return to the Caribbean via Jamaica, the head of the USIA, Mr Child, talked to me for a last time. His office was laid out with plush carpets and furniture in expensive woods that might have come from a Caribbean rainforest.

"In addition to your award certificate, here's a copy of the official recognition of your essay by the United States government."

He handed me an excerpt from the US Congressional Record. The page read:

A 6798 US CONGRESSIONAL RECORD – APPENDIX
August 6
EXTENSION OF REMARKS
OF
HON. JOHN SHERMAN COOPER
OF KENTUCKY
IN THE SENATE OF THE UNITED STATES

Thursday, August 6, 1959

Mr COOPER. Mr President, I ask unanimous consent to have printed in the Appendix of the RECORD an essay on Abraham Lincoln written by Christopher Vanier, of St. Kitts, British West Indies. This excellent and beautiful essay was the prize-winning essay in a contest sponsored by the USIA in the British West Indies, in which 54 schools participated.

Young Christopher Vanier, 17 years old, is now in the United States studying our institutions and visiting Lincoln shrines. We are honoured that he is the guest of our country.

There being no objection, the essay was ordered to be printed in the RECORD, as follows:

Lincoln and Us
"Lincoln was not a god. Lincoln was not even a demigod; he was a man like us ... 'Now he belongs to the ages'."

I was surprised that, in small print, my entire essay held in three columns on a single page – not much for my weeks of work.

"I've been happy to meet you," Mr Child said to me. "Do you think you've been changed by this visit to Lincoln's country?"

I thought of the TV, the newspaper articles, the congressional representatives, the VP's chair, Dr Bunche, the air-conditioning, my self-interrogation about skin colour, and my sympathy for the dead President; but also of the humble beginnings of my essay and Lincoln's own simple rail-splitting origins.

"I don't think so," I lied. "I just have more questions."

"But it must mean something that your name and your essay are in the same congressional record that might have recorded Lincoln's speeches. I'll bet you a dollar that someday you'll be President, Chief Minister, or whatever's appropriate, of your country."

So, the schoolboy champion of today might be a politician to contend with tomorrow? Something held me back from this ego inflation. I could feel the weight of his assessment, well intended as it was, dragging me down to a rough and conflict-ridden future: a friend of America, an enemy of my father's enemies, poised dangerously between Caribbean social forces I could not control. "I wish all men to be free," Lincoln had said. I would not succumb to a stereotype of myself. Instead, I would apply the same healthy scepticism I had applied to Lincoln's greatness – disbelieving, until its value was proven to me.

"No," I said. "With all due respect, if the price of fame is anything like Lincoln's, I'd prefer to remain unsung. I don't know what I'll do with myself, but I have learned that." I clasped both hands behind my head and rubbed the spot where I imagined Lincoln had been shot. "In addition, I wouldn't like to be distracted from good theatre."

Indiscretions

In the years afterwards, I had an occasional nightmare that the incident would be discovered. And I would be blamed, though it could be argued I didn't initiate things. You are still guilty if you don't speak up, or opt out of an illegal, collective act. And then, of course, the authorities would annul the exam results retroactively. This might lead to annulling my entry into university. The university would then consider I had enrolled under false pretences, and would thus annul my degree. Consequently, my employer would consider I was not qualified and fire me. As a result, my wife would leave me because I had lied and could no longer support my family. In short, my whole life would unravel, because of that single indiscretion in St. Kitts, long ago, in December 1959, my year of all the dangers. It was just a dream, of course, and ghosts from the past can easily be dismissed in daylight.

I was full of my own importance when I returned from America to St. Kitts in the summer of that year. The trip did my ego a lot of good and my studies a lot of harm.

I had just been selected as the English-speaking-Caribbean essay champion. In three months, I would sit the Cambridge Advanced Level exams for the second time. A little more work, and who could possibly beat me for the scholarship? I could take things easy, I thought. If Father Brown had been there, he would have taken me to task for arrogance, and he would have been right, though in a watered-down, more socially acceptable form, this annoying arrogance might one day become a healthy self-confidence.

I was about to make the same miscalculation as the year before, because essay writing is all very well, but it only counted for 10% of the exam. It took an unpleasant classroom episode to shake me off my cloud.

"Your compositions this week were interesting," Fitzroy Bryant said to us, "but uneven. When you choose a subject, you must develop it in a coherent manner. Think of a mango: peel it with your fingers, enjoy the flesh, and then meditate on the kernel. Just so for your essays: define your subject, develop the theme, and conclude what you have learned."

I wondered who was going to be raked over the coals. Out of the list of proposed topics, I had chosen a quotation from Lincoln: *You can't fool all the people all the time.* How could I not choose a man I was supposed to know a lot about? However, I could find nothing of Lincoln's life in this quotation. It was different from my usual topics, but I hoped I had worked my way around it. At least it hadn't required any reading or research, the way some essays did.

"I had a good essay from Albert," Fitzroy continued. "He chose to write on *Electricity is better than sunshine,* and I want you to read his essay and note how logical it is. He researched it thoroughly. I graded him seven out of ten. His writing is creditable, if not inspired, and he makes a good argument for investing more money in electricity generation in the Caribbean. To develop light industry, we need a reliable power grid. The sunshine-type of economic activity, such as tourism, should come later." He handed Albert his essay book. I had not understood this topic, it was true, but I was glad I hadn't chosen it, as it sounded so dull.

Had I been prescient, I would have seen this essay as a premonition of Albert's future role as Director of a large power system.

"And now for our champion," Fitzroy said, turning towards me with a large show of teeth. "One would think that a Lincoln essay winner, writing on a Lincoln quotation just a month later, would produce something wonderful."

I didn't like this conditional formulation. It made me sit up in my chair and clench the sides of my desk, waiting for something.

"Well, you would be wrong. Christopher's essay is, as it turns out, substandard, for he deviated from the subject. I think most of you will agree this essay should be about politics. When we hear, 'You can't fool all the people all the time,' the people concerned are probably an electorate. I was expecting Christopher to analyse a government's promises or at least the proclamations of prominent men. He did, in fact, begin creditably with the example of Columbus, who claimed on his voyages to the Caribbean he had discovered a new route to India. This was not maintainable, although Columbus died believing it. Unfortunately, Christopher got his dates wrong, mixing up 1493 when Columbus sighted St. Kitts, and 1623 when Sir Thomas Warner took possession of it. From then on, the essay goes downhill, because instead of politicians or public figures, Christopher writes about fictional characters, Fu Manchu and the Saint, fooling the rest of the world to carry out their nefarious schemes. It's fun, but it's not real – not what a serious subject requires. If you wanted current examples of 'fooling the people', you could have examined the labour issues around sugar in St. Kitts. On one side, the estate owners claim they'll be ruined if they pay the cane cutters more, on the other, the trade unions say the sugar industry is so profitable it must be nationalised. Who is right? Who is fooling the people? Why didn't you choose a real example, one of this sort, Christopher?"

Because the last thing I wanted was to talk about politics, I thought. I knew so little about it, and my father was too involved in industrial disputes. Fitzroy was being unfairly personal: he had recently taken part in a public debate with my father on "*Is sugar the purse or the curse of the Caribbean?*" My father had won; now Fitzroy was getting his revenge, or so it seemed to me.

"I gave Christopher five out of ten, and that's generous. Let that be a lesson to all of you. Style alone will not get you through, not even if you have been sitting in a Vice-President's chair." More wolf's teeth appeared, as he turned to face me square on and said pointedly: "You have to think about the subject and not write fantasy, Christopher. Come and see me after the class, please."

This stung. I had been so proud of occupying Nixon's chair. Pretending to be a Vice-President had nothing to do with essay writing, I began thinking, until I remembered that my trip to America and the White House had been part of an essay prize.

Later, there was worse to come from Fitzroy. My classmates filed out after the class, leaving me to my fate; some of my friends gave me a clenched fist salute, but Albert just smiled as he went by.

"You're angry," Fitzroy said, "I can see it in your pout – but it's for your own good. OK, let's say I did humiliate you – a little. But the Headmaster asked me to wake you up. This is the first time you've written a bad essay. You won't contest that, I presume? Our consensus in the staffroom is that, since your return from America, you've been slacking off. All your grades have dropped. If you think you can succeed in the Cambridge exams on reputation only, there'll be more than egg on your face. Guess what – those English examiners don't give a donkey's twat about your Lincoln essay. They might even hold it against you for fraternising with the Yanks, who speak another kind of English. And why should the scholarship committee be any different? Buckle down, if you don't want to blow your chances."

I didn't reply and didn't tell any of this to my parents. In fact, I didn't speak to many people for the next three days, despite my duties as Head Prefect. I was too busy disliking the world and preparing a damage report for myself. The world didn't seem to care, but I began to panic. How silly to have imagined I had no competition. Albert was so modest I had forgotten about him. He had been in Form 6B when I last tried for the scholarship. Now he was neck and neck with me in 6A, and I could see he was ambitious. The trauma of last year with my friend Clive was all set to repeat itself. Albert's Physics was better than mine. And my strong points in the previous year's exams might be vulnerable – all the hours of cramming I had done in Literature and Chemistry. The examiners didn't want to make it too easy for repeat students. They had changed half of the texts to be studied in Literature. Wordsworth was still current, but Keats had taken over from Blake. Shakespeare's *As You Like It* had remained on our syllabus, but *Othello* had dethroned *Henry V*. This meant more studying. My Chemistry looked secure, however hard Albert worked in the lab, but that wouldn't be enough. More willpower, I thought; my only hope was to work harder.

I plunged into additional studies, some to no avail. I had bought a literary guide in America at a Kentucky bookstore, hoping it would give me an advantage. It was entitled *The Misunderstood Othello*. I read 70 pages before I realised the author considered Othello to be a white man. According to him, the phrase "an old black ram / is tupping your white ewe" was a vulgar figure of speech, not real. The noble Othello was Caucasian, and the real black in Shakespeare's story was the black-hearted Iago. Quoting a certain Mary Preston from Maryland, the book went on like this for 200 pages. I didn't think it would convince my English examiners, however erudite the Southern intellectual who had written it. The book felt slimy in my hands. Perhaps, I realised, I should distinguish between unconventional books and evil ones. Precious hours of study time had been wasted, and now I had to return to "Beauty is truth, truth beauty".

This business about beauty was disturbing if I took it too seriously. I imagined a statue in unctuous marble of a half-clad Grecian damsel. That was what Keats was telling me, after all. Was his truth to be found in the perfect form of the marble or in the warm flesh it was based on? Ideas of girls plagued me, and even under pre-exam stress I had crushes. I would dream of female classmates I thought I was in love with and consigned my dreams to a diary. In these dreams I would rescue pulchritudinous females from warm waters full of hungry crocodiles. Or, on some nights, they would save *me* from the crocs' sharp teeth.

A certain family confusion over nudity didn't help. The little blue book on childrearing my Uncle Beezie had given to my mother advocated total frankness between adults and children. So, my father, and especially my mother, often showed themselves naked in our home. I remember thinking for the first time at ten that they were fat. This lack of modesty was all very well when my brothers and I were young, but adolescents are *not* children, and excessive openness can lead to exhibitionism. I was often embarrassingly interrupted in the middle of my studies to pin up a corset or a bra for my panty-clad mother. It was not the right sort of chemistry to help me study.

Two weeks before the exams, with exam stress dribbling out of every pore in my body, and a full night's sleep becoming an unobtainable paradise, I received an urgent message from Sammy. In the middle of my Saturday afternoon studies, my mother told me a friend had asked me to come at once to the Physics lab.

Twenty minutes later, I was there, on my bicycle. Sammy was pacing up and down in the corridor outside the lab.

"What's got into you, Sammy? I was studying." We went into the lab and perched on a bench between scales and burners.

"This is more important. We have to go and see Mr Ribeiro."

Tony Ribeiro was teaching us Physics again this year and was now the Headmaster. He taught us Physics and Mathematics, not my best subjects. Still, I didn't hold this against him. He was a short and quiet man, who never seemed to lose his temper, the lightest skinned of our teachers, and of Portuguese descent. If his administrative responsibilities hadn't made him cancel so many of his classes, I might have understood his subjects a lot better. Unlike Fitzroy Bryant, who gave his opinion on everything, Mr Ribeiro was discreet.

The lab door opened and Albert entered.

"This had better be important."

"Look, Chris, Albert, here's the story. You know Ribeiro is helping me in Physics?"

We were aware Sammy had been having catch-up classes with Mr Ribeiro. This didn't bother me; Sammy had failed everything he sat the previous year except Biology. What was troublesome was that our class hadn't finished half the Physics syllabus. Mr Ribeiro was often taken up with other duties, and extra tuition to Sammy was part of it. Unfortunately, I couldn't force myself to study Physics on my own, so his absence mattered. Chemistry was mostly memorising, and I was finding that easy, but the problems in Physics were frustrating.

"Well, Mr Ribeiro made a mistake this morning, opened the wrong envelope or something, and during my lesson he showed me the questions for the Physics practical exam."

"The Cambridge exam in two weeks' time? But that's – "

"Not right? Yes, I know, and that's why I had to get you both here. The fairest thing is to go and talk with him at his house, right now."

Mr Ribeiro lived in a single-story house with a shady garden – full of bay rum trees and Colville's Glory – a short walk from the school at the top of Victoria Road, almost opposite the church-owned house where my grandparents lived. Not knowing what to think of the leak, we trudged there in silence. Unlike the other exam papers, the Headmaster had the duty to open the Physics and Chemistry practicals two weeks in advance so he could prepare the equipment in secret.

Mr Ribeiro led us into his house and seated us around a bare table. I had never visited his home before so I looked curiously at the dark furniture and sniffed the spicy odour of cooking. "I'm glad you could come so quickly," he said. "I have been indiscreet. I'm sorry to mix you up in this, believe me. You have other things to worry about. I suppose Sammy has told you about my lapse?"

"You showed him the Physics practical?" asked Albert.

"It was an accident," he said.

"I'm sure you didn't mean to do it, Sir. But what does it have to do with us?" I said.

No one spoke for a while. Mr Ribeiro looked at us, his eyes hooded. He blinked from time to time, and I remembered he could be quite timid. I felt sorry for the overworked man and hoped he wasn't going to apologise again.

"Don't you understand? I'm not worried about the examiners, but I've given Sammy an unfair advantage over you."

I still didn't get it. Who cared if Sammy had a little helping hand? He was starting from so low. We would be happy to see him pass at least one paper.

"You three are not only my entire Physics class, but also each one of you is a candidate for the scholarship."

I hadn't thought of that. But yes, every student signed up for the scholarship as a matter of course. We had never considered Sammy as a bona fide competitor, though he was on the list.

"It's a question of fairness. I can't let Sammy be favoured over you two, no matter how small his chances are. Therefore, my solution is to share the information with you."

Impossible! I couldn't believe my ears. How could our Headmaster propose cheating on an official Cambridge exam with a four-year all-expenses-paid scholarship at stake? Memories of the Antigua Grammar School tumbled back out of the recesses of my mind. I had been inveigled into helping to steal a French exam paper, despite my best intentions. Mr Ribeiro's scheme was not for me.

"I know this may be upsetting for you, but it's the best thing to do. You can refuse, but I would be disappointed, trust me. Your friend Sammy insisted I tell you, and now you three have to come to an agreement among yourselves."

He got up and left us alone for a minute.

"Albert, let's not do this. It doesn't matter about Sammy."

"But I agree with Mr Ribeiro. It's necessary that all three of us see the paper. Otherwise, you and I will be trying to find out just what Sammy knows." Albert pointed his index finger at him. "And our friend here, he can't keep a secret, can he?" He turned back to me. "Chris, you have to agree to this. I can't guarantee what I'd pick up from Sammy. But I'd use it!"

I was cornered – Sammy and Albert worked together a lot. Damn and damn – an impossible situation. I couldn't let Albert walk away with a clear advantage. He was already too good. Even if I didn't cooperate, I was now an accomplice, I thought. Still, it wasn't as bad as if we were being let in on one of the theory papers. Who would care about a Physics practical exam? It counted for only 20% of the overall Physics grade and Physics was only one of our four major subjects.

So we agreed to go ahead. Of course, Mr Ribeiro bound us to secrecy. No one, not my father, nor mother, nor anyone else was to find out we had prior knowledge of the Physics practical exam. From the year before, Ribeiro already knew I would not betray him. Up to a point, he was right to see loyalty in me because not until today, fifty years later, after he had left all official functions, would I disclose his actions. He placed the infamous exam paper neatly in the middle of the table, and we copied the questions into our notebooks. But that was not all.

Mr Ribeiro told us: "You must first study the theory behind these two experiments, one in optics and the other in magnetism. When you've done that, next Saturday, you three come back here – in my home, not the school – and I'll show you how to proceed and give you the answers. I started with Sammy, so now I have to do the same thing with you. This will work out, trust me."

He was as good as his word. We went back to his house a week later and found he had set up some bits of glass and metal on his dining table to help us understand. When I had read the chapters at home and had seen how difficult the questions were, I realised I could never have passed the exam on my own. I had failed that paper the year before, and even now with more detailed knowledge, I wasn't sure I could do the experiments in time. It became much simpler when he explained things – we learned how to tell the concave and the convex lenses apart, and how to measure their focal lengths. Then we navigated magnetic fields with a tiny compass. Mr Ribeiro checked we knew what a gauss was, and how many were likely to be found wandering about on exam day. Albert and I were amused when Sammy kept calling it a ghost. I wondered why we couldn't have done all this in regular classes, but after a while the clandestine atmosphere became fun, especially when Mr Ribeiro's wife brought out some cakes and soft drinks.

Another week later, and the dreaded practical exam was there. It was held, of course, in the Physics Lab this time, with our instructions in sealed envelopes and an examination monitor who was not in the know. It was strange not to be able to talk to each other, but I got used to it. The exam took three hours and when I came out I was able to assure the waiting Mr Ribeiro it had gone smoothly – I had almost finished it. I asked Sammy if he had found his ghost.

I couldn't say the same for most of the other papers. More tired than I knew, I botched my essay by choosing a poor subject. Instead of something abstract, a demon incited me to write "A Portrait of My Best Friend". I had never done character or physical descriptions, and to cap it all I chose a girl in my class I fancied. A disaster, I realised as I turned in my paper. All my written exams took place in the cavernous main assembly hall; twenty desks in a room made for two hundred gives a lot of elbowroom. As I had been placed in the front row, to my frustration I couldn't even see my model. Anyway, what would the Cambridge examiners care about my inane reflections on her skin and hair?

Mathematics and Physics theory were so-so; I felt I hadn't improved since the year before. Chemistry was solid, but no more. And then, horror of horrors, I fell ill on the day of my Literature exams. You can't enthuse about poets and playwrights when your stomach is churning on stormy seas. I couldn't admit I was ill – we had no provision for re-sitting exams. I remembered my fears on my first day in the Sixth Form; each try at the scholarship might turn out *worse* than the preceding one.

I chose breakfast to tell my father I wasn't happy about my exams.

He stopped sprinkling salt on his egg. "Maybe it'll turn out better than you imagine," he said. "It's your second try and you have worked hard."

But I had a bad feeling about it. Two months later the results were there. As if it were a ceremony that started with my competitor Clive of the previous year, Albert and I compared grades in the Prefects' room. Despite a handshake, the tension built up around us; would the winner be him or me? We were equal in Chemistry, Mathematics and the essay paper. My Literature was better than his Geography, but his Physics was better than mine. A close thing, once more. This time I had no distinction papers, thanks to my treacherous stomach, but no failures either, thanks to Sammy. Albert and I wished each other good luck, but I could see him smirking.

I began to steel myself for another failure. My second attempt at the scholarship was not going to succeed. If Albert beat me, I would have to stay on for yet another year. That would be my third and final chance at the scholarship. Looking ahead, I could hear them all – family and friends – telling me I mustn't give up, and start working from day one, and so on. More and more convinced of my inadequacy, cheating on the Physics practical did not – at first – seem of great consequence. Until my fretful mind, having run out of other things with which to plague me, began to speculate that somehow the Cambridge examiners would realise we three had seen the paper beforehand. I had been careful, and probably Albert too, but who knew what clues Sammy might have left in his answers? I thought again of the incident in Antigua with Michael and Melford, and it hit me that dishonesty with the English examiners had then seemed the ultimate crime. And I had done it. If I were found out, not only would my family be dishonoured, but also I would be banned from taking the scholarship for ever after.

This was what was in my mind: tension, discouragement, and disillusion with the idea that hard work could lead anywhere useful. Then, to my astonishment, a few weeks later, the scholarship committee awarded *me* the Leeward Islands Scholarship.

I don't know how long a heart can stop beating without serious consequences, but I must have approached the limit. The scholarship was a precious stone, beautiful and mysterious from a distance but awesome when you had it in your hands.

This time, Mr Ribeiro interrupted our class in the Sixth Form to read the official letter: "...to our distinguished Lincoln Scholar, and now Leeward Islands Scholar, good luck..."

I went to Mr Ribeiro's office after the handshaking was over and the others had left. "I don't understand, Sir. I'm not going to turn down the scholarship, of course, but my grades were no better than Albert's. What happened?"

"Well, it's true the committee couldn't ignore your Lincoln essay."

"But Fitzroy Bryant told me – "

"Ah, he was a bit severe. But it did galvanise you, didn't it?"

I waited.

"And this year, the cards were in your favour. Albert has another try next year, as I suppose you know? He may well succeed.

"And one more thing." His eyes were definitely twinkling. "Your most dangerous competitor was, in reality, not Albert but a student in Antigua. He was your equal, but had the bad luck to fail a Physics exam. The committee didn't like that.

"Lastly, Christopher – discretion – I know I can count on you."

"Thank you, Mr Ribeiro."

So, I couldn't tell my father the inside story, once again. I was bursting with joy as I cycled home. One year before, in 1958, when I had failed in my first scholarship attempt, I remembered going at breakneck speed down Jones' Hill. In the back of my mind that sad day, I may have thought that if I had an accident nothing much would be lost – there was no future ahead of me. This glorious day in 1959, I cycled as slowly as I could, savouring all the rays of the sun splashing on my head after travelling such a colossal distance from heaven just for me, and rejoicing as I crossed the shadows under the old trees providing a counterpoint of cool and calm. In the midst of joy I saw Simba's green eyes and I felt him howl victory. I forgave our neighbour for his death because that's what moments of epiphany are for.

I thought of how lucky I had been. Of course, if I hadn't fallen ill on the day I wrote my exam in English Lit, or if I hadn't chosen a silly essay question on the General Paper, I would have been a clear head and shoulders above my competitors, above Albert and the Antigua student. But that was the land of 'if': the fact was, I had not performed well, and - though I couldn't be sure - only Sammy had saved me with his Physics practical imbroglio. Or rather, Mr Ribeiro had saved me. He had done an honourable job at repairing the leak to Sammy. It was thanks to him, finally, I had gained extra credit in Physics and won the scholarship. I hoped he would never regret his good deed, his actions on my behalf. It was a pity I couldn't confide in my father. But it was only fair to protect

Mr Ribeiro from any ill-conceived criticisms, I rationalised. He had cheated on – let's say reoriented – the Physics examiner's intentions, but only to correct a previous accident of disclosure and to avoid a possible injustice. It had been the honourable thing to do and no fair-minded person would find fault with his conduct. And if Mr Ribeiro was exempt from blame, then so was I, and I could be happy with my winner's status. No one could take exception, except perhaps the Antiguan student who had almost won. On account of him, that Physics Practical "arrangement" would have to remain secret. I was getting quite good at self-justification.

When I reached home, my father had already heard the good news from someone in town. "Cheers!" he greeted me. It was the time for his evening drink, and he had taken a double measure of rum. He leaped up and hugged me, on the same veranda where we had been so downcast just a year before.

"You did it, Chris, you broke the spell!"

"I did it for you," I said, and it was truer than I knew.

I could see he was thinking not so much of a voodoo hex by Bradshaw, but of himself thirty years before, frustrated and bewitched for so long, then caught up painfully in the War. He knew how wonderful it was to be young with all possible futures open. It felt humbling. How to measure the hard work over the years, by him and by me? But in the end, it was not enough, I thought. A little luck, a little goodwill, and a lot of trust; these too were necessary.

"Now you can begin to live," he said.

"I didn't think I was good enough, but events proved me wrong. Did you work any magic?"

"I have never been so well behaved," he opened his eyes to the sky, looking across the sea, and beyond. "If you call that magic, all year, ever since your first attempt at the scholarship failed, I have been polite and considerate to the powers-that-be, from the Premier down to his lowliest policeman, never the slightest criticism." Then he laughed, "But I'm sure your studying counted a lot more!"

I refused his offer of a drink, but we dined well later. However, at the edge of my conscience, something began bothering me, again, like a stray hair in my soup. I felt uncomfortable at my father's attributing my success either to hard work or to his diplomacy. Whatever our efforts, the scholarship victory seemed partly due to exceptional circumstances. Exceptional: there had been no real cheating, just that incident, I repeated to myself. And poor Mr Ribeiro had no choice but to proceed as he did, and we to follow. But what if… After all, the scholarship was so valuable it might disturb people's judgement. Did my *friends* accept the outcome as being entirely fair to them and to me?

The next day, I needed to talk to my comrades in crime. Albert was not upset; he had competed hard, but – to my surprise – never thought he would win that year.

"I hope you don't regret the Physics exam," I said, as he was packing his bag to go home for lunch.

"What Physics exam?"

"The Physics practical, Albert."

"Oh that! Well, we all worked hard for those results – even Sammy passed the paper, though not much else."

"But Albert, the special conditions – Mr Ribeiro – "

Albert raised his eyebrows and picked up his schoolbag.

"What special conditions? No more ghosts, OK? There was nothing special about that exam, Chris, and don't you ever forget it."

Ever? My future bad dreams, when they came, usually began with Sammy. After confronting Albert, I had found him by himself eating a strong-smelling sardine sandwich for lunch. I guessed he was going to stay on for an extra year in the hopes of improving his results.

"Sammy, sorry you didn't get through your exams, but I want to thank you."

"What for?" he asked, stuffing a mouthful of bread into his face.

"You know, the Physics thing. If it hadn't been for your sense of fair play, Ribeiro might not have talked to us, and I would have failed the practical – "

"Hold on, you say sorry and thanks together – it's too much for one bite! There's something you don't know."

What else could there be?

"Promise this stays between us?"

"My discretion is total."

"Well, when I called you that Saturday, it wasn't exactly as I said. Almost, but not quite. Ribeiro felt guilty about us, *all* of us. He hadn't taught us enough. It's true he was indiscreet, but only *after* he had all three of us together. Alone with him that morning, I only saw the outside of the Cambridge envelope, and he knew it. But he asked me to tell you I had seen the whole paper. As if he *wanted* to be indiscreet."

"You know, this is the fourth consecutive scholarship victory he's managed for the school. He's a very able Headmaster."

I can do it

St. Kitts, Mount Misery, 1960

The scholarship had been a goad, driving me harder and harder, higher and higher, until I was released by victory. In the turbulent descent that followed, many things crowded in on me that I had pushed into the background: new concerns and old, desires and ideas, and especially people. To give these things their proper importance, I must interrupt my narration of the immediate consequences of the scholarship and jump ahead to the summer of 1960. While I was writing my Lincoln essay, one person who had been particularly absent from my thoughts was my sister, Hazel. Naturally, she wrote to us, but her hand-written script was hard to decipher and full of strange references. Hazel had been to three different schools in England, each catering to handicapped children, but in such un-Caribbean surroundings I couldn't visualise her struggles. I was too preoccupied with my own adolescent survival to look that far, so it was a good thing for family unity my parents were able to find the money to bring her back home for a few weeks of summer vacation that year.

She was almost sixteen and I eighteen. She was coming from England and I might or might not be going there. All her scars were still there, and remembered; I had some new ones. Both of us were full of confidence, she because of coming home and me because of my scholarship. I was under-exercised, and though I couldn't know it at the time, she was in the prime of her life, physically. The insidious conspiracy between her spastic movements and the arthritis of her joints had not yet begun. Not before, and never afterwards would she attempt what she did that summer

To begin with, among handicapped people and even among the athetoid spastics – who have, at least, freedom of movement – mountain climbing is not a favourite sport. Yet that was what my sister insisted on doing. To be precise, it was not mountaineering in general, just one particular exploit. Early in her stay, I planned an expedition up the volcano, and to my surprise and dismay she decided to come with us.

"Sorry, Haze, you can't come to the crater with us – it's not called Mount Misery for nothing." Strictly speaking, Mount Misery was a separate climb, at least 900 feet higher than the lip of the crater, but the two were less than a half-mile apart and locked in a tight geological embrace. After all the academic trials of the year, I was looking forward to a simple outing and didn't want the complications of my sister. In the heated discussion that followed, I forgot all about Hazel's speech difficulties.

"Why not? You boyth can't haff all the fun."

"It's not because we're boys – "

"The lath time you left me behind, you bot loth in the foweth. I wouldn't get loth!"

"Some things are impossible! It's because of your handicap."

"Andicap, nothing! I'm stwong!" Proving the point, she punched me. "Andicap gives me the wight to twy!"

My father looked at me sharply, and I could see I was going to lose.

"Look, even I get dirty, bruised, and worn out. It would be a five-hour climb for you! And how would you ever get up the steep places?"

"I know how to scwamble on my kneeth petter than you!"

I couldn't deny that my sister had spent a lot more of her first fifteen years on her hands and knees than I had, but still I wasn't happy, fearing the complications. Maybe we would have to abort the climb halfway.

"We won't carry you, you know."

"Don't, then! Ath long ath you wait for me fwom dime to dime."

The doctors who first diagnosed Hazel's cerebral palsy considered her "uneducable". If that means "stubborn", I thought, they were right from the start. I could never make Hazel change her mind.

My father said, "You'll have to start earlier," and so the matter was sealed; and the next day Hazel clambered into the jeep, clad in a thick T-shirt and the toughest pair of trousers and shoes she could find. Together with my brothers Peter and Noel, we took along several friends: Patrick, Harry, another Peter, and Ann. My father found us a guide, but both parents opted out of the climb.

On level ground, in those days, my sister hardly ever fell. Her gait was still uneven – more like a controlled stagger – but she had learned to windmill her arms to provide balance when in doubt. She was reliable, as long as you didn't restrict her geometry to a straight line, as in the hand-rail walk my mother tried to teach her ten years earlier. During the first part of the climb, through the low rainforest levels, under the sickly-sweet mango groves, she may have tumbled a half dozen times, not more. Hardly black and blue, I thought, but the worst was ahead. When we reached the steep upper slopes, the mountain became brutal. Our path became a deep cut in the ground, slippery, and filled with obstacles. All of us fell at least once, and we had to use our arms extensively. Hazel did what she had promised – she took all of it on her hands and knees for a full hour.

Once started in this mode, she seemed driven by a relentless clockwork force pushing her through mud, dead leaves, fallen branches, gravel, and over mossy surfaces. But her headway was cruelly slow. Close behind, I expected that when granted a few yards of less precipitous trail, she would want to rise upright for four or five steps of normal walking. On the contrary, she remained on all fours, and used the easier stretch to creep forward a fraction quicker. I couldn't look too closely at her progress or I would begin to feel the impact of the bent tree roots and angular rocks on her knees as if they were mine.

The guide led the expedition, and I brought up the rear. After a while, he stopped, called me aside, and pointed to Hazel, struggling to get over one of the many fallen tree trunks blocking the path.

"Help her," he said.

"She doesn't want me to!"

"She will."

It was only after Hazel slipped and rolled several feet back down a lichen-covered rock that I had my chance to intervene. I pulled her upright, and she let me push her past the next bit. We could never have made the last few hundred feet to the crater's lip without helping Hazel. She was exhausted and would nod at Peter or myself when she got to an impossible bit. No request, just a look meaning, "I know I said I'd do it by myself, but a small hand up would go a long way."

On the crater's lip, the high point of our climb, there was never any question of going down into the volcano with Hazel. She took one look at the yellow-green vines trailing almost vertically into the sulphurous depths, sat down, and shuddered. We ate without talking, wolfing our sandwiches, simply marvelling that she was really there, 2700 feet above the sea, after four gruelling hours of struggle. I tried not to think of the descent back to where our vehicles were. We left Hazel to rest with Ann while we explored the crater. When we returned she was asleep.

I hadn't thought Hazel could make it up to the top – I'd imagined we'd have to leave her halfway and come back for her, but incredibly she'd made it.

I had a small space within me from which I could truthfully see my sister's handicap, away from not-seeing, and from seeing-but-not-caring, and from pitying. That day, I saw more clearly than ever that what she needed was a chance to compete – the handicap limited her body, not her will. And this should be respected.

Then, I was awed by her tactics for going down the mountain – almost as efficient as mine. I tried to stay upright, and straddled or jumped painfully over the bad stretches. She simply slid on her bottom when she had to, and when she couldn't slide, she rolled. I regretted her bruises and pain, but it was too late for that. Even had she yelled, I didn't have any energy left to help. The art of *not* falling down along a slippery trail had taken a high toll on my own untrained muscles.

At last, the trail became more level, and our numbed minds could begin to detach themselves from our numbed bodies and emerge into the twilight. No more whooshing and thumping as Hazel slid over yet another obstacle. I knew we mustn't stop. Hazel was so worn out she would not be able to start again after a pause. Along the rutted-but-level cane-field track to the jeeps, I began to rise above my tiredness. I had been wrong about my sister. We were now, several of us, sweatily arm-in-arm with Hazel, savouring her victory. None of us could walk steadily, so Hazel's extra imbalance didn't matter. My sister was strong. She had done the impossible, just as she had said she would, and if she could climb to the crater, she was strong enough for whatever else the world could throw at her.

Bruised from head to toe, her jeans torn, my sister thanked us with a mud-stained look of satisfaction, which put my own scholastic victories into a more modest perspective. She had another sort of willpower, almost frightening: the passion to succeed – to pay the price, in blood if necessary.

The Tennis Game

"I want it, Chris! Honey, you know what to do!"

I threw up my eighteen-year-old hands – metaphorically – in despair. In reality, those hands were busy fondling the girl beside me. Things were not meant to happen so quickly. The Chinese proverb zipped through my mind: cursed is he whose wishes come true.

"Sorry, Delores, I can't. I don't have any – you know – protection. We'll have to make do." She sighed, and we made do. What could she expect from an inexperienced virgin like me?

It was midnight, an hour after the movie, on an unlit back road somewhere near Conaree beach, on the Atlantic coast of St. Kitts, my father's Rover hidden by the tall cane stalks. The fever of my Caribbean island pounded in my veins. This was our first date, and I felt like a ramshackle house that has been through the eye of a hurricane, first shoved on one side by the winds of fear and timidity, and then shaken in the opposite direction by a gale of desire and frustration. But my house stood firm.

Once I was the boy who didn't date. Girls were strange, I thought, but that was their problem, after all. You couldn't be friends with them in the same way as boys. There had been no girls to complicate things in my boarding school. In my mid-teens, I found the idea of sex ridiculous, the butt of jokes, even grotesque. This is not to say I didn't develop crushes, but for me this was romantic infatuation, a thing of the imagination, with no immediate physical implications. My body wasn't ready. And if sex were necessary for reproduction, then the future would take care of that for me.

Then I learned to masturbate and everything changed. I could hardly control my urges. What stopped me was the need to study. At first my private episodes didn't involve thinking of girls. But I learned fast, and soon every second woman I saw gave me a hard-on: black, brown, and white – as long as she had good tits, a shapely bottom, and smelled slightly sweaty. While I still had my exams to sit, I forced the volcano to stop exploding. I had to. But after my scholarship was secured and I started teaching, I had more time and only one restraint.

I was sure my grandfather wouldn't approve of my intense sexual desires. My liberal parents were more ambiguous. I didn't talk to any of them about it, but it was my priestly grandfather, John George, whom I feared. Perhaps I was abnormal. In the bible, all sorts of bad things occurred because of sex. Sex was sinful, Grandpop seemed to say, and only marriage could sanctify it. I wondered what all the single adults did with their urges, priests included. In boarding school I had suspected the unorthodox desires of those in charge of me. No one else my age seemed to ask these questions, increasing my confusion. I spent weeks debating with myself. Several boys in my class – Arnold, Desmond, and Jones to begin with – were reported to have girlfriends, but they never admitted it, much less what they got up to. We teased each other all day long but I had nothing to observe – nothing to tell me whether our jokes were based on myth or reality.

The library rescued me once again. I found a book titled *Sexual Relations in the Modern World* that changed my life.

I opened it to page one: *"Sex is not love, and love is not just sex,"* it said.

"There is nothing wrong with sex in itself. It is a pleasurable physical activity, just like a game of tennis. It's a game of tennis between a man and a woman – nothing more or less than that. Now, a game of tennis doesn't need to involve a contract or a commitment to be fun, does it? Perfect strangers can play a game of tennis together and enjoy it. It's the same way with sex. So long as you don't hurt anyone, you don't have to feel guilty about sex. Generations have been oppressed by Church, family, and moralisers into feeling shame about sexual intercourse. Once you realise it is comparable to a game of tennis, you can be free."

I was astounded. No one had ever said anything so revolutionary to me before. It all seemed so simple. Just a game where the man throws his ball into the air, and – wham! – sex is there. Not only could I jack off in peace, but also if I found a willing female partner, we could play the delightful game together. Yes, sir!

But wait, I thought, books could be wrong. Maybe this one was all propaganda for makers of condoms. Maybe the American author of my book knew nothing about the Caribbean. My grandfather would not be convinced. Tennis, indeed! Perhaps he would say the body was holy and marriage was sacred and sex was only about babies and not something you could do or have just like that, for the pleasure of it. And what about the Pope? I knew my Anglican grandfather didn't agree with the Pope on many subjects, but perhaps on sex they would see eye to eye, excluding all fun and games. Maybe every tennis match needed an umpire.

I batted the issue back and forth in my mind for another fortnight. There was no one disinterested I could talk to. My brothers were too young and my parents too concerned I would "spoil my future". Besides, I didn't really want advice, much less warnings and constraints, on this vital subject. I wanted a sounding board to help me make up my own mind, irrespective of what everyone else was thinking and doing. If other people were clear in their own minds, the conclusions would be out in the open. I guessed that most were confused, and keeping their secrets, once again. My only clear source of information was this book. Books had always given me the freedom to explore new ideas. So eventually, I accepted the argument. Sex was just like a game of tennis. And you were a good player or a bad player. I did a little reading on that aspect too.

Behind the moral tension, I had another deep anxiety. Suppose other people were not confused after all, and I was like a donkey lost in a group of savvy horses? This was not an obscure subject like belladonna or nitro-glycerine; people probably thought a lot about sex and practised it; I was a ridiculous outsider who would look foolish.

And beyond this anxiety was another fear. My body and I were friends, but I wasn't sure I could relate to a girl, another person. The idea of confronting another with my desires was painful. What would happen to my ego if she just laughed at my naked self – if she considered me unworthy? How could I take on her desire, or lack of it, when I could barely accept my own?

This was as far as self-examination could take me at the time. Larger issues of relationships were obscure. I would soon be leaving home and had no intention of being tied down by a girl for the duration of my studies, which I already knew would be long. The right girl, the real soul mate, would turn up eventually, I imagined. In the meantime, I was drawn towards desire. All my intellectual hesitations could not disguise the physical call of the fertile tropical soil on which I had been born.

At least I could *look* for a tennis partner, I decided. Most of my classmates were still around, and although the school was all-boys up to Fifth, my Sixth Form had been excitingly mixed. My lustful eyes envisioned this girl or that girl in different, non-academic roles. How much of what followed was deliberate and how much was instinctive is hard to say. Among the girls I was attracted to – that meant most of them – who was currently unattached? Surely not Kristine: with her curves she must have someone. Of course, my judgement on this point was close to zero, because it wasn't written on their faces, but I selected anyway. And among this group of unattached naiads, I needed those who were unknown to my family. Kristine's father worked with mine for the factory, which made her a double negative; and Lorna's father was in real estate, and so might have legal contacts with mine – and anyway Bug seemed interested in her. I could sense the complications of playing tennis with someone who might visit our home or greet my parents on the street. The people who hadn't had my advantage of reading that book mightn't understand the modern tennis game concept. The field narrowed down and down to finally arrive at one candidate: Delores.

She had the English version of a Spanish name, Dolores, meaning sorrows, and I thought it matched her quiet personality. But had I studied the etymology of it, I would have learned that her pet names –

those she might have been given elsewhere – were more provocative: Dolly in England or Lolita in Spain. I had known her for the last two years of Sixth Form. She was about three years older than me, and it was her over-sized, liquid eyes and large mouth I noticed first. A little browner than myself – walnut to my cinnamon – she was always in a neatly pressed uniform. Her beige skirt, following school regulations, hugged her flat hips and stopped so far below her knees that my imagination had nothing to work on, but not even the starched pleats of her tan blouse could hide her swelling bust. Like most girls in the class she spent a lot of time straightening her crinkly black hair into a neat bob.

The school was not a social centre. After class we went home, and I knew nothing of most of my classmates' lives. There was no reason to think Delores ever dated. Except for my intuition. And then I went into a blue funk. I would have to ask the girl to go out with me, something I had never done.

It might all have come to nothing, except that my parents were keen for me to "develop normally" and go out with my friends in the evening from time to time. They encouraged me to borrow the family car. I had recently been hired as a teacher, along with several others, including Delores, who had passed two A-levels. And thus it was that, having nothing else planned one Friday evening, I mentioned to her: "…and I'll probably go to the cinema tonight if I can find someone to go with me…"

"What's showing, then?"

"The new weekly film – don't recall it's name – but it's in Technicolor."

"I'll come…" and in less time than it takes to say "scaredy cat" I found myself with a willing date.

Somewhere that night, I must have had a plan, however quickly it evaporated. It went like this: invite your prospective tennis partner out for a walk near the courts, find out if she has a racquet and a desire to play, reserve the court for another rendezvous, and then start worrying about contraceptives. The reality was being frozen in my seat in the cinema for an hour trying to work up the courage to hold her hand, and inhaling an intoxicating mixture of body odour and perfume I had never been so close to before, then finding how difficult it was to stop a roller coaster speeding downhill towards its sensual destiny.

Many notions in my book on sex had been hazy – pleasure centres, Kama Sutra, and so on – but one thing was clear. Sex can get a girl pregnant. Hell, that was one of the few things I had known since I'd been very young.

Years later, when I looked back at that night – my first real sexual encounter – I was grateful my parents had taught me the ins and outs of pregnancy early on, for my Caribbean school system had no sex education classes. If the birds and the bees could discover reproduction on their own, then the conservative elements in my society thought it would be scandalous to give love-making any more publicity. I realised I had been living in a glorious free-for-all between two poles: the warm and tribal lower classes who had little respect for "white people's" marriage – why pay for pleasures you could get for free – and the puritanical, upper-class, white-and-brown churchgoers, who upheld family institutions rigidly and had only scorn for "those who didn't know any better". Given the population ratios, I was not surprised that the laissez-faire attitude won. Thus, a good majority of Caribbean babies were born out of wedlock and raised by their mothers. And even in some "respectable" families, knowing one's real father could be tricky. My own mother never missed an opportunity to warn me of the danger of "bush babies", by which she meant a child out of wedlock with a woman of lower class or darker skinned than me. On average, Caribbean males were a feckless lot, though the responsibility of their temptress partners should not be downplayed. My own family background, filled with lawyers and a priest, put me on the orthodox wing of this moral spectrum. The stable family, "until death us do part", was a lifetime goal. So I had the opposite problem: how to break free of my sexual inhibitions without pulling the whole house down.

Although I welcomed the tennis idea, in 1960 I didn't want to be stuck with a casually chosen sporting partner as a long-term commitment. Pregnant meant baby, and baby meant marriage – on this account, I was in total agreement with my grandfather, who had been married to my grandmother for over fifty years. I was not ready, not at all, at age eighteen, for those chains. So contraception it must be, and at least the book had explained how the male condom worked. One of my favourite songs was by an American comic, Tom Lehrer, giving advice to boy scouts entitled *Be Prepared*:

"If you're looking for adventure of a new and different kind,
And you come across a Girl Scout who is similarly inclined,
Don't be nervous, don't be flustered, don't be scared,
Be prepared!"

My generation would not go the irresponsible, Caribbean way, I resolved.

The embarrassment of that night with a willing Delores but without contraceptives was total. I had imagined myself incapable of convincing a partner to frolic with me, but not the other way around. I had to obtain the magic ticket to rapture before the occasion was lost and someone closed down play on the tennis courts. But even though I knew of the usefulness of contraceptives, my book had omitted the logistics. I had no idea how to procure condoms, so the next day I pinned my hopes on a friend.

"Carl, tell me something."

"Your nose looks out of joint."

"Where do you buy prophylactics?"

"How do you mean, broken-nose-man?"

"Quit it – you know – stuff with a girl – to prevent babies."

"I thought it was out of joint. You mean rubbers."

"I guess so. But they're against disease, too."

Carl took my shoulder. "You're moving up in the world, Chris. City Drugstore has what you need. But they're not cheap: $10 per pack."

"You just walk into the Drugstore and ask for them?"

"Just like that, in broad daylight."

"But the pharmacist knows me; I go there all the time with my mother."

"Ho! You expect to remain anonymous?"

"Carl, be a friend and buy some for me."

"If you give me the money now." I passed it over. "Let's say next week?"

I knew Carl wouldn't let me down. He was more streetwise than I was. And our friendship went a long way back. But how was I going to wait a week?

"Fitzroy, I have a personal favour to ask." We were alone in the staffroom – a concrete-walled office crammed with large desks. It was clean, but the bare walls would have startled a modern observer: no pictures, no posters, no printed notices, just one lonely calendar. In 1960, almost everything in the school was handwritten and it was all on the desks, overflowing piles of exercise books to be marked, dog-eared textbooks, and odd scraps of paper.

"Ask me, young sire."

I dragged a chair in front of his desk as he continued to splash rivulets of red ink over some student essays.

"I'm right out of rubbers. Could you loan me one?"

He seemed to strangle.

"You know what you're doing? Is it for who I think?"

Unlike me, Fitzroy, my mentor and ex-English teacher, knew exactly who was seeing whom in the Sixth Form, the staffroom, and a good bit of Basseterre.

"Yes." I hoped he wouldn't ask for details.

He gave me a long look, and then searched his wallet.

"OK, but on several conditions. One, it's a gift; two, it's the only time I do this; three, it never happened; and four, you better be damned careful."

"Deal." I pocketed the precious protection while waiting for Carl's supplies. Now I was in business, or rather, in tennis.

With all this preparation, I had high hopes the game would give the proper results on my second date. Considering all the other unknown variables, I had blindly repeated the previous week's arrangements. We were parked at the same spot near Conaree beach, within a yard or two, at the same midnight hour, with the same sea sounds.

Delores looked curiously at my pack of rubbers. "Do you really need that, honey?" she whispered.

"Yes," I insisted, and for a moment she seemed to want to help me slip one on, before my masculine vanity asserted itself.

This time, there *was* a climax. Despite the limited space in the back seat of my father's car, there was certainly a climax. Beyond the perfume, her hair smelled of something oily and aromatic, like benzene, which repelled and excited me at the same time. But – disappointment – although Delores was warm and soft, and entering her brought cries and moans I had not imagined, it was no better than doing it by myself. What was the point, I thought, afterwards. All the trouble, the expense of gasoline and condoms, and my reward is just wet lips and the same jolt as by jacking off. My penis was not, ultimately, too small to fill the space of such a welcoming girl, and I was not inert. But I couldn't see where the paradise was. Why did people bother? I hesitated between several explanations. It was probable that the use of the condom, however thin, diminished my male sensations, but this couldn't be the whole story. Either I was so expert at masturbation that other forms of sex had difficulty competing, or my technique in two-person intercourse needed to make a lot of progress. On the other side of the tennis court, I couldn't be entirely sure whether Delores was satisfied, but it certainly appeared that way from her sighs.

And then again, looking back, my dissatisfaction may have come from language allergies. I couldn't stand being called "honey" – it sounded like a corny American B-movie. The English would at least have said "darling". I had nothing against endearments as such, but if they took place I wanted them to be original. References to piracy, war, or even science fiction would not have been out of place.

In the weeks that followed, I applied myself with courage and assiduity. Front seat of the car, back seat of the car, trunk of the car, school staffroom, anywhere we could be alone, and as long as my supply of condoms held out, we kept at it. At last I knew what went on behind closed doors, and I felt in tune with the island world around me.

In what was perhaps a perverted vision, sex in the school toilets became the most exciting of scenarios. The back seat of a car is so traditional, whereas, public toilets – even those reserved for staff – have a forbidden connotation. Drug dealers, prostitutes and assorted criminals use toilets for their rendezvous. As lovers, we were engulfed in this wicked aura. There was constant tension someone might enter the outer toilet room and hear our rejoicing behind a booth door. The sitting position had its merits, too. In fact, the sole inconvenience was the fear that our delicious movements might dislodge the low-cost porcelain bowls from their rivets in the ground. At this point, jacking off seemed definitely inferior.

"More! Push it in, sweetie!" and other encouragements burned their way into my psyche, though this endearment was in no better style than the previous one. At first we were prudent and avoided being seen together, but as the weeks went by I became bolder and hid less from the public eye. This carelessness did not extend to the contraceptives – the condom remained king.

One late night, we were parked in the enveloping darkness of the foothills above Basseterre. A half-moon and some distant yellow glimmers from the town were all we could see by. Only the crickets in the nearby cane field were listening to us.

Embracing across the steering wheel of my car, I had evoked my future university studies, then getting closer. I had just mentioned I didn't yet know where and when I would be going, when Delores asked me, "Chris, do you love me?"

The question cut through my post-coital satisfaction like a razor. I had no doubt about my feelings, but the tennis-game idea was at stake. I had never pretended more than a physical interest in Delores, so what right did she have to ask this question? I had done nothing to merit such a breach of faith. If I told her the truth, I quickly realised, it would be hurtful, maybe very painful. But if I embarked on a lie...

Suddenly, I didn't care about the game of tennis any more. I could accept we never made love again if only I could settle this matter of *being* in love.

"No, I don't love you, not in the way you mean. I like you, I desire you, but you mustn't think I love you, Delores."

"I thought, I thought..."

Not for the last time in my life, such idiotic frankness betrayed me and produced an emotional storm of tears. Recriminations might have been easier to handle, but it was just tears. I was submerged by the wave of Delores' disappointment. Perhaps she had hoped for romantic outcomes: that I would send for her once I went off to study, or I would come back for her, or at least I would write to her, or promise her something. I never found out when she had crossed over the invisible lines of our tennis court. If I had the right to my sexual rationale, then she did too, and doubtless, instead of a game, hers would have been a Cinderella-type story with me as a specialist in slippers for small feet. She expected a promise from me I could not give.

In the midst of this trauma, I knew that this was the first, and possibly the last, serious conversation I'd had with Delores. I was hungry for the volcanic smell and taste of her, not talk, and she was searching for some force in me that could only be felt, not heard. Ever since the frustrating night without rubbers our insatiable intercourse had had nothing to do with words.

So, I tried to make up for lost time by apologising for any false impressions. I explained gently it had always been sex, sex, and sex for me. I was not ready for love in any sense. I was too young; I had no resources; I was being catapulted like a service gone wild into the world beyond St. Kitts with little control over my trajectory; and I had a tight ball inside my chest instead of a heart that I couldn't open for a woman any time soon. But, as she felt better and better, because I was painting it as my fault and not her unsuitability, I felt worse and worse. My guidebook had said sex was all right, "so long as you don't hurt anyone." And now, whether I told the truth or not, I was inflicting pain. From my side of the court, she seemed to be trying to change the rules of the game, and this was not fair play. My symbols had become inadequate: she was not a tennis player at all, but a marriage seeker.

While I was talking to her, and more so afterwards, I wondered what love felt like. Was it sudden and magical, or did it need considerable practice like other adult games? Would I even recognise it in time? It might be invisible to the beginner. I could even – without knowing it – be in love with this girl who wanted a permanent union. And then I remembered I was going to leave soon, abandoning my native island. It would not be practical to be in love; there was nothing permanent in my situation.

But though the youth I was that night found it natural not to be enamoured, when I searched years later, I knew why I hadn't loved her. Under the guise of the tennis game, I had unconsciously chosen someone I *couldn't* love. Since my parents hadn't known her, it meant she had come from a much poorer family and I didn't have the courage to cross such a social barrier. And since she was three years older and had been in the same form, it meant there was a difference in intellectual abilities on top of the social one. To be fair, my conceit was not limited to Delores, who, after all, had passed her A-level exams and been hired as a teacher, like me. I had not met *any* girl or boy on the island of compatible spirit, with the exception of my nearest scholarship competitors. This was partly the result of living in a small community and partly my teenage arrogance. It was a lonely time but I didn't know I was lonely. And finally, Delores represented the St. Kitts I wanted to leave, and she called me "sweetie" and "honey" to my despair. I needed more than Delores, more than the place where I was born. I desired – I didn't know what – but it had to be *other*, and that other had to call me something I had never heard before. Prior to my first date with Delores, I had been terrified of the *other*, the yin for my yang, but now otherness was the siren that drove me, and it was not hers.

After this, I thought it would be impossible to go out with Delores again, but I was wrong. She insisted we meet a few more times, and it wasn't awkward as I had feared, but calm, as calm as it could be for lovers squeezing the last sexual drops out of a tangy lime. At around this time, I had a brief but painful quarrel with my mother. She had found out I was seeing a local girl from a poor home and she demanded I stop because this girl was surely a honey trap. I was outraged that she should be dictating my sex life to me, and doubly so because she was telling me to do what I had already decided to do. I agreed to nothing. But I knew I couldn't prolong the ambiguous situation; I had to make a gentle but clean break.

We were walking away from the school, dusk was gathering, and an orange sunset seared the sky. "Next Saturday night, I can take you to the end-of-term party for teachers at Old Road Town," I said.

"Are you sure you want to? I didn't think I would go."

"Well, it's up to you, but after that I'm afraid I won't have much time. I have papers to work on and preparations to make."

"Let's do it, then," she said.

At the party, we behaved with circumspection: we didn't sit together, didn't touch, and didn't talk. Yet I felt no one was fooled. I retained nothing I said or that was said to me, until it was time to go and I offered to drive Delores home.

"Drive safely," Fitzroy said.

We stopped off on a convenient side road, and I shut off the car engine. Above us, unusual clouds drifted across the night sky, alternating shades of dim light and darkness. Delores seemed hesitant. The reason soon became apparent in the tenderness of caresses. It was the wrong time of her month, and intercourse was messy. She warned me, but we did it anyway, and then she cried again because it would finish like that. I assured her it was all right: that I didn't mind; and that it was my fault for insisting. And it was all true.

In the cold moonlight I looked at the drops of blood on the translucent condom and wondered if carefulness was worth the effort. The blood did not disgust me, as it did her. Maybe it should have been on my skin and not the plastic. Perhaps that would have produced a real communion between us. But I had opted out, kept the enormous barrier of a tenth of a millimetre of synthetic rubber between us. Momentarily, I doubted my resolution and planning for protected sex. How could I be feeling and caring if I was so careful?

Yet my use of condoms for safe sex had little to do with feelings and everything to do with consequences. Two years later, in my rooms at university, I had occasion to remember this with no regrets. Far from home, I was reading a letter from a Caribbean friend about his sexual misadventures. Just before leaving for studies abroad the girl he was seeing had announced her pregnancy, putting him in a moral quandary.

I meditated, shivering into an English winter around a dull gas fire.

The world has to continue, I thought, knowing that he was placing his trust in my discretion. I suddenly felt hungry, took out some fresh bread and a toasting fork, and began grilling the tender slices on the flames.

Leaving home, I thought, was never a simple affair. Through the women, my friend's nameless pregnant girl and my Delores, I felt the pull of the islands, taut erotic strings vibrating in our flesh. The brutal choice was to tear these connections or lose our newfound freedom. Or maybe it was the other way around: the brutality of leaving – the loss of home and island culture – anaesthetised our relations and we mistook it for freedom. Either way, in the brashness of our youth, not one of us would give up his studies, and we lacked the courage to shed tears.

After eating, I wrote back to him: "You'll have to live with it. But why – why didn't you use a protection? You're supposed to be intelligent!

"And don't tell me it just happened, that she took off her clothes and you couldn't stop yourself!"

But it was like that throughout the islands for so many, my generation included. It made me question, in my own affair, what had really happened. Had I seduced Delores or was it the other way around? I didn't ask whether my friend intended to recognise his child. I knew that, at least, he would give support. A selfish tremor of relief ran through me that I was not in his shoes. I guessed he would leave her, and I thought of his unborn child without a father to welcome him into the world, and the many Caribbean mother-only homes, and I felt lucky to have had a father and a secure family, and I was grateful to the inventor of condoms. This family smugness would have been quite tarnished had I known of the three out-of-wedlock cousins secretly begotten by my philandering Uncle Jack in St. Kitts, or the parallel family my distinguished grandfather Cecil Rawle had fathered in Dominica, which even my mother hadn't yet discovered. As for Delores, I never saw her again, but she continued to feed my solitary fantasies until it no longer seemed appropriate. Shortly after my meditation of that day, news reached me she had married one of my classmates. I was pleased for her. Though not a tennis player, she had won her match.

Parting of Ways

My own way in the world, that was what mattered. Forget the mistakes and drudgery to get where I was, but keep the dreams. My Leeward Islands Scholarship put the means of independence within my grasp. The world was out there beyond my island shores, a huge magnet beckoning, and I was an iron filing ready to fly off along a line of force to some unknown pole, North or South. No sooner had I won the scholarship than I was pulled in several directions. My university destination – and hence my future career – was undecided; my affair with Delores – with all its possible complications – was about to take off; and I had neither compass nor calendar to guide my trajectory.

"When can I leave, Dad?"

It was shortly after the scholarship had been awarded to me, before the crater expedition with Hazel, and before Delores – I was still seventeen.

My father laughed, reclining on a soft chair after dinner. We were alone in the living room. There had been talk of Canadian campuses the year before and more recently – since my parents' last trip to see my sister Hazel – it had been English universities, but now *I* favoured Jamaica. Perhaps I could leave in a month or so, I thought. My brothers Peter and Noel were supposedly busy with homework, although the noises coming from their bedroom sounded more like pillow fighting than penmanship. My mother had stepped onto the veranda, from where I had just come, and was staring out over the bay of Basseterre, seeking the cool night air, and admiring the full moon that made sharp metallic lines of the wavelets. The ever-present sea breeze brought a tang of salt to our noses. On a night like this, the harbour was a silvery painting, even more intriguing for its shadows than the grainy sunlit picture that would succeed it in a scant ten hours. But I had no time for moon gazing.

"You won't be going anywhere soon. You have to be accepted first," said my father.

"But I have a scholarship."

My father shook his head, "The scholarship is a guarantee of funds from the British Government. That's essential, but it doesn't get you *into* a university."

"Not more entry exams, Dad!"

"No, but you'll have to apply to specific places, and the committee will have to approve your choice."

"OK, let's apply. To whom do I write?" I was ready to make a start that night.

"There are procedures. You'll need entry forms – it'll take a few weeks."

"Weeks? But when will I be able to leave?"

"Not this year, of course. It's too late."

I gasped. We had sat our scholarship exams in December of 1959 and it was now March of 1960. I would be eighteen in three months. My father implied I would have to wait until 1961 to enter university. I did not enquire why he had not started applications based on the previous year's quite acceptable A-level results. We knew and accepted, my brothers and I, that the scholarship was a family dream. Until all chances of it had been exhausted our futures would remain in limbo – it was all or nothing. But now that it was "all", the consequences remained to be spelled out.

"You can't mean it! I thought the university year began just after the hurricane season. Surely, at the worst, I can enter in September of this year?"

He gave another shake of his head and a half smile, "Afraid not. You see, entrance procedures for big universities close more than eight months beforehand; add to that the necessary approval of the scholarship committee. You must apply in November to get in for September of the next year. Our Caribbean schools sit their Cambridge exams too late. We should move them forward to June, like the British schools."

I was not amused. "You can't mean I have to stay another year and a half in St. Kitts!"

I should not have been surprised. Under the Caribbean sun, time dilates. *Everything* takes longer: months to obtain a bank loan, years to build a house, indefinite waiting to get government agreement on anything. The time to close a transaction is never known in advance. Decisions are not synchronised. Few care about delays; things are always "coming to come". But I was seventeen, eager, and naive.

My mother heard our voices rising and came back into the room. "Don't you like being with us, Chris?"

"That's not the point! I'm decomposing – I mean vegetating!"

My father said, "Nothing's lost. You're still young – less than the usual university entry age – and your scholarship won't disappear."

"But what the blazes will I do?"

"There's a lot to decide yet. For a start, go and talk with your school. Maybe the Headmaster will have some ideas. You might think of working."

I couldn't remember being so impatient with my father before. Maybe *his* dream had been fulfilled to see me win the scholarship, but mine had barely started. It was idiotic I couldn't leave sooner. I feared Mr Ribeiro was going to suggest extra studies to reinforce my entrance qualifications.

Next day, I found the Headmaster in his office during the mid-morning break, that same office where scholarships had been announced, boys had been caned, and our characters had been forged – though the furnace still held a few surprises. The first term of the year would end in a few days, mid-March, and I would be able to put away my school uniform for good. For the next term, in April, new Prefects would be chosen to replace any departures, and a new set of hopefuls would start competing for following year's scholarship. My time was over, I thought.

"Christopher, are you sure you wouldn't like to re-sit Mathematics and Physics to improve your grades? I could coach you with pre-university problems," Mr Ribeiro said.

"Not specially. But I'll borrow any first-year university books you have."

"Well, what about teaching?"

"Me, a teacher?"

"Yes, you could earn some money for university. The scholarship stipend pays your fees and lodging, but there's never enough."

"But I'm not trained to be a teacher."

"Doesn't matter. Most of your former teachers weren't trained."

I imagined what it would be like to hold a stick of chalk in my fingers and have twenty pairs of eyes boring into me. If I had survived the role of Falstaff on stage then I could surely vanquish teaching Algebra. I remembered Mr Barnes, my Mathematics teacher in Antigua, who had not passed his Cambridge A-levels, nor obtained any qualification other than fast bowling for the Antigua Grammar School cricket team. I had liked him.

"Your friend Clive taught for a few months. We need teachers desperately. One or two of your Sixth Form classmates will join the staff in addition to you."

"What would I teach?"

"I need an Assistant Mathematics teacher to take over 6B. I'm sure you could do it, and learn some more Mathematics at the same time. I also need a Mathematics and Physics teacher for the Fifth Form. The rest is easy: English and Literature in Second and Third Forms to fill out your timetable. That sort of stuff."

I thought of the students in 6B: some were two years older than I was, and six inches taller. I cringed.

"Will Sixth Formers accept me as their teacher?"

Mr Ribeiro laughed. "Of course – that won't be your problem. If you have any problems, which I doubt, you should be more worried about your two brothers in Third and Fifth Form. I hope they won't give you a hard time."

I sighed in relief. "No difficulty there."

Living at home, all my basic needs were taken care of, my only expenses being cinemas, books, and condoms. As a teacher, I was paid a hundred dollars a month, out of which I saved eighty. It was a small fortune for me – another step towards the independence I craved. This almost reconciled me with the year and a half I would have to spend in St. Kitts. Now all I had to do was to become a teacher, manage my upcoming sex life, and choose my university.

But this new freedom required me to make all sorts of difficult choices. I sensed that each decision from now on could have uncharted consequences. Like a looming fork in the road: one branch goes left, one right; one to sunshine and one to winter. You take your path; your companions take another. Clive had chosen Jamaica; Lee Moore was studying Law in London; Felix was at school in Barbados; Willie John had been sent somewhere in the north of England to a polytechnic college; Hart would soon leave Trinidad for an unknown destination; Rosemary was at a finishing school in Switzerland; I had lost track of my Antiguan classmates, but I thought some had gone to America to become doctors or soldiers. Maybe the roads would meet up in some huge circularity, maybe they wouldn't.

To start with, I was most apprehensive about teaching Mathematics to my ex-Sixth-Form comrades. Teaching the lower classes, despite what Mr Ribeiro had said, seemed easy. But the Sixth Form – why should they take orders from someone younger and smaller than most of them? There was a good chance they would laugh at me, and then I would have to resign. I spent many days preparing for my class in Applied Mathematics.

When I entered the Sixth Form classroom the first day, in mid-April, I was still clad in the long khaki trousers and white shirt students wore. The only new element was my necktie; it was no longer the green-and-black school colours but a blue pattern I had borrowed from my father. I hoped the class could see the difference in my status and I smoothed the tie as I reached the teacher's desk. Then, my pages of notes dropped, and they all got mixed up. A boy in the front row helped me pick them up and I stood in front of my students fumbling and cursing myself for not having numbered the sheets. I'd planned to write the whole chapter on the blackboard, and now it was impossible. It was early afternoon, and through the glass jalousies the sun dappled the room. A row of black heads was grinning at my confusion, and without thinking, I grinned back. This was their second term of the year, and they already had their textbooks open to the point where Mr Ribeiro had left them.

I abandoned my notes and said, "I'm here to help you for a year, more than to teach you. I've just done the A-level Mathematics exam myself, as I'm sure you all know, so I'm only a few steps ahead. Any questions?"

"Well, we find Mathematics difficult. How was it for you?"

"No picnic." There was some laughter. I continued, "Maybe where I can be most useful to you will be in showing some of the mistakes I made, and how to avoid them." Interested looks followed this.

I picked up a piece of chalk, threw it into the air, and then caught it.

"See that chalk? The chapter you just opened is about falling bodies. This sort of problem upset me a lot at first. For example, if I throw the chalk up with an initial speed of eight feet per second, how high will it go?" No one answered, so I prodded, "Test your instincts!"

"Eight feet," said one.

"More," said another.

"Less," said a third.

We spent an hour showing that it would peak at the ridiculously small height of one foot, and why. I astonished myself at scribbling on the blackboard: once started I couldn't stop. The bell at the end of class was another surprise – it seemed we had just begun. The students were still copying my untidy chalk script as I left the room. Mr Ribeiro was right: they wanted to learn, and if I didn't look down on them (I couldn't), it would be a good class.

But this initial success as a teacher did not carry over into other areas. Outside of the classroom, where I had social and emotional needs, an incident occurred that severely hurt my sense of independence. I have related my affair with Delores, a fellow teacher, but scarcely the reaction of my parents. It was September of 1960 and I was eighteen. I realised that although I might be earning a salary, I was still living at home, so I had to be discreet. I felt I had the right to choose my girlfriend, but – conveniently for my privacy – I had been attracted to a girl who had nothing to do with my family. And then, one evening, overconfident, I walked with her and a group of colleagues down the main street of Basseterre, towards the Bay Front, after a soccer match. The social dynamics of people being seen together had not been part of my studies. I became aware of my mistake when my mother took up the subject.

"Something serious has happened, Chris," she said. I'd been reading in bed when she'd strode into my room after work, with a stern face. "A good friend tells me he saw you near the Post Office with a girl from your school. You were holding hands."

It's so reassuring on a small island to know everyone; it's so alarming that everyone knows you.

"So what, Mum? Can't I hang out with whomever I like? I'm earning my own money now."

She stopped mid-room and looked down at me. "Don't be aggressive, Chris. I'm talking to you for your own good."

I sat, then stood up and faced her, dropping my thriller on the bed. "I'm not being aggressive – I just don't see what business it is of yours." For our soft-speaking family, these were unusually harsh terms.

"Stop! Listen, Chris, you're our eldest son, you're the island scholar, and you will be going to university in the near future. This is the wrong sort of girl."

"You know her?" I was nearly sure she didn't. This had been one of my reasons for courting Delores. I remembered other incidents from the past – just annoyances at the time – like the occasions when my mother had steered me away from some potential girlfriend and towards another. I began jerkily pacing my room from the small desk to the porcelain washbasin and back; my mother followed me a few feet behind, a tiger looking after its precocious young.

Her ideas flowed from our tropical Caribbean context, where the warmth of the sun parallels the carnal heat of bodies, and the extreme fertility of the volcanic soil mirrors the frequency of pregnancies, giving us one of the highest birth rates in the world. What would seem a mild token of affection in frigid northern climates – a man and a woman holding hands – was in St. Kitts a clear indication they were probably screwing the hell out of each other and might soon contribute to the population explosion.

She blocked my path and put her hands on her hips, lifting her eyebrows. "My friends have told your father and me about her. She lives in a poor part of town with her unmarried mother. I've always warned you about girls like this. They're up to no good. Next thing, she'll have your baby and want to marry you."

So, I was being spied on. "Mum, you may mean well, but don't interfere! I'm the one who decides which girl I see." I gathered myself as tall as I could so as to be above her. "I know what I'm doing."

"You could ruin your future, Chris. Don't commit yourself to anything. Promise me you'll stop seeing her."

This may have been the effect of my early whistle regime: however scornful, I could not be rude to her.

"All I can promise is I won't embarrass you, and I'll be a responsible adult. I don't take stupid risks."

She looked at me as if she didn't know what I meant. By this time, I was so red in the face I couldn't continue the discussion. Usually frank with my parents, I was certainly not going to spell out the virtues of contraception to my mother. She turned and walked out of the room, leaving her reproachful glances floating in midair. I wondered how I had got into this fight. Afterwards, I thought, in her defence, that contraceptive choices had not been part of her own adolescence in the 1930s. But still, what infuriated me most was to be lectured at (not a good sign for a future university student) on issues about which I suspected she was right. Of course, despite the safe sex, I shouldn't be making any promises that I couldn't keep. Of course, I might have to dump Delores at some point. But, damn it, I hadn't asked for advice! I doubted my ability to quickly cool down an amorous entanglement at boiling point, and I certainly wouldn't lose face by agreeing to do so.

If this girlfriend incident took a bite out of my power to decide things, it was just a prelude to university discussions. It wouldn't be the first time I had found myself in conflict with my mother about girlfriends or other matters, but I'd never had a real fight with my father.

My plans for university crystallised in the company of my ex-classmates. Clive, the scholarship winner before me, had just returned from the newly opened campus of the University of the West Indies (UWI) in Jamaica. He had started his medical studies and enthused to Albert and me about life on campus. We strolled on the Grammar School grounds, smelling the dry grass and a sweet-and-sour odour of burned cane coming from the nearby sugar factory chimney.

"What I appreciate," he said, as we looked at the afternoon athletics practice, "is to work with the other Caribbean students in medicine from Barbados, Jamaica itself, and all the little islands from the Leewards and the Windwards. I've never met so many young people of my age and interests. It's a real community, and we feel part of a Federation."

I remembered how, six months before, Clive had witnessed a boy break his arm during high jumping, not far from where we were walking, and had fainted. At the time, I teased him that he could never be a doctor, but now, after a short spell at UWI, he looked so self-assured. We envied him. It underlined for us how small St. Kitts was with its sixty-eight square miles of territory. Albert said if he got funds the following year, he, too, would go to Jamaica.

"What about you, Chris? Where are you applying?"

"I'm not sure; my father is getting the application forms. But UWI sounds good to me."

"It *is* good – let's all meet there!"

But it didn't sound good to my father when we talked later that evening. I had gone to find him in his study where we could be alone. He sat at his grey metal desk penning a legal brief. The room smelled of ink and leather. My father, despite his respect for technology, would never learn to use a typewriter, whereas, twenty-five years later, my mother would work enthusiastically on a PC. On the wall above him were bookshelves with dozens and dozens of fat law books – those he had brought back from London twenty years before, with dark blue covers and gold lettering on their spines, and an equally impressive set concerning Caribbean and St. Kitts law. Beside these, were his precious Complete Oxford Dictionary of English and Roget's Thesaurus, references he used daily, and his Freemasonry books. Years later, the only survivor to stay in my hands would be *The Constitution and Laws of the Grand Lodge of Ancient Free and Accepted Masons of Scotland* (1940 edition). I told my father of my firm decision to go to UWI.

"Hold on, hold on, just think a little. UWI may be a friendly place, but it has no international reputation," he said.

"Why should I care?"

"You've just won a big scholarship, one of the biggest. Even though you come from a pinprick of an island, students all over the world might envy you. The British Government will pay your expenses and sponsor you at *any* university, anywhere. Why not pick the best? There are many fine universities in Britain, but Cambridge is reputed to be the top for science. Their overseas board sets the exams for the British Caribbean that you have taken. I've thought about it a lot, and it's where you should go."

"But I don't have any friends there! All my friends are going to UWI. I've promised to meet them in Jamaica."

"You'll make friends anywhere. Don't be short-sighted. Your university is a lifetime choice. Do you think you'll still have the same friends in five years' time?"

A chill went through me when I saw how opposed he was to the idea of my going to Jamaica. What would it take to make him understand?

"But Dad, England is hostile. They have winters there. It gets cold; all the books say so. I've heard of people freezing their toes off. I'd prefer a little sunshine." I looked at his feet.

He followed my gaze and calmly took off his shoes and socks.

"Look, I went to London for four years, cold winters included. Want me to count my toes?" He counted up to ten.

"Ah," he said, "one's missing."

I stared in puzzlement.

"My eleventh toe. I don't have it any more – the one that wouldn't fit inside my warm shoe. I gave it a name. I called it 'stubborn'."

I didn't think this plea would win him any court cases. "OK, Dad, but I still won't go to England."

Looking back, the reasons for denying my father's wishes went beyond good friends and cold winters, even if I couldn't formulate them. I wanted to leave, but I sensed I might lose something important. I could see a canyon gaping in front of me. Childhood literature aside, I didn't know faraway England. Jamaica would have been continuity, a way to keep my Caribbean perspectives open. All my life I had been opening doors but rarely closing them. With both Science and Literature to my credit, I could study many things. Even God was an option – my grandfather's shadow flickered on and off – for I had not yet decided whether I was a true believer or not. I was deeply reluctant to close any of these doors, to exclude a possible future. Years later, this reluctance to choose would be good for prudent scientific research but only when I learned to abandon the non-essential would I be in balance. Only by letting go of things would their possession become meaningful. But that day, I was not ready to let go of anything.

While thinking about how I could persuade my father my future lay in the Caribbean, I was assigned to teach Physics to the Fifth Form. This was my brother Peter's class.

It would be a piece of cake, I thought. I'd studied all that in Antigua, four years earlier. If I could survive teaching the Sixth Form, then I should be an expert in the Fifth. Besides, none of the students in that class were taller than I was.

"It's an exceptionally bright Form," Mr Ribeiro instructed me. "The Farrier brothers are gifted in languages, Beach is strong in science, and then there is your brother, who shows great promise all round. I'd like you to start a special class in Additional Mathematics, which the school will offer for the first time."

If the Sixth Form had been cooperative, this Fifth Form was hungry to learn. They sucked knowledge out of the air like plants absorbing carbon dioxide. My lessons with them, even Mathematics, were to be in the Physics lab. The day I started, I noticed the quiet – no one talked. Less harassed than when I had taught my first classes, I had time to find it strange I should be standing in front of the students, in Mr Ribeiro's place, rather than sitting behind a lab bench daydreaming. The moment passed. In the front row sat the two leaders: Leroy Beach, a year younger than most of the class, with his gentle features, ready replies and quick, birdlike handwriting; my brother Peter, a year again younger than Leroy, smaller, but energetic, with unflinching eyes. In the row behind was one of the Farriers, squat and more muscular, always smiling. Ten others completed my class – the rest of the Fifth were not in the science stream. I taught the scientists heat and electricity.

Quite unnecessarily, I had told Peter in private, "You'll have to work hard in my class. You won't get good marks just because I'm your brother."

During the first few weeks, no student dominated. The class worked so well I had to speed up the teaching programme. Every lesson entailed homework or a quiz, and I graded it all scrupulously. Sometimes Peter would get the best mark, sometimes it would be Leroy, but never anyone else. Then, as we got deeper into the coursework, and balancing circuits took over from simple voltage/current/resistance calculations, a fixed pattern set in. Peter would always manage to get one more mark than Leroy. If Leroy got seven out of ten, Peter got eight. If Leroy got eight, Peter got nine.

I began to feel immensely proud of my brother. I looked at him fondly when there was no one around, and a previously unlit candle inside me flared up. Was this really my brother? The fun we'd had all our lives playing together had been bounded on one side by sibling rivalry – although I wouldn't have known it by that name – and on the other by feelings of responsibility, as when I had hypnotised him or hurt him. The teacher/pupil relation liberated me from these constraints, and I could take unrestrained pleasure in his intelligence. I astonished myself by hoping he was smarter than I was and would do better in his exams.

In the midst of this generosity, I overheard a conversation not intended for my ears. Two lesser lights of the class were comparing notes after the lesson.

"What you got in Physics? I reach six!"

"You bang me up. I only got five and a half."

"Who first?"

"Peter, with eight, then Leroy, seven. They always first. Teacher's brother keep an advantage. What you bet that with another teacher, Leroy bang Peter?"

I was tempted to intervene, to explain, but I did not. It was hard to digest. I had done everything to be rigorously fair, and was still suspected of favouritism. For a moment, I wished Peter were *not* so smart. Wielding the power of a teacher was fraught with danger.

I had to find a way to counter any suspicions of preferential treatment. The week after, when I had corrected the Fifth Form's latest homework, Peter and Leroy were – unusually – tied with eight marks each. I spent half an hour re-examining Peter's work, and eventually found the little imperfection I had been hoping for. On one question, he had worked out all the thermal equations and numbers correctly, but had forgotten to state the units in the answer. In thick red pencil, I wrote "Calories", and subtracted one whole mark, exorbitant by any means. So, it was Leroy eight, Peter seven, the first such reversal for a month. No one could say I was one-sided now.

One mark. You wouldn't think it would make that much difference, but it had the effect of a bomb. When I read out the grades, there was a moment of silence, then sharp whispers and stares. Leroy looked at me, and smiled beatifically. Peter concentrated on his copy and refused to raise his eyes. Then I rubbed it in by explaining why Peter had lost a mark, and pointing out that several others had made the same mistake and got away with it.

"The better you are, the more rigorous you should be," I said to the class.

Peter never protested, never told me, as he might have, that I had been unfair to pick on him alone. But he got his revenge. I could see him spending much more time than usual on his next homework, and at first, I thought this was good. What I found not so comfortable was that it was perfect. I had no excuse to take off even a half-mark. Peter scored ten, Leroy seven. After that, I couldn't control Peter's momentum any more, if I ever had. He went to enormous lengths to have impeccable homework and superb exam results. Leroy remained competent, but he stopped competing at the top end. He never got closer to Peter than two or three marks. He seemed to think he had no chance any more, and I suspected he blamed me for trying to clip Peter's wings. I was ashamed at the pressure I had put on Peter, but there was no going back. At least, he had solved my problem. He was so impressive no one ever complained of favouritism again.

But I had no shortage of other problems as the months went by. I was still seeing a lot of Delores, despite my mother's admonitions. She had become known as my girlfriend, a teasing term in our youthful circles covering any connection with a girl, friendly or not. This gave me status, but I was finding the charms that seduced me at night looked less enticing in the daylight. I walked her back to her home several times and I suddenly saw her neighbourhood differently. The road we used was only half paved, her house was small and in need of paint, and stray dogs yapped at my heels. Delores did not invite me inside, and I was angry with my mother for making me notice these things.

I learned to my discomfort about Delores' previous boyfriends. And I found myself wondering how I could be going out with a girl who had failed her A-level Shakespeare paper. I remembered Falstaff telling the future Henry V, "Thy wish was father, Harry, to that thought."

Meanwhile, the disagreement was less and less cordial between my father and me as to which university I should apply to.

Once again in his study, I could see a lizard moving outside the window. Killing the reptiles had been good sport for me as a boy, even though they were inedible. I doubted there was an equivalent in England. On the other hand, if I had to change countries, I could do without the rats periodically infesting our Caribbean homes. My father brought me back to earth by wagging a finger at me, "I'm not saying UWI is worthless, or even mediocre, but you can't compare it with a good English university. It's just a start-up. Apart from hanging out with your friends, why do you want to go there?"

"Because it's *our* Caribbean university. Until this new West Indies Federation came along, there hasn't been a regional campus – a meeting place. It's not just my friends – can't you see most of my generation will go there? They'll head for Jamaica from all the Sixth Forms across the islands, including the scholars I met on my Lincoln tour. They'll build the future of the islands, and I want to be part of it."

My father shook his head. "And your English heritage? Your grandmother Elsie Sophia Garrett was born in Hackney. Her mother was Deputy Mayor of that town. And what about your two grandfathers, John George Vanier, Bachelor of Arts from Durham University and Cecil Rawle, getting his Law degree in London? And don't forget me, your own father, who studied and shivered at the Middle Temple Inns during the war. And your sister, who is at school there right now. Does all this mean nothing to you?"

"It's old stuff, not the Caribbean of today."

"Pronounce it properly, Chris, 'Caribbean', the English way."

"Dad, don't you think I have some sort of duty to the community, to the island of St. Kitts? It must cost them less to send me to Jamaica, and it prepares me for a career in the region."

"Cost less? Of course, but what do you get for your money? The minimum cost would be for you not to enter university at all. Think quality, not just cost. You've got a good mind – perhaps – but who's going to make the most out of it, Jamaica or England?"

My father was becoming animated. This must mean a great deal to him, I thought. But I couldn't give up. He was making me feel impotent and angry.

He continued, "Federation of the West Indies, you say? It's just a sham! Bradshaw's gone to Trinidad to be Finance Minister, but it won't last. Read the papers: not the local *Labour Spokesman* or the *Democrat*, but the Trinidad and Barbados papers. You'll see: born only two years ago, our baby Federation is about to break itself up in a temper tantrum. Maybe ten islands are too many to agree on anything. Norman Manley in Jamaica doesn't think much of the 'little eight'. Nothing good has come out of this attempt at a Federation except the UWI, and that's not good enough for you."

I would learn later that the big islands didn't want to pay for the small islands, and the small islands didn't want to surrender their sovereignty. At the time, I was naïve enough to believe we could all work together in a rosy political fusion. I didn't know the power of fissile energy, nor the entropic tendency to disorder. The Premier of Trinidad, Eric Williams, had not yet made his dismissive quip: "If Jamaica drops out, one from ten leaves zero".

"Why are you so anti-Caribbean and pro-English, Dad? Don't you want me to find a job and a home out here?"

"Ah, that's the nub of it. I'm not anti-Caribbean, but I want you to have a *choice*, not to be trapped like most of the preceding generation. If you go to the UWI, you won't have a real choice. You'll be committed to the Caribbean. If you go to Cambridge, you can choose to live and work anywhere in the world. I wish you that freedom."

"But in practice, you studied in England, as you say so often, and you came back here. There was no extra choice. Shouldn't you have studied Law in Jamaica?"

"There was no Law school in the region in my time. That saved me from the mistake you are contemplating. I had to go to England, and it changed my horizons. I returned because of your mother."

"What horizons?"

"Jamaica is like St. Kitts, but bigger. Rough sunshine, rough houses, rough people, everything going in circles with no aspirations. We hide from both the ugly past – slavery and crushed rebellions – and the morose future – ignorance and sloth. There's no vision of how to improve things, no way forward."

I shrugged my shoulders. "I can't see what you find so wonderful about England."

"When you land there, you break through into the twentieth century. For better or for worse, that's where all the culture of our Caribbean colonies comes from."

He clasped both hands behind his head and mused, "You can't understand until you've been there, Chris. For people like us, England is enchanted, despite the winters, or perhaps because of them. As immigrants, we West Indians don't know how to talk about the experience, about how it expands our minds. Later on, we still don't want to discuss it for fear of looking pretentious. The only way to get it out of our systems, this wonder of being in England, is to make jokes about it. We've been dreaming the English dream all our lives: St. Paul's, London Bridge, red double-decker buses, trains from King's Cross, the Underground at Tottenham Court Road, Big Ben chiming, Buckingham Palace, the pigeons in Trafalgar Square, Speaker's Corner in Hyde Park, and so much more, without ever seeing it. Steps so deep under the streets you need a moving stairway to climb them; streets so crowded with people you could lose your companions, not to mention yourself; stores and cities packed with faces you don't know; weather, weather, where there was just the monotonous sun before; rain nearly every day, and people who think nothing of walking in it, protected by skinny black umbrellas like you've never used before; cold and snow that existed only in stories, and which introduce you to the joys of warm underwear; books, bookstores, and libraries where you can find anything, really, anything at all. We know these things in our heads. How could we not know them when the English wrote all of our literature? But in the immigrant's heart, it doesn't exist before arrival. Not until you have walked in Autumn leaves, caught a snowflake in the air, seen a glass of water freeze on your windowsill, felt the pulsing of a hundred thousand people and machines around you. Then that hidden part of you comes to life. You are in England. What you learned was not a lie. And you have all the time in the world to dislike it afterwards."

I was hard-pressed by this recital: I didn't want to succumb to the attraction of Britain, though I felt the pull of his words. Still, I knew my Newton: every force creates an equal and opposite reaction.

"I'm sorry, Dad, I know you liked your time there, and England means a lot to you. I, too, saw lots of skyscrapers and cars in America, but it didn't impress me."

A pang ran through me as I said this. I was lying, of course. What if there were no skyscrapers in Jamaica? "I'd still prefer to go to UWI."

"Just tell me son, who are your favourite writers?"

I cited a few, all English, plus Zane Grey.

"And what about Caribbean writers, whom do you prefer?"

"That doesn't make sense, Dad – you know there aren't any."

"Wrong – there are a few. I guess you haven't read George Lamming's *In the Castle of My Skin*, from six years back, or V.S. Naipaul's *Mystic Masseur* and *Miguel Street*, more recently. That should make you reflect on what your tastes really are. You say you want to participate in Caribbean culture, but everything you've read, every scrap of literature, points to England. And, anyway, both Lamming and Naipaul went to England."

"Never mind about literature, I'm going to be a scientist, Dad."

I opened my eyes wide and looked at him. I had to find something convincing. "What about the evils of slavery and colonialism? Why should my generation ingratiate itself with our former oppressors?" Even as I said it, I wondered where *that* had come from.

"Look son, the colonies *happened*. It's the past. It's a bit like being a child born as a result of rape. You want to know how it occurred, and you regret the circumstances, but you're not going to regret yourself out of existence. We are what we are and it's the future that counts."

When he said such things, I would reflect afterwards – sometimes long afterwards – that as a Freemason in his Mount Olive Lodge my father wanted things in the world to function. A craftsman's goal is the beauty of his craft. And although I would never become a mason myself – too much religion for my taste, strong belief in God being a membership prerequisite – this feeling things should work, and that we had the responsibility to make them work, was transmitted to me whether I wanted it or not.

At the time, I couldn't recall ever having such a furious divergence of opinion with my father. He received application forms and pamphlets from universities everywhere, but they all went unanswered, stacked up on his desk while we battled it out.

The more I talked with him, the less sure of myself I became. I didn't want to be angry with my father. Combined with some new teaching difficulties at school, life as an independent adult began to seem like a jungle filled with traps. My current teaching concern was my youngest brother Noel, in Third Form. It had started with a query from my mother.

"Chris, don't you have to teach Noel's form?" she asked.

"Yes, I teach them three times a week, but I've got other things to worry about, Mum."

"I don't think he's doing very well. Could you look at his marks and help him?"

"Not doing well in what subject? I only teach them English."

"Not doing well in anything, really. I think he placed near the bottom of his class."

This was an unpleasant surprise for me. I had noticed Noel seemed a little quiet in my classes, but he answered questions well enough. Was he going to have achievement problems? Why couldn't he be brilliant like his brother Peter? Yet, I also remembered periods in Antigua when I was not at all interested in schoolwork. I sensed that if I didn't do something to encourage him now, his failure would be my fault.

That evening, I took Noel aside in the living room and found out he had Latin homework. Just my luck.

"What mark did you get in Latin last week?"

"None."

"What do you mean, 'none'?"

"I mean, I got zero out of ten. I don't understand Latin. I was absent when we started the book, and now I can't read it. Nobody speaks Latin, anyway; I don't like it."

That makes two of us, I thought. The last time I had done Latin was four years ago, under the infamous Mr Blackett.

We opened his book on the mahogany dining table, and, fortunately, he had only missed a few declensions and conjugations. Even I remembered those. He had ten short sentences to write, and I helped him with nine.

"Did you understand?"

"Not all, but it's less stupid than I thought."

I worked two or three sessions with him in the following days and he began to hold his own in Latin. I breathed a sigh of relief. Maybe he wouldn't be a laggard in his class from now on.

A week later, the Third Form did a bad job on my English homework, so I put everyone under half marks in detention during the morning break period of thirty minutes. Noel was among them.

Of course, I had to stay with the detainees. I sat down behind the Master's desk, took out my red pencil and started grading a pile of Mathematics exercises from the Fifth. I heard a few grumbles when, looking through the half-opened windows, the boys saw the rest of the school hopping off to the playing field.

"Quiet! I want the exercise done without errors this time."

After a few minutes, I became aware of a rhythmic, thumping noise, like a jackrabbit running along loose boards. I looked up and it stopped. Where had it come from? I had no sooner crossed out the next mistake than it started again. Thump, thump. I pretended not to hear, then looked up suddenly. There it was! Young Terence was swinging his rigid legs up and down so that he bounced in his seat and jerked his whole desk.

"Terence! Stop bouncing at once! The next boy to make a noise will be severely punished. You are already in trouble."

Calm settled on the classroom and I must have graded three entire papers unimpeded. Ten minutes to go before I released them. Then the jackrabbit came back to life, bouncing even harder than before. Like a puppet on a string, I shot to my feet.

'That's it! You were warned. Now you will be – " at that moment, I identified the rabbit more precisely: it was no longer Terence, but Noel, " – caned. Vanier report this minute to the Headmaster's office."

The little devil, I thought. I couldn't pardon him, or again I might be accused of favouritism. How could he do this to me? I had been so glad to escape from the caning system in Antigua I had hardly ever used my teacher's disciplinary prerogatives in St. Kitts. Anyway, I had mostly Fifth and Sixth Form classes where the problem didn't arise. But the Second and Third Forms were considered 'untamed', and received lots of corporal punishment.

Noel got two strokes, and at home, I explained things to him as well as I could.

"I couldn't make an exception for you. It wouldn't have been fair. If only you had kept still another few minutes."

"But we weren't doing anything wrong! It was just a *little* noise. Terence and I do it all day. It's a nervous thing – a reflex."

"You had been warned. What's to become of you, Noel? Your grades are low, and soon I won't be here any more."

He didn't seem in the least impressed, so I wondered what sort of platitude I could offer. Not hoping for much, I said, "You know, if you wanted you could get better results than either Peter or me," which turned out – in the long run – to be true.

But it wasn't Noel for whom I needed to clarify the situation the most. Later in the day I had to explain to my parents why, instead of taking care of my little brother, I had let him be brutalised by the Headmaster. It did no good to point out I had survived far worse in Antigua. Family relations became even more strained.

I broke up with Delores in pain and guilt. The pain was mostly for her and the guilt for me. One moment it had seemed like an exciting game, and sex was fun for both of us, the next she began to take things seriously and I could no longer avoid looking at the future. There was no place there for Delores, and I told her so. We agreed we should stop before honey turned to poison. Although I didn't look at it this way, it was a first step in learning to let go. At the time, I was displeased with myself, and despaired of communicating my need for independence. I left her body; I abandoned the sensuality and sweat of it all; and it was just a prelude to deserting my island.

But my priority was to understand the quarrel with my father. Why was I so disappointed not to go to Jamaica? I felt bitter, as if I were losing something essential. I couldn't counter his arguments, and it would be impossible to go it on my own, to reject my family. I tried to bargain. People continued studying a long time, I had heard; they took a Master's degree after a Bachelor's. So, I could do a first degree at UWI and still go on to England afterwards. No, my father told me, because the scholarship only supported a first degree. Better the other way around: first a top-level English university, and then whatever I wanted if I couldn't go further in Britain. He was depressingly convincing, and I could already feel my toes congealing in the evil English Winter, one by one.

As things were settling into a sort of ice age between us over this university conflict, I received a letter from my Lincoln scholar friend in Trinidad, Hart Edwards. I had kept in touch with him and mentioned my indecision about universities. He had no such hesitations.

"I don't know to whom you've been talking," he wrote, "but down here in Trinidad we don't think UWI is worth a poop for the moment. Forget the Jamaican propaganda – the university has just started up, it's full of confusion, and they can't yet recruit proper teaching staff. My school is well informed about further studies, and hardly anyone is applying to UWI. On the other hand, your father's idea of Cambridge seems exciting to me. I can confirm it is the best, or one of the best, in the world. And how satisfying to beat the Brits at their own game! But it's not easy to enter from the Caribbean, even with scholarship credentials. My Headmaster has discovered what may be a loophole. One of the Dons at Cambridge comes from the Caribbean, a certain Professor King at Pembroke College. By a strange coincidence, it seems he was born on your island, St. Kitts. He's our only bit of influence in the whole of Cambridge. Do you know the man? If so, please send me any useful details. That's where I want to go, and I'd love to see you there. Oh, I should add that Edmonds of Jamaica, whom you met on your tour, is also interested."

I stuffed the letter away in defeat and decided to talk to my father. If even my most knowledgeable friends were going to betray the Jamaican cause... I ruffled my hand through the dark hair on the nape of my neck in what threatened to become a lifelong gesture – a search for primal inspiration – and what came to mind was the image of Simba, my beautiful black cat whose flesh had long since been reclaimed by the soil. If he could send me a message, it would be that fences are meant to be climbed and risks to be taken. Had it been worth it, the taste of our neighbour's stolen hens that night, in the time he had left to live? And what would I find in the neighbour's yard, across the Caribbean and Atlantic waters?

I went to see my father in his "honey room", thinking this might give me some leverage. My father had been a beekeeper for many years and was gearing up to turn his hobby into a business. It was a family affair, and he roped in help from us all: my mother for the accounting, my brothers and myself for the reaping and extractions, and paid assistants for the heavy lifting. He had a hundred hives at four locations: Conaree, Wingfield Estate, Stone Castle and our Harbour View back garden. A few years later, when his job as Secretary of the Sugar Association was terminated by the nationalisation of the industry, he would add two more apiaries and boost the number of his hives to three hundred. Since there was no winter, he reaped honey throughout the year, but especially between March and July, before it got too dry.

There were no pre-Columbian bees on St. Kitts. The early French colonists introduced these "immigrants" and in the 1950s the local variety was an aggressive brown bee. My father – the only beekeeper on the island – was trying to replace these wild bees with a gentler and more productive Italian species. To me, they all stung the same, barbs full of venom, but not as badly as the local wasps, which we called Jack Spaniards as a relic of the wars with Spain, centuries before. My father's imported bees, plus our eternal summer weather, meant St. Kitts had much higher hive yields than the US. Those golden bees gave my father a reason to love his island, though he dreamed of London.

The day before, we had reaped a crop from the apiaries. I liked the work, hard as it was, and the disagreement over my future was forgotten while the honey flowed. I had been detailed to use the smoker to calm the bees while my father checked the hives to separate honey frames from brood frames. My calming technique was not perfect – I'd been stung once despite my protective mask, and my father and his assistant twice each. There's always a vulnerable bit of skin somewhere. We had brought home ten "supers" – superposable wooden hive bodies full of honeycomb frames – in my father's jeep.

Later on, we had helped him extract the honey through a centrifuge technique. We used a metal drum with a perforated inner basket that could take several frames at a time, positioned around the circumference. In later models the positioning would be radial. First, we uncapped the comb on each side by slicing off the outer two millimetres of wax with a sharp, hot knife. This was delicate work – my father's job. I often wondered what would happen if the huge knife slipped. Would it lop off a bit of a finger, and would it spoil the frame of honey? And would we have to change our logo: *Pure honey, untouched by hand*? But that day, no fingers were lost.

As soon as there were sufficient frames in the basket, dripping with uncapped honey, Peter and I spun the centrifuge by turning a crank wheel and timing up to fifteen minutes until the first side of the comb was dry. As the combs spun, honey was forced out of the bees' delicate wax structure, through the basket mesh, and onto the inside wall of the drum. That's me, I thought, sucked out of my natural matrix. Then I thought how strange it was for me to compare myself to honey when Delores calling me by that name had upset me. When the whirling ceased, I could see the honey flowing down the wall and oozing towards the centre of the drum. In truth, I liked the colour, the smell, and the viscous texture, but I didn't much care for the taste of honey – too sweet, too cloying. I was the only family member to put sugar on my morning porridge and not honey. I had to be careful – spinning the centrifuge too fast could break up the frames, preventing reuse. To finish, we inverted the frames and extracted the other side, until the lower drum filled and we could filter the liquid off into storage containers. I realised now it was my turn, at least metaphorically, to be spun and filtered.

As I approached him the next day, with Hart's letter in my pocket, my father was bottling the clear amber honey from a storage drum into one-pound glass jars. The room smelt of warm wax overlaid with a thick odour of flowers. My father's bees sucked their nectar mostly from fruit trees – coconut, citrus, cashew, mango, avocado, and tamarind – but they also danced on hibiscus, yellow bells, and "bee bush", the pink coralita climbing vine that decorated the roadside. A few bees had infiltrated the wire mesh windows and were dying in ecstasy on the sticky floor.

"Dad, do you know anyone called Professor King?"

"Do you mean Mr King next door who shot your cat?"

"No, no, I'm talking about a Professor at Cambridge."

"Oh! Rufus King! Yes, of course. He visits St. Kitts from time to time. He's at Pembroke College, I think."

"Why didn't you tell me about him before?"

"Well, there wasn't any point. You wanted to go to Jamaica. And, by the way, Rufus can't guarantee you entry to Cambridge – admission is tough."

"We can still discuss it, can't we?"

"I was waiting. Here, help me to stick these labels on to the jars, please."

I sat on a stool next to him and wet the labels. They were smart, yellow-and-black designs announcing *Vanier Honey*. Years later, when he had formed his company, in which I would invest, he would change the logo to *Caribbees Honey*, with a stylish painting of the flamboyant flower, the *royal poinciana*.

This was the moment, if there was a single one, when everything changed and the door leading to the Caribbean slammed shut. And it shut not just for me, but also for my brothers who would follow. Damn the books, I thought. Outside knowledge, foreign worlds, and dreams of England – this was what it led to. How bitter – and yet challenging – to accept my father's plan and leave the islands. I knew I would not be able to come home for vacations – too far, too costly. I would be gone for a long time. In all my dreams of leaving the details had never been clear. Now, I could see myself wandering around the world, a tree uprooted and defoliated, having to choose between one country of exile and another. It lasted a while, this moment of bitterness, but my story could have only one ending.

I was astonished at my lack of constancy. For months, I had held firm and sharpened my resistance, and now, capitulation came because of one letter... I never told my father of Hart's comments – no point pouring salt on my wound. Once I was guaranteed to find a bit of the Caribbean in Cambridge, I agreed to exchange the hardly dry concrete of the UWI campus at Mona, Kingston for the fourteenth-century stones of Pembroke College, Cambridge – if the bloody Dons would have me.

I found to my relief my father was a gracious winner and did not gloat. We worked as a team. I was reassured he had taken the same difficult road in his youth and yet had thrived in England.

"Now, we have to decide what subject you will apply for."

"What about Chemistry?"

"That might be a problem. There's some politics involved. You see, there are others who want to build up the UWI campus at whatever cost to the early graduates. If you choose a subject that is offered by UWI, the British Government might not support your application to Cambridge. They might think it was unfair to the Caribbean to steal the islands' best students. My contacts in the Jamaican sugar industry tell me UWI doesn't yet have a Chemistry faculty – they offer mostly Liberal Arts, Medicine and Law – but next year they might offer Chemistry. Then you would be stuck. What I propose is Chemical Engineering, which only sophisticated places like Cambridge can offer."

"What is Chemical Engineering?"

"I don't know, to tell the truth. It obviously has a lot of Chemistry in it, and it seems to be about building chemical plants. Not much of that in the islands. You'll be able to change subjects later, if you don't like it."

I thought of his honey room, with all the pipes, pumps, thermometers, and valves, connected to control and purify the viscous liquid. It sounded like a Meccano game. And so, we filled out the application forms for me to study Chemical Engineering at Pembroke College, Cambridge.

"Dad, did you realise if Chemical Engineering isn't planned at UWI, and if there are no new factories in the Caribbean, then there won't be any jobs for me here?"

"I know, son. I said you would have a choice, but to be honest, I don't expect you or your brothers to make your future here. Long ago, the Europeans colonised these islands. Now it's time to colonise them."

This shunted my thoughts onto a picturesque track, of hordes of coloured Caribbean settlers, cutlasses and whips in hand, bent on enslaving the British and the French on their green lawns. Maybe, in return for the early European colonists' gifts of influenza, measles, and smallpox we could give them our tropical mosquitoes. It was too much fun to be true. No doubt the natives would have a thing or two up their sleeves to repel the mixed-blood invaders. I substituted the image of my father's centrifuge: when the spinning stopped, the honey oozed its way back from the periphery to the centre, just as I would move back to the cultural centre of my world. I wondered if the original English colonisers of the Caribbean had imagined that by imposing their language and civilisation on Amerindians and Africans alike they were creating linguistic return tickets to Britain for their descendants. I had to accept my father's wishes, I thought: it was cultural destiny.

Honey was an apt emigrant symbol in another way, too, I realised. If the beekeeper overheats his precious crop, it will turn out dark and more difficult to market. The best selling honey was clear amber, like the colour of my skin. I knew, and sometimes was ashamed of it, that I would be able to pass for white as I oozed towards the European roots of my island culture.

Down to earth, I asked, "And you and Mum – what'll you do?"

"We'll make do. Just go out into the world and remember us." But I was not surprised he didn't expect me to return home. This was the thing I had seen lurking, and I had to put it out of my mind.

I gave little pause at the time to my mother's role in the heated debate, because she always sided enthusiastically with my father. She thought England a pleasant country – her mother's birthplace – and ignored the consequences of rupture. My father was a gift giver who understood the nature of sacrifice. A true gift does not materialise out of nowhere – it is part of the giver's substance.

At about this time, I changed my dialectical stance concerning that holy-of-holies, the West Indies Cricket Team. I was not much of a cricket player myself – the hard, red ball scared me – but my friends were forever talking about the game. Test matches between England and the West Indies were our equivalent of bullfighting. I liked a good argument, and for the past four years in St. Kitts, I had supported the English team, applauding the exploits of Len Hutton, Fred Truman, Peter May, and Colin Cowdrey, to the despair of my St. Kitts friends.

Now that I was sure to leave the Caribbean, perhaps for good, I discovered the virtues of the West Indies team, and Weekes, Worrell, and Walcott, followed by Gary Sobers, replaced the English icons. I was all set to grind minds with the Cambridge cricket fans.

Apart from this, since I was committed to England, every trace of the Caribbean had to be cleansed. I began to think of impossible foods like apples and chips instead of mangoes and sweet potatoes. From all points on my small island of St. Kitts, I could see the mothering sea; it had always centred and reassured me; now this seemed childish, and I began – clumsily – preparing for a borderless world of towns, forests, hills, the unknown landscapes of Britain. How curious that, forever after, the sight of a lake, a river, or even a pond of muddy water, would instantly attract my eye. I still had ten months to wait, but events flew by in 1961. My application to Cambridge, ardently supported by Rufus King, was accepted. From September, I would read four years of Chemical Engineering, starting with the Natural Sciences Tripos. A small part of my Caribbean world would go with me. Rufus helped my friends, and Pembroke accepted Hart Edwards to read Economics, as it did Dennis Edmonds of Jamaica and Tony Williams of Barbados – I would be arriving alongside a tiny islander clique.

Like an accountant trying to close his books, I took stock of what I was leaving behind. My teaching results were better than I could have hoped for, with good grades for my mathematics students in the Sixth, and distinctions for Peter and Leroy in their Cambridge O-Level exams. Noel had not improved enough at the end of the year, and, gritting my teeth, I persuaded Mr Ribeiro to make him repeat the class. I hoped the extra year would get him on track. He was not an all-rounder like Peter, but, by focusing, he might yet succeed at what he wanted to do.

I need not have worried about my brothers' future. Three years after I left, Peter would grab the scholarship on his first try, and follow me to Cambridge. Farrier would win the scholarship the year after. Another three years on, and Noel would win it, ironically beating Mr Ribeiro's son Alvin into second place, and would follow the Pembroke tradition. But it would no longer be called the Leeward Islands Scholarship. Mr Ribeiro was too clever a Headmaster and – on occasion – too good a fixer. The Antiguans would grow so frustrated by St. Kitts winning the scholarship *twelve* years in a row, that they would decide, in concert with the British Government, to fund a separate scholarship for each island. Noel would be the first recipient of that St. Kitts Scholarship. The change to an island award was only fair, but it spelled the end of a magic era, the demise of the inter-island scholarship that had reigned for 40-odd years over the Leewards' schools.

The astonishing thing about the school in St. Kitts, I saw looking back, was how wrong some of my perceptions were, in particular the idea that there was no future for us without the scholarship. Every single member of my Sixth Form – to the best of my knowledge – succeeded in obtaining further education abroad, university or professional, an astounding success rate for an out-of-the-way little island. Even Sammy became a highly qualified professional. Perhaps we were all suffocating, and the desire to breathe the outer world's fresh air had forced us to overcome the obstacles. But once the birds have flown their cage it's hard to get them back.

Over the next years, a desire for independence was manifest on a much larger scale than my personal concerns. One-third of the population of St. Kitts-Nevis is estimated to have emigrated to Britain between 1955 and 1965 when the UK immigration laws changed – less for questions of money than of expectations. It is unknown how many eventually returned. The West Indies Federation would be dissolved in 1962, as my father had forecast, and Bradshaw would come home, frustrated, to reign over St. Kitts' politics for the next sixteen years, until his death in 1978. Each island wanted autonomy. Bradshaw's greatest trauma would be the Anguillan Rebellion. The islands of Nevis and Anguilla had long formed a tiny federation with St. Kitts, but were justifiably unhappy with their small share of the central resources and decision-making power. On June 10th, 1967, when I was far away in the USA, the Anguillan leader, Ronald Webster, threw out the Kittitian representatives on his island and foolhardily dispatched a boatload of third-rate mercenaries and armed Anguillan supporters to kidnap the Premier of St. Kitts at night. The invasion was so inept that only two policemen were slightly injured before a few rebels and their considerable arms were captured (but not the mercenaries). Unfortunately for Bradshaw, he bungled their subsequent prosecution as badly as the invasion itself had failed, and all the plotters and their local sympathisers – including my old school friend Billy Herbert – had to be set free. I followed the trial for months by subscribing to the local newspapers, reading them excitedly a week late on the coffee table of my student apartment. My father played a prominent but undocumented role – he advised the Counsel for Defence.

At around this time I would – at my father's request – succeed in smuggling a TV set into St. Kitts in the form of a Heathkit. Importing TV sets was not authorised, though several had already reached the island. It was said the Labour government feared criticism from abroad. My set was impounded at the airport but the Customs later released it, as the law did not cover kits, which my father knew.

Where arms had failed, Webster eventually succeeded by cunning – petitioning the UN and embarrassing Britain for his island's freedom. To Bradshaw's chagrin, Anguilla and its 5000 inhabitants became de facto independent; it was proclaimed a self-governing British colony in

373

1980. St Kitts itself would gain independence from Britain in 1983, five years after Bradshaw's demise, under a non-Labour government. My own independence, when I left home for England in September of 1961, had the same elements of pain, conflict, and ambition.

On the day of departure, I was nineteen years old, and I stood with my hand luggage at the Golden Rock airport just outside of Basseterre, clad in a new, blue suit, waving goodbye. My attire was too warm; the sun bathed me and its rays reflected from the concrete, together causing trickles of salty sweat to run down my armpits. My father stood next to my mother and brothers at the edge of the strip, watching me. This was the ideal my parents had planned: liberty for their children.

The plane on the tarmac was waiting. Like swatting mosquitoes on my arm and fingering the blood, I savoured retrospectively my little battles for independence. One could love people and fight them back at the same time. I had been assailed by my grandfather's call for a faith too intense, the Reverend Mother's taste for confessions, and Father Brown's quiet, intellectual pressure. I was still a believer of sorts, but cuts and tears were showing around the edges. My mother's outlawing of my girlfriend had outraged me. Delores had given me a packet of pink envelopes and a pad before leaving, which I donated to my mother without explanation. I had resisted, but lost out to, my father's preference for an English university, but whether it was the right subject or the right country, I no longer cared. I had struggled with my own lazy instincts and become a half-serious student; now my Caribbean molecules were free to fuse or to explode, as they wanted. I had lost forever my cats and my virginity. It was better to think of all these little wounds than of the trembling earth under my departing feet.

I hoped it would be cooler in the plane, but for the moment I could only envy my excited brothers in their short-sleeved shirts. My smiling parents were also lightly dressed, in their office clothes. They were building their own prison, because, as they grew older, their island world would close in around them, and there would be no way to maintain close contact with their liberated offspring, as they flapped their wings in the larger world. Letters took up to a month to arrive and transatlantic phone calls were unheard of at the time. I looked at my father with love, knowing I was very like him but not yet acknowledging in his gentle hands the hammer that had shaped me. It was an age and a moment to be myself, to strike out on my own, and to imagine self-determination. Later, I would see my father had fashioned three clones, destined to lead the life he had wished for himself abroad.

Turning to follow the other passengers, I fought for inner calm and imagined I was not leaving my island at that time, because I had left in spirit long before. After all, I had been an emigrant in waiting ever since finding buried treasure in my first book – a chest full of English dreams

– and every other book had taken me a step farther away. If I looked back, there were many signs of my transience. I had envied the scars on my grandfather's leg from the lost country of his forbears, and I had seen myself wandering the world like him to earn my own scars. I had dreamed of alternate worlds where the beauty of cats and Caribs could reign supreme. I had learned from my stay at boarding school that loss of home, even painful, can give you strength, and I envied the ancient pirates their freedom. Having broken out of my boarding school cage on occasion and survived my fears of the Antiguan night, I was biding my time to escape from the thicker bars of my island life. My brief and sultry affair with Delores had only served to convince me my heart was destined to be elsewhere. So why did the blue sky seem so dark?

As I boarded the plane, the small figures of my family waved to me a last time. I turned to take my seat and tried to hold that moment. I suppressed the idea of leaving the Caribbean behind; instead I thought of finding a future. I didn't doubt I would be back and the guava trees would still be fruiting, the sand still warm, the little waves of seawater still cool, and my parents still a haven of love and wisdom. Yes, I could return, I might return, I would return, and it would all still be there.